CW01369810

Ballets Russes

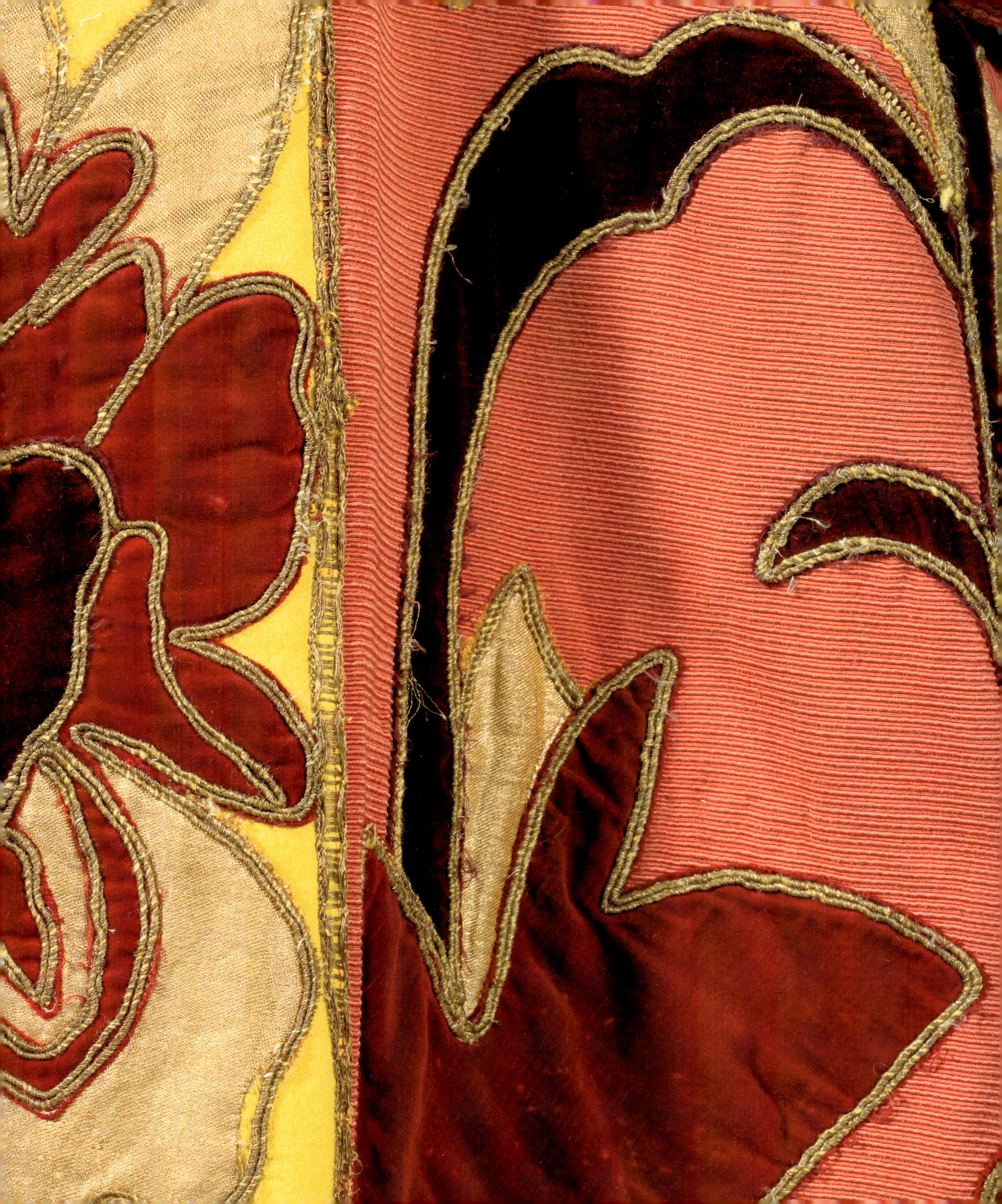

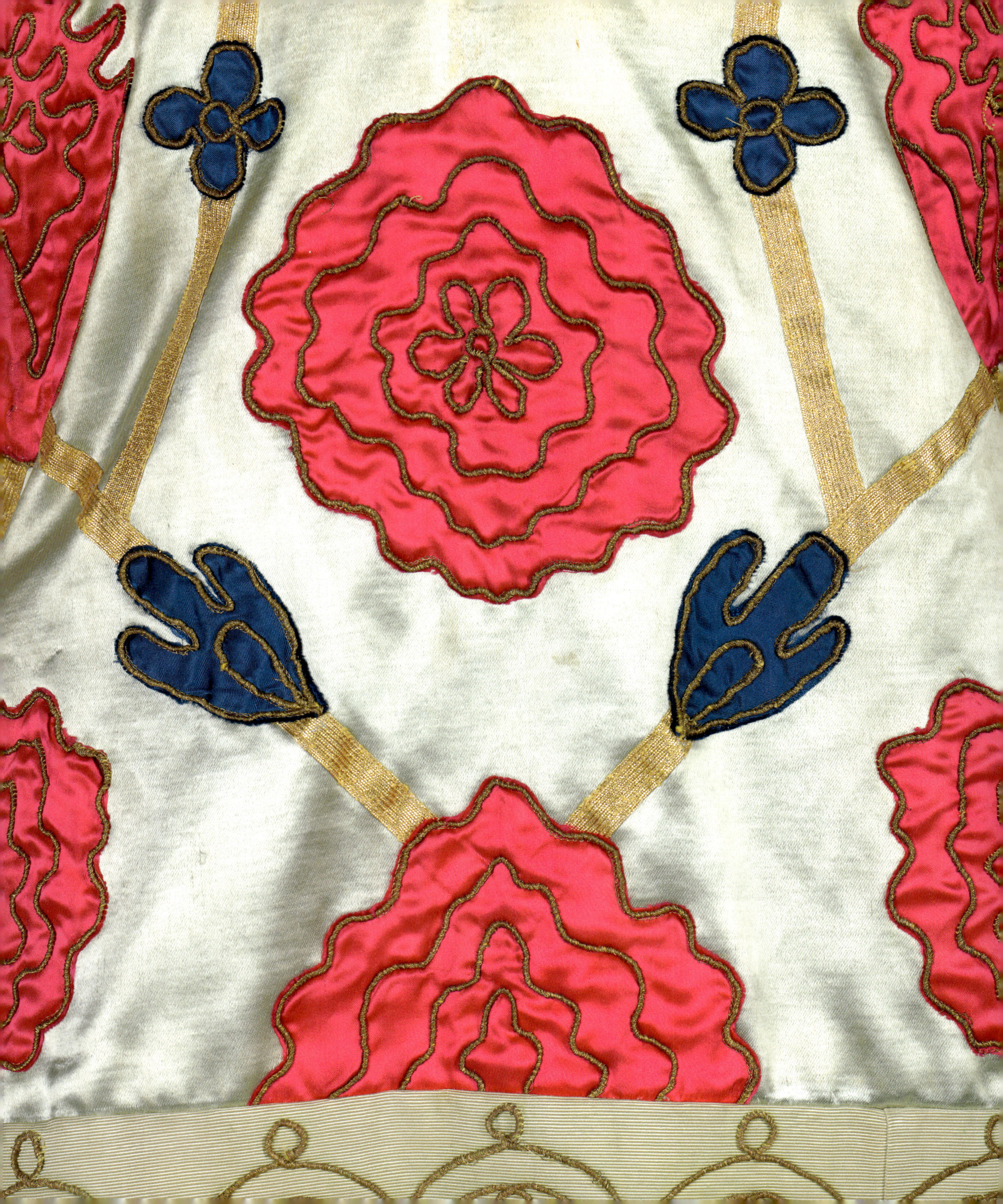

BALLETS RUSSES

THE ART OF COSTUME

ROBERT BELL

with essays by Christine Dixon, Helena Hammond,
Michelle Potter and Debbie Ward

NATIONAL GALLERY OF AUSTRALIA

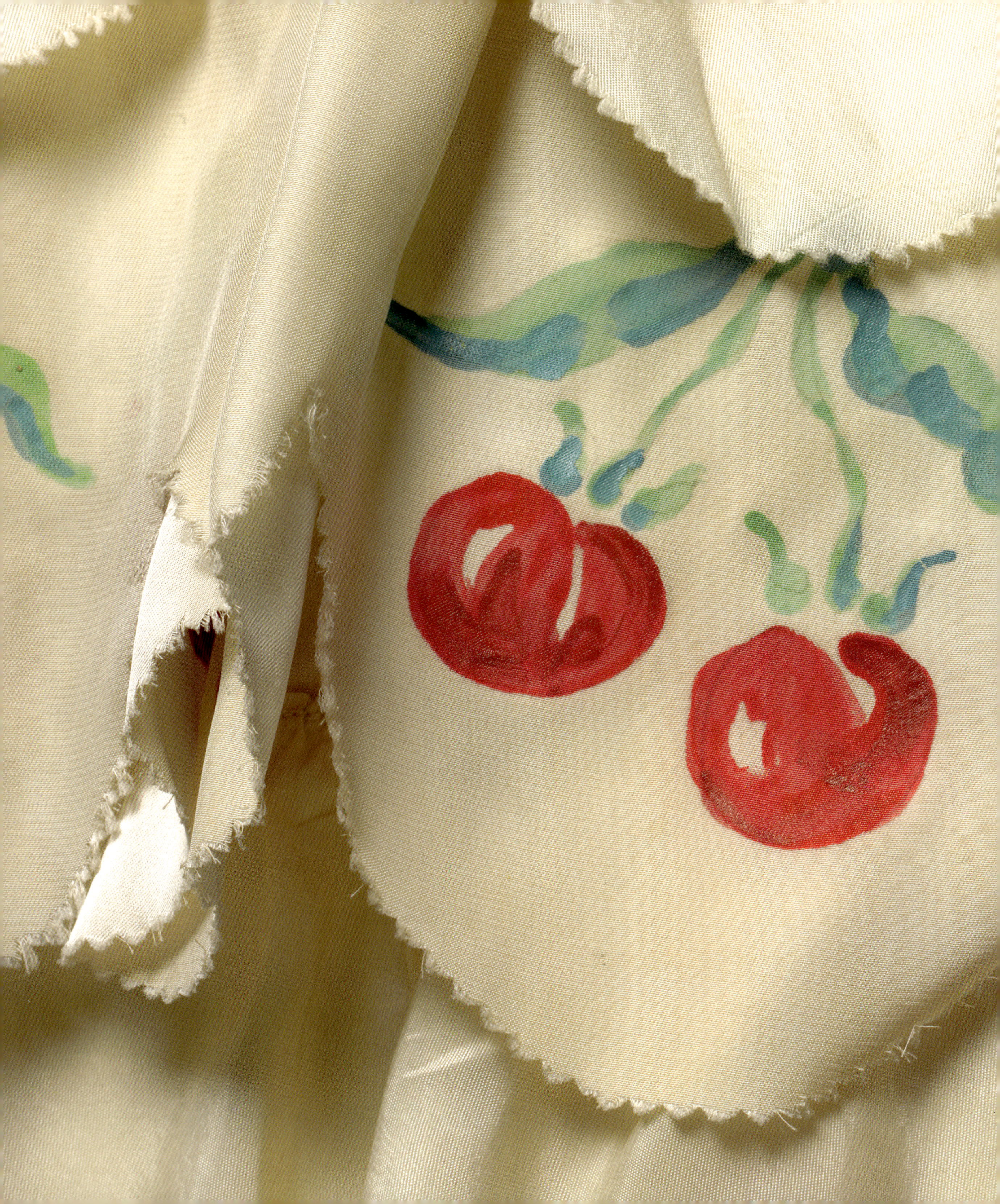

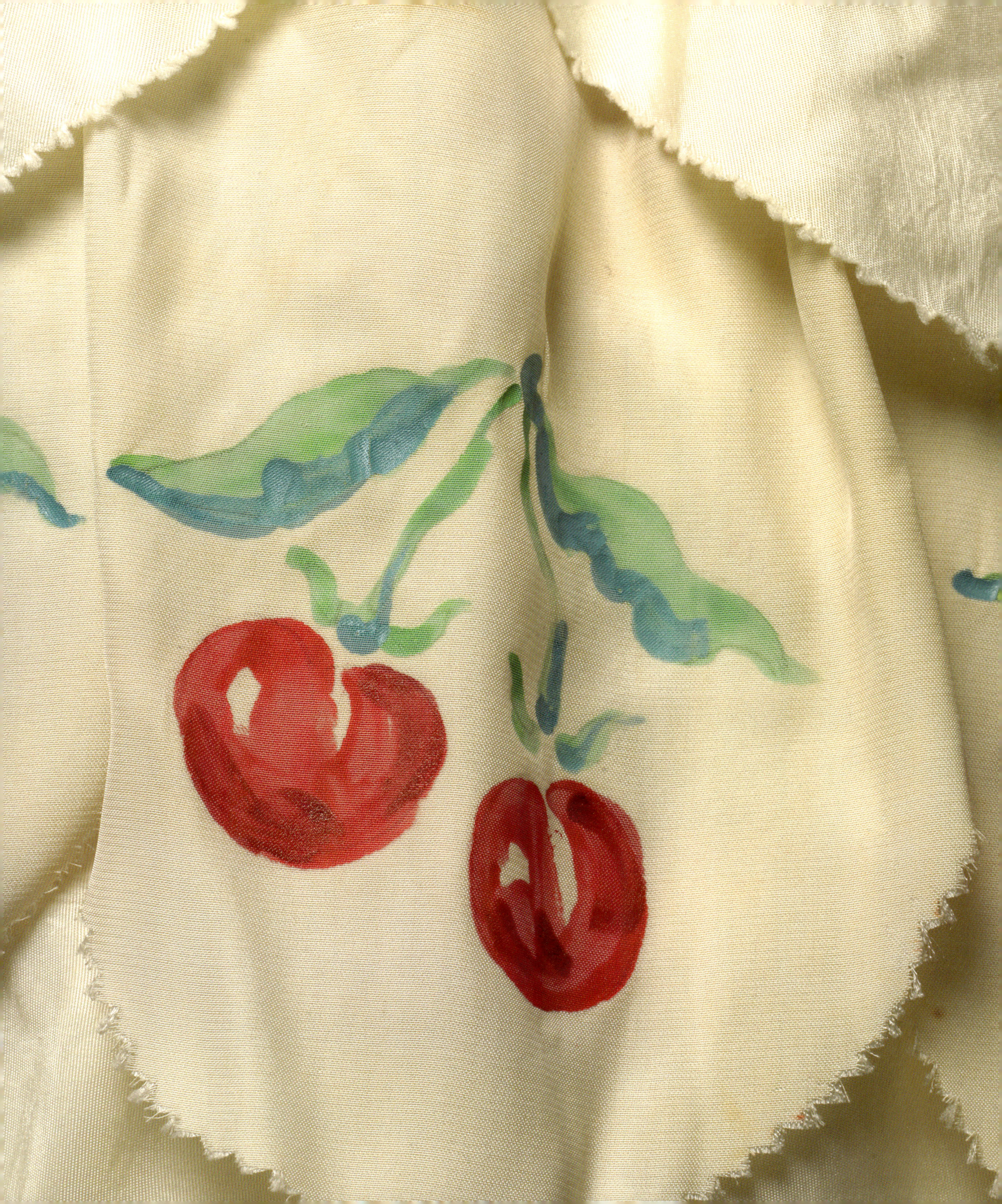

Author's note

There is variation in the text of the spelling of Diaghilev's name. Diaghilev called himself Serge de Diaghileff in France and America, but is commonly referred to by the French variant of his name, Serge Diaghilev. Diaghilev's first name in Russian, Sergei, is used in this publication when referring to the man. Serge Diaghilev, the French variant and commonly used version of his name, is used in reference to his dance company, Les Ballets Russes de Serge Diaghilev.

(pages 2–3) **Natalia Goncharova**
Robe from costume for King Dodon c 1937 (detail) from *Le Coq d'or*

(page 4) **Natalia Goncharova**
Tunic from costume for an Ivan c 1920s (detail) from *Le Mariage d'Aurore*

© Natalia Goncharova/ADAGP. Licensed by Viscopy, 2010

(previous pages) **Léon Bakst**
Dress from costume for Columbine c 1942 (detail) from *Carnaval*

(following pages) **Léon Baskt**
Costume for Queen Thamar c 1912 (detail) from *Thamar*

CONTENTS

Forewords — 13

The Ballets Russes costume legacy — 19
Robert Bell

Wild dream: imagining the Ballets Russes — 23
Robert Bell

Spectacular histories: the Ballets Russes, the past and the classical tradition — 51
Helena Hammond

Modern art, modern ballet — 69
Christine Dixon

Costumes for Les Ballets Russes de Serge Diaghilev 1909–29 — 83
Robert Bell and Simeran Maxwell (synopses)

Costumes of Colonel de Basil's Ballets Russes de Monte Carlo 1931–40 — 165
Robert Bell and Simeran Maxwell (synopses)

People, patronage and promotion: the Ballets Russes tours to Australia, 1936–40 — 181
Michelle Potter

Sights unseen: tags, stamps and stains — 195
Debbie Ward

Notes — 209

The designers — 215
Simeran Maxwell

Ballets Russes timeline — 228
Robert Bell and Simeran Maxwell

List of works — 239

Selected bibliography — 253

Contributors — 257

Acknowledgments — 259

Index — 260

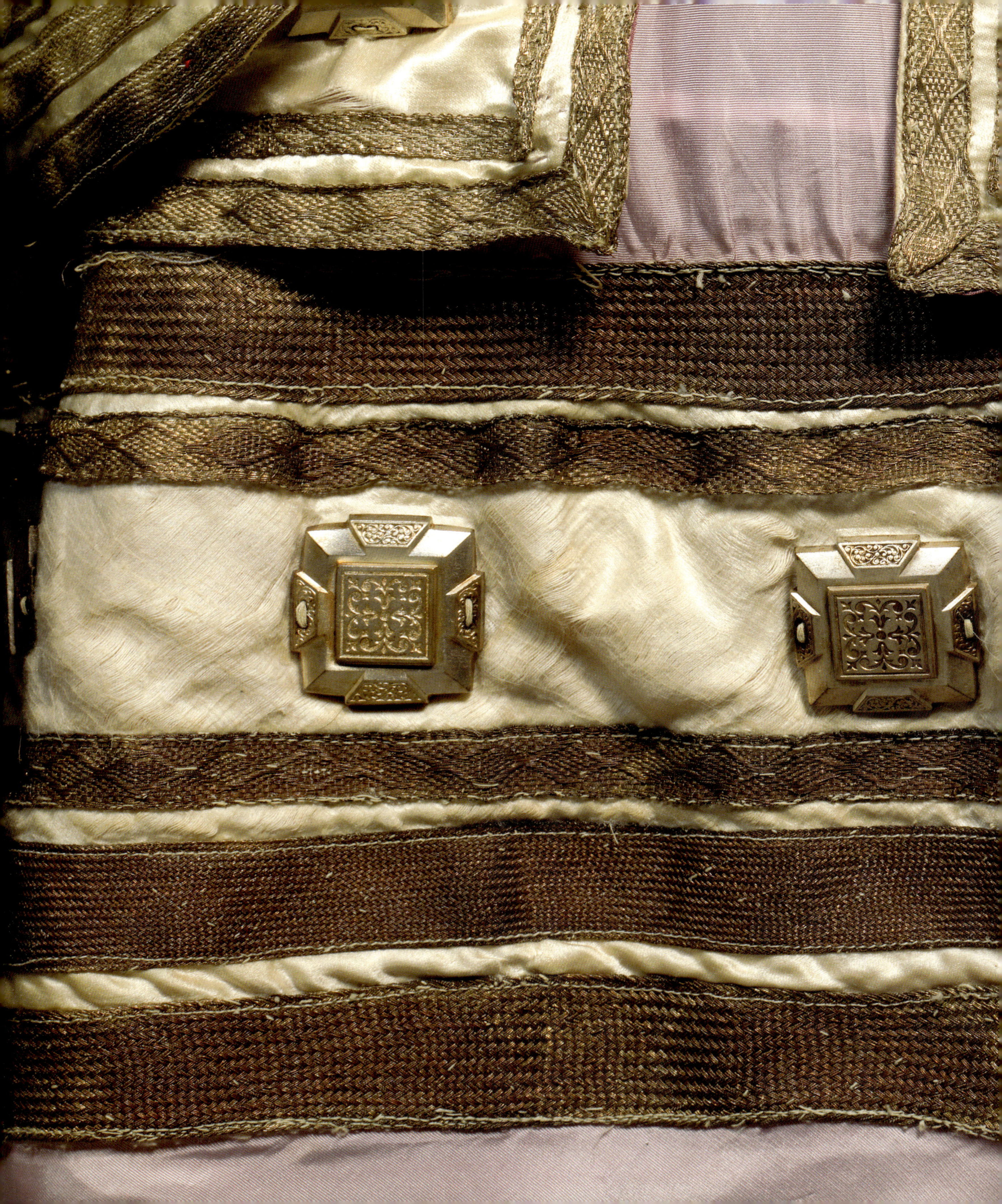

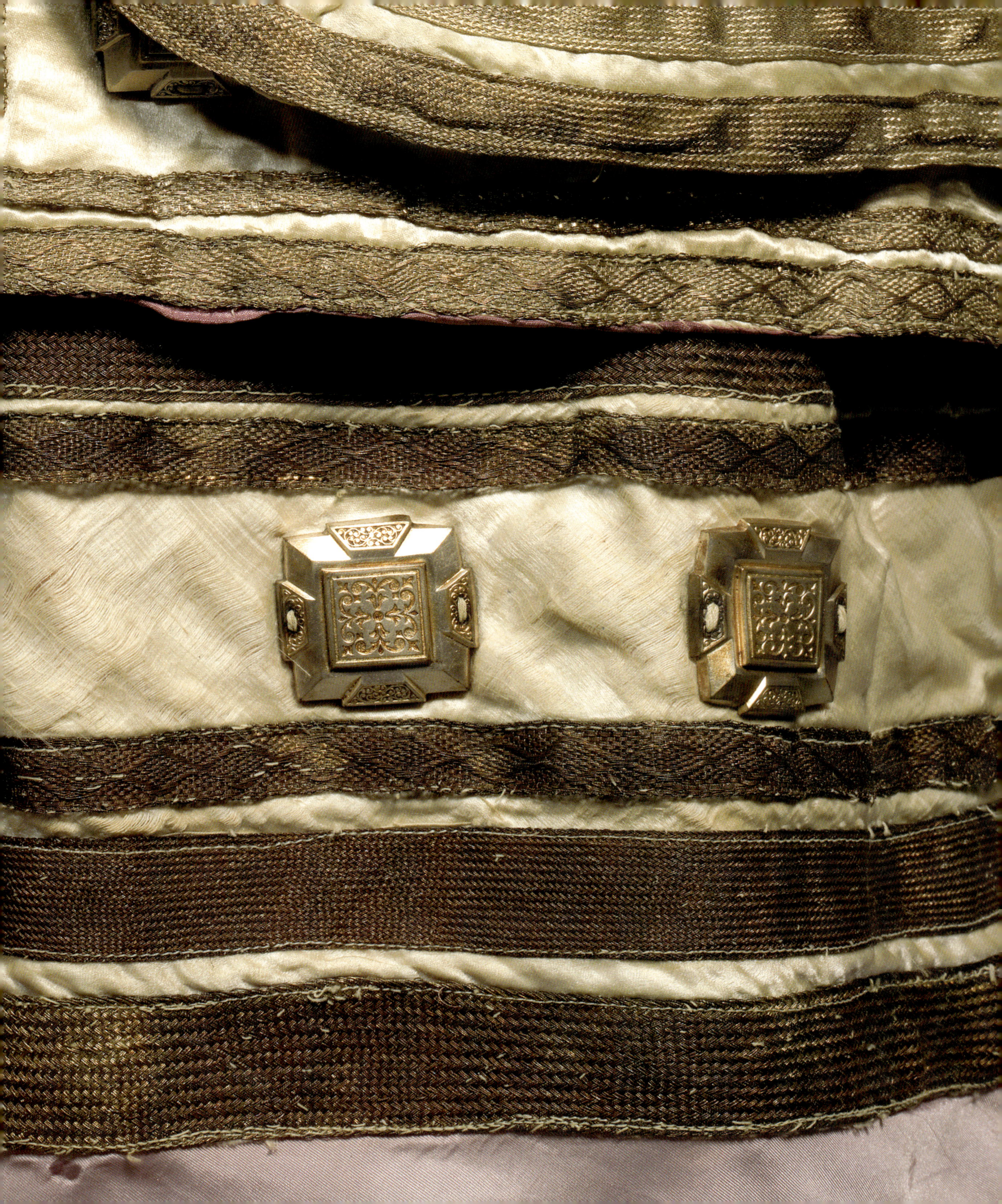

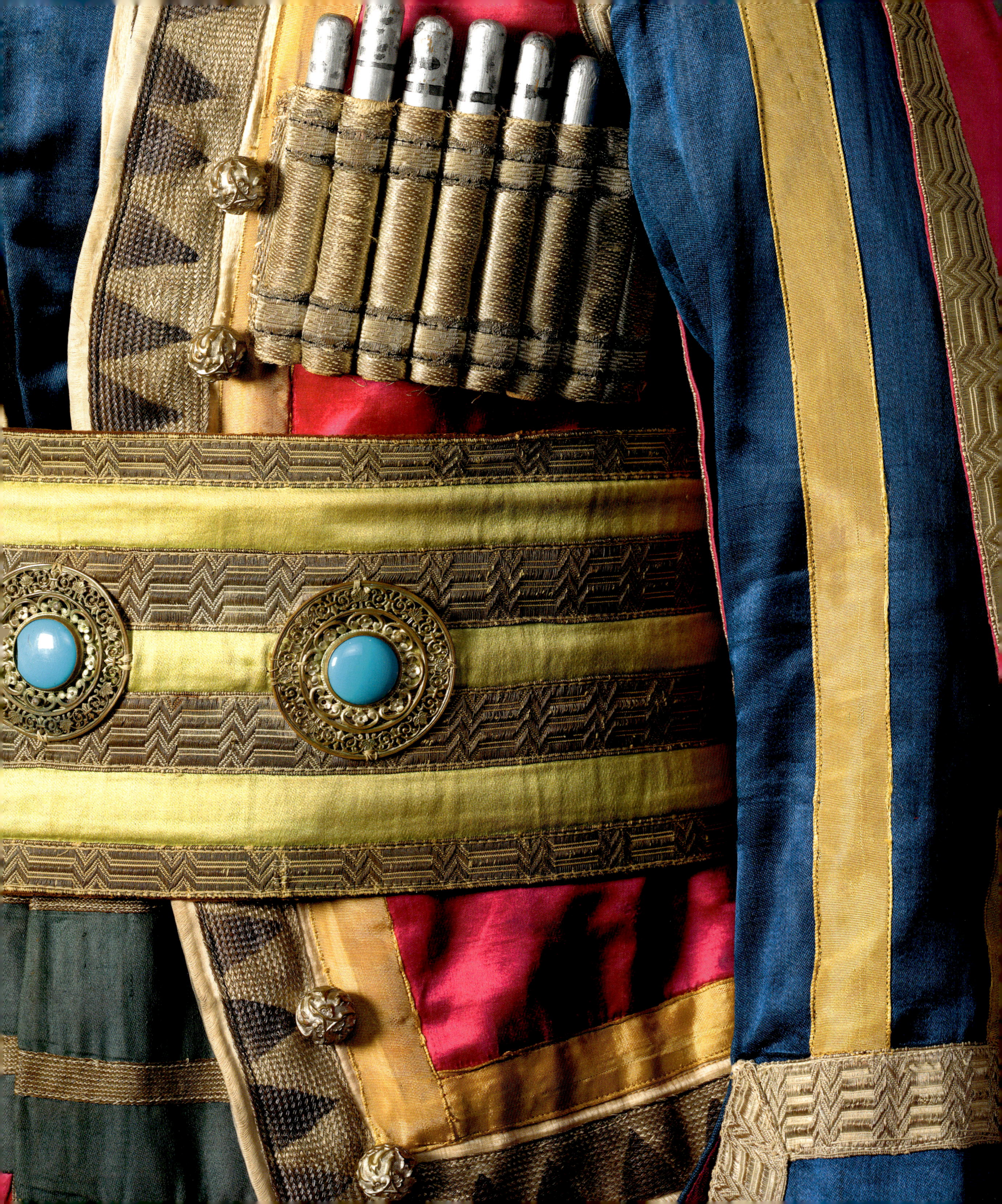

FOREWORD

The story of the Ballets Russes has engaged people for the past one hundred years, ever since Sergei Diaghilev brought together some of the most important artists of the twentieth century and infused new life and creative energy into the theatre and the wider world of design. For the brief period of its existence (thirty years in several incarnations), the cultural phenomenon of the Ballets Russes, which was not just a Russian company, was linked to the most accomplished choreographers, dancers, composers, designers and artists of the time, creating not only exotic, extravagant and charming theatrical spectacle but excitement, critical discussion, technical innovation, glamour and scandal wherever it appeared. The Ballets Russes was formed entirely for touring, its peripatetic existence giving audiences in Europe, North and South America, New Zealand and Australia a view of a remote world that was continually re-imagined by Diaghilev and his collaborators.

Centenaries offer us many ways to reconsider the past and to make connections between events. Diaghilev established his Ballets Russes company in Paris in April 1911, the same month that the competition for the design of Australia's new capital city, Canberra, was announced. He could not have imagined that this yet-to-be-conceived city would eventually be the home for one of the three largest collections of the costumes of his great Ballets Russes.

When the National Gallery of Australia was established, one of its central aims was to celebrate Modernism and to show how arts across all media contribute to an understanding of its influence. The Gallery's prescient purchase in 1973, early in its collecting history, of the foundation of its Ballets Russes collection is vivid evidence of this commitment.

As this collection has grown and we have developed major displays from it, continuing research and extensive conservation have been priorities, resulting in a collection rich in depth, condition and provenance. As the most important group of works in the Gallery's International Decorative Arts and Design collection, the Ballets Russes collection spans a revolutionary period of European design, creating potent links between decorative arts, craft, painting and photography.

Included in the exhibition—entirely from the Gallery's collection—are 150 costumes and accessories from thirty-five productions of the Ballets Russes de Serge Diaghilev and Colonel de Basil's Ballets Russes de Monte Carlo. Many of these are illustrated in this book and reveal the extent of Diaghilev's creative engagement with some of the most influential artists of the early twentieth century. Painters such as Matisse, Picasso, Braque, Gris, Goncharova, Larionov, de Chirico, Bakst, Benois, Derain and Delaunay delighted in the opportunities offered by the collaborative nature of work for the theatre, to expand their practices beyond the studio, and in doing so revitalised the world of stage design.

The revived post-Diaghilev Ballets Russes reached Australia in 1936 in performances by the various touring companies of Wassily de Basil. These tours had a profound impact on not only the emergence and development of Australian ballet, but in raising overall expectations for the potential of the arts in Australia.

The Gallery's curator, Robert Bell, has absorbed the Ballets Russes into his passion for twentieth-century design. Over the past five years he has reviewed and

Léon Bakst
Costume for a Lezghin c 1912
(detail) from *Thamar*

re-catalogued the collection. His essay in this book provides a new account of the history of the Ballets Russes. He has built upon the fine work of previous curators of the Gallery's Ballets Russes collection and has been ably assisted by Exhibition Assistant, Simeran Maxwell. The other essays in the book—by Christine Dixon, Helena Hammond, Michelle Potter and Debbie Ward—also offer new perspectives on the Ballets Russes.

Robert Bell has worked closely with all of the Gallery's departments to assist him in bringing his vision for the exhibition and this book to fruition. The resulting quality of their work is evidence of the pride and skill that the Gallery staff demonstrate in handling, protecting, documenting, interpreting and publicising this unique and precious part of the national collection.

The Gallery's conservators have worked on the Ballets Russes costumes for nearly thirty years, giving them a unique insight into these remarkable costumes. During the past six years, they have restored and conserved forty-eight costumes that have previously never been able to be shown, as well as undertaking further work on many previously restored costumes to bring them up to current display standards. The result is that the majority of these costumes can now be displayed on mannequins and be seen in the round as originally intended. The newly restored costumes include some which had previously been considered unsalvageable and their present fine condition is evidence of the continuing research and skill development that makes the National Gallery of Australia's textile conservation department a world leader. New photography of the costumes reveals them in three dimensions to give the viewer a sense of their form and quality of their materials as they drape and catch the light.

We are grateful for the generous support of our Presenting Partner in this project, ActewAGL, which has enabled this important collection to engage our audience and make the collection widely accessible through this book and the exhibition website.

We would also like to acknowledge the support of our Principal Partners: the National Australia Bank as our ongoing Art Education and Access Partner, and Channel Nine; and Supporting Partners: JC Decaux, ABC Local Radio, Fairfax Media, PricewaterhouseCoopers, Moët Hennessy Australia and the Novotel, Canberra.

I sincerely hope that visitors to the exhibition, and the readers of this book, will be stimulated by this new interpretation and presentation of one of the world's greatest collections of Ballets Russes costumes, and take pleasure in seeing newly restored costumes along with well-known favourites. Each is a fragile reminder of the passion, achievements and collaboration of those who made the Ballets Russes the twentieth-century model for the fusion of dance, music and visual arts.

Ron Radford AM
Director, National Gallery of Australia

Henri Matisse
Costume for a Mandarin c 1920
(detail) from *Le Chant du rossignol*

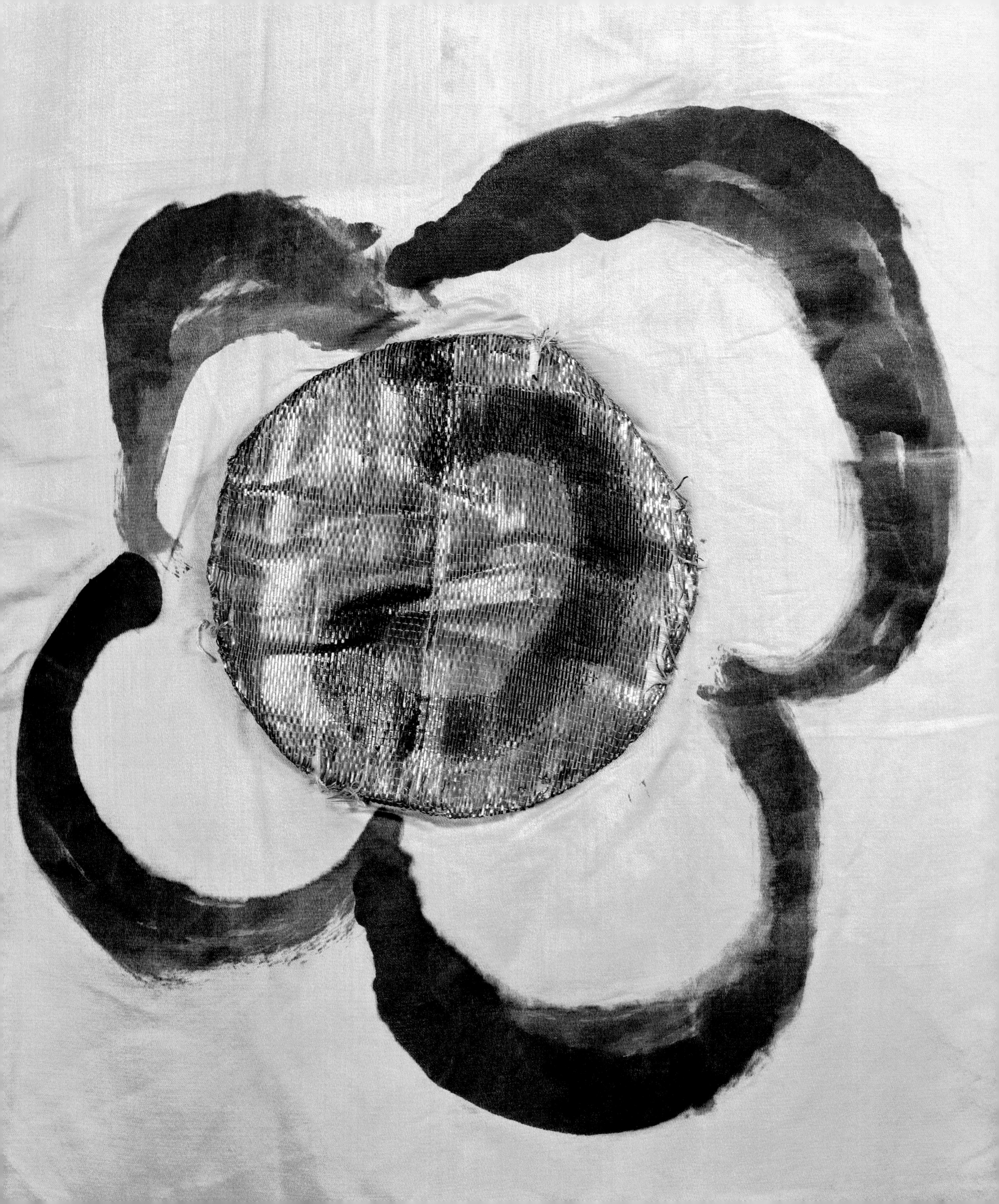

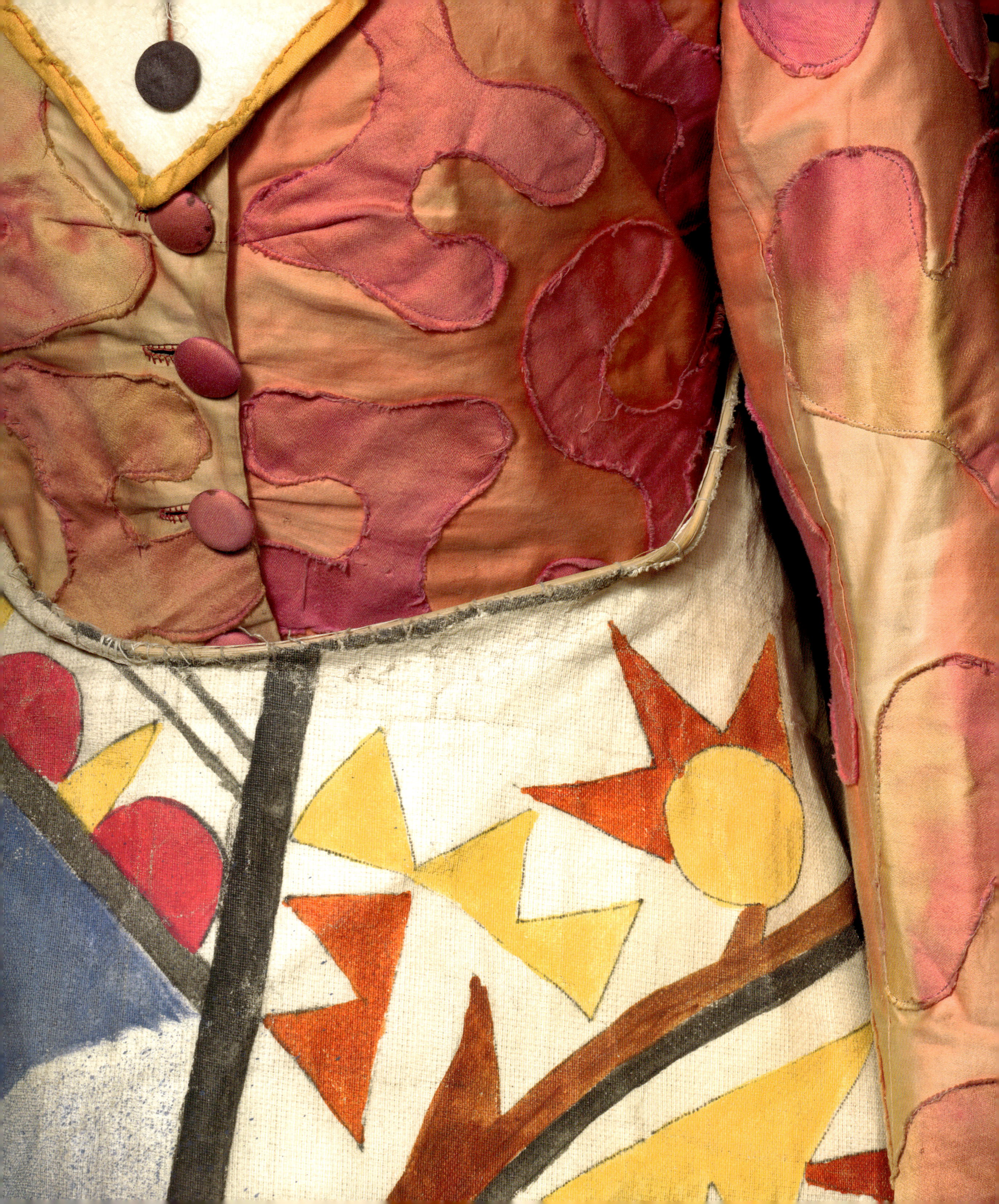

PRESENTING PARTNER

ActewAGL is delighted to be the Presenting Partner of the National Gallery of Australia's 2010–11 summer exhibition *Ballets Russes: the art of costume*. Audiences will have the opportunity to view costumes, drawings and film from one of the most cutting-edge and influential theatre companies of the twentieth century. ActewAGL and our predecessors have been supplying energy and water services since 1915. We are firmly committed to supporting the community, from artistic and cultural events to charities, schools, community groups and sporting teams.

As we mark our 10th anniversary as ActewAGL, it is timely to reflect on the extensive sponsorship we have provided to the National Gallery of Australia's exhibitions and acquisitions. It has been a privilege to support the following acquisitions, programs and exhibitions: *Chihuly: masterworks in glass* (1999–2000); *Jackson Pollock's Blue Poles* celebrating its fiftieth anniversary (2002–03); the acquisition in 2002 of Neil Dawson's *Diamonds* 2002; the Bill Viola Fund in 2005; *George W Lambert retrospective: heroes and icons* (2007); and *Degas: master of French art* (2008–09).

Ballets Russes: the art of costume presents the Gallery's renowned collection of costumes from Sergei Diaghilev's and Wassily de Basil's Ballets Russes, painstakingly restored and dramatically presented. The exhibition includes costumes by artists Natalia Goncharova, Michel Larionov, Pablo Picasso, Henri Matisse, André Derain, Sonia Delaunay, Georges Braque, André Masson and Giorgio de Chirico.

We believe this exhibition will be a drawcard for tourists, who will want to experience this amazing exhibition and see the many other exciting and unique attractions across the city that make Canberra such a rewarding destination.

I would like to congratulate the council and staff of the National Gallery of Australia for their commitment to presenting world-class exhibitions such as *Ballets Russes: the art of costume*. ActewAGL looks forward to continuing our strong partnership with the National Gallery of Australia into the future.

Michael Costello
ActewAGL Chief Executive Officer

Mikhail Larionov
Costume for a buffoon's wife
c 1921 (detail) from *Chout*

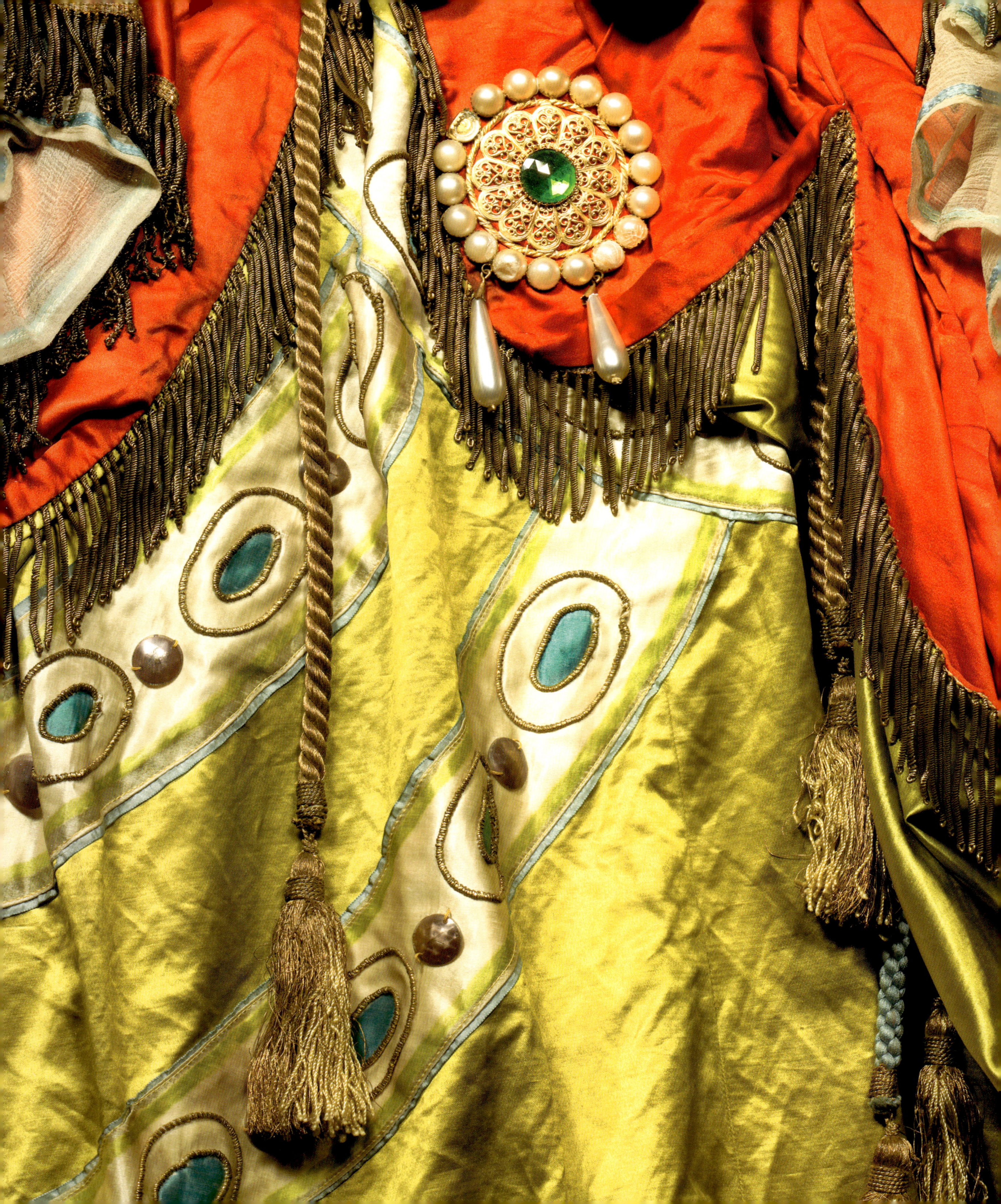

THE BALLETS RUSSES COSTUME LEGACY

Robert Bell

While ballet is a synthesis of music, illusion, art, artifice, narrative and the nuances of gesture and movement, it remains ephemeral, an art of the moment, dependent on the exquisite timing and interpretation of these elements. Dancers on stage can transcend, or ruin, planned choreography, stagecraft and music can transport an audience to another reality, and the timing and relevance of a production in the real world of society and politics can raise it to the canon or condemn it to obscurity. Musical scores, stage design and choreography can be re-created but costume remains the only really tangible part of productions and performances given before the advent, and different dimension, of film and video recordings of ballet.

The costumes designed and made for the Ballets Russes were conceived in the context of powerful and emotional artistic collaboration and command attention as persuasive works of art in their own right, long after they ceased to be worn on stage. Their ingenious design, cut and construction, innovative colours and patterns, the use of a variety of fabrics and trim materials, come together with the purpose of being worn in complex action by athletic dancers for maximum visual impact on stage. Even now, bearing the ravages of time, use and neglect, they are tangible reminders of the craft of their makers and their wearers.

The National Gallery of Australia's collection of over three hundred costumes from the productions of the Sergei Diaghilev and Wassily de Basil periods of the Ballets Russes is an important part of the international legacy of dance and stage design from the early twentieth century.[1] The question often asked is: how did these costumes come to be in Canberra? After Sergei Diaghilev's death in 1929, his theatre properties, including stage sets, costumes, designs and musical scores, were assembled by his choreographer Léonide Massine and sold (to cover the debts of the estate) in 1930 to the New York composer and theatre producer, E Ray Goetz (1886–1954), who planned to use them for his ambitious project to revive the Ballets Russes with Massine in the United States. Goetz's losses in the 1929 Wall Street financial crash forced him to abandon the project—and Massine—in 1931, leaving Massine as the owner of the Ballets Russes properties. In 1934 Massine was forced to sell the entire collection (then stored in Paris) to a group of de Basil's supporters in London through the Educational Ballets Ltd Foundation (established in 1932 by Anthony Diamantidi, a Greek-Russian businessman and enthusiastic supporter of Diaghilev and his enterprises since 1911). The Foundation allowed de Basil to use the collection and joined with him (as the Russian Ballet Development Company) in presenting his 1938 and 1939 seasons at Covent Garden in London and in a number of Australian and New Zealand cities.

On de Basil's death in 1951, the collection, and de Basil's company, returned to Diamantidi's control, becoming part of the assets of his new company, the Diaghilev and de Basil Ballet Foundation, and giving him renewed hope that he could interest others in establishing a ballet company to continue the artistic legacy of the Ballets Russes.[2] While public interest in the Ballets Russes was revived in 1954 with *The Diaghilev exhibition* at the Edinburgh Festival, organised by the renowned Diaghilev expert and

Léon Bakst
Costume for a lady-in-waiting
c 1921 (detail) from
The sleeping princess

biographer Richard Buckle, over the next several years Diamantidi failed to find a buyer. The success of a Sotheby's auction on 18 July 1967 of other Diaghilev material encouraged him to consign his collection to the auction house. A celebrated sale, catalogued under Buckle's supervision, took place at La Scala Theatre in London on 17 July 1968. Students from the Royal Ballet School modelled the costumes for the catalogue photography under the supervision of the School's English founder, the former Ballets Russes dancer Lydia Sokolova (Hilda Munnings 1896–1974). Subsequent auctions of additional costumes and properties from the collection were held by Sotheby's on 19 December 1969 and 3 March 1973.

Many of the works offered in the first three auctions were acquired for the collections of London's Theatre Museum (now part of the Victoria and Albert Museum collection), the Los Angeles County Museum of Art, the Dansmuseet in Stockholm, the Theatre Museum in Amsterdam and the Wadsworth Atheneum in Hartford, Connecticut. The Australian National Gallery (now the National Gallery of Australia) was the major bidder at the last auction in 1973, securing forty-seven lots comprising over four hundred items for a little over £3000. The National Gallery's establishment in 1968 offered its founding director, James Mollison, the opportunity to shape a collection that would showcase modern art in all its forms. He seized upon the early developmental opportunity offered by the Sotheby's sales to extend the European modernist collection, and aggressively and successfully bid for the works that now form one of the world's major collections of Ballets Russes costume.

A further group of Ballets Russes costumes was acquired at auction in 1976, with a number of individual costumes being purchased at auction since that time. The costumes are supplemented by a collection of artists' design drawings for costumes and sets, among them works by Léon Bakst, Alexandre Benois, Natalia Goncharova, André Derain and Juan Gris. They reveal the designers' original visions of the costumes as they would be seen by audiences—in movement and completed by the dancers' bodies. The Gallery's Research Library collection of Ballets Russes programs and other ephemera is a valuable research resource for curators, conservators and dance specialists.

The first group of costumes arrived in Canberra in the condition in which they had been consigned to storage twenty-three years earlier. The British ballet historian Philip Dyer was contracted by the Gallery to identify and catalogue them, allocating the dates of their original use and the subsequent revivals for which they were used or modified. Some were relatively pristine, but most showed the effects of accumulated sweat, dried make-up, fugitive dyes, dirt, insect damage, mould or moisture. The evidence of modifications and alterations, both skilled and hastily done, remains as clues to the costumes' use on stage and their long use by many performers of varying sizes and body types. Other modifications to the costumes were made to extend their use in later productions and to align them to changes in dress and stage fashions. We can also see weakened or torn areas that are the consequence of particular, repetitive movements and gain insights in to the 'performance' of the actual fabrics in heavy use. The costumes presented a stimulating challenge to the nascent Gallery's newly recruited team of conservators as they began to prepare them for display. Their patient research, carried out over the past twenty-five years, on the fabrics and the costumes' histories of use, combined with their development of advanced textile conservation skills, have contributed to the high reputation and fine condition of the Gallery's collection.[3]

Selections from the Ballets Russes costume collection have been exhibited regularly since the National Gallery of Australia opened in 1982, initially in a small dedicated space for theatre arts and fashion costume and later as an integral part of collection displays in the International Art galleries. Two major exhibitions have previously been mounted at the Gallery: *From studio to stage: painters of the Russian Ballet 1909–1929* in 1990 and *From Russia with love: costumes for the Ballets Russes* in 1999.[4] In 2004, fifteen of the Gallery's Ballets Russes costumes were lent to the Groninger Museum in the Netherlands for its exhibition, *Working for Diaghilev*. These projects accelerated conservation work on the costumes, as has the exhibition associated with this publication, resulting in 51 newly restored costumes being exhibited for the first time.[5]

Diaghilev commissioned leading couturiers and theatrical costumiers to make costumes designed by his artists and to bring sketchy ideas to fruition as practical and durable performance garments. Among them were the Paris couturiers Jeanne Paquin, who made the costumes for *Parade* (*Sideshow*) and *Jeux* (*Plays*), Germaine Bongard (the couturier Paul Poiret's sister), whose firm Jove made the costumes for *Chout* (*The buffoon*) and *Cuadro flamenco*, and Gabrielle 'Coco' Chanel, who designed and made the costumes for *Le Train bleu* (*The blue train*). Regularly commissioned professional theatre costumiers included Marie Muelle (Muelle & Rossignol), Vera Sudeikina, Helen Pons, A Youkine, Pierre Pitoeff, M Landoff, Caffi and Vorobier, Grace Lovat Fraser and Barbara Karinska. Luxurious materials and the highly developed craft skills of the professional costumier are evident in costumes made for costly productions, while leaner times for the company are revealed in the use of cheaper materials and painted *trompe l'oeil* decorative effects, executed in some cases by the designer's own hand.

Inevitably the dance costumes became seriously worn and had to be constantly repaired, even re-made for use in extended tours, long-running productions or later revivals. Original, repaired, remodelled and new costumes, made by various costumiers, might be used in the one performance. Replicas were also made to be worn by guest dancers at private and fund-raising events. The costumes worn in staged publicity photos may not always have been those worn on stage and there are few contemporary colour photographs that would allow us to verify whether a designer's intentions for fabric, colour and texture were fully and accurately carried out. These factors make the exact attribution of costumes to actual productions, performances and performers difficult to confirm. As the first-hand recollections and experiences of those who wore the costumes fade over time, only forensic investigation by conservators and ongoing research by curators, writers and dance historians will reveal more of their histories.

Many of the costumes are associated directly with known performers, identified through names or initials written inside them, or in contemporary performance photographs that indicate how many dancers might have worn a particular costume. One of the most important costumes in the collection is that worn by Vaslav Nijinsky in the role of the Blue God in *Le Dieu bleu* (*The blue god*). While it is a costume of fascinating design and construction, the traces of blue body make-up on its lining capture forever a physical and intimate moment of Nijinsky's commanding stage presence.

The Gallery's costumes are only part of the larger context of the productions for which they were made, but each one retains the power to evoke the intimacy and emotional charge between performer and audience that was at the heart of the Ballets Russes experience. These disembodied and endearingly vulnerable costumes engage us like fragments of a dream that appear, overlap and disappear, populating a half-remembered world of imagination and memory. We cannot share our dreams, but through these fragments we can catch glimpses of the work and passion of Diaghilev and his collaborators and successors, glimpses that reveal their understanding of this precarious equation of memory and reality.

WILD DREAM: IMAGINING THE BALLETS RUSSES

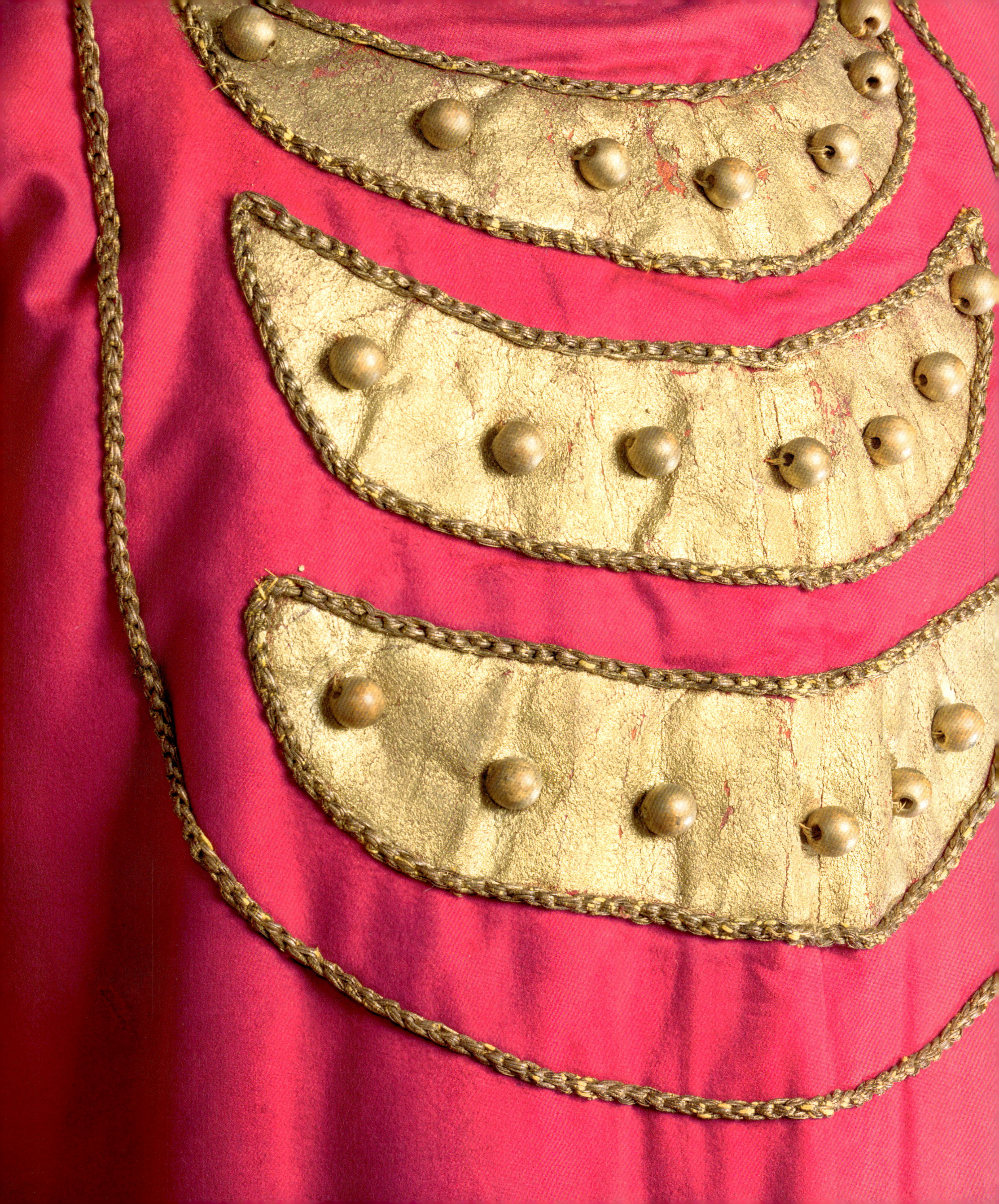

WILD DREAM: IMAGINING THE BALLETS RUSSES

Robert Bell

> They say that one should never return to a first love, or look at the rose which one admired the evening before.
> *Omphale*, Théophile Gautier[1]

Aurora, Carabosse, the Firebird, Petrouchka and Giselle are among countless figures of the imagination that have been given substance and character through the world of ballet. Their legendary status has grown through the generations as they continue to inspire the re-tellers of stories from deep in the European imagination and are re-interpreted by flesh and blood performers reflecting the manners and fashions of their own time and place.

The arts of choreography, stagecraft and dance costumery have their foundations in the sixteenth century. The French *ballet de cour* (court ballet) grew from the acrobatic and folk dance court entertainments of the Italian court of the 1490s, being introduced to France by Catherine de' Medici (after her marriage to Henry II in 1533) as an element of elaborate staged allegorical spectacles of song, music and dance in celebration of the microcosm of man.[2] The organisation, structure, narrative and plot conventions of ballet performance began to be defined, allowing an enormous range of characters—mythic, comic, folkloric, historic and aristocratic—to take to the stage in elaborate and luxurious costumes based on the silhouettes and constructions of everyday and fashionable dress.

From about 1610 onwards, the introduction of the proscenium arch and mechanically operated painted perspective scenery allowed ballet designers and choreographers to integrate costumed singers, actors and dancers into an overall visual spectacle to be viewed, as we do today, from an auditorium. With the establishment of the Paris Opéra by King Louis XIV in 1669, ballet's move from court spectacle to public theatre, and the subsequent development of the ballet company and the professional performer, began.[3]

Ballet costumes based on everyday dress restricted movement and inhibited the development of dance techniques. By the eighteenth century, choreographers and costumiers were designing adjustments to costume and footwear to allow for greater leg exposure and movement for both male and female dancers. Innovations in costume design by artists employed by the Paris Opéra influenced ballet masters in opera houses in other European centres and stimulated further developments among those innovators of the newer, more expressive *ballet d'action*, in which dramatic narrative was expressed not through formal spectacle but directly by the dance steps and movements of principal dancers and the corps de ballet.[4] The choreographic freedom of *ballet d'action* was well served by the spirit and style of the neoclassical movement that began to infiltrate the theatre from the 1780s. Stage and costume designers drew from the movement's focus on naturalism and its stylistic references to classical mythology, developing simpler costumes in lighter, diaphanous fabrics that revealed more of the dancers' bodies and allowed more fluid and athletic movement. Technical virtuosity became more evident to the audience, encouraging the perfection of formal dance movements and the development of techniques specific to ballet, such as

Natalia Goncharova
Costume for finale c 1926 (detail)
from *L'Oiseau de feu*
© Natalia Goncharova/ADAGP.
Licensed by Viscopy, 2010

pointe work for female dancers and lifts for males in the pas de deux.

The Romantic movement of the late eighteenth and early nineteenth centuries offered newer and more varied subject matter for the ballet, less influenced by the strictures of classical antiquity and scientific rationalism. It was more reflective of the new readings of history and folk legend, the expression of melancholy and nostalgia and the growing movements of nationalism, in themselves reflecting the uncertainties of a society challenged by the new industrial age. The first significant expression of Romanticism in ballet was the Paris Opéra's 1832 production of *La Sylphide*. Its character costumes, the work of an independent designer, the French painter Eugène Lami (1800–1890), contrasted with the simple, ethereal tutus worn by the *sylphides* (forest fairies). White, calf-length and full-skirted, these costumes suggested the weightlessness and purity of the characters and allowed female dancers to dominate the stage. The cult of the Romantic ballerina was born with the Opéra dancer Marie Taglioni's skilled and expressive pointe work in this production.[5]

The increasing eclecticism of Romantic subject matter during the nineteenth century created important, but seldom credited, roles for costume designers and makers employed by opera house and ballet company directors. Earlier costumes and costume books provided sources of design detail for costumiers as they sought to reflect the ballet characters' nationality, ethnicity, personality or historical roles.

By the late nineteenth century, ballet's reputation in Western Europe had begun to decline due to its rigid adherence to classical technique and a lack of program freshness and of new choreographic ideas. Costume and stage design had become formulaic, and music subservient to dance techniques and their rhythmic conventions. Relegated to light divertissements and interval acts at opera performances or to part of the program in music halls and vaudeville, ballet had become almost entirely reliant on female performers (including those playing male roles), resulting in an aura of eroticism and voyeurism. Costume and scene designers, however, found greater freedom and expressive possibilities working in the music hall context, and the consequent widening of ballet's subject matter from the confines of the classical and Romantic traditions of the opera stage incorporated contemporary themes and narratives, exotic imaginings and popular culture. Ballet's new audiences began to expect theatrical spectacle and artistic novelty.[6]

The re-emergence of ballet as one of the most dynamic and engaging forms of modern cultural production in the early decades of the twentieth century is synonymous with the spectacular success of Les Ballets Russes de Serge Diaghilev (Sergei Diaghilev's Russian Ballet). From the emerging troupe's first performances in Paris in 1909, this dance company, and those that evolved from it in the following three decades, drew together the performing and visual arts in provocative and entertaining creative collaborations that continue to inspire. While its original productions exist now only through photographs, music, costumes and sets, choreography, published memoirs and the direct memory of a dwindling few performers and collaborators, one hundred years after those first productions the term 'Ballets Russes' signifies not just the history of this particular ballet company but also the triumph of audacity and creative vision. The surviving costumes of the Ballets Russes offer some of the most tangible links to these endeavours. Intimate, intricate, sensuous in material and form, and bearing the evidence of hard and continuous use, they are poignant reminders of their wearers' physicality and performances, the visions of their designers and the experienced hands of their makers. This book and the exhibition of costumes it documents mark the centenary of the Ballets Russes and reveal the richness of the National Gallery of Australia's renowned collection of Ballets Russes costume.

Sergei Diaghilev, creator of the Ballets Russes

The story of the Ballets Russes is also that of founder and director Sergei Diaghilev, a Russian dilettante and impresario whose passion for the arts was matched with curiosity, charm, determination, risk-taking and attention to detail. He was born Sergei Pavlovich Diaghilev on 19 March 1872, the only son of Pavel Pavlovich Diaghilev (1849–1914) and his first wife, Yevgenia Diaghileva, who died three months after Sergei's birth. The Diaghilev family's position came from its minor connections to the nobility, while its

Perm, where, in his large town house, the musical Pavel Diaghilev led the town's cultural life by holding regular musical and literary events and soirées. Sergei (known to family as Seriozha) attended the boys' grammar school in Perm, excelling in music and arts before enrolling in 1890 at the University of St Petersburg to study law, in preparation for a presumed future career in the Imperial civil service. The move coincided with the family's descent into bankruptcy, leaving Sergei with only a small inheritance (from his mother) which enabled him to set up a residence in the city. With a stocky figure and a dramatic streak of white in his dark hair, he presented himself as a grand and elegant aesthete, immaculately dressed and, later, monocled, providing good subject matter for the innumerable artists, photographers and caricaturists who depicted him during his life.

Before embracing his law studies, Sergei stayed regularly at the home and estate of his father's elder sister, Anna Pavlovna Filosofov (1837–1912), a wealthy and prominent social reformer in St Petersburg, and formed a close relationship with her son Dmitri ('Dima'). As was usual for young men of their class and standing, the cousins embarked on a grand tour of Europe in 1890 before settling into university life. They attended theatre and opera and visited art collections and historic sites in Germany, Austria, Italy and Switzerland. For Diaghilev, the romantic intimacy and intellectual challenge of Filosofov's company boded well for their future relationship and travels together.

The world of art

In their private life and as a fellow student, Dima Filosofov, a dandyish aesthete with a deep knowledge of theatre and literature, exerted a strong influence on his cousin's emerging literary and artistic tastes and interests. Most important was Filosofov's introduction of Diaghilev to his existing circle of school and university friends, artist Alexandre Benois (Aleksandr Benua), writer Walter Nouvel and artist Konstantin Somov. The artists Nicholas Roerich and Léon Bakst (Lev Samoilovich Rosenberg) joined the group at the same time.[7] This group expressed its diverse arts and literary interests through a club known as the Society for Self Education, or the 'Nevsky Pickwickians', which held music performances,

wealth derived from its land and the operation of its vodka distilleries at Bikbarda near the provincial town of Perm in the province of Novgorod, at the gateway to the Urals. Pavel Diaghilev had risen through the military to become Squadron Commander in the prestigious Chevaliers Gardes (cavalry) regiment. After his wife's death, he joined his family with that of his widowed sister, Maria Koribut-Kubitovich, and her three children, and moved the combined household seasonally to enjoy a more urban life in St Petersburg. In 1874 he married Yelena Valerianovna Panayev, a union that produced two sons, Valentin and Yury, and provided a warm and supportive stepmother for Sergei.

By 1878 the financial constraints of maintaining a home in St Petersburg had forced the family back to

Unknown photographer
Serge Diaghilev, New York 1916
Bibliothèque nationale de France, Paris, Fonds Kochno, Album Photo Diaghilev 6

lectures and discussions on aspects of the latest ideas and movements in the world of the arts. The club held subscriptions of literary and art journals from abroad (such as *La Revue Blanche*, *Studio*, *Pan* and the *Yellow Book*), stimulating among its members a desire to publish their own journal to disseminate new ideas, arts criticism and the work of both Russian and foreign artists.

By 1892 Diaghilev's interest and growing passion for music had begun to overtake his formal university studies. He undertook singing and composition lessons and became a regular figure in St Petersburg's musical circles as an audience member and occasional performer. In the summer of that year he travelled to Austria and Germany to immerse himself in the music culture of Salzburg, Nuremburg and Bayreuth, where he indulged in what would become a lifelong passion for the work of Richard Wagner, attending numerous opera performances. In 1894, with Filosofov, he travelled again to Italy, and to France for the first time, where his experiences and the connections he made provided an even stronger stimulus to pursue a career as a composer. Later that year, Diaghilev was sufficiently confident of his work to approach the Russian composer Nikolai Rimsky-Korsakov (1844–1908) with a work that he hoped would convince Rimsky-Korsakov to take him on as a theory student. The composer's response, however, was both dismissive and demoralising, leading Diaghilev to reassess his expectations of a career in music and turn his attention to a period of concentrated and necessary final university study, followed by the diverting task of furnishing a new apartment in St Petersburg. Exercising his developing taste for luxurious decorative and fine arts, he began to build a collection of works by progressive Russian and French artists which he exhibited for the edification of those in the widening cultural circle that was beginning to form as a result of his entrepreneurship. From 1898, Diaghilev's exhibitions of progressive Scandinavian and Finnish artists established his credentials as a curator.[8] In these projects Diaghilev was mentored and encouraged by Benois, whose family was prominent in the artistic life of St Petersburg, and whose own developing career, even as a young man, as illustrator, stage designer, art historian and critic was beginning to place him as an influential figure in Russian art.

Léon Bakst
Portrait of Diaghilev with his nanny 1904–06
oil on canvas
161 x 116 cm
State Russian Museum, St Petersburg
© 2010 State Russian Museum, St Petersburg

While the Nevsky Pickwickians had been discussing the publication of their own journal since 1893, it was Diaghilev who in 1898 developed this idea into reality by inaugurating Russia's only art journal, *Mir Iskusstva* (*World of Art*). His connections and cultural authority had allowed him to secure for the journal the patronage and sponsorship of Princess Maria Klavdievna Tenisheva (1867–1928) and the wealthy industrialist Savva Mamontov (1841–1918). The aristocratic Tenisheva, formerly an opera singer, had founded the progressive artists' colony of Talashkino, near Smolensk, in 1893 and was committed to the preservation of Russian folk art, while the middle-class Mamontov, heir to a railroad fortune and an ardent supporter of Russian opera, had since 1870 developed a community of artists at his estate at Abramtsevo, near Moscow. Both centres encouraged the new expressions of Russian nationalist art and design in the spirit of the Arts and Crafts movement that had taken hold across northern and eastern Europe in the 1890s.[9] Importantly, Diaghilev's membership of these progressive circles provided ready access to contributors to, and subjects for, the journal.

28 Ballets Russes: the art of costume

Mir Iskusstva was a work of art in itself, lavishly produced with colour illustrations, interesting typography and innovative graphic design on quality imported paper with fine bindings.[10] From an editorial office within his apartment, each issue was conceived by Diaghilev and developed in collaboration with an editorial team consisting of Filosofov, Nouvel, Bakst and Benois, each contributing to aspects of content and design and bringing in other writers, critics and artists. This group, known as the *miriskusniki*, ensured a diversity of views and provided a framework of progressive Russian thought to the journal's international outlook. In addition to articles on aspects of Russian historical and progressive art, literature and music, subscribers were introduced to new and fashionable works by Western European artists such as the English illustrator Aubrey Beardsley, the French painter Pierre Puvis de Chavannes, the Swiss painter Félix Vallotton, the French Symbolist writer Stéphane Mallarmé, the Scottish architect Charles Rennie Mackintosh and the designers and artists of the Vienna and Munich Secession groups. By 1900, however, Tenisheva and Mamontov's financial backing had come to an end, forcing Diaghilev to seek new sponsorship to keep the journal in print.[11] He succeeded in gaining financial backing for three years from Tsar Nicholas II, adding the lustre of imperial support for the progressive views of the *miriskusniki*.

His imperial connections placed Diaghilev in a favourable position for advancement and in 1900, on the recommendation of Prince Sergei Volkonsky, a contributor to *Mir Iskusstva* and Director of the Imperial Theatres, he was appointed to the civil service as a 'functionary for special missions' of the Theatres' directorate. Among his roles was the editing of the Imperial Theatres' annual journals, to which he brought some of the panache that he had been developing in *Mir Iskusstva*. Gaining confidence in this new position, he proposed the staging of what he planned to be his first production, the ballet *Sylvia*, employing the skills of his close colleagues in the *miriskusniki*.[12] Diaghilev's entry to the higher echelons of the Imperial Theatres, however, had caused disapproval among entrenched opponents to change, which eventually led to his abrupt dismissal by Volkonsky in March 1901. Finding himself increasingly excluded from official theatre circles, he resumed work towards curating and producing a large exhibition of Russian portraiture since 1705, a project that had grown from his research into the history of Russian art. Extensive travel in Russia and abroad, with introductions often facilitated by his imperial connections, had given Diaghilev access to numerous old private collections from which he was able to assemble, and properly catalogue, a monumental exhibition of over 4000 works at the Tauride Palace in St Petersburg in February 1905.

(above left) *Savva Mamontov*, title page of *Mir Isskusstva*, vol 4, no 4, 1903
National Library of Australia, Canberra

(above centre) Page in *Mir Isskusstva*, vol 3, nos 12–13, 1900
National Library of Australia, Canberra

(above right) Maria Yakunchikova, title page of *Mir Isskusstva*, vol 2, 1899
National Library of Australia, Canberra

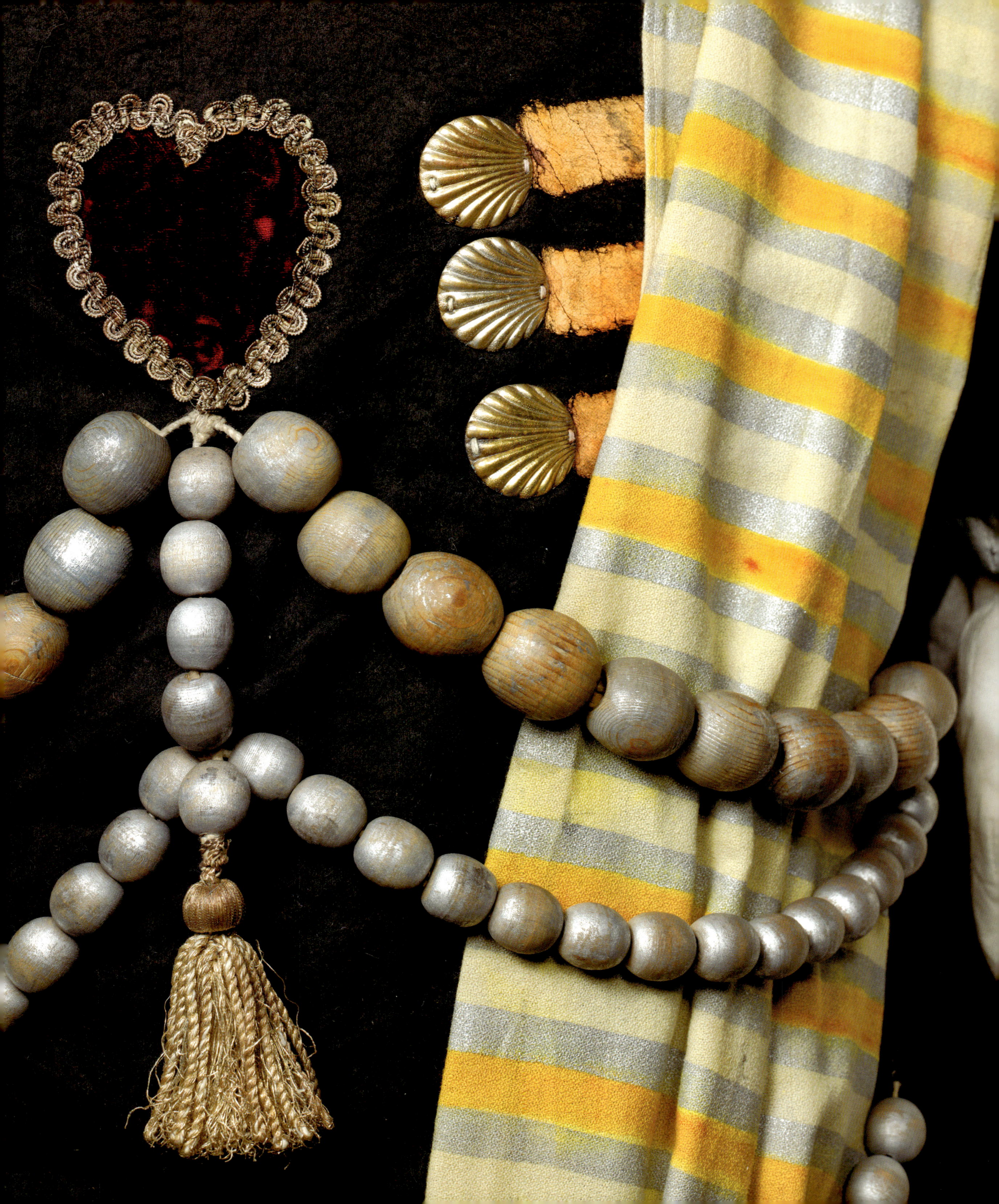

The eventual cessation of *Mir Iskusstva*'s publication in 1904 freed Diaghilev from what had become the emotional and financial burden of its precarious financial situation, for he had been forced to make the decision to sell a number of works from his collection to meet the journal's costs. *Mir Iskusstva*'s and Diaghilev's swansong was an exhibition in St Petersburg of the work of the *miriskusniki*, along with that of a younger group of progressive artists which included the painter Mikhail Larionov, who would later become one of the designers for the Ballets Russes.

Although he was lauded for his organisational skills and discerning eye in bringing ambitious exhibition projects such as this to fruition, Diaghilev understood that opportunities for more intensive and independent entrepreneurial and directorial work would lie outside Russia, particularly given the country's deteriorating political environment. Diaghilev was confident in his openly homosexual life in the gay subcultures of upper-class St Petersburg and Moscow and the other European cities he regularly visited, but he was no doubt aware that his activities and associations might be a reason for official repression in a more conservative political environment. His circle of leading arts figures was stimulating, intellectually challenging and well connected, and placed him in a wider and more radical European cultural environment.[13] Diaghilev resolved to avoid potential problems at home by working abroad for the promotion of Russian culture, and left for Paris in 1906.

Diaghilev's formative years in St Petersburg had placed him in the period when ballet in Russia was controlled by the Imperial Ballet School, founded in 1738, and the Imperial Russian Ballet, founded a few years later. By the late nineteenth century these organisations had trained and later employed some of the most accomplished figures in ballet and introduced most of the standard classical works into the repertory. The period's towering figure was the French-born choreographer, Marius Petipa (1822–1910), who was employed from 1847 to 1903, initially as a dancer and then as ballet master from 1869. His lavish fairytale productions were characterised by the spectacle of massed dancers, elaborate (but formulaic) sets suggesting exotic locations and highly structured classical dance interspersed with folkloric character dances in multi-act performances. Among his most celebrated productions were *Don Quixote* (1869), *Giselle* (1884 revival), *The sleeping beauty* (1890), *The nutcracker* (1892), *Cinderella* (1893) and *Swan lake* (1895). The production of these ballets was under the control of the Imperial Theatres' director from 1881 to 1898, Ivan Vsevolozhsky (1835–1909), who also designed most of the costumes.

One of the School's most impressive graduates was Michel Fokine (Mikhail Mikhailovich Fokin 1880–1942), who made his debut as the partner of Anna Pavlova in 1898.[14] In 1902 he began teaching for the School and choreographic work for the Imperial Russian Ballet, culminating in his first production, *Le Pavillon d'Armide* (*Armida's pavilion*), at the Mariinsky Theatre in 1907. Fokine's work in expanding Petipa's disciplined and structured approach to include more expressive possibilities for the dancer aligned him with innovators such as Isadora Duncan, the *miriskusniki* and eventually, through Benois' introduction, with Diaghilev, for whom he became chief choreographer with the Ballets Russes in Paris

(opposite) **Alexandre Benois**
Jacket from costume for a musician c 1909 (detail)
from *Le Pavillon d'Armide*

(above) **Auguste Bert**
M Fokine and Mme Fokina in L'Oiseau de feu
page 17 in *Official program for the Ballets Russes at the Théâtre du Châtelet,* June 1911

Léon Bakst
cover of *Official program for the Ballets Russes*, Théâtre national de l'Opéra, Paris, 1910

from 1909 to 1912, before returning to the Imperial Theatre in 1913.[15] His acrimonious split with Diaghilev in 1912 centred on the impresario's favouring of Vaslav Nijinsky's choreography, but Diaghilev was able to persuade him to work again for the Ballets Russes as choreographer for several productions in 1914. To publicly reinforce his approach to choreography at this critical time in his career, Fokine published his 'five principles' of dance in a letter to *The Times* in 1914.[16] He emigrated to the United States of America in 1919, founding his own ballet school in New York in 1923. But by 1909 it was Fokine's record as a creator of ballets, his talent and audacity as a choreographer that were the catalysts for the visual and musical spectacles that Diaghilev had devised.

The Russian seasons 1909–14

When the Théâtre du Châtelet's curtain went up on 19 May 1909 for the opening performances of Diaghilev's fourth Saison Russe (Russian season) consisting, for the first time, of ballet and opera, it was to a Parisian audience already primed to expect the extraordinary. Beginning with the Orientalism that had engaged French artists and composers through the nineteenth century, a wider taste for exoticism had developed in the city since the eclectic spectacle of foreign cultures presented at the Exposition Universelle of 1900. Since then dancers such as the Americans Loïe Fuller and Isadora Duncan, and their followers, had opened the eyes of Parisians to new forms of expressive individual dance and to non-Western dance styles.[17]

In 1906 Diaghilev had presented an extensive exhibition of historical and contemporary Russian art, *L'Exposition de l'art russe*, as part of the Salon d'Automne at the Grand Palais in Paris. It was based on his last exhibition in St Petersburg and, while well received, did not equal the energy of the contemporary French visual arts scene in the host city. This led Diaghilev to concentrate on the lesser-known field of contemporary performing arts as a more viable, and potentially profitable, vehicle for the promotion of Russian arts abroad.[18] Following his success with five concerts of Russian music in 1907[19], he presented an extravagant production of Modest Mussorgsky's 1874 opera *Boris Godunov* at the Paris Opéra in 1908.[20] This production broke new ground for this most famous of Russian operas, with its costumes, an eclectic mix of traditional ethnic dress from across the Russian empire, offering a foretaste of the production values and style that were to become the trademark of Diaghilev's enterprises.

Diaghilev's 1909 Saison Russe began with the ballet *Le Pavillon d'Armide*, which had premiered on 25 November 1907 at the Mariinsky Theatre in St Petersburg.[21] A production of the Imperial Theatres, it was the first to bring together the talents of choreographer Michel Fokine and prominent dancers such as Anna Pavlova and the seventeen-year-old Vaslav Nijinsky with a leading member of the *miriskusniki*, the designer Alexandre Benois. Diaghilev, not previously been involved in the promotion of ballet, was introduced to this production by Benois and saw the possibility of including it in a season of ballet and opera in Paris that would showcase the work and the artists of the Imperial Theatres, and set about seeking patronage, funding and venues. The program Diaghilev devised for the first night of this Saison Russe included the ballets *Le Pavillon d'Armide*, *Danses polovtsiennes du Prince Igor* (*The Polovtsian dances from Prince Igor*) and *Le Festin* (*The feast*). The full season included the ballets *Giselle*, *Les Sylphides* (previously staged as *Chopiniana* in 1907) and *Cléopâtre*, previously staged as *Une Nuit d'Egypte* (*Egyptian nights*) in 1908, and the operas *Ruslan and Ludmila*, *Ivan the terrible* (*The maid of Pskov*) and *Judith*.

After two months' rehearsals in St Petersburg, the 330 Imperial Russian Ballet dancers, singers, musicians and technical staff that had been released by the organisation and assembled by Diaghilev arrived in Paris in early May 1909. The Théâtre du Châtelet had been used for musicals and, although run-down, was the only venue suitable for a 'mixed' music and dance program. Diaghilev requested that it be extensively refurbished to accommodate his company and orchestra in a grander style, with larger and more efficient facilities befitting this inaugural season. This contributed to serious financial losses over the season (Diaghilev's properties, sets and costumes were seized by the Châtelet management as security until overdue accounts were settled), requiring the entrepreneur to secure further loans to continue with new projects—a situation that was to become a pattern in his enterprises.

The 1909 Saison Russe marked the restoration of the art of ballet to the higher levels of the performing arts. The presence of so many of the Imperial Russian Ballet's female stars—Anna Pavlova, Ida Rubinstein, Vera Fokina, Tamara Karsavina and Ludmila Schollar—brought drama and authority to their performances as central characters in the program, which was designed to allow their individual skills to be explored and displayed to the full.[22] However, it was the powerful presence of the male dancers that galvanised audiences unused to seeing dominant male roles and unprepared for the overt physicality, athleticism and bravado that dancers such as Vaslav Nijinsky, Adolph Bolm, Michel Fokine, Georgi Rosai and Mikhail Mordkin brought to their roles.[23] The costumes designed for these performers, and for the members of the corps de ballet, allowed for fluid and energetic movement and revealed and sexualised the dancers' bodies in a manner that shattered ballet's genteel, feminised image.[24] The sexual ambiguity of dancers such as Nijinsky was exploited in Ballets Russes publicity images and in the illustrations and photographs appearing in fashion and theatre magazines such as *Le Théâtre* and *La Gazette du Bon Ton*. The male dancers were shown in revealing costumes designed to heighten homoerotic appeal as Diaghilev's productions moved away from ballet's previous sexual stereotyping.[25]

Diaghilev's engagement of leading Russian artists and designers (instead of conventional scenery painters and costumiers) for stage décor and costume provided a new type of visual spectacle and framework for Fokine's unconventional choreography and his dancers' powerful presence. The integrated design of these elements of theatrical production, and the singular vision they created, demonstrated Diaghilev's commitment to bringing the mid-nineteenth Wagnerian concept of *Gesamtkunstwerk* (total work of art) to the service of Modernism. The 1909 season's repertoire introduced themes of historical revival, Orientalism and Russian folklore in productions that revolutionised ballet, moving it beyond ossified convention to reflect current art movements and interests.

Diaghilev's deep musical knowledge led him to abandon works specifically written for ballet in favour of using, and sometimes rearranging and editing, the independent works of Russian composers such as Rimsky-Korsakov, Tcherepnin, Mussorgsky, Tchaikovsky and Borodin. Parisian audiences were also introduced to the imaginative artistic visions of the designers Benois and Roerich as they drew from the

Jean Cocteau
Poster of Vaslav Nijinsky 1911
from *Le Spectre de la rose*
(*The spirit of the rose*)
© Jean Cocteau/ADAGP. Licensed by Viscopy, 2010

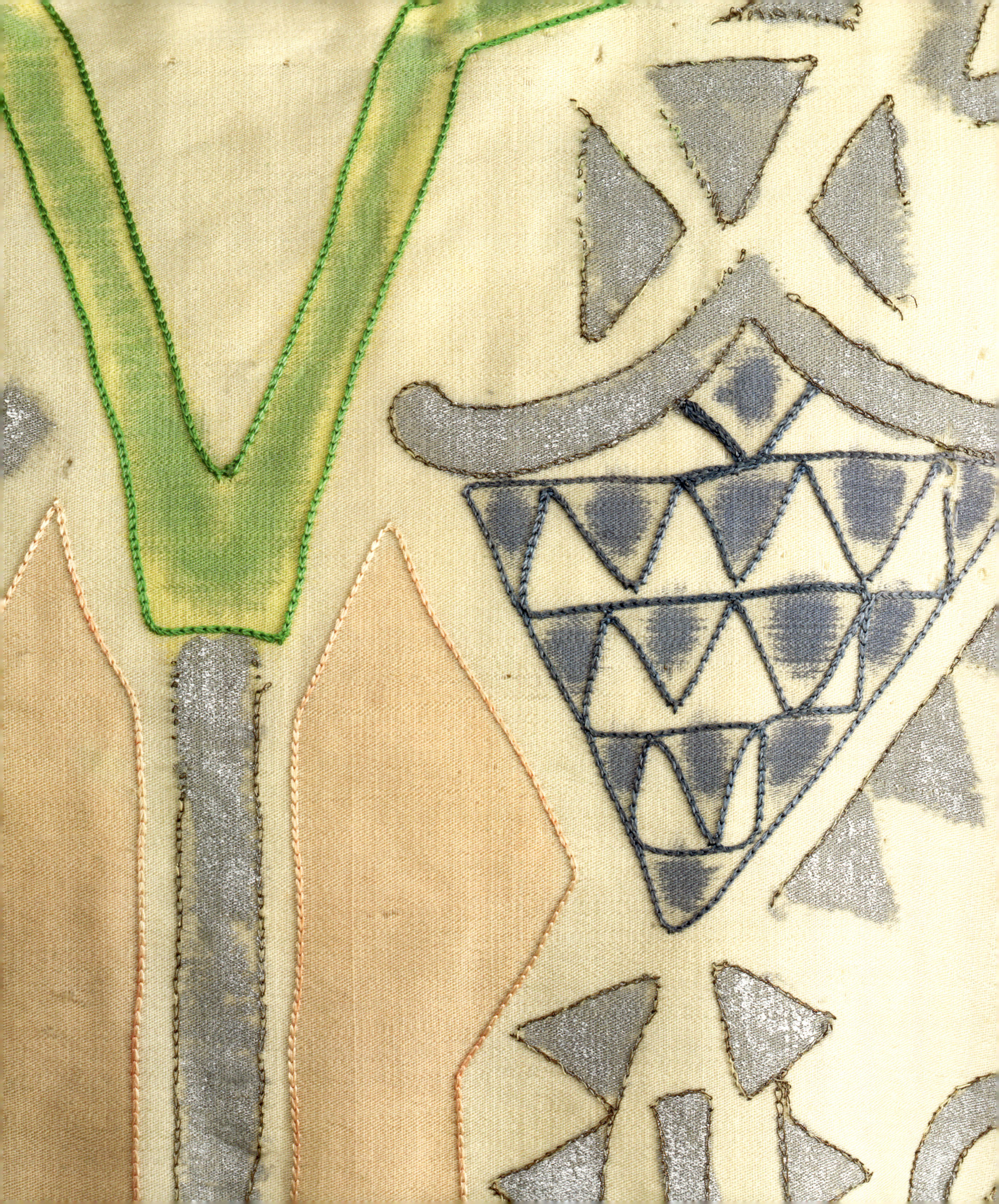

Russian Empire's vast cultural and historical depth, from its classical centres to its farthest central Asian reaches. Bakst's costumes for *Cléopâtre*, a living interpretation of the sinuous and rhythmic Art Nouveau style, shifted ballet into a new visual dimension where the dancers' exposed bodies joined with the patterns of their jewellery and the sheen of metallic textiles in abstracted Egyptian motifs on their costumes.

Diaghilev's Russian troupe returned to Paris for a second ballet season (the fifth Saison Russe) in May–June 1910 at the Théâtre national de l'Opéra with a program that included *Schéhérazade*, *Giselle*, *Les Orientales* and *L'Oiseau de feu* (*The firebird*). Bakst's rich orientalist design for *Schéhérazade* was realised with an equally vivid Fauvist-inspired colour orchestration that influenced fashion and interior design for the next decade, particularly through the work of the French couturier Paul Poiret, whose *Schéhérazade*-inspired designs changed the silhouette and cut of women's clothes.[26] Set to Rimsky-Korsakov's symphonic poem of the same name, *Schéhérazade* was the first ballet entirely created by Diaghilev and his collaborators. Its sensual choreography established Fokine as a dance dramatist and its male star, Vaslav Nijinsky, was immortalised by the role of Zobeïde's Favourite Slave. By that stage, Nijinsky was also Diaghilev's favourite, as lover and protégé, in the first of a number of highly visible and controlling homosexual relationships with young dancers in the Ballets Russes.

L'Oiseau de feu's contribution to change was even more enduring and revolutionary than that of *Schéhérazade*, for it introduced to the Western stage the work of the Russian composer Igor Stravinsky (1882–1971), who Diaghilev had met in St Petersburg in 1909 and with whom he would develop his most enduring and creative, although often argumentative and acrimonious, professional partnership.[27]

Diaghilev began to move away from the work of Russian composers for his 1912 season, commissioning scores for new works from contemporary French composers such as Reynaldo Hahn for *Le Dieu bleu* (*The blue god*), Claude Debussy for *L'Après-midi d'un faune* (*The afternoon of a faun*) and Maurice Ravel for *Daphnis et Chloé*, further establishing the Ballets Russes as a Western European and internationally focused company associated with the musical avant-garde.

By 1911 Diaghilev had resolved to free himself from his dependence on the Imperial Theatres to release their dancers during their vacations for his European seasons. Indeed, support in Russia, even from the Tsar, was disappearing as Diaghilev's reputation was being eroded by those envious of his success abroad. In 1911 he founded his permanent company, Ballet Russe de Diaghileff (named in his correspondence and publicity as Les Ballets Russes de Serge de Diaghilew) and, with rehearsals and management no longer possible in St Petersburg, chose Monte Carlo, Monaco as his headquarters, base for rehearsal and the location for annual spring seasons at the Théâtre de Monte Carlo.

A growing repertoire of successful ballets enabled Diaghilev to plan for more regular and extensive touring programs in Europe. Dancers were recruited for the new company from Russia and Poland, and among Russian and Polish émigrés already working with dance companies in Paris and other European capitals. Diaghilev's key collaborators, Benois and Fokine, were formally integrated into the company as artistic director and choreographic director, while his stars, Nijinsky and Karsavina, were persuaded

(opposite) **Léon Bakst, Aleksandr Golovin and Natalia Goncharova**
Costume for a princess c 1910, modified c 1934 (detail) from *L'Oiseau de feu*
© Natalia Goncharova/ADAGP. Licensed by Viscopy, 2010

(above) **Unknown photographer**
Flores Revalles and Adolf Bolm in Schéhérazade
page 29 in *Souvenir program for Serge Diaghilev's Ballet Russe*, Metropolitan Opera, New York 1916

to sign contracts. Nijinsky had been dismissed from the Imperial Theatres in 1911 after scandalising its aristocratic audience by deliberately wearing a revealing costume while dancing in *Giselle*, and was thus available full time. Nijinsky's sister, the Imperial Theatres dancer Bronislava Nijinska (Bronisława Niżyńska 1891–1972), resigned in protest at her brother's treatment and came to Monte Carlo to join Diaghilev, along with another colleague, Adolph Bolm. The respected Italian ballet master Enrico Cecchetti (1850–1928), who had taught Pavlova, Nijinsky and Karsavina in St Petersburg, was recruited as ballet master and a mime.[28] Diaghilev had hired the dancer and ballet master Serge Grigoriev (1883–1968) as *régisseur*, or business manager, in 1909 and now relied on his business skills to manage the company on a permanent basis. Timetabling, program planning, rehearsals, negotiating venues, budgeting and juggling finances, along with contracting and managing dancers, stage technicians, musicians, scenery painters and publicists, were indispensable skills that Grigoriev exercised for Diaghilev until the impresario's death in 1929, and for subsequent Ballets Russes companies until 1948.[29]

The April–June 1911 season from Diaghilev's consolidated base in Monte Carlo included the new productions *Le Spectre de la rose* (*The spirit of the rose*), *Narcisse* (*Narcissus*), *Sadko* and *Petrouchka*. The first two focused on male dance, with *Le Spectre de la rose* particularly devised as a showcase for Nijinsky's ethereal and fluid style in the role of the Rose. *Narcisse* was the first of three Greek-themed ballets designed by Bakst, whose research on ancient classical art and culture had taken him to Greece in 1907, at a time of heightened interest in that country's ancient culture influenced in part by the Olympic revival of the 1890s. His striking visual spectacle for this production was interpreted through Fokine's athletic and lively choreography, demonstrating the collaborative creative relationships that characterised Diaghilev's productions. *Petrouchka* was the highlight of this season, with its vivid and emotional synthesis of Russian folk themes, an expressively tragic performance from Nijinsky, Stravinsky's music and its quintessential Russian décor and costuming by Benois, together echoing the heritage of the homeland that was receding from Diaghilev and his fellow émigrés.

Nijinsky's first choreographic role was for *L'Après-midi d'un faune*, in which he danced the central role of the Faun in a highly stylised Grecian setting by Bakst. The ballet was a triumph for its synthesis of music, movement and graphic design, although it gained opening-night notoriety for Nijinsky's highly eroticised ending. It was the most publicised production of a rich

(above left) **Elliott & Fry**
Portrait of Vaslav Nijinsky c 1913

(above right) **Unknown photographer** *M Waslaw Nijinski* (*Le Dieu*)
page 36 in *Comœdia Illustré*, special edition, no 16, 15 May 1912

(opposite) **Léon Bakst**
Costume for character The Blue God c 1912 (detail)
from *Le Dieu bleu*

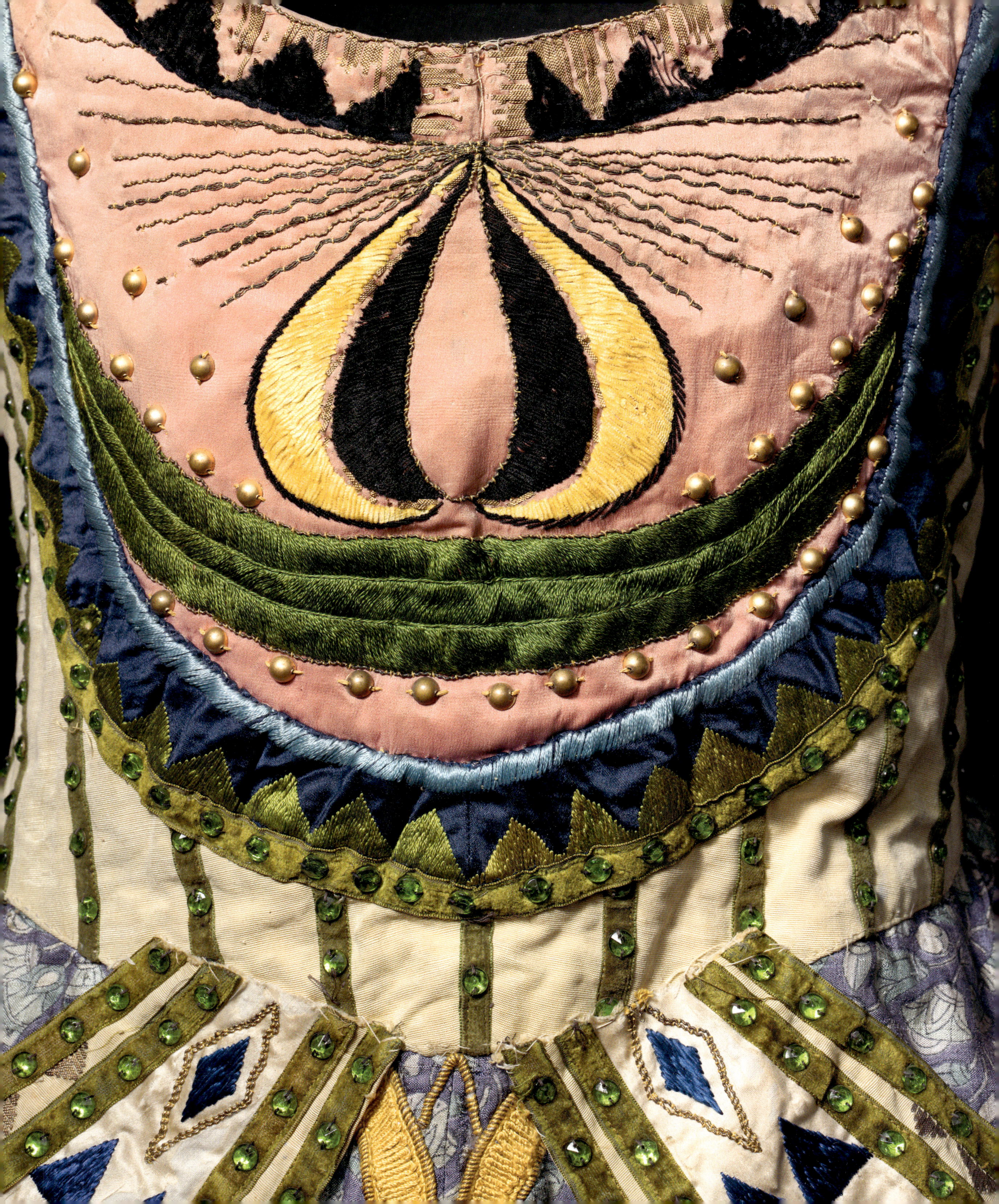

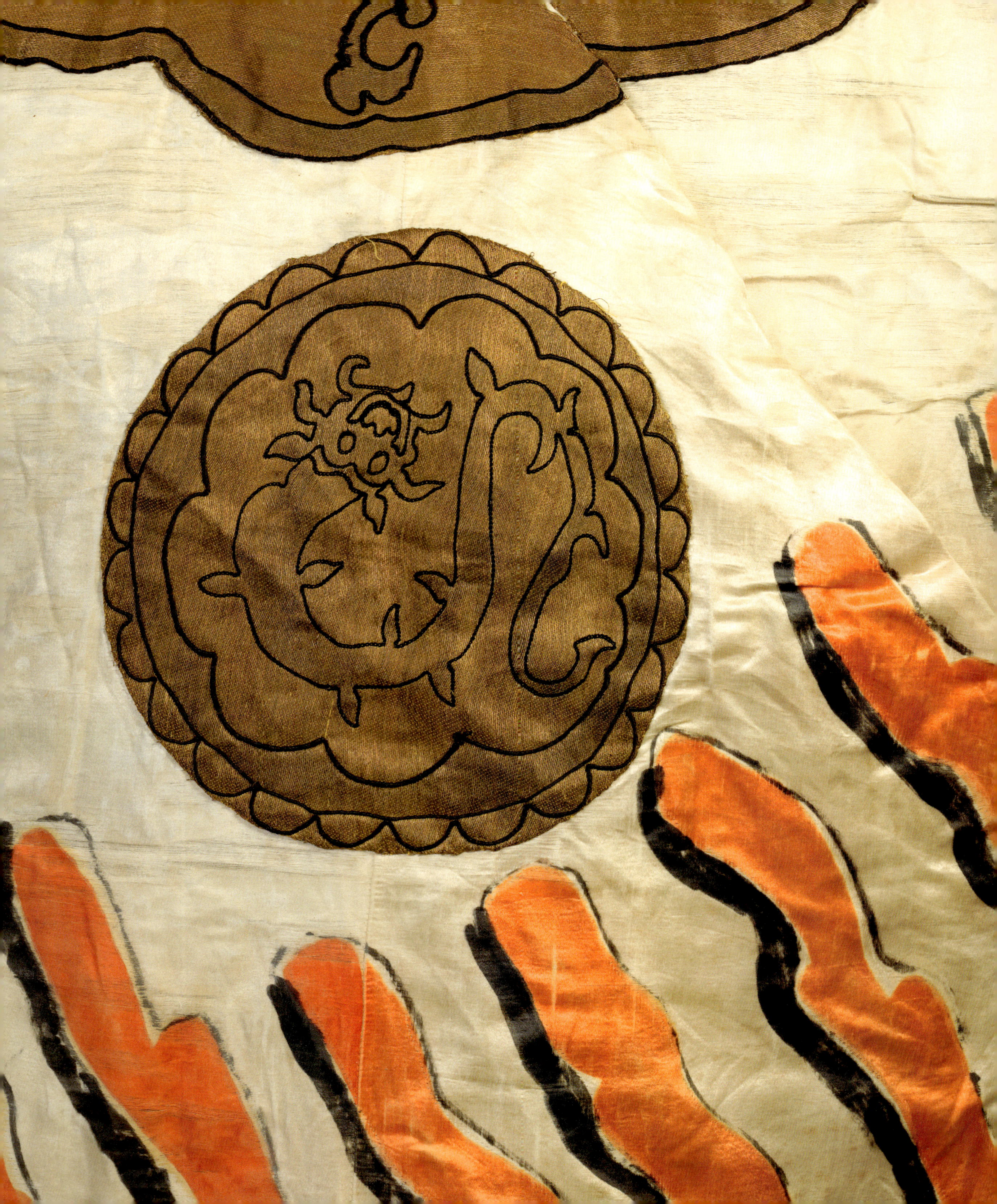

and exotic 1912 season that included Diaghilev's last orientalist ballet, the Georgian drama *Thamar*, and Bakst's two other 'Greek' ballets, *Le Dieu bleu* and *Daphnis et Chloé*, all choreographed by Fokine during a period of heightening tension with Diaghilev over the relatively inexperienced Nijinsky's ascendance as choreographer.

The years 1913 and 1914 were a time of tension and drama for the Ballets Russes, as they were for a nervous Europe on the brink of conflict. Of the eight new ballets presented in 1913–14, two brought the Ballets Russes to a turning point. *Le Sacre du printemps* (*The rite of spring* 1913), a close collaboration between Stravinsky, Roerich and Nijinsky, broke all conventions of ballet in calling forth the forces of nature through violent and convulsive dance movement, a fragmented and dissonant musical score, and coarse and unflattering 'folk' costumes. The performance created a furore at its Paris première, outraging conservatives while indelibly marking Diaghilev's and Stravinsky's first engagement with uncompromised modernity.

Nijinsky was to cause a new direction for the Ballets Russes with his unexpected marriage to the wealthy Hungarian dancer, Romola de Pulzsky, in Buenos Aires on the company's tour to South America in 1913 (which Diaghilev did not join). Diaghilev reacted to cabled news of this union and betrayal of their already deteriorating relationship with histrionic anger, summarily dismissing Nijinsky from the company, and leaving himself without a choreographer for the forthcoming season. Fokine, who had fallen out with Diaghilev in 1912 and left the company, was enticed to return, but in 1914 Diaghilev introduced his new protégé, the Mariinsky dancer Léonide Massine (Leonid Myasin 1896–1979). Massine, intellectual and knowledgeable about art, took over Nijinsky's roles in the company and in Diaghilev's personal life, rising to choreographer from 1915 to 1928. Nijinsky rejoined the company for its two tours of the United States in 1916 and 1917, during the second of which he began the descent into the debilitating and socially isolating schizophrenia that would consume the rest of his life.

By 1913 Diaghilev was beginning to view Bakst's decorative Orientalism as counter to his vision for the Ballets Russes. With Bakst's subsequent gradual separation from the company, the design of Rimsky-Korsakov's opera-ballet, *Le Coq d'or* (*The golden cockerel* 1914), was entrusted to two members of the Moscow avant-garde, Natalia Goncharova (1881–1962) and her partner Mikhail Larionov (1881–1964). They were the first artists not associated with the *miriskusniki* to work for Diaghilev, although their work had been included in his 1906 exhibition. Their vivid, neo-primitivist interpretation of Russian folk art brought the Ballets Russes into the world of the Futurists and Cubism. As Diaghilev's new artistic advisers they encouraged him to commission more independent artists to take the stage and costume design of his productions into untried territory. Diaghilev would go on to invite the collaborations of contemporary European artists Sonia and Robert Delaunay, André Derain, Giacomo Balla, Pablo Picasso, José-María Sert, Henri Matisse, Georges Braque, Giorgio de Chirico, Juan Gris, Marie Laurencin, Henri Laurens, Maurice Utrillo, Georges Rouault, Max Ernst, Joan Miró, Nuam Gabo, Anton Pevsner, Georgy Yakulov, Pavel Tchelitchew and André Bauchant. Their work transformed the Ballets Russes stage into a site of artistic experimentation and design innovation, at the same time expanding the dimensions and applications of their practices beyond their easels and studios.

The embrace of Modernism 1914–22

The outbreak of the First World War in 1914 left Diaghilev's increasingly multinational émigré troupe in a precarious position, with return to Russia

(opposite) **Henri Matisse**
Costume for a chamberlain
c 1920 (detail) from *Chant du rossignol*

(above) **Unknown photographer**
Léonide Massine, Natalia Goncharova, Michel Larionov, Léon Bakst and Igor Stravinsky—Lausanne, Switzerland 1915
Bibliothèque nationale de France, Paris, Fonds Kochno, BN 81

Massine to Spain's traditional folk music and dance. Velázquez's celebrated painting, *Las meniñas*, was the inspiration for Diaghilev's ballet of the same name which premiered at the Teatro Victoria Eugenia in San Sebastián in August 1916, the only new work presented that year. Massine's choreography was based on a Gabriel Fauré pavane, while the costumes by the Catalan painter, José-María Sert (1874–1945), were based on those depicted by Velázquez. Goncharova and Larionov joined Diaghilev's diminished entourage in Spain, along with Robert and Sonia Delaunay, who had been forced to stay on in the country after vacationing there at the outbreak of war. Although he was fastidious in keeping up appearances, Diaghilev was reduced to very poor circumstances in Spain, unable to commit to, or pay, any of his troupe, many of whom had already dispersed across Europe looking for whatever work was available.

increasingly difficult for some of its members, and the prospect of confirmed European seasons diminishing. During 1915 Diaghilev travelled in Italy with Massine, meeting the Futurist artist and provocateur Filippo Marinetti, and building networks in Rome, before moving his base to a rented property, the Villa Bellerive at Ouchy, near Lausanne in neutral Switzerland, where Stravinsky also lived. Goncharova and Larionov joined Diaghilev there as the company was assembled and prepared for the American tours of 1916 and 1917.[30]

Diaghilev, superstitious and harbouring a life-long fear that he would die on water, reluctantly joined the first of the two gruelling tours, which included performances in sixteen cities yet did not prove to be the profitable venture that he had hoped would bring financial security to the company. The equally stressful return journey from New York in May 1916 brought the troupe through increasingly dangerous North Atlantic waters, not back to France but to neutral Spain, where Diaghilev had arranged a tour.

This began a lengthy and enforced sojourn in Spain, during which Diaghilev secured the interest and patronage of King Alfonso XIII for performances in Madrid as Los Bailes-Rusos. He formed a working relationship with the composer Manuel de Falla, who introduced both Diaghilev and

Sert's wife Misia, a prominent patron of the arts, had been Diaghilev's ardent supporter since 1908.[31] She had introduced him to the young French poet Jean Cocteau in 1909, a meeting that would bring him into the milieu of the Ballets Russes, most notably through a challenge, issued by Diaghilev in conversation in 1912, to '*Etonne-moi!* (Astonish me!)'. In 1916 Cocteau responded by proposing a new ballet, *Parade* (*Side show*), from his scenario, with music by Erik Satie and costumes and design by Pablo Picasso.[32] Diaghilev approved and was taken to meet Picasso, with the result being the landmark 1917 production that brought Cubism and the Ballets Russes together for the first time. *Parade*'s triumph, along with Picasso's marriage to one of the Ballets Russes dancers, Olga Khokhlova, brought the artist to the centre of Diaghilev's circle, ensuring a wider clientele for his work. It also marked the return of the Ballets Russes to Paris after almost three years. In March that year, shortly after the downfall of the tsarist regime, Diaghilev was approached by a newly formed cultural committee to return to Russia as Minister of Culture. With commitments in place and the new modernist focus of the Ballets Russes as a priority to develop, he declined.

A second tour to South America in 1917 (again without Diaghilev) proved disastrous, with the destruction of some of the company's precious sets and costumes by fire, financial losses and the further

(above) **Unknown photographer**
Karsavina, Diaghilev, Matisse and Massine 1919
Bibliothèque nationale de France, Paris, Fonds Kochno, Album Photo Karsavina 3

(opposite) **Léon Bakst**
Costume for a Jew c 1909–20s
(detail) from *Cléopâtre*

40 Ballets Russes: the art of costume

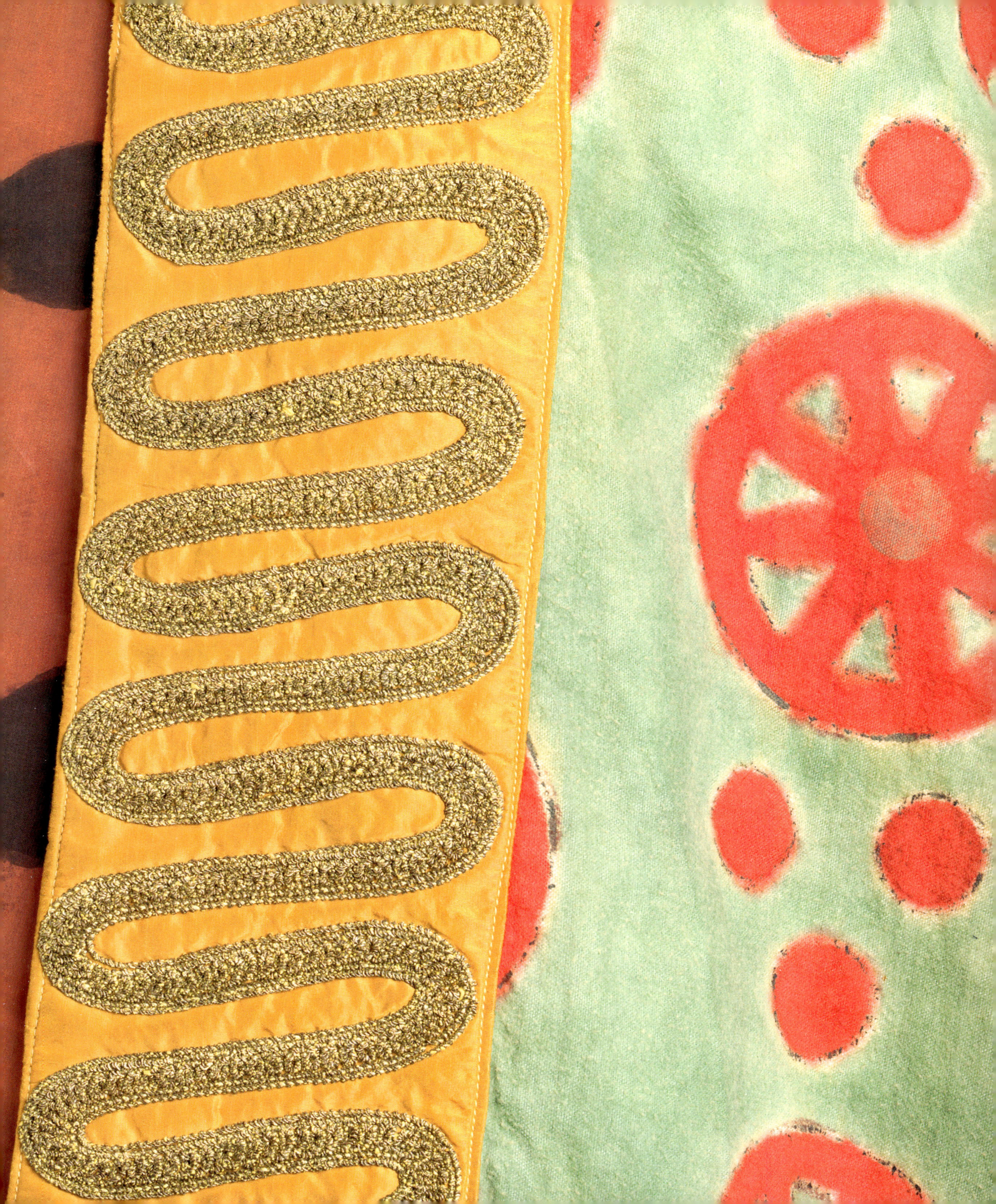

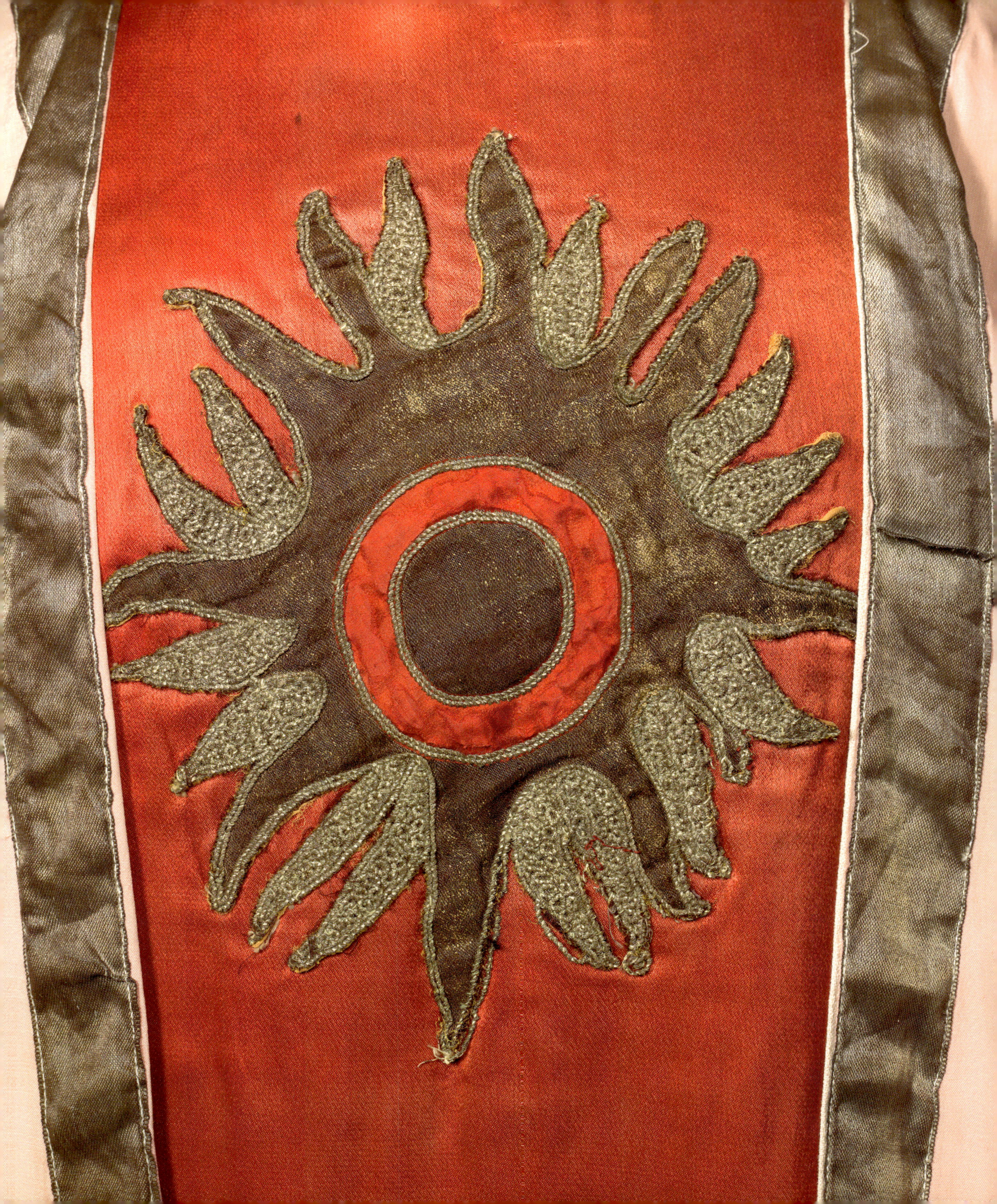

deterioration of Nijinsky's sanity—he danced on stage for the last time in Buenos Aires in December 1917, performing *Le Spectre de la rose* and *Petrouchka*. Back in Europe, Diaghilev and most of the company found themselves stateless as a result of Lenin's signing of the Peace of Brest-Litovsk in March 1918, and cut off from their homeland forever. Diaghilev organised for some of the troupe to be issued with League of Nations Nansen passports (official travel documents for stateless refugees) from 1922, but from the time of the signing of the treaty the Ballets Russes, a perennially touring company with no permanent home base, would always be shadowed by this fracture from its roots.

The company's heightened visibility and credibility within modernist circles, as a result of Picasso's success with *Parade*, and later with *Le Tricorne* (*The three-cornered hat*) and *Pulcinella* in 1919, opened dialogues with other major artists. André Derain designed *La Boutique fantasque* (*The magical toyshop*) in 1919 and Henri Matisse, who had been impressed with Stravinsky's and Massine's work, agreed to design the new ballet production of *Le Chant du rossignol* (*The song of the nightingale*), which premiered in February 1920.

These works, and a new interpretation of *Le Sacre du printemps* in late 1920, provided an impressive platform for Massine's talents as a choreographer. His new creative authority created tensions with Diaghilev who shortly afterward, in a rage on discovering Massine's burgeoning relationship with the British dancer Vera Savina (Vera Clarke), dismissed Massine from the company. Diaghilev soon contracted the services of the young Russian dancer and poet, Boris Kochno (1904–1990), as secretary and personal companion and, eventually, his main collaborator.

The company's 1921 production of *Chout* (*The buffoon*) provided an opportunity for Larionov as both designer of its radical Cubist set and costumes and choreographer, in partnership with the Polish dancer Thadée Slavinsky. This ballet also introduced the work of the composer Serge Prokofiev (Sergei Sergeyevich Prokofiev 1891–1953) to the Ballets Russes.

Despite its artistic successes of the previous seasons, the company's financial position remained precarious, leading Diaghilev to make the seemingly counter-revolutionary decision to stage a re-creation of Petipa's 1890 *Sleeping beauty* as *The sleeping princess* in November 1921 as a potential money-earner in a London season. This production and its impact are discussed by Helena Hammond elsewhere in this publication.[33] Featuring extravagant production and Bakst's expensive costuming, it was perhaps inevitable that *The sleeping princess* generated the loss that would almost bankrupt Diaghilev. Returning to Paris with no funds for the development of new productions, he developed as a ballet the 1916 opera-ballet *Le Renard* (*The fox*), which Stravinsky had devised as a commission for the wealthy Winnaretta Singer, Princesse de Polignac, a supporter of the Ballets Russes and host of an important private musical salon in Paris.[34] Singer-Polignac's support gave Diaghilev the opportunity to instate Bronislava Nijinska as his principal and first female choreographer, a role she would play until 1926. Her austere 1923 production of Stravinsky's *Les Noces* (*The wedding*) was a landmark in modern choreography. Based on a traditional Russian peasant wedding, its plain, simple costumes were designed by Goncharova to enhance Nijinska's expressive and Constructivist movements and composition. Her other well-known productions include *Les Biches* (*The house party*) and *Le Train bleu* (*The blue train*) of 1924, both of which explored the lighter subjects of elegant modern urban life in the 1920s.

Monte Carlo and beyond 1923–29

By the end of 1923 the Ballets Russes had returned to a permanent base in Monte Carlo thanks to the interest and enthusiastic financial support of Pierre de Polignac (Prince Louis II of Monaco's son-in-law and Winnaretta Singer-Polignac's nephew), an avid promoter of cultural development in the principality. Based at the Théâtre de Monte Carlo, Diaghilev could return to the experimental program that had been the company's hallmark in the pre-*Sleeping princess* period. He also entered into a new personal and professional relationship with the British-born dancer, Anton Dolin (Sydney Francis Patrick Chippendall Healey-Kay 1904–1983), who had danced in *The sleeping princess* in London.

In Paris in 1925 Diaghilev met and signed up George Balanchine (Georgi Melitonovich Balanchivadze

Alexandre Benois
Costume for a courtier c 1909 (detail) from *Le Pavillon d'Armide*

Maurice Seymour
Col W de Basil
page 3 in *Program for Col. W. de Basil's Ballet Russe, Théâtre national du Palais de Chaillot,*
7–8–10–12–13–14–16–17 October 1947
National Gallery of Australia Research Library, Canberra

1904–1983) and several other recently arrived Soviet defectors (including the first of Balanchine's four wives, Tamara Gevergeyeva), most of whom had been dancers at the Mariinsky Theatre (by then the State Academic Theatre of Opera and Ballet). With Nijinska's departure from the company, and following the brief return of Massine, Balanchine became the principal and the last choreographer of the Ballets Russes.[35] The company's work of the later 1920s was a reflection of the interests in French music and the art world connections of Diaghilev's younger team of Kochno, Balanchine and Diaghilev's last premier dancer and companion, Serge Lifar (1905–1986).[36] The historical, antiquarian and folkloric visual character of the earlier Ballets Russes repertoire was left behind with the architectural and Constructivist design of *La Chatte* (*The cat*), *Le Pas d'acier* (*Step of steel*) and *Ode* in 1927 and 1928. The works of this period are discussed by Christine Dixon elsewhere in this publication (see p 78).[37]

Diaghilev's final season in Paris in May 1929 included the surrealist fantasy *Le Bal* (*The ball*), designed by Giorgio de Chirico, and Prokofiev's *Le Fils prodigue* (*The prodigal son*), designed by Georges Rouault.

Diaghilev had been particularly enthusiastic about *Le Fils prodigue* at a time when his long exile and the diminished contact with his family in Soviet Leningrad finally seemed permanent. His life as a *bon viveur* had taken its toll on his health, with the problems of diabetes and debilitating skin problems and abscesses exacerbated by his denial of their seriousness. He retreated to Venice, the city he had first visited in 1890 and to which he continually returned for periods of contemplation and rejuvenation with his friends and lovers. Staying at the Grand Hôtel des Bains de Mer in the company of Lifar, Kochno and old friends Misia Sert and Coco Chanel during his final days, he succumbed to blood poisoning on 19 August 1929, aged fifty-seven. He had died, as he had feared, on water and was buried in Venice's San Michele cemetery. Nouvel and Lifar acted as executors and began the arduous task of dealing with Diaghilev's estate.

The rebirth of the Ballets Russes 1930–40

Diaghilev's death left the Ballets Russes leaderless, with no provisions for continuity of programming or security of tenure for its dancers and other staff and collaborators. A committee of directors including Nouvel, Grigoriev, Lifar and Kochno began to divide the estate, cancel planned tours and release the dancers from their contracts. The Diaghilev 'diaspora' had begun and with it an industry of writing, research, reminiscences and re-creations of his repertoire that would keep the Diaghilev tradition and legend alive. Lifar arranged exhibitions of works associated with the Ballets Russes in 1929 in Paris, and London in 1929 and 1930, and staged a major exhibition of this material at the Musée des Arts Décoratifs in Paris in 1939, further increasing the allure of the Diaghilev period. Some of the company's prominent dancers and choreographers found themselves free to pursue their careers elsewhere, among them Balanchine with his American Ballet in New York in 1935 and Lifar with the Paris Opéra Ballet in 1930.

Diaghilev's role as ballet and artistic director of the Monte Carlo Opera was taken by the French writer, critic and publisher René Blum (1878–1942). In 1932 Blum formed the Ballets Russes de Monte Carlo (La Société des Ballets Russes et Ballets de Monte-Carlo) in partnership with the Russian impresario Wassily de Basil (Vassily Grigorievich Voskerensky 1880–1951) as business manager. De Basil had a colourful military career before becoming an émigré in 1918, styling himself Colonel (or Col) W de Basil, later in the 1930s. His involvement with ballet began in 1925 as director of the Georgian Prince Alexis Zeretelli's Opéra Russe à Paris, which from 1930 presented seasons of ballets choreographed by Bronislava Nijinska. The formation of the Ballets Russes de Monte Carlo presented opportunities to re-engage important former Diaghilev associates: Grigoriev was appointed as *régisseur général* (production manager), Balanchine as ballet master, Kochno as artistic director, Roger Desormière as orchestral director and, for a first-season production of his ballet *Cotillon*, Massine. Very young dancers were recruited to provide the new company with a youthful image befitting Balanchine's new ideas. Among them, three of the youngest Russian émigré dancers, Irina Baronova (1919–2008), Tatiana Riabouchinska (1917–2000) and Tamara Toumanova (1919–1996), were promoted as the 'baby ballerinas', even as they became the most experienced and accomplished of the de Basil troupe.[38] Costumiers included Barbara Karinska (Varvara Andreievna Jmoudsky 1886–1983), a Russian émigré who was to go on to become a leading theatrical costumier in London and New York.[39]

By 1934 Blum and de Basil, an unlikely coupling of opposing personalities, had reached serious disagreement on the company's priorities and strategies, with de Basil favouring an international touring company rather than one focused on Monte Carlo. Their partnership ended in 1935, beginning a period of diverse, competitive and often confusing dance company businesses operating under the flag of the 'Ballets Russes'. Blum inaugurated his Ballets de Monte Carlo in 1935, hiring Fokine as choreographer from 1936 to 1938. The company was acquired that year by the Russian-American banker Serge Denham, who operated it in the United States as the Ballet Russes de Monte Carlo until 1963, with Massine returning as choreographer from 1938 until 1942. The Jewish Blum's involvement ended tragically in Occupied France when he was deported by the Nazis and killed in the Auschwitz concentration camp in 1942. In 1935 de Basil formed Col W de Basil's Ballets Russes, with Massine as choreographer, a role he was to play until 1938 when he left the company after a legal battle with de Basil over his claim for copyright ownership of ballets he had produced.[40] De Basil's company, then based in London with Covent Garden sponsorship, continued as the Russian Ballet (presented by Educational Ballets Ltd) in 1938, as the Covent Garden Russian Ballet (presented by Educational Ballets Ltd) in 1939 and as the Original Ballet Russe from 1939 to its demise in 1951. In 1937 Fokine was contracted for two years as its choreographer.

Through these business reconfigurations, de Basil's companies maintained a prodigious output of new productions during the 1930s, continuing the spirit of Diaghilev in their engagement with contemporary artists and designers, including re-commissioning many from the earlier era, as among them Goncharova, Larionov, Benois, Dufy, Tchelitchew, Delaunay, Derain, Messel, Miró, Rouault and de Chirico, for new or revised ballets.

The Ballets Russes in Australia 1936–40

Touring internationally had become the lifeblood of de Basil's companies, gaining him new audiences for older, proven and loved works from the Diaghilev repertoire as well as allowing him to trial new works in countries with different cultural histories to those that had generated and nurtured the original Ballets Russes. The scale of international touring meant that several troupes of the de Basil Ballets Russes would appear concurrently in various cities and towns, providing valuable experience for newer recruits. The idea for an Australian tour had its genesis in Monte Carlo in 1932 when de Basil met Daphne Deane (Theodora Robinowitz), an Australian ballet promoter who proposed herself as an impresario for any future Australian tour.[41]

De Basil assembled a second company, billed as the Monte Carlo Russian Ballet and led by the Polish ballet master Léon Woizikowsky (1899–1975), to present a program of twenty-one ballets in Adelaide, Melbourne, Sydney and Brisbane from 13 October 1936 to 14 July 1937, with a mid-tour diversion to New Zealand where they played in Auckland, Wellington, Christchurch and Dunedin. The tour, organised by the Australian entrepreneurial

Sidney Nolan
Set design for Icare 1940
© Sidney Nolan Trust/Bridgeman Art Library

organisation J C Williamson Theatres Ltd, was a resounding success, giving Australian audiences a visceral connection to the music, dance and art forms that had brought the Ballets Russes to the forefront of European Modernism only a few years earlier.

While those interested in the fields of art and design would have been well aware of the impact that the Ballets Russes had made in Europe, the majority of the Australian audiences would have their first experience of extravagant theatrical spectacle and stage and costume design by some of the most avant-garde artists of the period. They may have been unaware of how much they had already absorbed through the movies, as early Hollywood films had drawn inspiration from the Ballets Russes' explorations into musical and choreographic exoticism. Among the highly experienced dancers engaged by de Basil for these tours were Woizikowsky, Dolin and Lubov Tchernicheva (1890–1976), all bringing the lustre of their former association with Diaghilev to their Australian performances. The three 'baby ballerinas',

Baronova, Toumanova and Riabouchinska, also joined the tours, gaining enormous publicity. These dancers and the productions in which they performed offered Australians a different reality in the midst of the Depression and for many, balletomanes or not, this magic would be sustained and recalled though a lifetime.[42]

De Basil's company, billed as the Covent Garden Russian Ballet, toured Australia a second time, from 28 September 1938 to 27 April 1939, playing in Melbourne, Sydney and Adelaide. Mid-tour they again played Auckland, Hamilton, Wanganui, Palmerston, Wellington, Christchurch and Dunedin in New Zealand. Michel Fokine joined the Australian tour to supervise his ballets, intensifying the experience of those balletomanes who were able to watch rehearsals. The dancers, many of them the undisputed stars of de Basil's companies, brought a new European glamour to the local scene and were fêted wherever they went. They were sketched, painted and photographed by professional and amateur artists and regularly appeared in the popular media, from the social pages to feature articles. Staged photographs of the dancers were commissioned for souvenir programs, giving Australian photographers such as Max Dupain the opportunity to work with new subjects. Amateur photographers provided a lasting record of some of the de Basil companies' actual stage performances in Australia: solicitor Hugh P Hall regularly photographed performances in Melbourne, while ophthalmologist Joseph Ringland Anderson and dermatologist Dr Ewan Murray-Will filmed a number of performances.[43] Ballet historian Michelle Potter discusses aspects of the media impact of the Ballets Russes in Australia elsewhere in this publication (see p 189).[44]

The third and final tour, as the Original Ballet Russe (also known as Colonel Wassily de Basil's Covent Garden Ballet), went to Sydney, Melbourne, Adelaide and Brisbane from 30 December 1939 to 21 August 1940. De Basil travelled to Australia for the first time on this tour. With the outbreak of war in Europe in 1939 and the subsequent uncertainties of return transport, the planned ten-week tour stretched to almost eight months, allowing the company to develop its work (through the financial imperative to keep giving performances) and to become a welcome part of Australia's theatre and dance scenes. The extended stay gave a number of Australian artists the chance to become professionally involved. The painter Sidney Nolan was commissioned to work on the re-staging of *Icare* (*Icarus*) in Sydney in 1940, designing its set and costumes as his first work for the theatre.[45] The artists Kathleen and Florence Martin, sisters from Melbourne, designed scenery and costumes for Igor Schwezoff's ballet *La Lutte éternelle* (*The eternal struggle*), staged by the Original Ballet Russe in Sydney in 1940.[46]

From the late 1930s the worsening political situation in Europe meant that the prospects for some of the stateless émigré members of the company were uncertain, and several remained in Australia after the tours to work as dancers or to establish their own schools and companies. Among them was Hélène Kirsova (1910–1962), who settled in Sydney in 1937 and in 1940 founded her own school and company, the Kirsova Ballet (1941–44), Australia's first professional ballet company.[47] Between 1939 and 1943 the Czech dancer Edouard Borovansky (1902–1959) and his wife Xenia worked tirelessly towards the establishment of an Australian ballet company, and in 1944 the Borovansky Australian Ballet Company Ltd gave its first performances in Melbourne as a fully professional company. Following Borovansky's death in 1959, Peggy van Praagh was appointed artistic director of the Borovansky Ballet and subsequently became the first artistic director of the Australian Ballet, a company that drew significantly in its early years on the legacy of the Borovansky Ballet. Kira Bousloff (née Abricossova 1914–2001) remained in Australia after the 1939 tour and in 1952 moved to Perth to establish the West Australian Ballet. The Australian-born dancer Valrene Tweedie (1925–2008) joined de Basil's company in 1940, dancing as Irina Lavrova with the Original Ballet Russe until her return to Australia in 1952 as a dancer, choreographer and influential teacher, eventually founding Ballet Australia in 1960.

The full story of the influence of the aesthetic and culture of the Ballets Russes on Australian performing and visual arts from 1940, although beyond the scope of this publication and its accompanying exhibition, has been the subject of a major four-year collaborative research project, *Ballets Russes in Australia: our cultural revolution*, commenced in 2006 by the National Library of Australia, the Australian Ballet and the University of Adelaide.[48]

The Ballets Russes story was played out in Europe, North and South America, Britain, Australia and New Zealand through the most tumultuous decades of the late nineteenth and early twentieth centuries and has a resonance that belies the size and precariousness of Diaghilev's companies. Diaghilev's cultural knowledge, determination and audacity, combined with fearless business acumen and a pleasure in risk-taking and controversy, made him a model of the modern entrepreneur. His ballets showed that creative collaboration and cultural inclusiveness was the future, and from the vantage point of a hundred years on we can see how the legacy and the legend of the Ballets Russes continue to challenge us.

(following pages)
Giorgio de Chirico
Front and back of jacket for costume for a male guest 1929 (detail) from *Le Bal*
© Giorgio de Chirico/SIAE. Licensed by Viscopy, 2010

Wild dream: imagining the Ballets Russes   47

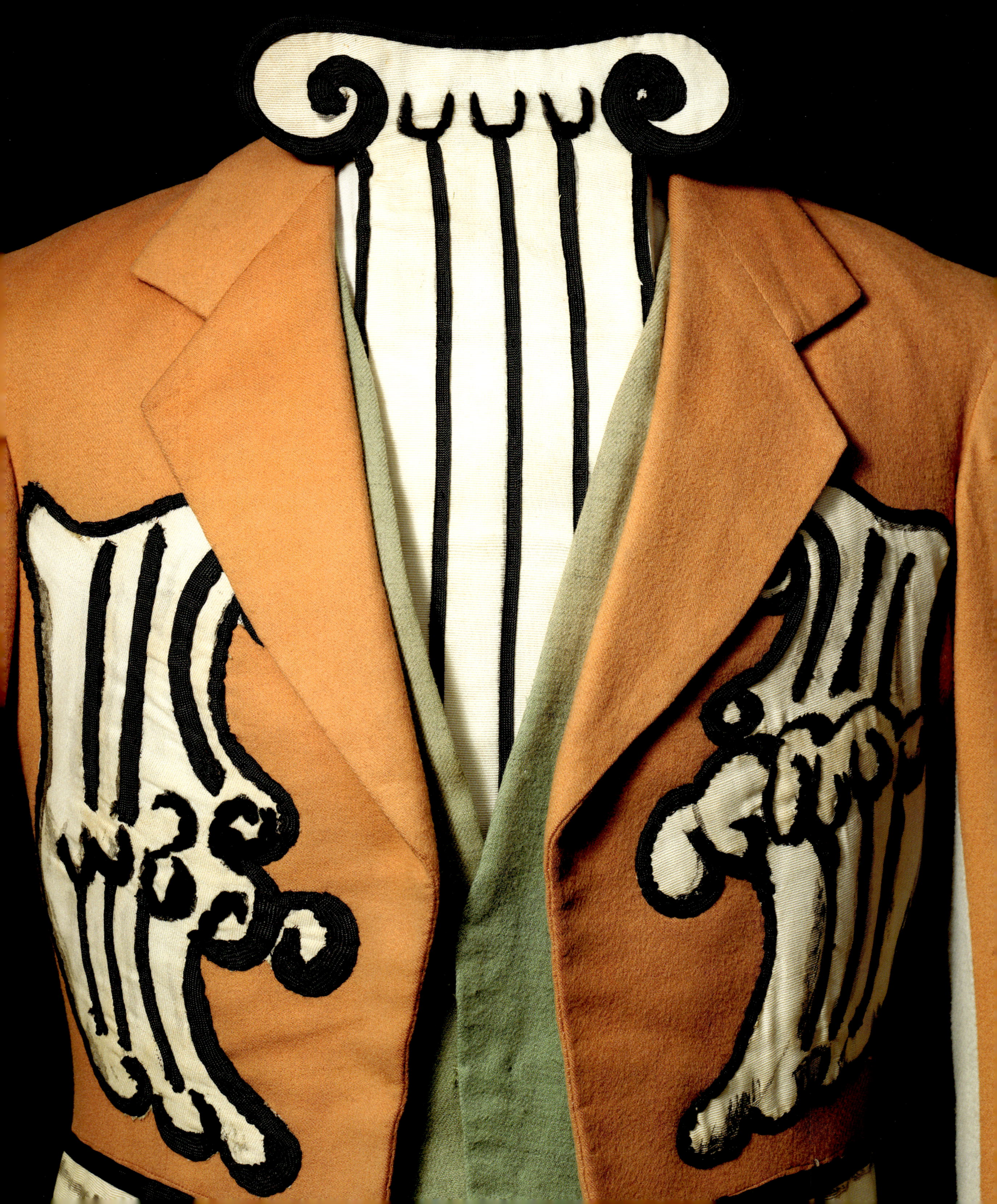

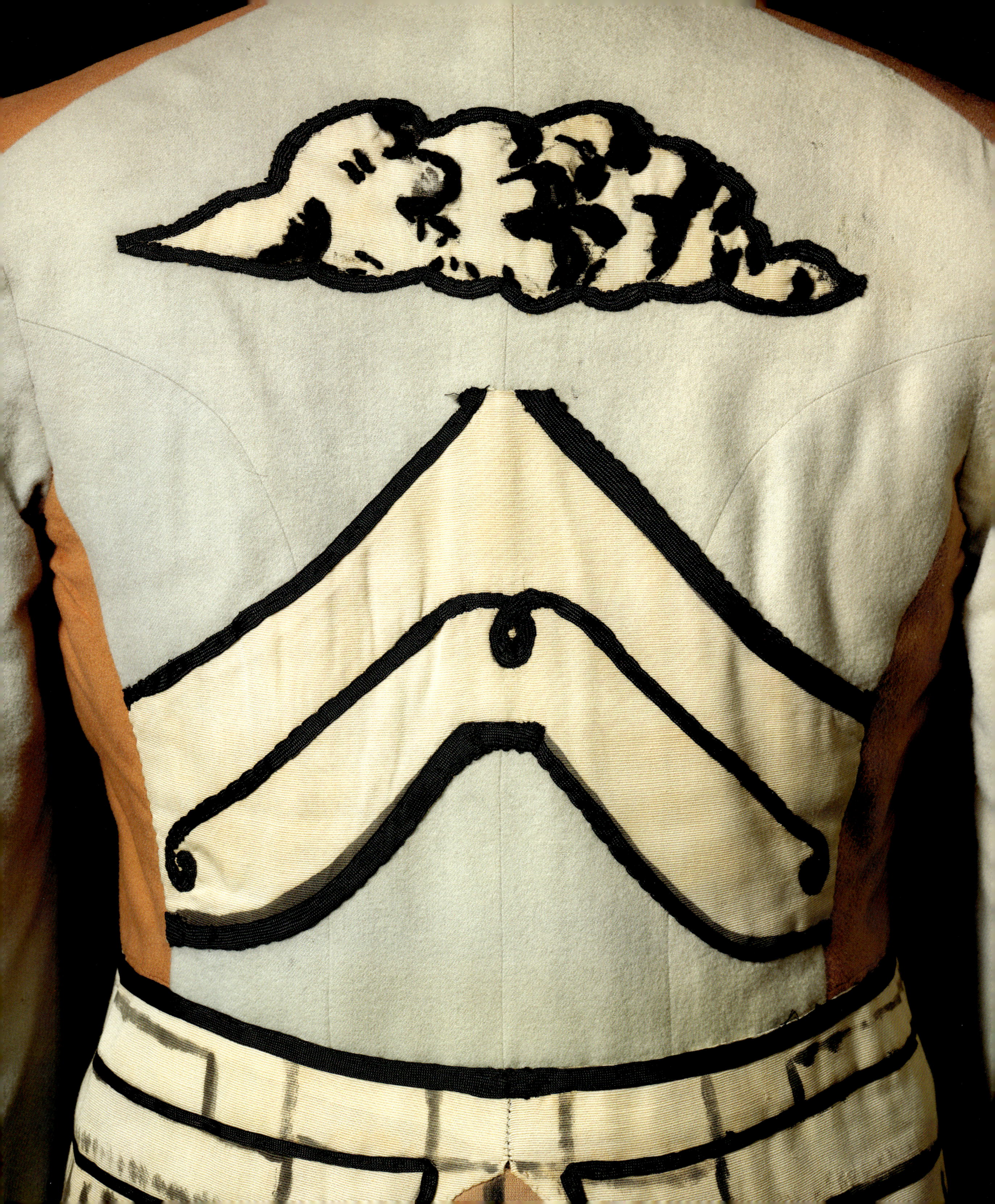

SPECTACULAR HISTORIES: THE BALLETS RUSSES, THE PAST AND THE CLASSICAL TRADITION

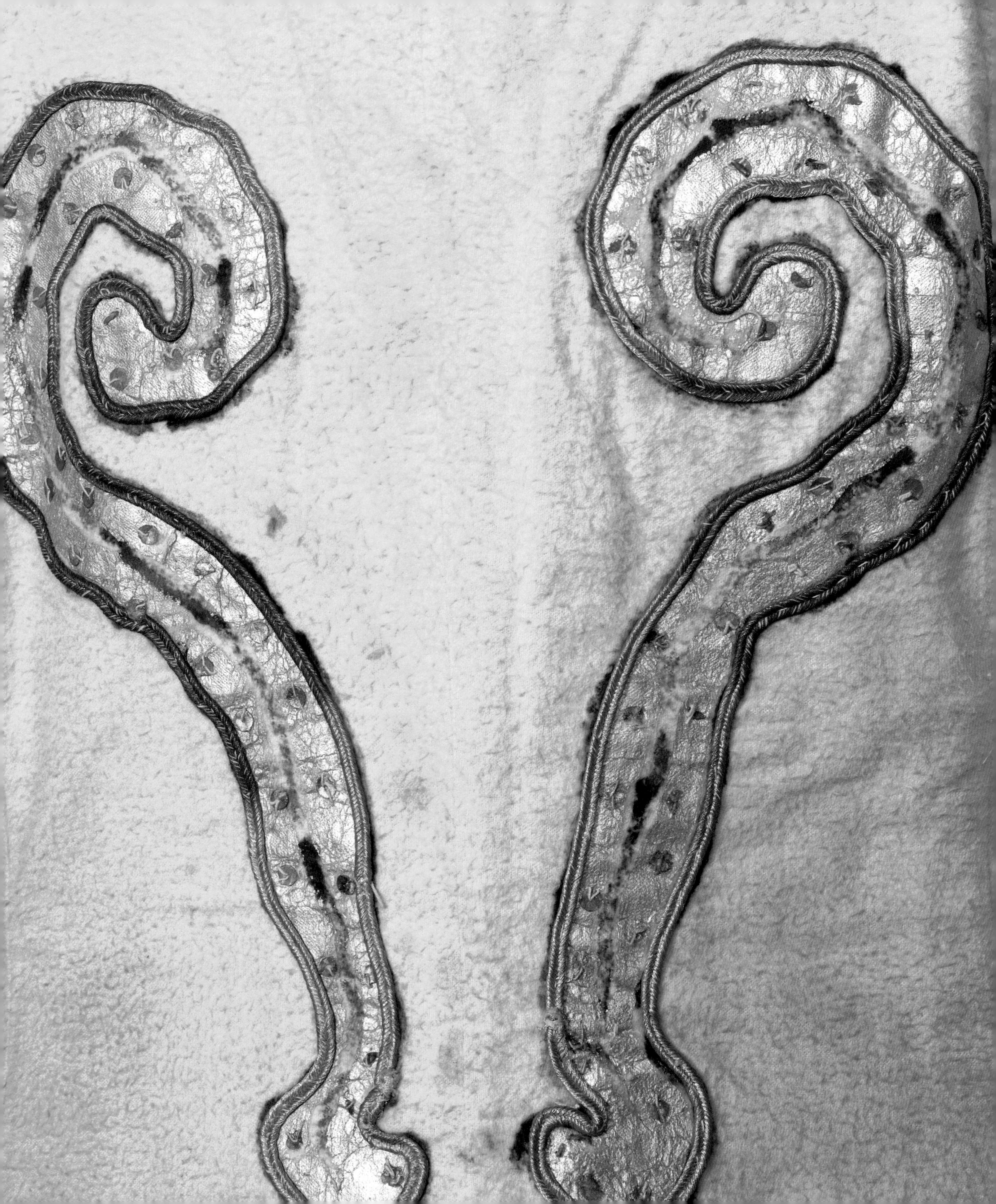

SPECTACULAR HISTORIES: THE BALLETS RUSSES, THE PAST AND THE CLASSICAL TRADITION

Helena Hammond

The productions of the Ballets Russes were driven as much by the past as the future. For all the company's perceived iconoclasm, the enduring image of Diaghilev's enterprise as an avant-garde project interested only in breaking with the past and in severing all connection with the classical tradition is highly distorted. Diaghilev's description of the Exhibition of Russian Art which he brought to Paris in 1906, as offering 'a faithful image of artistic Russia today, with its sincere training, its respectful admiration for the past and its ardent faith in the future', could also stand as a kind of manifesto for the Ballets Russes enterprise which he would bring to Paris three years later, and for which the exhibition served in some sense as a rehearsal.[1]

The seminal importance to the very inception of the Ballets Russes of the landmark Russian nineteenth-century ballet, *The sleeping beauty*, highlights the need to reclaim a preoccupation with history as a defining concern of the company. This was a concern which designers such as Alexandre Benois and Léon Bakst, taking their cue from *The sleeping beauty*'s privileging of historical epochs, consistently explored through costume in their designs for Diaghilev.[2] The enormous impact of this ballet on these three men is just one index, and a highly significant one, of the retrospectivism which powered their collaborative project, even if this dimension has tended to be under-acknowledged in standard histories of the company. As Hanna Järvinen has recently pointed out, Diaghilev himself:

> never hesitated to feed the prejudices of his Western audiences—after all, he was running a business.

It was profitable to obscure the troupe's relationship to the Russian ballet tradition and to Russian culture in general, so that the works performed by the Ballets Russes could appear more innovative and avant-garde, even [more] politically progressive than they were.[3]

If Diaghilev advocated selective amnesia when it came to acknowledging formative influences on the company, Benois was always at pains to emphasise the seminal role played by the culminating work in the soon-to-be exhausted Imperial Russian dance canon as the touchpaper that ignited the Ballets Russes project, later recording:

> The Ballets Russes themselves would never have seen the light of day, had not *La Belle au Bois Dormant* [*The sleeping beauty*] awakened in a group of Russian youths fiery enthusiasm that developed into a kind of frenzy … later on he [Diaghilev] also became infected.[4]

The 1890 premiere of this ballet, a danced essay of unmatched classicism, 'was an outstanding event for us, in comparison with which even the arrival [in the same year] of Seriozha [Diaghilev] was just an episode of minor importance', Benois remembered.[5] During the 1890 carnival celebrations, Benois was said by Prince Peter Lieven, a close commentator on the Ballets Russes, to have seen *The sleeping beauty* six times within a week, even attending two performances in one day[6], a situation confirmed by Benois himself: 'as soon as possible I saw *La Belle au bois dormant* a second time, and then a third and a fourth … Gradually my visits … became almost a sort of obsession'.[7]

Alexandre Benois
Back of jacket from costume for a spirit of the hours c 1909 (detail) from *Le Pavillon d'Armide*
© Aleksandr Benois/ADAGP.
Licensed by Viscopy, 2010

Such was the lure of this ballet that Bakst was equally keen to source the origins of his career to its premiere, crediting his vocation as a designer to an improbable meeting with Tchaikovsky which, he maintained, occurred at an 1890 performance, although his biographer Charles Spencer thinks it unlikely that Bakst saw the ballet so early on.[8] Bakst singled out as a special catalyst for his artistic formation the transformative power of Tchaikovsky's score, the way in which it 'impels our thoughts to the broad decorative lines of the seventeenth century and the magnificence of the Roi-Soleil [the Sun King, Louis XIV]'.[9]

Bakst was not alone in nominating as one of the ballet's strengths its power to transport its late nineteenth-century Russian audience to the royal courts of sixteenth- and seventeenth-century France, for chief among its great attractions for Benois were 'the historical reminiscences that it evoked. No music had ever so successfully resuscitated the distant past as was done in the hunting scene and in the last divertissement'.[10] Benois described his outlook on life as 'to an extreme degree sentimentally reminiscent. I find it hard to destroy even an old slip of paper. After all, the past is the only real thing in life, the future does not exist and the present is merely fiction'.[11] The sleeping beauty's special appeal thus lay in its purchase on the past. Benois particularly praised the way in which Ivan Vsevolozhsky, Director of Russia's Imperial Theatres and The sleeping beauty's librettist, set Perrault's French fairytale in two contrasting and different epochs, 'divided by a hundred years [so that Princess] Aurora falls asleep in the middle of the sixteenth century and wakes up in the days of the youthful Louis XIV'. Such was the historicising power of this staging that 'even people who knew nothing of the history of the *Grand Siècle* seemed, during the dance, to achieve a clear vision of the distant past'.[12]

For Benois *The sleeping beauty*'s most striking twin aspects were this ability to conjure up the past—'something we once referred to with the faulty term "epochal quality" and which, finding no better expression, we then called by the no less faulty term "passé-ism"'—and its status as a genuine *Gesamtkunstwerk* or total work of art. This process of 'collective mastery [whereby] the charm of each artist flowed together in the beauty of the ensemble', enabled *The sleeping beauty* 'to possess a "genuineness" which is not at all the same as an intelligent counterfeit of antiquity or some kind of stylization'.[13] In other words, *The sleeping beauty*'s ability to render history with unprecedented veracity lay in its no less innovative total art work qualities—the way in which the ballet, as the product of intensive collaboration between choreographer, composer and librettist, fused dance, music, costume and design into an apparently seamless whole. It was this special conjunction of *Gesamtkunstwerk* and history that would be so significant for the Ballets Russes. The evening-length, highly classical *Sleeping beauty* might seem at first sight to be an unlikely prototype for the radical avant-gardism of Diaghilev's one-act ballets, but in its pioneering deployment of the total art work as a tool for bringing history to the dance stage lay the blueprint for the extraordinarily innovative history ballets Diaghilev's company would go on to devise.

The total art work qualities and exploration of historical themes which, as the twin legacies of *The sleeping beauty*, would come to define so much of the Ballets Russes enterprise, were piloted in the various collective projects launched by Diaghilev, Benois and Bakst in the years preceding the company's first 1909 Paris season. These schemes, consistently characterised by their commitment to retrospectivism, were frequently realised through embryonic versions of the total work of art that, in more fully developed form, would eventually characterise their Ballets Russes collaborations. The Russian dance and literary critic André Levinson's own championing of classicism—he has been aligned with T S Eliot and those other classical revivalists of the late 1910s and 1920s who strove to restore classical values to artistic production—made him especially receptive to the innate historicism of those pre-Ballets Russes collaborations of Benois, Diaghilev and Bakst.[14] In their hands, said Levinson:

> the brush became a means of interpreting a history perceived with a sort of sentimental homesickness mixed with irony … Is it surprising, then, that the retrospective attitude got the upper hand more and more, and that the offshoots of this movement were sacrificed to a propaganda for the past?[15]

For Levinson, the work of the Nevsky Pickwickians and, later, of the *miriskusniki* (Benois, Bakst and Diaghilev were key members of both groups) served as a much-needed corrective against 'preceding generations [which] going into Russian extremes, became infatuated with the idea of progress. Accordingly they either ignored or misunderstood their national past'.[16] Levinson recalls how he:

> was himself brought up in this atmosphere of hateful contempt [for] the unique and grandiose beauty of the structures in the [overtly classicizing] style of the Empire and of Louis XVI, buildings without parallel in the occidental world. … The implacable hatred [borne by] the public … toward the regime that had erected and was maintaining them [meant, for example, that] an educated Russian could not possibly find anything beautiful about the Winter Palace, this fine masterpiece of Rastrelli. … Benois and his friends discovered this slandered beauty and became enamoured of it.[17]

As early as 1900, Diaghilev was entrusted with editorship of the Imperial Theatres Yearbook in his capacity as Official for Special Missions under the new director of the Imperial Theatres, Prince Serge Volkonsky, transforming this report from, to quote Benois, 'an utterly bureaucratic publication, lacking any artistic quality [into] a book of exceptional elegance and taste which was full of altogether priceless artistic and historical documents'.[18] A clear indication of Diaghilev's desire to rehabilitate classicism in the eyes of his compatriots is his inclusion, in the 1900 volume, of an illuminating essay by critic and Ballets Russes supporter, Valerian Svetlov, on the classical origins of choreography in the dances described in Homer and Aeschylus, and of another essay by Benois on the classical architecture of the Alexandrinsky Theatre in St Petersburg.[19] The rehabilitation of eighteenth-century Russian classicism continued through the trio's activities as members of the *miriskusniki*, a movement characterised by Russian art expert Ann Kodicek in terms of its imaginative nostalgia and retrospective concerns.[20] The journal *Mir Iskusstva* (*World of Art*) bore the direct imprint of the Grand Siècle—for, said Lieven, 'unable to find a suitably elegant type, they unearthed old eighteenth-century founts and used them'—and featured numerous articles on 'days gone by', with much of the historical material attributable to Alexandre Benois[21], to the extent that 'the magazine's consistently avant-garde element concerned its presentation of art history'.[22]

In 1904, Diaghilev turned to portraiture as a means of resuscitating Russia's past, its classical Grand Siècle in particular. Benois would later recall how Diaghilev, having established his credentials as an authority on portrait painting with the publication of the first volume of *Russian painting in the eighteenth century*, on the portraitist Dmitry Levitsky:

> spent the whole summer of 1904 in ceaseless travelling all over Russia, visiting provincial museums, country seats, and private collections in his search for everything of historical interest … He was now entirely engrossed in his new undertaking, which was to surpass any exhibition yet held … The result surpassed even his own expectations.[23]

The huge *Historical exhibition of Russian portraits*, featuring over 2000 works of art, opened in St Petersburg the next year. According to Benois, 'all Russia's past seemed to have been resurrected' in its displays. Of special significance for the future Ballets Russes enterprises is the way in which Diaghilev's conception of the exhibition as a means of staging a national history depended on distinctly *Gesamtkunstwerk*-like methods of display and installation. Thousands of portraits, statues, busts, water-colours, bas-reliefs, miniatures and drawings, collected from all over Russia, were integrated as part of chronologically-arranged displays featuring furniture and exotic plants especially loaned for the exhibition by the tsar, who was also the exhibition's patron.[24] Benois observed how:

> The effect was greatly enhanced by the way in which the most important portraits were grouped together in the centre of each group, under a special canopy, hung the portrait of the Emperor or Empress indissolubly identified with the epoch.[25]

Bakst, the exhibition's designer, had transformed the hall of the eighteenth century, for instance, into a grove, with trellis surrounded by vases.[26]

Reflecting on Bakst's installation with the benefit of hindsight in the 1920s, when the total art work mobilised by the Ballets Russes was at its zenith, Levinson paid particular to attention to the designer's 'conception of an exposition hall forming an organic whole, making a coherent ensemble, and therefore having a distinct atmosphere … Is not this, again, a gift belonging to the Russians?' he asked rhetorically in his biography of Bakst, implying that in anticipating the vivid historical visions conjured by the Ballets Russes fused synthesism of dance, design and music, there was something intrinsically Russian about Bakst's use of the integrated schema of the total work of art to organise and stage Russia's history.[27]

A reduced version of the exhibition, which had drawn 45 000 visitors over six months in St Petersburg, was exported to Paris in 1906, where it was exhibited in the Salon d'Automne at the Grand Palais, and then toured to Berlin and the Venice Biennale. Diaghilev next offered Paris an image of Russia's history through its music, returning in 1907 with a season of Concerts Historiques Russes, said by Levinson to have caused the greatest excitement, and in 1908 with a production of *Boris Godunov*.[28] Again, total art work qualities were key to the images of sixteenth- and seventeenth-century Russia which the opera brought to Paris. Benois, who designed Act III (the Polish act), described how some costumes were sketched by Ivan Bilibin:

> one of the greatest experts on old Russian history. On the basis of these Diaghilev and I supervised the rest. We scoured all the Tatar and Jewish shops of the markets as well as shops that were famous for their silk and brocade materials … we found many genuine headdresses and folklore costumes, kerchiefs embroidered in gold and spangles. All this museum splendour later staggered the Parisians.[29]

The historical specificity and detailing sewn into the costumes, so intrinsic to the opera's sense of period, and themselves echoes of the rich historicism of the costumes and sets of the 1890 *Sleeping beauty*, set an important Diaghilevian precedent which the Ballets Russes would follow.

The works Diaghilev selected for the inaugural Ballets Russes Paris season in 1909 extended and amplified the historicism of the opera season the year before. Although all the chosen ballets were choreographed by Fokine in the first years of the twentieth century, they variously recalled particular key works in the nineteenth-century Imperial Russian ballet canon so that, viewed together, says Järvinen, they presented 'the history of ballet in a Russian nutshell'.[30] All but one of the ballets had originally been performed at the Mariinsky, the Imperial Theatre in St Petersburg from which Diaghilev recruited most of his dancers.[31] If, as Diaghilev says, ballet classicism was created in the eighteenth century and developed in the nineteenth century[32], by the 1870s it had made the Mariinsky its Russian home. The classical purity of the dancing of the Mariinsky-trained Nijinsky in *Le Pavillon d'Armide* (*Amida's pavilion*), the first ballet on opening night on 18 May 1909, may have been something that had never been seen in Paris, notes Lieven, but the first Ballets Russes Paris season offered its audiences much more than a historical primer in ballet style alone.[33]

In the words of Benois, the ballet's designer:

> the purpose of *Le Pavillon d'Armide* was to show the Russian conception of eighteenth-century France, in the story itself as well as in the manner of its presentation, in the scenery, the costumes, the manners, the groupings, and the dances … those Frenchmen who still retained the capacity of understanding that period from Versailles, the Gobelins tapestries, the Sèvres … those who understood the actual spirit which breathed through this delicate art, felt and understood the meaning of *Le Pavillon d'Armide*. Its aim was achieved; Russians had shown that they were not only supreme but that they could outvie the French on their own ground.[34]

It was this fusion of different artistic dimensions that first opened Diaghilev's eyes to what he came to perceive as ballet's unmatched potential as total work of art. This must be shown to Europe, he had told Benois, marvelling at the ballet's synthesis at its Mariinsky premiere in 1907, thereby sowing the seeds for the inception of the Ballets Russes.[35]

The way in which *Le Pavillon d'Armide*, based on a story by Gautier about a Gobelins tapestry that comes to life, harnessed a total art work fusion of dance, music and design to mobilise a historical tableau must have resonated deeply with Parisians. French audiences, inspired by their national writers to view cathedrals as total art works which brought their history to life through a harmonious ensemble of architecture, liturgy, speech and sculpture, would have come to the Ballets Russes already accustomed to the spectacle of history restored through the total art work. 'A performance of Wagner at Bayreuth is not much

Alexandre Benois
Costume for a spirit of the hours c 1909
from *Le Pavillon d'Armide*
© Aleksandr Benois/ADAGP.
Licensed by Viscopy, 2010

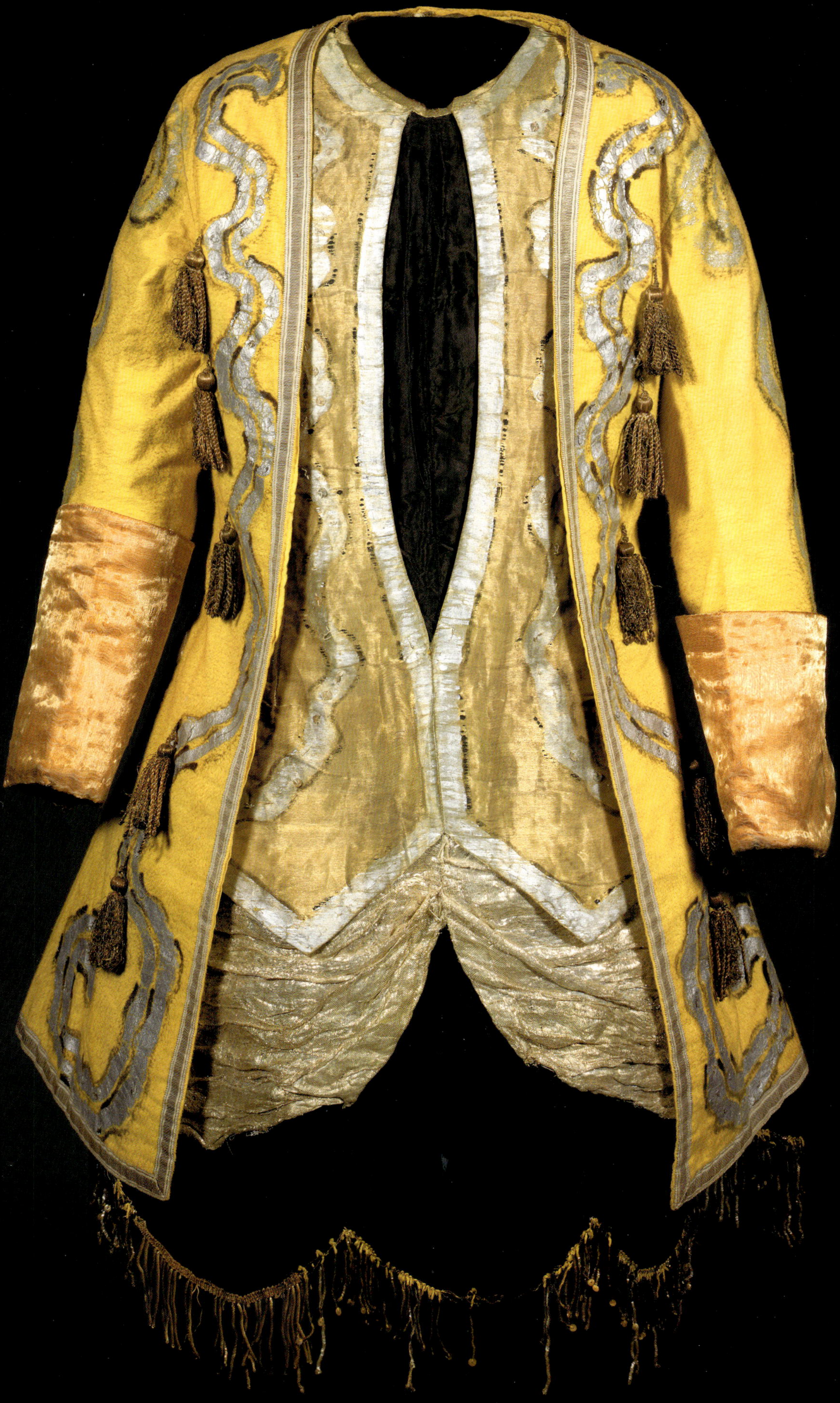

compared to high mass in the cathedral of Chartres' argued Marcel Proust, pitting the French medieval cathedral against the Wagnerian *Gesamtkunstwerk*. Proust was only the latest in a long line of French writers, artists, journalists and politicians from different backgrounds, stretching back to the early nineteenth century, for whom the 'Gothic cathedral … served as a kind of *ur*-museum in which different media … fused into a unique experience'.[36] Such was the cathedral's status as historical *tableau vivant*, resting on 'an inherently *French* tradition that pre-dated the theory of the [Germanic] *gesamtkunstwerk* by hundreds of years', that Proust urged the French government to subsidise religious services as performing arts.[37] He soon came to view Ballets Russes performances in similar terms, as theatrical total art works which brought history to life with an unprecedented veracity.

In *The captive*, volume V of *In search of lost time*, Proust likened the way Fortuny gowns:

> brought before the eye that Venice saturated with oriental splendour where they would have been worn and of which they constituted, even more than a relic in the shrine of St. Mark, evocative as they were of the sunlight and surrounding turbans, the fragmented mysterious and complementary colour [to] the theatrical designs of Sert, Bakst and Benois, who at that moment were re-creating in the Russian ballet the most cherished periods of art impregnated with their spirit and yet original.[38]

'Everything of those days had perished but everything was being reborn, evoked and linked together by the splendour and the swarming life of the city, in the piecemeal reappearance of the still-surviving fabrics worn by the Doge's ladies', Proust wrote of the gowns' power to conjure up history, a power he soon came to recognise in Ballets Russes costume and set designs.[39] Proust even read the actual remains of Renaissance Venice against their representation in the Ballets Russes, not the other way round, as if Venetian history existed more palpably in the total art work tissue of the ballet than in the surviving urban fabric of the city itself:

> Then my eyes travelled from the old wooden Rialto to that fifteenth-century Ponte Vecchio with its marble palaces decorated with gilded capitals, and returned to the canal on which the boats are manoeuvred by adolescents in pink jackets and plumed toques, the spitting image of those avowedly inspired by Carpaccio in that dazzling *Legend of Joseph* by Sert, [Richard] Strauss and Kessler.[40]

Here, again in *The captive*, Proust was referring to the Ballets Russes production choreographed by Fokine in 1914 and conceived by Léonide Massine, who danced the titular role, in the style of Venetian Renaissance painters Veronese, Titian and Tintoretto, with costumes designed by Bakst.[41]

To characterise the Ballets Russes' pervasive sense of history merely as dry, pedantic antiquarianism would therefore be to misread, fundamentally, the intense power of the living museums which Diaghilev's ballets brought to the stage. A more archaic and antiquarian attitude to the past, out of step with contemporary French notions of history, would not have registered with Parisian audiences with anything like the same impact of the Ballets Russes. If, as historian Stephen Bann says, early nineteenth-century France had 'developed the Romantic cult of history with an unequalled degree of clarity and explicitness'[42], by the end of the century, in the wake of the Franco-Prussian War and the Paris Commune especially, the cult had accelerated into an unprecedented 'phenomenon of revivalism'.[43] In the aftermath of these events a shared understanding of the national past across the population at large was identified as vital to ensuring national unity and history acquired a new urgency. Within this climate of rapid and intense popularisation of history, the past staged as total art work emerged as an intrinsic element of the new orthodoxy. It was as easily encountered in the new and innovative national museums, as in allied cultural practices such as grand opera or the diorama, and even in the birth of the modern era Olympic movement of Pierre, Baron de Coubertin. The launch of this movement in 1894 with de Coubertin's founding of the International Olympic Committee, its Hellenic revivalism, its reliance on spectacle and its origins in France's defeat in the Franco-Prussian War, can be read as another mobilisation, this time on a global stage, of the total art work as vehicle for staging the historical past.

The Musée des Thermes et de l'Hôtel de Cluny's new installation, an:

ensemble display [of] different media from the same period, including furniture, sculpture, tapestries, suits of armor, paintings, ivories and enamels, … often placed in a single room, creating a kind of total environment in which the visitor could imaginatively occupy the role of lord or knight,[44]

was so uncannily close to the Ballets Russes concept of ensemble display that its description is interchangeable with Benois's account of *Le Pavillon d'Armide*, quoted above. The new Parisian national museum's ensemble display worked with an extraordinary sense of theatre to draw visitors inexorably into its extremely vivid historical tableaux, so that they 'felt as if they had stepped into the Middle Ages', just as the ballet's fused ensemble furnished characters which stepped out from its animated tapestry with an unprecedented sense of historical veracity. The museum's aim of 'mak[ing] the medieval past live again'[45], from its opening in 1842 under the curatorship of Edmond Du Sommerard, who would hold this post until his death in 1885, was matched by the ballet's 'lifelike quality, the truthfulness, [its] actual re-creation of the eighteenth century which astonished people with a knowledge of the period'.[46] *Le Pavillon d'Armide*'s overriding sense of verisimilitude was rooted in deep and direct knowledge of the Palace of Versailles, on which its garden setting was based.

Benois, whose ancestral roots lay partly in France, had lived at Versailles with his family and, says Levinson, was fascinated by the regal splendour of the palace.[47] Benois recalled that he had given himself up entirely to painting, 'sketching in my beloved Versailles and creating a series of pictures on themes from my favourite epochs, the seventeenth and eighteenth centuries'.[48]

Benois, a deeply cultured art historian who directed the graphic arts department at the Hermitage Museum until 1923, like his counterparts in France did much in his native Russia to generate interest in the country's past.[49] As Lieven observed, his influence was apparent in the museum and in collections, in his promotion of 'interest in provincial monuments, old palaces, furniture and country mansions [to] … a wide public', and in triggering a revival of interest in Russia's history, art and antiquities.[50] And Benois was as steeped in France's culture and history as in that of Russia; in fact,

according to the French poet Robert de Montesquiou, 'there emanated from him the epoch of Louis XV'.[51] Lieven was quick to recognise the novelty of Benois's historical revivalism, commenting from the relative proximity of the 1930s that this cult of the past proved to be something new: 'the love of things historical, so deeply imbued, was the motive power of Benois's innovations'.[52]

Chief among these innovations was Benois's embrace of the French phenomenon of the total art work as the very embodiment of history, so different from its Germanic cousin, the Wagnerian *Gesamtkunstwerk*, marked by its retreat *away* from history, into the universalising realms of Niebellungen myth. And the mobilisation of history in this way, through the vehicle of the Gallic total art work, must help account for the intensity of the reception of the Ballets Russes in Paris. In Proust's view, the company registered with French audiences as nothing less than 'a revolution as profound as Impressionism itself'.[53]

If *Le Pavillon d'Armide*'s success was due in part to the way its intense evocation of Louis XV's Versailles resonated with a 'cultural and scholarly elite interested in rococo style [and for whom] the eighteenth century came to be associated with nostalgia for the Ancien Régime'[54], other ballets in the opening Paris season conjured up alternative historical vistas no less powerfully. Benois was quick to credit to Bakst's designs, the dynamic historical veracity with which *Cléopâtre* staged Ancient Egypt for the audience at its Paris Ballets Russes premiere on 2 June 1909:

> The fresh aspect Bakst gave Egyptian antiquity in *Cléopâtre* seemed at the time the ballet was created, like a surprising discovery in the field of archaeology … Diaghilev told me that Kaiser Wilhelm II, after having attended the opening night of *Cléopâtre* in Berlin, had called together the members of a society of Egyptologists of which he was president to talk to them about the cultural significance of the ballet and to urge them to study Bakst's mise-en-scène.[55]

As Lieven makes clear, this *mise-en-scène* resulted from careful historical research:

> Bakst, who had to design the costumes, shut himself up for several days in the Hermitage Museum making sketches with beautiful results. Cleopatra was draped

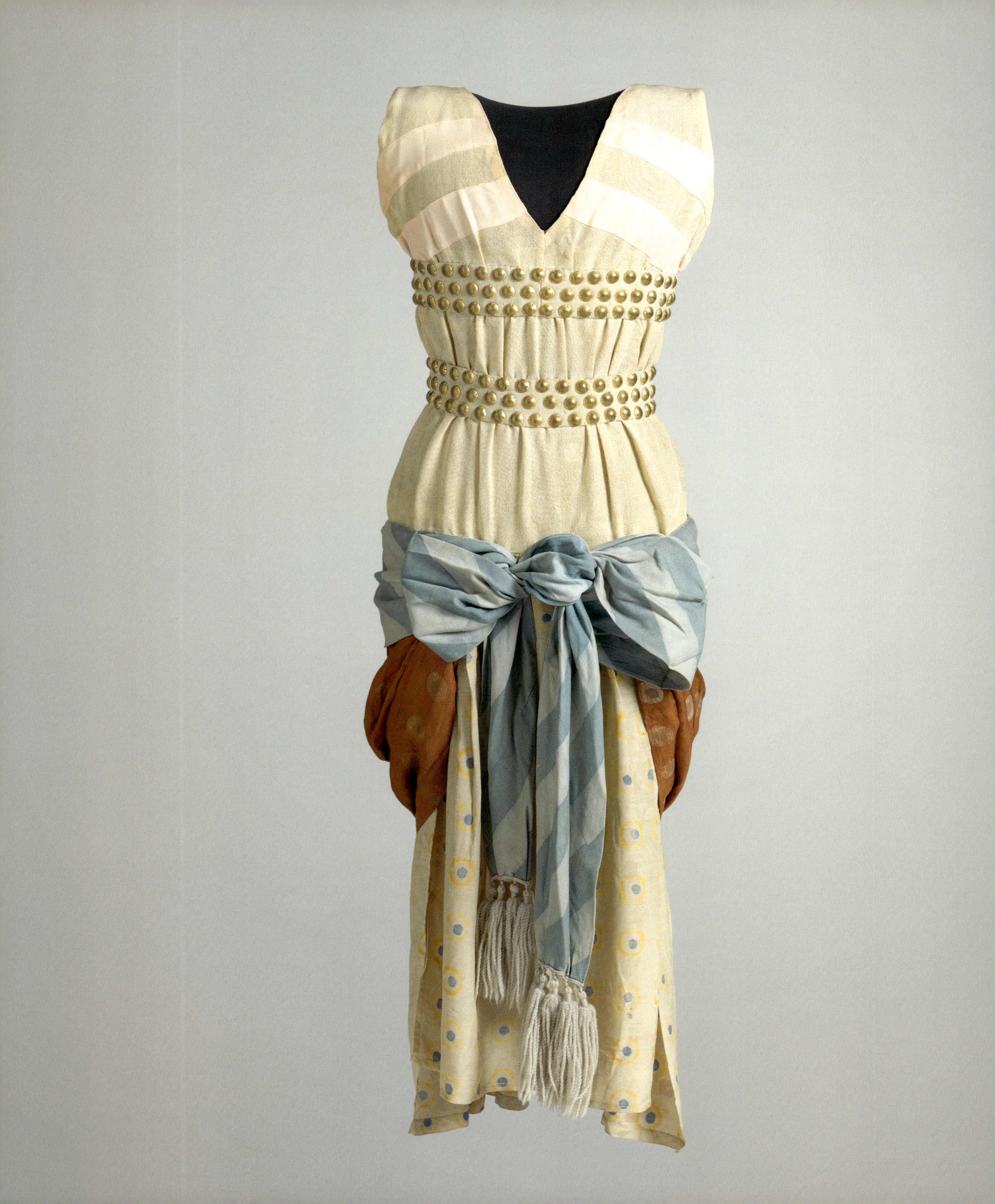

in a long strip of linen sumptuously designed with Egyptian hieroglyphs and motifs.[56]

In an article written in 1909, Benois again attested to Bakst's unswerving commitment to historical research: 'He must have seen the Department of Antiquities at the Hermitage or the Louvre, methodically making sketches of ornaments, details of costumes and objects, in order to avoid historical superficiality.'[57]

The historical plausibility that Bakst had invested in *Cléopâtre* was shared by *Les Sylphides*, designed by Benois and programmed with *Cléopâtre* as a double bill.[58] According to Lieven, *Les Sylphides* was 'filled with the sentimental and spiritual romanticism of the 1830's, with all its conventions—the moon, tombs, hopeless love, etc.'—and offered an elegy to the period.[59] He went on to comment:

> As *Le Pavillon d'Armide* was the reincarnation of eighteenth-century France, so *Les Sylphides* was a return to the thirties of the last century, a faithful return, in which even the accurate detail of the long *tutu Taglioni* was not omitted.[60]

Lieven was alert to this all-encompassing accent on historical revivalism:

> If one recalls the direction which the development of the *Ballets-Russes* took in the sense of theme one can see the early touch of Benois's leaning to the past ... Thus in all the pre-[First World] War productions there is an element of the revival of the past, the only ballet of pre-War days which broke the link with the past was *Les Jeux*. This was modernism, quite up-to-date and devoid of any historical tradition.[61]

This otherwise all-pervasive historicism, this vision of the distant past, even extended to *Le Sacre du printemps* (*The rite of spring*) which, Lieven emphasised, was 'a prehistoric vision, confused, awe-inspiring, but true'.[62]

This view was shared by Levinson, for whom this ballet, 'conceived against an historic background of pagan Russia', imagined 'the sacred rites of an ancient cult'.[63] For Levinson the plangent, post-war *Les Noces* (*The wedding*), for all its harsh Modernism, also came 'straight from the soil of Russia. In the whole history of art it would be hard to find anything more poignant than the mother's lamentation on bidding her daughter farewell'.[64] Thus even at their most radical, Ballets Russes productions were almost always highly retrospective, revealing the extent to which our perception of the company as a wholly iconoclastic enterprise, concerned only with breaking with history and focusing exclusively on the future, is distorted and extremely partial.

By 1923 the historicising powers of the Ballets Russes were being called on by the French state itself to vivify and restore French history at the heart of the country's most celebrated palace complex. Diaghilev was approached by the impresario Gabriel Astruc and Henry Lapauze, a wealthy fundraiser, to create a performance to be staged in the Galerie des Glaces at the Château de Versailles on 30 June 1923 as part of a gala charity evening to raise funds for 'the upkeep of the palace and restoration of the park'.[65]

This gala evening (termed La Fête Merveilleuse by the French government) was to evoke the Versailles of Louis XIV and the Grand Siècle. Diaghilev's original idea of using music of the period for the ballet *Les Tentations de la bergère* (*The temptation of the sheperdess*), after he found a musical score by

(opposite) **Léon Bakst**
Costume for a Syrian woman
1909 and 1930s
from *Cléopâtre*

(above) **Juan Gris**
Costume for the Countess
c 1924 from *Les Tentations de la bergère*

Bodies of history: the Ballets Russes, the past and the classical tradition 61

Michel Pignolet de Montéclair (1666–1737) in the library of the Paris Opéra, would have been especially appropriate. (Under Louis XIV dance had become an instrument of state and the king had founded the ballet company at the Opéra and established the Académie Royale de la Danse.[66]) When the Society of Ancient Instruments was unable to make the music ready in time, Diaghilev staged instead *Le Mariage d'Aurore*, the final act of *The sleeping beauty*, which had recently entered the company's repertory. *The sleeping beauty* is set at the royal courts of sixteenth- and seventeenth-century France, and ends in a glorious apotheosis of Louis XIV, so this was a highly appropriate substitution made more apt by the introduction of a preceding fanfare by Rameau and an oration in the style of the period.[67] The ballet was followed by songs by Rameau and Lully, composers to Louis XIV, before the figure of the Sun King, wearing a magnificent blue and gold costume, ascended or descended—there are conflicting accounts—'the stairs to his throne … with his enormous blue velvet cloak embroidered with *fleur de lys* covering the stairway'.[68]

The Cubist artist Juan Gris may have seemed an unlikely choice to dress the ballet in high baroque designs to match the Hall of Mirrors performance space but, according to *Le Figaro*, 'with the collaboration of the Keeper and the Architect of the Château, Juan Gris has created a décor worthy of Mansart' (referring to one of the original architects of Versailles).[69] Several of Gris's carefully researched costumes, including the blue and gold outfit with its ermine-trimmed, embroidered train for the Sun King, were used for *Les Tentations de la bergère* when this ballet was eventually staged the following year. In its Versailles-based conjunction of dance, historical re-enactment and public history, the Fête Merveilleuse drew on a precedent set in 1837 when the July Monarchy mounted the Fête de Versailles to celebrate the opening of the Museum of the History of France at Versailles. The museum, itself the culmination of an earlier project to renovate Versailles, was inaugurated through a performance featuring historical figures, opera and also dance.[70] This celebratory performance:

> connected the greatness of the king-centred ancient régime, best represented by the court of the young Louis XIV at Versailles, with the constitutional monarchy [of Louis-Philippe], in theory returning the past grandeur of France to the people of the present.[71]

Some eight decades later the French republican government, through the Fête Merveilleuse, sought

Léon Bakst
Costume design for the Queen and her page (in Act I) 1921
from *The sleeping princess*

62   Ballets Russes: the art of costume

to cement the same connection between itself and the illustrious history encapsulated in the chateau, doubtless spurred also by the publicity potential of such a gala at a time when Versailles, like its sister palace at Fontainebleau, was a well-established destination on a tourist itinerary and in easy reach of Paris.

The commitment of the Ballets Russes to valorising history through the vivid evocation of the past as danced total art work reached its apogee in *The sleeping princess*, Diaghilev's 1921 attempt to bring to London and Paris audiences a vision of the 1890 Imperial Russian *Sleeping beauty* that had first inspired him, Benois and Bakst to collaborate creatively. Indeed, Diaghilev's reconstruction, which was 'mounted as the ultimate tribute to the vanished glories of imperial Russia'[72], must have been at least in part an attempt to recreate the notion of the total art work enshrined in the original 1890 production, the aspect of the ballet which proved such a catalyst for the founding figures of the Ballets Russes. The historical gaze of *The sleeping princess* was thus twofold or, if you count the *two* early modern French époques, separated by an intervening century of sleep, which are the ballet's settings, threefold. Bakst's designs for the ballet transported audiences to the same baroque court societies that had been one of the 1890 *Sleeping beauty*'s twin historical settings. In evoking the original St Petersburg production, said by Benois to be the Russian Ballet's highest achievement, the 1921 *Sleeping princess* conjured a no less vivid vision of the fin-de-siècle Romanov Russia in which *The sleeping beauty* had been created.[73]

Igor Stravinsky, commissioned by Diaghilev to orchestrate two items for *The sleeping princess*, was all in favour of the revival.[74] In an open letter to Diaghilev published in *The Times* and included in the souvenir program for the London opening, Stravinsky said:

> this work appears to me as the most authentic e xpression of that period of our Russian life which we call the 'Petersburg Period', and which is stamped upon my memory with the morning vision of the Imperial sleighs of Alexander III, the giant Emperor and his giant coachman, and the immense joy that awaited me in the evening, the performance of *The Sleeping Beauty*.[75]

Bakst, writing in the same souvenir program, regarded the ballet's music as the principal conduit for its bifurcating historicising gaze, observing that 'through the absolutism of Alexander III, with its pomp and splendour, Tchaikovsky's genius impels our thoughts to the broad decorative lines of the seventeenth century and the magnificence of the Roi-Soleil.'[76] And Benois, whose special affinity with the period of Louis XIV would have made him Diaghilev's first choice as designer were he not still living in Russia and employed as curator at the Hermitage Museum[77], was equally keen to credit Tchaikovsky's music, which he described as imitative of the earlier, Baroque style of Lully and Couperin, with the same role. No music had ever so successfully resuscitated the distant past for Benois as much as Tchaikovsky's score for *The sleeping beauty*: 'Not only did I know the score by heart, but I *had* to hear it played by the orchestra again and again'.[78]

Writing elsewhere, Benois told how:

> I experienced at that time a feeling of profound gratitude to Tchaikovsky. It was as if he had opened doors for me through which I penetrated further and further into the past, and at certain moments this past became more comprehensible and closer to me than the present.[79]

The figures most closely involved with, or surrounding, the Ballets Russes creation of *The sleeping princess* were keen to stress what they perceived as the gulf separating the ballet's unprecedented synthesis of dance, design and music from Wagner's conception of the total art work, a gulf which they detected in the music especially. According to Levinson:

> Igor Stravinsky loudly proclaims the genius of Tchaikovsky, upholding—in defiance of the shade of Wagner—the spontaneous melody of the Russian master against the 'leitmotifs' of the mage of Bayreuth, his delicate instrumentation against the noisy orchestration of the German composers.[80]

Similarly pitching the two composers against one another, Bakst evoked Stravinsky—after all the two were writing alongside one another in *The sleeping princess* program—in order to champion Tchaikovsky's melody over Wagner's thematism:

> That in the great struggle between melody and the musical theme, the doctrinaire Wotan of the Bayreuth

stock-jobbing market has already suffered eclipse by the lovers of music, by Mozart and Haydn, admits of no doubt. As Stravinsky expresses it, it is impossible to prefer celluloid to tortoise shell, to enjoy a theme as much as a melody. I have never feared to state my own opinion, even when it went against the tide, and I confess, without subterfuge, that beside Tchaikovsky's melody, the ruminated thematism of Wagner seems to me cerebral and tedious pompier [pomposity].[81]

Benois acknowledged the same distinction: 'the rapture it aroused in me was different from the thrill provoked by Wagner'.[82] And this antipathy extended to Tchaikovsky himself who, 'like most other Russians', as musicologist Richard Taruskin points out, 'felt a powerful aversion to Wagner'.[83]

From these firsthand commentaries, the need to challenge the commonly held assumption that the Ballets Russes's pathway to the *Gesamtkunstwerk* was routed exclusively, or even particularly, via Wagner, is imperative. Wagnerian opera was, after all, only the latest in a series of formulations of the total art work that reach back at least as far as the Renaissance. The sixteenth-century *ballet de cour*, for instance, one of those paradigmatic earlier examples of the French total art work, as Mark Franko has shown, sprang— appropriately enough in the context of this essay— from the same French royal courts which were the settings of *The sleeping princess*.[84]

The special conjunction of *Gesamtkunstwerk* and history which drove so much of the Ballets Russes enterprise stemmed not from Wagner but from Gallic notions of the total art work, with their origins in the French Romantic rise of history, and in even earlier French precedent. Honouring the governing precepts of the French total art work, a range of key Ballets Russes works consequently endeavoured not to erase history in the Wagnerian sense of retreat into the realms of universal myth but rather to mobilise the fullest possible historical vision. In other words, in its creation of spectacular vehicles for staging the most thorough-going retrospectivism, the company joined the Gothic cathedral, diorama, French Grand Opera and a range of other allied total art works in re-animating the past with an unprecedented sense of vivacity. Contemporary critics viewed the Ballets Russes in precisely these terms, as allied to

earlier nineteenth-century French grand opera and therefore little connected to Wagner. In its 1921 review of *The sleeping princess*, *The Times* observed that 'Tchaikovsky's conception of the ballet was very much like the average attitude taken by opera composers towards grand opera before Wagner had turned the world upside down'.[85]

For the young British essayist, poet, aesthete and art critic Sacheverell Sitwell, seeing the Ballets Russes *The sleeping princess* in London, with its designs by Bakst, was:

> the most exciting first night of Ballet I have ever seen— or am ever likely to see … the great first scene … was like an intoxicating revelation to a young man of twenty-three … It reminded me of the [eighteenth-century] staircase in the Palace at Caserta, near Naples.[86]

'In Bakst's version the [period] transition was from Louis XIV to Louis XV', Sitwell went on, with dancers in the Act II hunt clad in 'riding habits of the time of Louis XV, as we can see them in Oudry's tapestries'.[87] The same strong evocation of period, Levinson notes, extended to the hunt dances for this act, boldly choreographed in the style of the Grand Siècle by Bronislava Nijinska, Vaslav's sister.[88]

Overall, Bakst produced five sets and 300 hundred designs for various versions of the ballet. (He had previously designed *The sleeping princess* for Anna Pavlova's company in a 1916 New York production that drew heavily on French costume of the seventeenth and eighteenth centuries.) Such were the historicising powers of this ballet that Bakst depicted *The sleeping beauty* in a series of seven painted canvases, the only murals he ever undertook. They were set in more remote historical periods, with some of the figures in medieval dress and others wearing Renaissance costume, as costume historian Deborah Howard has discussed. Begun in 1913, when Bakst's Ballets Russes fame was at its height, the paintings were not completed until 1922, coinciding with the London production.[89] Commissioned by the French-born James de Rothschild to decorate the drawing room of his London town house, the paintings, says art historian Diana Souhami, were 'designed almost as stage sets themselves', an expression of 'Bakst's preoccupation with costume design and textile', and again conceived as part of an ensemble display, originally to include specially designed furniture and interior design.[90] The canvases featured as actors de Rothschild himself, cast in the role of the prince, his wife and family, relatives and friends, employees and even household pets[91], so that they simultaneously amounted to a set of highly historicised group portraits of contemporary figures.

Researching designs for *The sleeping princess* in the Bibliothèque Nationale in Paris, Bakst had studied the dance costumes of Jean Bérain the elder, Jean-Baptiste Martin, and Louis Boquet, seventeenth- and eighteenth-century designers at the French court, where they worked on court ballets.[92]

Bakst's 1921 set designs for Tchaikovsky's most Imperial ballet were founded, architecturally speaking, on the experiments of the set designers and architects Giovanni Battista Piranesi and the Bibiena family and, in terms of costume, on surviving accounts of Viennese masques and Versailles ballets.[93] The costumes were notable for their extreme lavishness and use of the finest materials. 'I've had to make, with my own hands, more than two hundred maquettes, costumes and sets not to mention the accessories, the wigs, the shoes, the jewellery' Bakst wrote to Diaghilev in 1921.[94] Dance writer Cyril Beaumont remembered that some cost £40 to £50 each, a large sum at the time.[95] The *Daily Mail* described how 'this new ballet … conjur[ed] up … before our dazzled eyes all the pomp of dead and done-with kings and emperors— Bourbons and Romanoffs'.[96]

Bakst's totalising historical vision bore a striking resemblance to a phenomenon described by Emery and Morowitz as 'museumification' that was by then well established in France. Comparison with the Musée de Cluny makes this clear: 'The mixed media display of Cluny had as its aim the revival of the past', just as, according to Lieven, Diaghilev's underlying motivation in creating the ensemble display of *The sleeping princess* was to 'return to the past'.[97] Similarly, the conceptual logic underpinning Cluny's methods of display, possessing much in common with the eclectic display of the collector's parlour, as Emery and Morowitz put it, reverberated in the ballet also.[98]

The strong imprint of *mise-en-scène* and eclecticism on the museum's interiors and historical displays, coupled with an extraordinary sense of theatre is closely paralleled by the purposeful eclecticism underlying *The sleeping princess*'s retrieval of the past. Howard notes how its 'evocation of the periods of Louis XIV and XV was achieved without pedantic adherence to the historical sequence … In each act the costumes cover a range of historical periods'. She also points out how Benois recalled that 'there was never anything doctrinaire, scholastic or "borrowed" about him'.[99]

Diaghilev's determination to render history in terms that matched the splendour of the Imperial Russian *Sleeping beauty* ended in financial disaster. Beaumont commented that *The sleeping princess* was Diaghilev's Moscow.[100] The production was planned to run for six months in order to recoup costs, but Diaghilev had badly misjudged a British audience grown used to his one-act offerings and not yet ready for an evening-length ballet on an Imperial Russian scale. *The sleeping princess* closed after one hundred and five consecutive performances, and did not transfer to the Paris Opéra as planned in April 1922.[101] In its place Diaghilev mounted *Le Mariage d'Aurore* (*Aurora's wedding*), a one-act selection of highlights from *The sleeping princess*. With the lavish costumes and sets from *The sleeping princess* sequestered by Sir Oswald Stoll, the production's financial backer, some of the sets and costumes created by Benois for *Le Pavillon d'Armide* in 1909 were used for *Le Mariage d'Aurore*, augmented with additional designs by Natalia Goncharova.

Le Mariage d'Aurore soon established itself as a staple of the company and its popularity was to endure after Diaghilev's death in 1929. Incorporated into the repertory of Colonel W de Basil's Ballets Russes de Monte Carlo, the ballet was performed on the company's inaugural tour of Australia at the Theatre Royal, Adelaide, on 27 October 1936. Back in Europe, Ninette de Valois's recollections of dancing in Diaghilev's *Sleeping princess* formed the crucial yardstick against which post-World War Two productions of *The sleeping beauty* were measured; the ballet rapidly established itself as the signature work of the Royal Ballet, the company she founded. With the establishment of the Australian Ballet, founded by Peggy van Praagh on her return from England in 1962, *The sleeping beauty* enjoyed

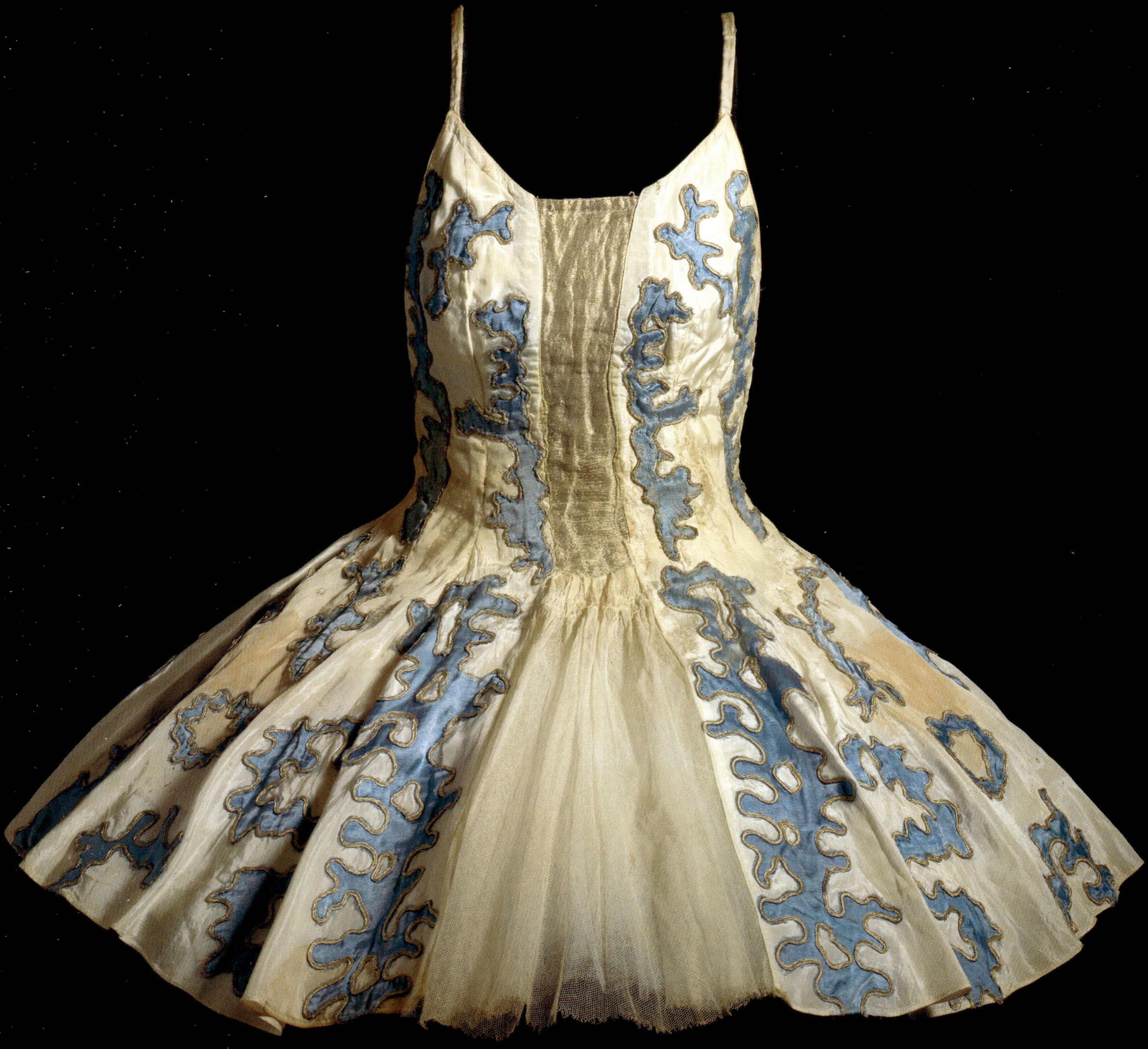

a similarly auspicious status in Australia, inaugurating the national company's first season at the Sydney Opera House in 1973.

Culminating in *The sleeping princess*, the company's project to stage *The sleeping beauty*, the ballet that was probably the greatest example of Russian classicism[102], the legacy of the Ballets Russes' overtly historicising tendencies was far-reaching. Sitwell saw *The sleeping princess* as the greatest achievement of Bakst's career, an astonishing success. And, as he recalled, if in 1921 the public was not in the mood to value this production, by 1940 *The sleeping beauty* was at last appreciated.[103] The historicism epitomised by *The sleeping princess* complicates those received histories of the Ballets Russes with their tendency to view the company's evolution, as far as its defining thematic preoccupations are concerned, in terms of a seamless progression from the Russian folkloristic revivalism of works such as *Petrouchka* to the cosmopolitan, international avant-gardism of ballets like *Parade*. In re-reading the danced total art work staged by the Ballets Russes as a potent and consistent vehicle for staging representations of the historical past, this essay also challenges those standard accounts of the company which view as straightforwardly Wagnerian the conception of the total art work that is so intrinsic to its enterprise.

This fundamental re-assessment of the Ballets Russes *Gesamtkunstwerk* proposes that the total art work on which key Diaghilevian ballets depended for their articulation of so vivid a historical vision had little to do with Wagner's conception of the *Gesamtkunstwerk*, with its retreat from history in favour of universal myth. Recovering the strong, if hitherto neglected, bonds binding the Ballets Russes to an abiding concern with representation of the historical past enables the identification of an altogether different conception of the total art work operating at the heart of the company, one much more closely allied to major contemporaneous developments in French attitudes to the past. History, to quote Stephen Bann, moved:

> from being a localized and specific practice within the [French] cultural topology' to become 'a flood that overrode all disciplinary barriers and, finally, when the barriers were no longer easy to perceive, a substratum to almost every type of cultural activity.[104]

It is not hard to recognise as axiomatic of this new, all-pervasive Gallic exploration of the past, the spectacular historical tableaux mobilised by a rich synthesis of dance, costume, design, and music which the Ballets Russes brought to the stages of London and Paris. In Diaghilev's hands, the key to ballet's progressive avant-gardism lay precisely in its radical retrospectivism.

Alexandre Benois and Léon Bakst
Overdress from the costume for Aurora c 1922
from *Le Mariage d'Aurore*
© Alexandre Benois/ADAGP.
Licensed by Viscopy, 2010

MODERN ART, MODERN BALLET

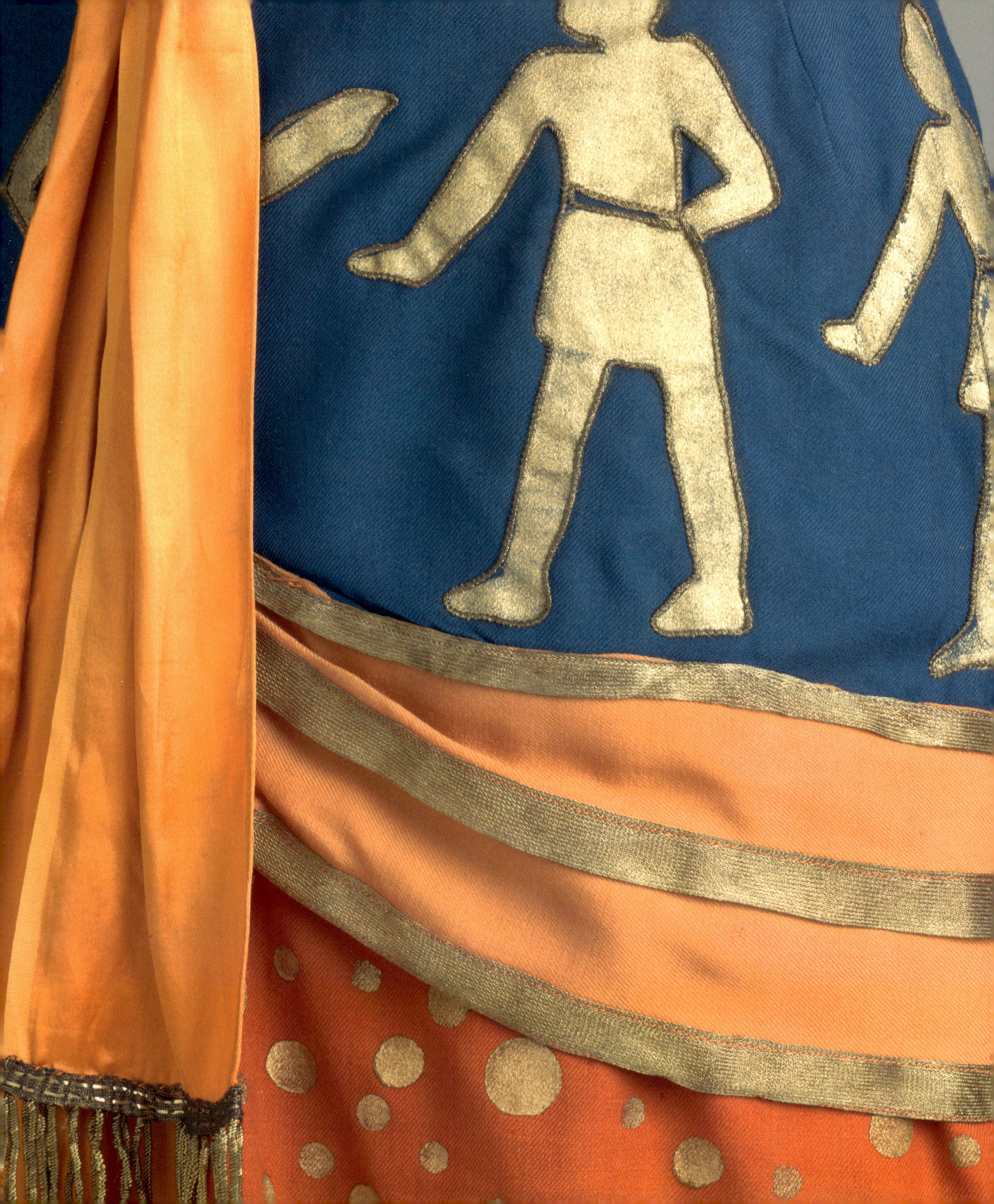

MODERN ART, MODERN BALLET

Christine Dixon

> Art must have perpetual youth; it must change and renew itself.
>
> Sergei Diaghilev[1]

Diaghilev's productions for the Ballets Russes are credited with transforming the stultified world of ballet. Music, choreography, and design: all appear modern. When the repertoire is examined closely however, a mere handful of works seem to be comprised of only avant-garde elements. Igor Stravinsky, Eric Satie and Nikolai Prokofiev were the most important and radical composers he employed, with Vaslav Nijinsky and Léonide Massine the most daring choreographers. Among the modernist painters who worked with Diaghilev, perhaps only Natalia Goncharova, Mikhail Larionov, Pablo Picasso, Sonia and Robert Delaunay, Henri Matisse, Georgy Yakulov and Giorgio de Chirico attempted to create sets and costumes as experimental as their painting styles.

The tumultuous premieres in Paris between 1909 and 1914 sometimes combined new music and choreography with unusual costumes and sets, *Le Sacre du printemps* (*Rite of spring*) 1913 being the most famously shocking example. But Nikolai Roerich's designs for this ballet, and particularly his costumes, belong to the tradition of Orientalism made famous by Léon Bakst in the previous few years, being adaptations of exotic patterns and motifs of the non-Russian realms of the Tsarist empire. The most avant-garde trait of Roerich's costumes is the flowing simplicity of the dancers' tunics. It was the ground-breaking multiple rhythms and rejection of conventional melody of Stravinsky's score, and Nijinsky's abstract choreography, which convulsed the audience, rather than the visual impact of the ballet. Never one to put all his aesthetic eggs in one basket, and in order to attract more conservative ballet audiences, Diaghilev also selected music by Romantic composers (Robert Schumann, Pyotr Ilyich Tchaikovsky) and more traditional designers, especially Alexandre Benois and Aleksandr Golovin. Often the Romantic scores were assigned to iconoclastic designers.

During and after the First World War Diaghilev increasingly chose young modern painters to visualise his ballets, rather than his older Russian colleagues from the days of *Mir Iskusstva* (*World of Art*). On the eve of the conflict, Goncharova's brilliant, blindingly colourful sets and costumes for *Le Coq d'or* (*The golden cockerel*) 1914 brought a new boldness and simplification to the stage. Instead of the sophisticated silken luxury of Bakst's Eastern fantasies (*Schéhérazade* 1910, *Thamar* 1912) she adapted Russian folk and peasant traditions such as the *lubok*, or popular wood-engraving, carved and painted wooden crafts and embroidery as necessary sources of her invention. This was part of a wider preoccupation in the European avant-garde: prehistoric and 'primitive' cultures also influenced the work of Amedeo Modigliani and Picasso. In Russia, as well as early stone sculpture, icon painting was valued for its severe and static, elongated images of the Holy Family and the saints. Another anti-classical resource was art made by children, which was seen as direct, unselfconscious and authentic.

Goncharova was an accomplished and prolific painter, and the life partner of Larionov from 1900 to 1962.

Sonia Delaunay
Costume for a slave or dancing girl 1918–36 (detail)
from *Cléopâtre*
© L & M Services BV Amsterdam

Exposure to such freedom from the old rules of structure and verisimilitude intoxicated Goncharova. She was inspired to paint a series of bold pictures depicting the lives of Russian peasants: working in the fields, picking apples, the harvest. Between 1909 and 1912 she experimented with intense colour contrasts, abstracted forms and simplified grounds. *Peasants dancing* 1911 shows the influence of Matisse and other Fauvist painters, as well as awareness of the heavy, statuesque works of Picasso's proto-Cubist period. Although idealised in their subject matter—it is always sunny, the peasants are happy at work and play—these works are both decorative and strong. Goncharova conveys the importance of the ordinary activities and feelings of the rural people of Russia.

When the Italian Futurist artist, writer and provocateur FT Marinetti visited Moscow in January 1914, the Russian *futuristi* were defiant. Larionov, Goncharova and other dissidents disrupted his lectures and performances. They could stage their own events, write all-but-incomprehensible manifestos, paint their faces with strange patterns and make radical films, such as *Drama in the Futurists' cabaret No 13*, December 1913, without any help from outside. So Diaghilev's suggestion that Goncharova should be asked to design his stylish new production—Pushkin's Russian retelling of the folk tale *Le Coq d'or*—frightened his associates. The choreographer Michel Fokine remembered his relief when they met late in 1913:

> After all the terrible stories I had heard about the Moscow Futurists, I found myself in the company of the most charming, modest and serious people ... how earnestly Goncharova discussed every detail ... I went away feeling thoroughly convinced that she would produce something unexpected, beautiful in colour, profoundly national, and at the same time enchanting.[2]

Fokine was not disappointed. Goncharova designed a distilled, intense decor which integrated the set and costumes in an extraordinary fusion of Russian and modern art. Her flat, bold patterns, a striking and simplified scheme of bright colours, and an acute understanding of dramatic values were applauded at the premiere in Paris on 24 May 1914. Diaghilev's ability to select enthusiastic collaborators was rewarded when *Le Coq d'or* was greeted rapturously

Natalia Goncharova
(top) *Study for the curtain for the prologue of* Le Coq d'or
c 1914–17
watercolour and collage on board
53.3 × 73.3 cm
collection of the McNay Art Museum, San Antonio, Texas, gift of the Tobin Theatre Arts Fund

(above) *Peasants dancing*
1910–11
oil on canvas
92 × 145 cm
© Natalia Goncharova/ADAGP.
Licensed by Viscopy, 2010

She was a central figure of the Russian avant-garde before the First World War, closely associated with Russian Futurism and a co-inventor of Rayonnism. Her exhibition of 768 works astonished Moscow in 1913. The purity and intensity of her hues were certainly influenced by Matisse, whose paintings *La danse* 1910 and *La musique* 1910 were installed at the city home of Sergei Shchukin in December 1911; the collection was open to the public on Sundays. Matisse's compelling and intense Fauvist palette is at its high point in these two large canvases where red figures traverse a deep blue and green flat ground.

by public and critics alike.³ Nikolai Rimsky-Korsakov's nationalist opera, which premiered in Moscow in 1909, was remade by Diaghilev into an opera-ballet, with singers at the side and dancers miming the action on centre stage. Goncharova suggested that the theatre be blacked out when the curtain rose⁴, an innovation which allowed the design to be seen all at once, a visual thunderclap. This fantasy Russia was still barbaric, but now dazzling in dissonant red, orange and yellow, enhanced by counterpoints of blue and green. Goncharova's set was highly decorative, with crowded townscapes of onion domes and towers, while curling, abstracted flower and plant motifs seemed to occupy every surface.

Diaghilev's great project, the Ballets Russes, can be seen as a continuation of the earlier search for an integrated work of art which would combine music, visual art and performance into a perfect, 'total' work of art—what Richard Wagner called a *Gesamtkunstwerk*. It would prove a futile quest, but sometimes on the stage as the company performed, the chimera seemed within reach. The outbreak of war in August 1914 was financially disastrous however, disrupting the company and forcing the postponement of most new productions. Diaghilev presented only four new ballets between 1915 and 1918, most notably *Parade* (*Sideshow*) 1917, which rejoiced in a scenario by Jean Cocteau, designs by Picasso and a score by Satie. Although today *Parade* is regarded as Cubist, only the Managers were constructed as characters fitting a Cubist painting, while the other characters were extremely conventional, especially the Little American Girl and the Chinese Magician.

Was part of the aura which surrounded Diaghilev's ballets an alien Russian quality, whether it was modernist or not? Less well-known than Cubist artists in France, the inventiveness of the Russian avant-garde in painting and sculpture in the second and third decades of the twentieth century was unique in its range and the courage of its artists. As well as their expressionist folk visual language, Goncharova and Larionov created a Futurist style they called Rayonnism, which was fast-moving, abstracted, and cinematic in its effects. Kazimir Malevich went as far against figurative art as possible, culminating in his Suprematist paintings such as *White square on white* 1918, a monochrome geometric form on a monochrome ground.⁵ Vladimir Tatlin made a new

(above left) **Unknown photographer**
The American Manager in Parade *(designed by Pablo Picasso)* 1917
page 34 in *Souvenir program for the Ballets Russes at l'Opéra, May–June 1920*

(above right) **Unknown photographer**
The final scene from Chout *(designs by Mikhail Larionov)* 1921
Bibliothèque nationale de France, Paris

Modern art, modern ballet 73

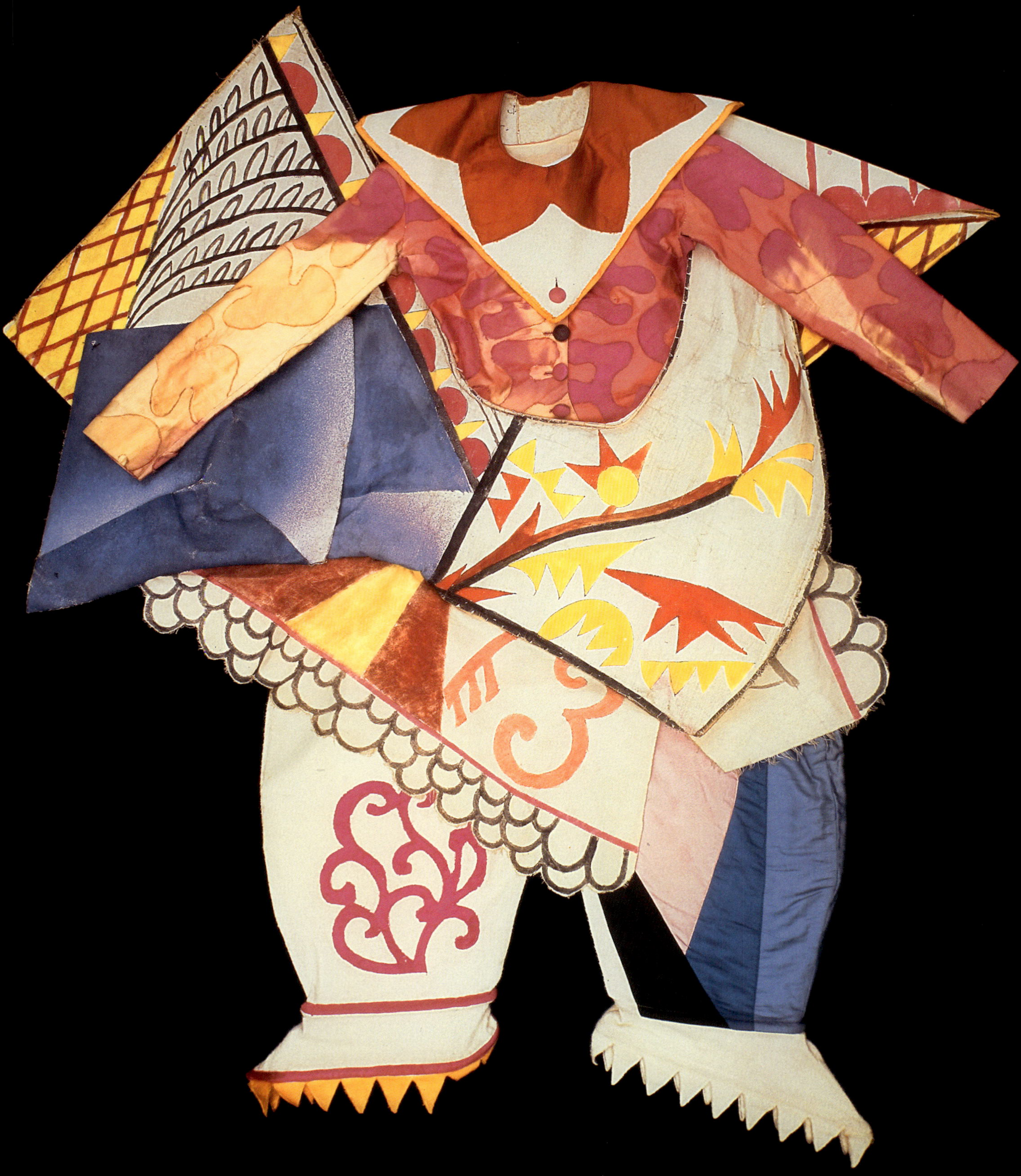

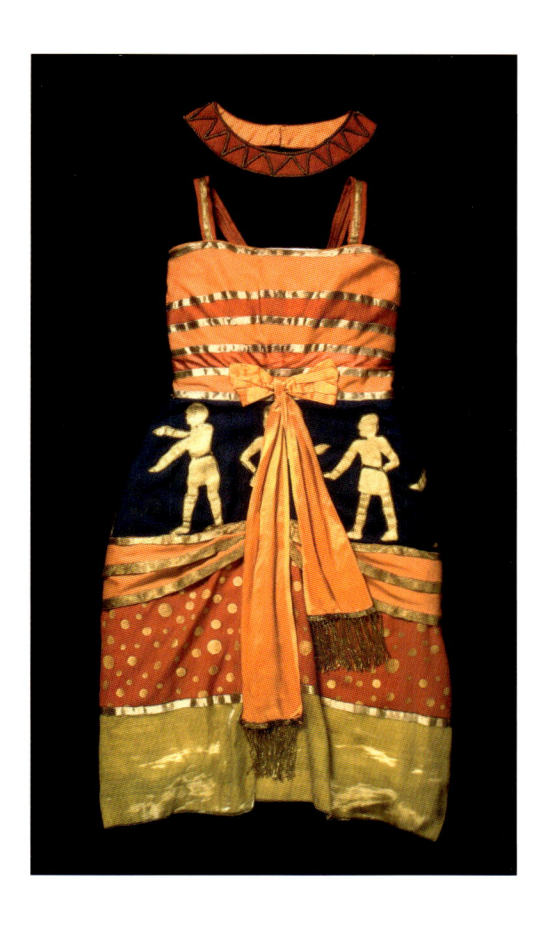

kind of sculpture, architectural in its ambition. After the war and the Russian Revolution of 1917, there was little contact between the Soviet Union and the West. Diaghilev commissioned fewer Russian designers, and those who were Russian tended to be long-term exiles such as Sonia Delaunay and Pavel Tchelitchew.

Larionov's designs for the costumes and set for *Chout* (*The buffoon*), designed in Switzerland and Spain between 1915 and its premiere in Paris in 1921, were more daring and abstract than any by the other artists who worked for Diaghilev. Brilliantly coloured, dazzlingly distorted and with visual echoes in the sets, the costumes animated the stage like living canvases. Larionov used heavy canvas or buckram with cane ribs to make the asymmetrical shapes for his foolish characters. The dancers found the costumes very heavy and cumbersome to move in. John E Bowlt notes that 'Diaghilev was even forced to threaten the dancers with penalties in order to make them dance in clothes that interfered with the very movements of their dancing'.[6] Diaghilev's use of painters as theatre designers emphasised the innate contradiction between a static, flat, inert canvas and moving, flexible costumes on living bodies. The idea of going beyond the frame, out of the picture, is realised best in the Cubist and Futurist work of Picasso and Larionov: they create three-dimensional paintings or two-dimensional sculptures. Unusually, the artist for *Chout* was also its choreographer, with technical assistance from Thadée Slavinsky.

Some of Bakst's original costumes and the sets for *Cléopâtre* 1909 had been damaged by fire on tour in 1917, so when Diaghilev wanted to re-stage the ballet in 1919 he commissioned Robert Delaunay to design the sets and Sonia Delaunay the costumes. They were stranded in Spain by the war, and Diaghilev seems to have tired of, or fallen out with, Goncharova and Larionov. Robert's sets were simplified and dramatic, totally unlike the orientalist excesses of Bakst and Benois, while Sonia's conception of Cleopatra as an unfolding mummy was extremely clever. Her costume for Amoun is richly coloured in red and green, with purple and black backing the gold Egyptian symbol on the trunks, and purple, black and gold for the halter. Despite the traditional royal

(opposite) **Mikhail Larionov**
Costume for a buffoon's wife 1915–21 from *Chout*
© Mikhail Larionov/ADAGP. Licensed by Viscopy, 2010

(above left) **Sonia Delaunay**
Costume for a slave or dancing girl 1918 from *Cléopâtre*
© L & M Services BV Amsterdam

(above right) **Léon Bakst**
Costume for an Egyptian 1914 from *La Légende de Joseph*
Private Collection, The Bridgeman Art Library

Modern art, modern ballet 75

palette, she achieves a contemporary look from its short and streamlined contours.

Comparing Bakst's 1909 costume for a slave or dancing girl with Delaunay's 1918 version is enlightening, as the claims of modern invention rest firmly on the shoulders of earlier designs. Bakst's work is pink, purple and dark blue, with gold netting, fringe and stencilled patterns, while the 'modern' one consists of pale and bright orange panels edged with gold ribbon, a red skirt with stencilled gold spots and gold lamé band, and a central panel with stylised Egyptian figures stencilled in gold on a blue ground. Both are sleeveless, Bakst's with a halter and Delaunay's with simple shoulder straps, and both have allusions to hip panniers. The 1909 dress is much longer and more sinuous in its effect, while the 1918 costume is shaped more simply, indicating the new conventions about desirable body shape soon to be adopted by women's fashion in the Jazz Age. While Delaunay seems to have shrugged off most of the Romantic Orientalism of Bakst, she is nevertheless indebted to him, but rather to his design for an Egyptian for *La Légende de Joseph* (*The story of Joseph*) 1914 than his conception for the original production of *Cléopâtre*. Here we see shoulder straps, horizontal bands, orange and gold, and similar stencilled figures around the blue torso. It seems probable that either Delaunay had access to Bakst's designs through Diaghilev, or they were described to her in detail.

The last years of the war and the 1920s saw a 'return to order' in literature and other arts, exemplified by André Derain, then by Juan Gris, Picasso and Georges Braque. Cocteau's *Le Rappel à l'ordre* (*Call to order*), a collection of his earlier essays republished in 1926, was an appeal for the return of the values of classical simplicity. In effect, artists rejected the multiple viewpoints and fragmentation of Cubism, the Futurists' glorification of war and the machine, and the seeming confusion of non-naturalistic art. Modernity seemed intertwined with that European culture which culminated in destruction and the mass deaths of industrial warfare in the trenches which had shattered the continent between 1914 and 1918. Visual consequences included a dominant palette of black, brown and grey, offset by white. In ballets designed by Derain, such as *La Boutique fantasque* (*The magical toyshop*) 1919, the artist looked to rococo lightness and charm rather than classical sobriety. Braque's costumes for *Zéphire et Flore* (*Zephyr and Flora*) 1925 harked back to ancient Greek ideas of the theatre, with masks, feathered helmets, kirtles and sandals, although the dancers bared their limbs rather more than had been considered seemly in earlier years.

Picasso's costumes and sets for *Le Tricorne* (*The three-cornered hat*) 1919 were simplified and bold, as befitted the most radical and Spanish artist of the avant-garde, but displayed none of the originality he had shown in *Parade*. Mañuel de Falla, a respected contemporary Spanish composer, wrote the music, but the ballet was an amusing trifle rather than aesthetically ground-breaking. Arabesques and flourishes in blue, black or white decorate the peasants' and officials' dress, backed up by chestnut brown, black and tan for the men, with red and yellow for the women. The production was notable for de Falla's and Massine's incorporation of Spanish folk and flamenco tunes, rhythms and steps into a classical ballet performance. Another, unintended, consequence may have been to spark Matisse's rivalry with Picasso again, this time to be played out on the London stage in *Le Chant du rossignol* (*Song of the nightingale*) 1920, the year after the debut of *Le Tricorne*.

Stravinsky's opera *Le Rossignol* (*The nightingale*), based on Hans Christian Andersen's tale, premiered in 1914. Diaghilev finally persuaded Matisse to collaborate on a ballet with him and the composer, which became *Le Chant du rossignol*. The story unfolds in the court of the Chinese Emperor, and concerns a live and a mechanical nightingale. Massine visited the artist in Nice, where:

> he lived in a penthouse flat in which one of the best rooms was occupied by a giant birdcage. He had hundreds of exotic birds from all over the world, and was so proud of them that he even carried about an official document testifying to the vocal range of his favourite nightingale.[7]

Matisse relied on a T-shaped motif for his costumes, derived from his knowledge of Chinese and Japanese traditional clothing. All his characters except the Nightingale wore such robes, short or long, conceived in two dimensions. Most were loose and made of silk: they draped around the dancers' bodies when worn.

The Mourners' heavy felt, on the other hand, was stiff and difficult to move in.

Most significant for the artist's future working methods was his making of the sets in the rush to prepare the production for its premiere:

> Matisse's paper cut-out technique developed from his working methods on the décor and costumes for ... Le Chant du Rossignol of 1920 ... Matisse had gone to London in 1919 to work on the décor with the Russian scene-painter Vladimir Polunin. He arrived without any sketches and 'set to work in the studio, scissors in hand, cutting out and piecing together a model' ... the décor was kept pure and simple (possibly as a reaction to the ornate profusion of earlier Russian Ballet décors).

The colours of the backdrop were restricted to black, white, blue, and turquoise green; the chromatic accents came in the costumes of the dancers.[8]

Yellow was used for the Mandarin, orange and gold for the Chamberlain; the costumes also had accents in black or orange-red (hand-painted by Matisse and others). Court ladies and servants wore pastel silks with appliquéd clouds or flowers, while the Mourners' cream was made more dramatic by midnight-blue velvet triangles on the body and chevrons down the spine.

In the mid 1920s Diaghilev was searching, as always, for the newest, the most modern. At the time this was Soviet revolutionary culture. He looked to Russia for possible directors such as the radicals Vesevolod Meyerkhold and Aleksandr Tairov, but it was already

Henri Matisse
Costume for a court lady 1920 from *Le Chant du rossignol*
© Succession H Matisse/Viscopy, 2010

(inset) Enriett
Group of dancers from Le Chant du rossignol (*court ladies' costumes designed by Henri Matisse*) page 18 in *Souvenir program for the Ballets Russes at l'Opéra, May–June 1920*

Modern art, modern ballet 77

(above left) **Unknown photographer**
Costumes for Le Pas d'acier *(designed by Georgy Yakulov)*
1927
Hulton Archive, Getty Images

Giorgio de Chirico
(above right) *Costume for a male guest* 1929 from *Le Bal*

(opposite) Cover of the *Souvenir program for the twenty-second season of the Ballets Russes de Serge Diaghilev* 1929
© Giorgio de Chirico/SIAE. Licensed by Viscopy, 2010

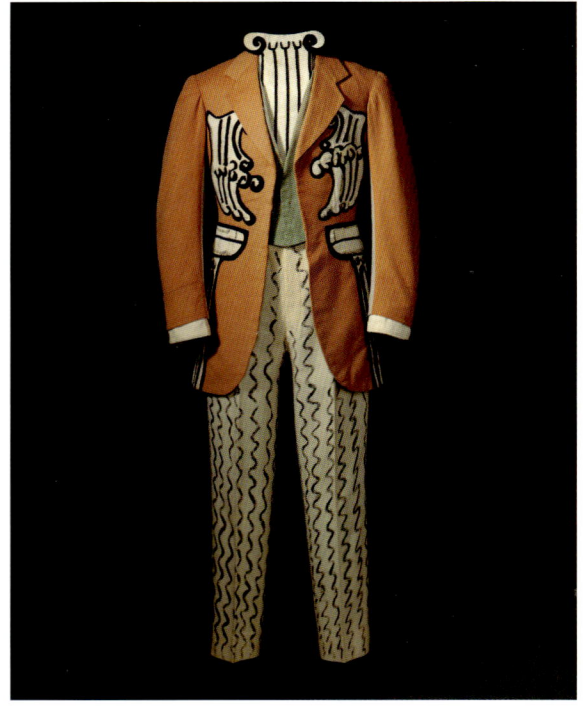

too late in the increasingly Stalinist climate taking hold in the Soviet Union. Following Lenin's death in 1924, revolutionary Constructivism was being displaced by conservative Socialist Realism. Artists were forbidden to travel, and Diaghilev's Ballets Russes was seen as hopelessly bourgeois, tinged with reactionary ideas of luxury and Tsarist nostalgia. Nonetheless, in 1925 Diaghilev commissioned a score for a 'Soviet' ballet from Sergei Prokofiev, then living in Paris. *Le Pas d'acier* (*The steel step*), the only Constructivist ballet ever created, in Russia or outside it, premiered in June 1927 at the Sarah Bernhardt Theatre in Paris. The title has been translated as 'Step of steel', 'Steel dance' or 'The steel leap'. In a violent break from the richly exotic themes and decors of the pre-war period, and the charming Russian folk fantasies of Goncharova and Larionov, *Le Pas d'acier* was set in a village market and a factory, with working-class heroes and heroines clad in grey, blue or brown clothes which displayed an industrial or 'utilitarian aesthetic'.[9]

The sets and costumes were designed by Georgy Yakulov, who had worked at the experimental Kamerny Theatre in Moscow, and was temporarily in Paris as a prize-winner at the International Exhibition of 1925. Massine was the choreographer, and described how the ideas behind the production informed the dance movements:

> [Prokofiev] wanted the ballet to distil the current conditions in the new Russia; to show how the Revolution had been the culmination of centuries of oppression; how the new régime was encouraging ideals of equality, discipline and work which would lead to national progress and knowledge ... [He] helped me to create the two contrasting scenes, the first set in the countryside and based on old legends and peasant types, the second demonstrating the force and virility of Communist youth. The wheels and pistons on the rostrums moved in time to the hammering movements of the young factory workers, and by strengthening the tableau with a large ensemble group in front of the rostrums, I was able to create a climax of overwhelming power.[10]

The National Gallery of Australia holds many costumes from this extraordinary production. Little evidence of the performances survives, although photographs, models and drawings for the machine-like set design have been examined by Lesley-Anne Sayers.[11] The socialist ideal of the triumph of the industrial worker was seen in the West at the most unlikely venue, a Parisian ballet stage, performed by a company mainly consisting of emigré White Russians,

78 Ballets Russes: the art of costume

g. de Chirico

Giorgio de Chirico
Coat for Death 1932
from *Pulcinella*
© Giorgio de Chirico/SIAE.
Licensed by Viscopy, 2010

with an anti-Bolshevik upper-class audience. Yakulov's costumes were made of the industrial fabric called 'American cloth', synthetic ponyskin and leather, as well as cotton and wool. The traditional luxurious silks, satins and lamés of Bakst were obviously inappropriate, as was the translucent mica used with oil-cloth by Naum Gabo and Anton Pevsner for *La Chatte* (*The cat*) 1927. American cloth, enamelled for waterproofing, was a shiny everyday material used in kitchens and laundries. The chosen colours were muted—Yakulov used grey, blue, a rusty red, light brown and black—yet the fabric conveyed the required sense of urban modernity. It was also cheap. In one of the ironies often attending Diaghilev's productions, the costumes were made by Barbara Karinska (1886–1983), another emigré from the Russian Revolution.

Among the ground-breaking productions of the Ballets Russes was *Le Bal* (*The ball*) 1929, the final ballet commissioned and overseen by Diaghilev before his sudden death in Venice that year. Vittorio Rieti's neoclassical score—he was indebted to Stravinsky and Georges Poulenc—and Georges Balanchine's choreography were joined by the visual inventions of the Italian metaphysical painter de Chirico. The genius of *Le Bal* lies in the designer's combination of architectural features, not only in the sets, but in the characters' costumes. Classical columns and capitals, brickwork, arches and cartouches decorate both dancers and the dominating backdrops. De Chirico's sets feature out-of-scale friezes, a giant painted horse and unexpected conjunctions of objects: uncanny relationships which figure in his painting. But he did not attempt to reproduce the brooding shadowed silence of his canvases, instead animating statues and buildings so that they come to life on stage.

The techniques employed by de Chirico in *Le Bal* include appliquéd elements, hand-painted decoration and patterning, as well as the use of tertiary and pale colours such as salmon and terracotta, light blue, and a dominant white. White is also the prevailing note in the costumes for his redesign of *Pulcinella* 1931 for the Ballet de l'Opéra Russes à Paris, originally a collaboration between Picasso, Diaghilev and Stravinsky in 1920. De Chirico enlivens his flared white tunics and tops with entertaining elements such as blue hearts, red and black stripes, yellow sleeves and pink flourishes. Black forms make up a skull on Death's costume, but all impart the jaunty world of Italian *commedia dell'arte*.

Ode 1928 was among the most innovative productions of the Ballets Russes, designed by Tchelitchew and choreographed by Massine to music by Nikolai Nabokov. The ballet's libretto was adapted from a hymn to the Empress Elizabeth by the eighteenth-century poet Mikhail Lomonosov, titled *Ode: a meditation on the majesty of God on the occasion of an apparition of the aurora borealis* 1746. The female costumes, for the Stars, refer to dress of the period, with fitted bodices and hooped skirts. They were decorated with lines of small mirrors making up a large starburst on the skirt, a small star on the neckline, with a black hood and mesh mask to suppress all elements of personality and to make the elements of the corps de ballet anonymous. The male dancers, the Constellations, were dressed in blue leotards and tights, with stylised constellations painted on their costumes in luminous paint. The stage is illuminated by backstage lights diffused through a grey screen onto which films of plants, animals and dancers were projected.

After Diaghilev's death, the company split and re-formed on several occasions under various names and managers, most notably René Blum, Vasily de Basil and Massine. New artists were commissioned, including Joan Miró, Jean Lurçat and André Masson. Masson created the décor and scenery for the first symphonic ballet, *Les Présages* (*Destiny*) 1933. The work was controversial because it was set to Tchaikovsky's Fifth Symphony 1888, by nature a non-narrative and abstract piece. Selecting a Surrealist painter such as Masson to conceptualise the music in a visual sense was also regarded as shocking, as Surrealism was seen as politically and artistically subversive. Against a backdrop of stars and comets, the main characters, such as Action, Passion, and Fate, are clothed in Greek-style flowing tunics, while the members of the corps de ballet are dressed in identical costumes. Men in simplified green woollen jackets with jagged maroon elements contrast with the women's simplified short dresses of silver-grey with red appliquéd abstract shapes. The Depression has arrived: the dresses are rayon, not silk.

Many elements central to modern art were flaunted on the stage in Diaghilev's productions for the Ballets Russes: boldness, simplification, asymmetry, layering and abstraction. How did the Russo-French designs by Goncharova, Larionov, Picasso, Matisse and de Chirico differ from those earlier creations by the painters of the World of Art? Benois's backdrops and costumes were historicist and traditional, based on descriptive evocations of the ballets' settings. Bakst, on the other hand, appeared to use formal, abstract patterns, for example on his simple Greek tunics for *Daphnis et Chloé* 1912. Their clarity, brightness and abstraction at first glance link him more closely to modern rather than naturalistic art, but it is the original designs to which he refers, rather than building up groups of intense colours or striking elements as a visual pattern of dancers on the stage.

The 'isms' of art in the early twentieth century—Fauvism, Cubism, Futurism, Constructivism and Surrealism—provided stars whom Diaghilev commissioned for his own artistic ends. A recurring theme was folk art, which Russian, Spanish, Italian and French painters, composers and choreographers all employed as a strategy to reinvigorate their own styles. Diaghilev's role in popularising modern art and modern music through his ballets was summed up in 1925 by the British critic Raymond Mortimer:

> He is the apostle to the Philistines. Thanks to him ... the idiom of contemporary composers such as Stravinsky receives the appreciation that only familiarity can breed. Thanks to him, too, the crowd has positively enjoyed decorations by the best and most ridiculed living painters. He has given us Modern Music without Tears and Modern Painting without Laughter.[12]

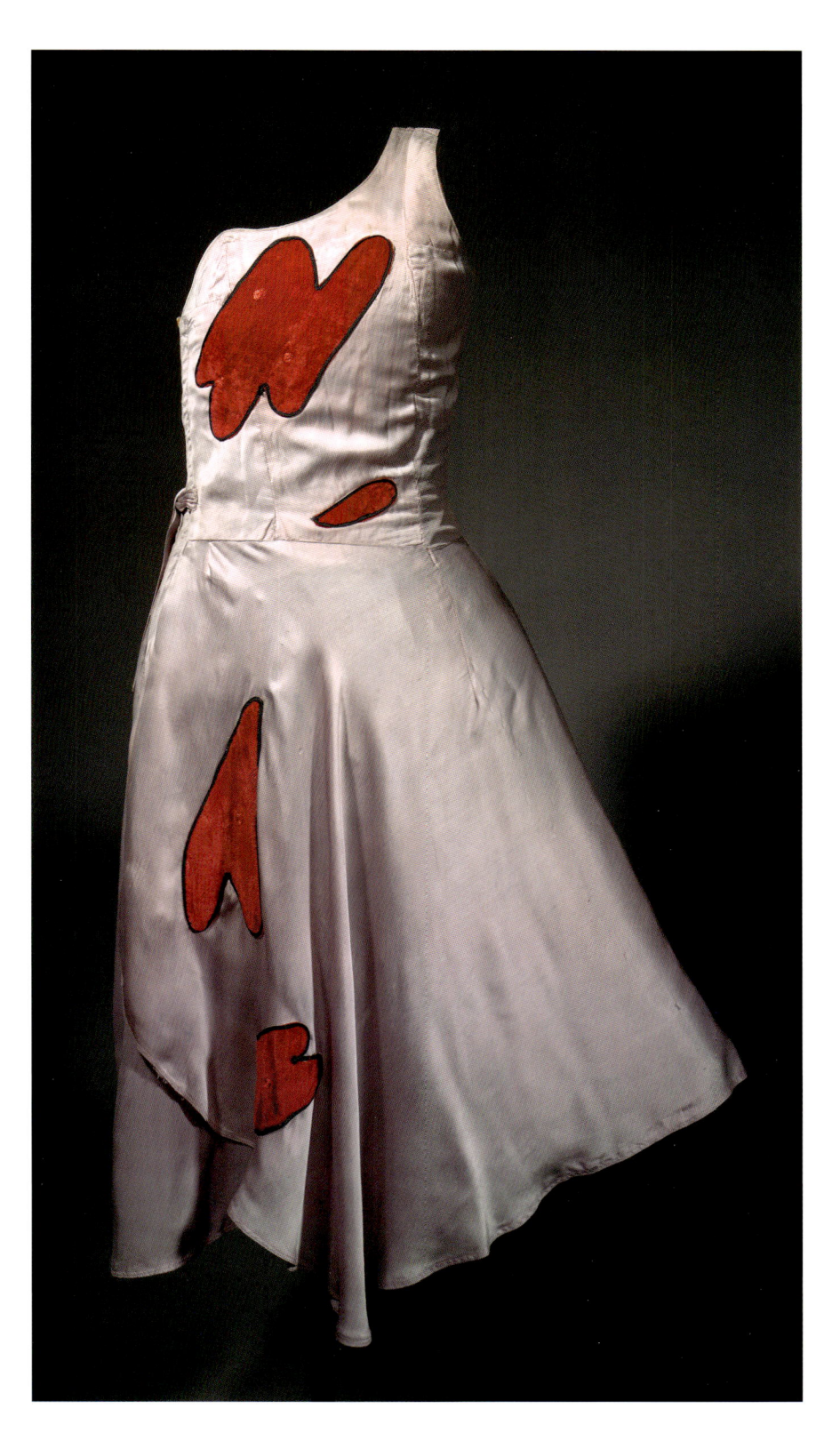

André Masson
Dress from costume for a female (in Scene 2) 1933 from *Les Présages*

COSTUMES FOR LES BALLETS RUSSES DE SERGE DIAGHILEV
1909–29

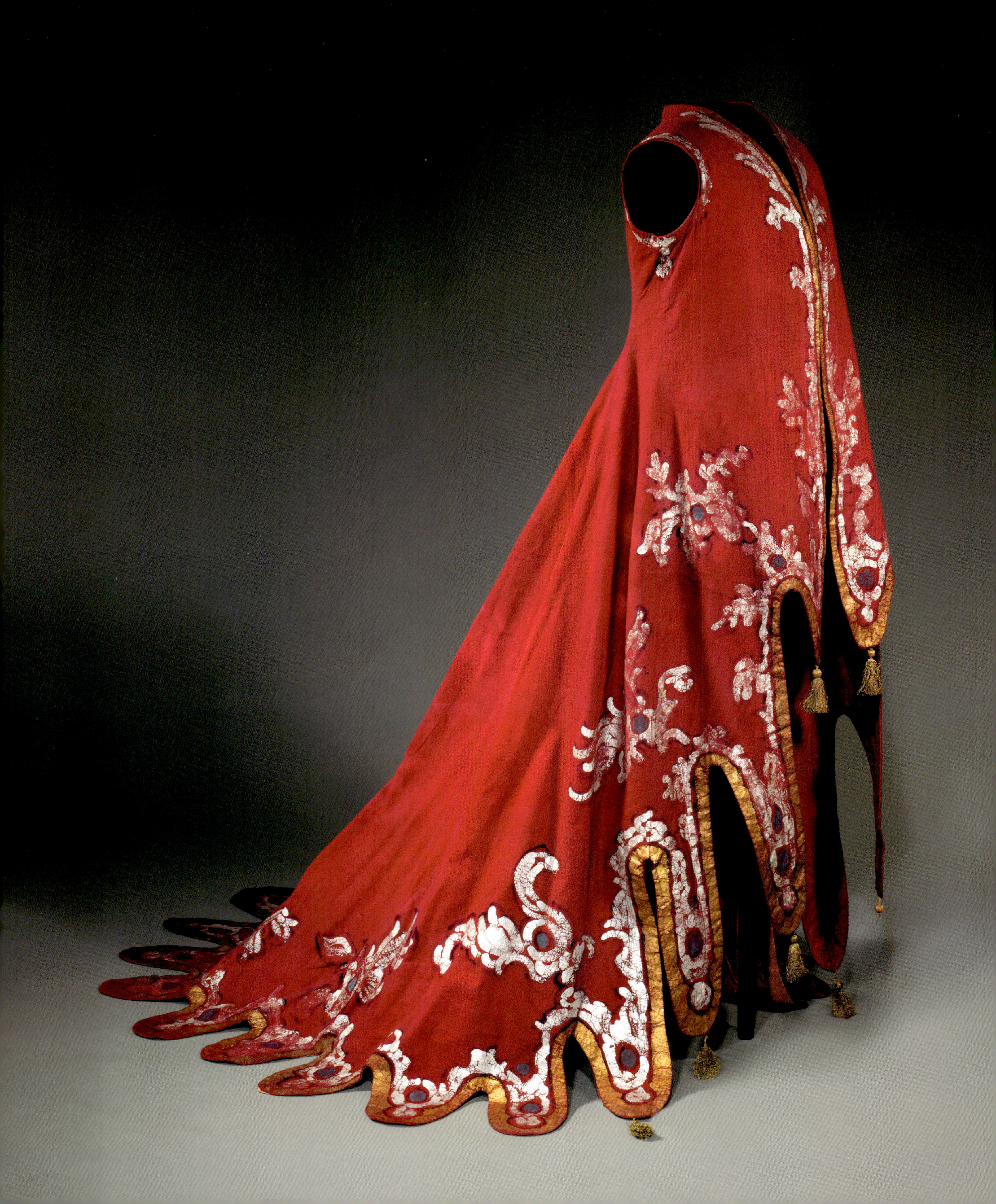

Le Pavillon d'Armide
Armida's pavilion

Ballet in one act

Producer:	Les Ballets Russes de Serge Diaghilev
First performed:	25 November 1907, Mariinsky Theatre, St Petersburg
Paris premiere:	19 May 1909, Théâtre du Châtelet, Paris
Costume design:	Alexandre Benois
Costumier:	Ivan Caffi (Imperial Theatres, St Petersburg)
Scenery design:	Alexandre Benois
Music:	Nicholas Tcherepnin
Choreography:	Michel Fokine
Libretto:	Alexandre Benois, after Théophile Gautier's story *Omphale*
Main characters:	Armide (Armida), Vicomte (Viscount) René de Beaugency, Armida's favourite slave, Marquis de Fierbois, King Hidraot, Confidantes of Armide, Vicomte René's servant Baptiste, Master of Ceremony[1]

The ballet is set during the reign of Louis XVI (1643–1715). During a storm, the young Vicomte René de Beaugency seeks refuge in a castle owned by an old magician, the Marquis de Fierbois. René spends the night in Armide's Pavilion, a wing of the castle, where he becomes mesmerised by a Gobelins tapestry hanging on the wall. While asleep he dreams that the tapestry figures of the sorceress Armide and her entourage come to life and perform a series of dances. Encouraged by King Hidraot, a member of Armide's animated court (and bearing a striking resemblance to the Marquis de Fierbois), René falls in love with Armide, who gives him her scarf as a token in return. Awakening, René discovers that he possesses Armide's scarf and that her woven tapestry figure does not. Shocked that his reverie was real, he collapses at the feet of the Marquis.

■

Benois's interpretation of Gautier's 1834 short story, *Omphale*, was influenced by the eighteenth-century Regency and Rococo costumes by the Paris Opéra designers, Jean Bérain (1640–1711) and Louis-René Boquet (1717–1814). Benois drew upon his deep love and knowledge of eighteenth-century French art, evoking the Rococo style's light elegance and design unity in this first Ballets Russes production. The leitmotif of the story's animated Gobelins tapestry is expanded to dominate the stage, with the costumes' painted silver patterns and metallic braids and fringes designed to catch the light as the performers, animated from their woven state, appeared to weave in and out of the overall decoration. This play of reality, memory and illusion also revealed Benois' interest in the dreamlike quality and supernatural subject matter in the work of the German Romantic composer and writer, ETA Hoffmann.

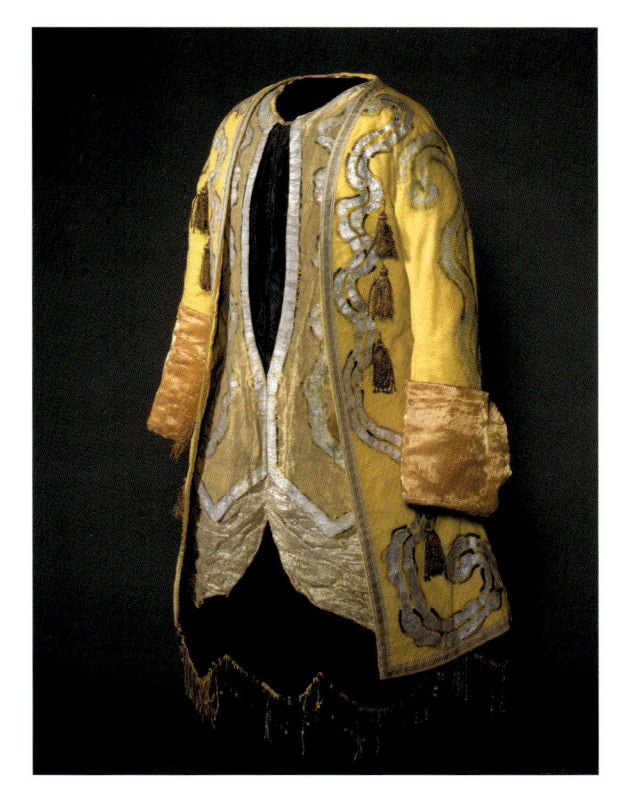

Alexandre Benois
(opposite) *Cloak from costume for a harpist* c 1909
(top) *Costume for a spirit of the hours* c 1909
(above) *Jacket from costume for a musician* c 1909
© Alexandre Benois/ADAGP. Licensed by Viscopy, 2010

Danses polovtsiennes du Prince Igor
The Polovtsian dances from Prince Igor

Polovtsian scene and dances

Producer:	Les Ballets Russes de Serge Diaghilev
Premiere:	19 May 1909, Théâtre du Châtelet, Paris
Costume design:	Nicholas Roerich
Scenery design:	Nicholas Roerich
Music:	Alexander Borodin (completed and orchestrated by Nikolai Rimsky-Korsakov and Alexander Glazunov)
Choreography:	Michel Fokine
Libretto:	Alexander Borodin, after a scenario by Vladimir Stasov
Main characters:	Igor Prince of Novgorod-Seversk, Vladimir, Polovtsian warriors, Polovtsian girls, Polovtsian boys, Oriental slave women

The ballet consists of a series of dances taken from the second act of Alexander Borodin's opera *Prince Igor*, based on a historical Russian epic. The ballet is set in the encampment of Khan Kontchak, leader of the twelfth-century Polovtsian army, following his capture of Igor Prince of Novgorod-Seversk, and his son Vladimir. Khontchakovna, Khan Kontchak's daughter, visits Vladimir at nightfall, but their tryst is interrupted by the magnanimous and hospitable chief, who calls for his warriors to entertain the royal party with a banquet and energetic, traditional dances.

■

While *Le Pavillon d'Armide* paid homage to France's *ancien regime*, the *Danses polovtsiennes* transported the Ballets Russes' first-night audience to a wilder world of Russian history set in the steppes of Central Asia. Roerich's interest in Russian folk art and nomadic tribal history resulted in his glowering and dusty sets evoking the smokiness of the Polovtsi's evening campsite, while his costumes for both male and female dancers presented a kaleidoscopic combination of traditional Central Asian folk dress patterns and shapes. Mauve, red, orange and green silk and cotton woven coloured-warp *ikat* textiles and braids were sourced from contemporary southern Russian nomadic tribal traders at markets in St Petersburg and made up into vibrantly patterned costumes that echoed the cultural interaction of the story, the ethnic diversity of the dancers and the savage rhythms of Borodin's score.

(above) **Unknown photographer**
Scene from Prince Igor
page 29 in *Souvenir program for Serge de Diaghileff's Ballet Russe*
1916–17

(opposite) **Nicholas Roerich**
Costume for a Polovtsian girl and a Polovtsian warrior c 1909–37

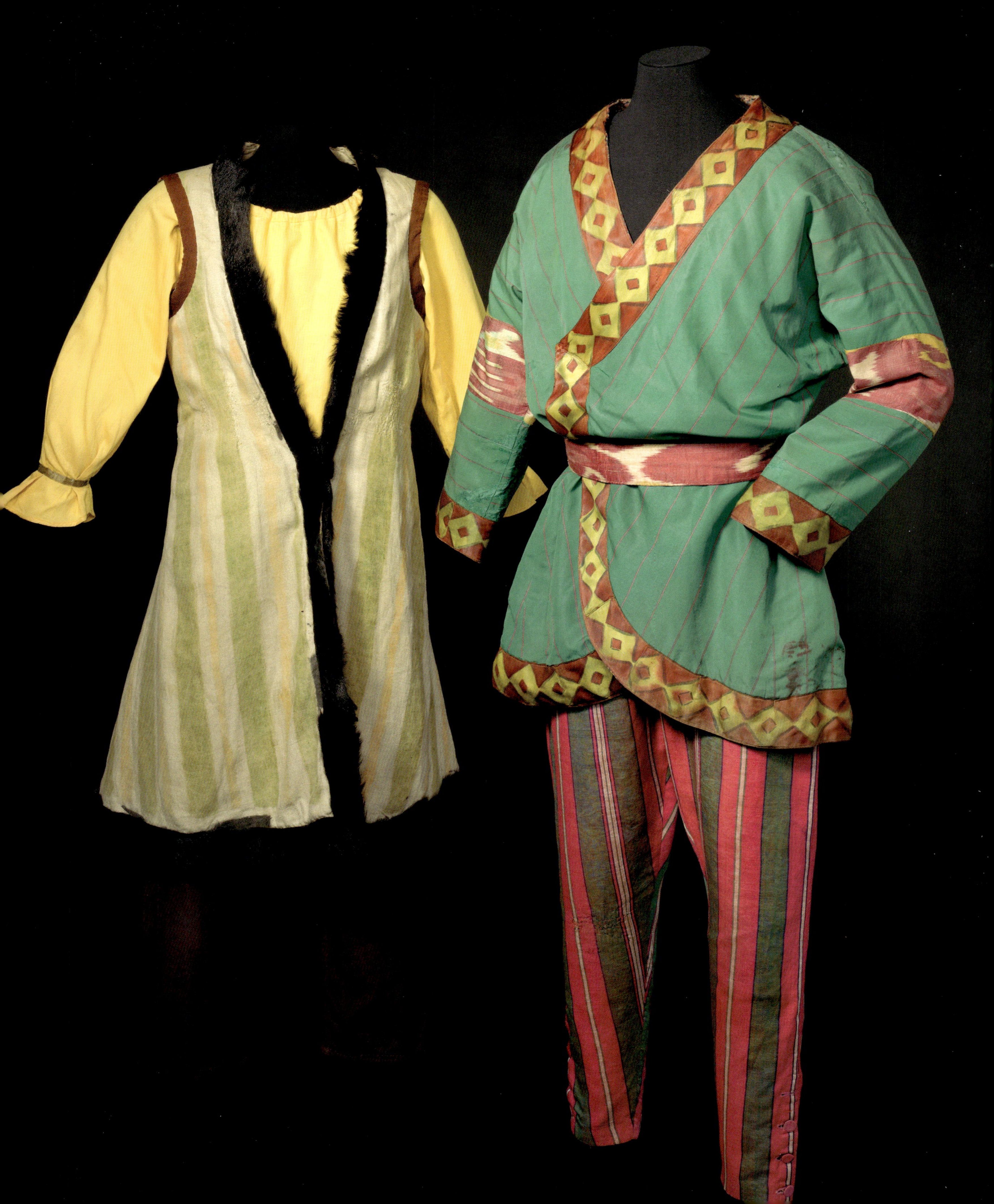

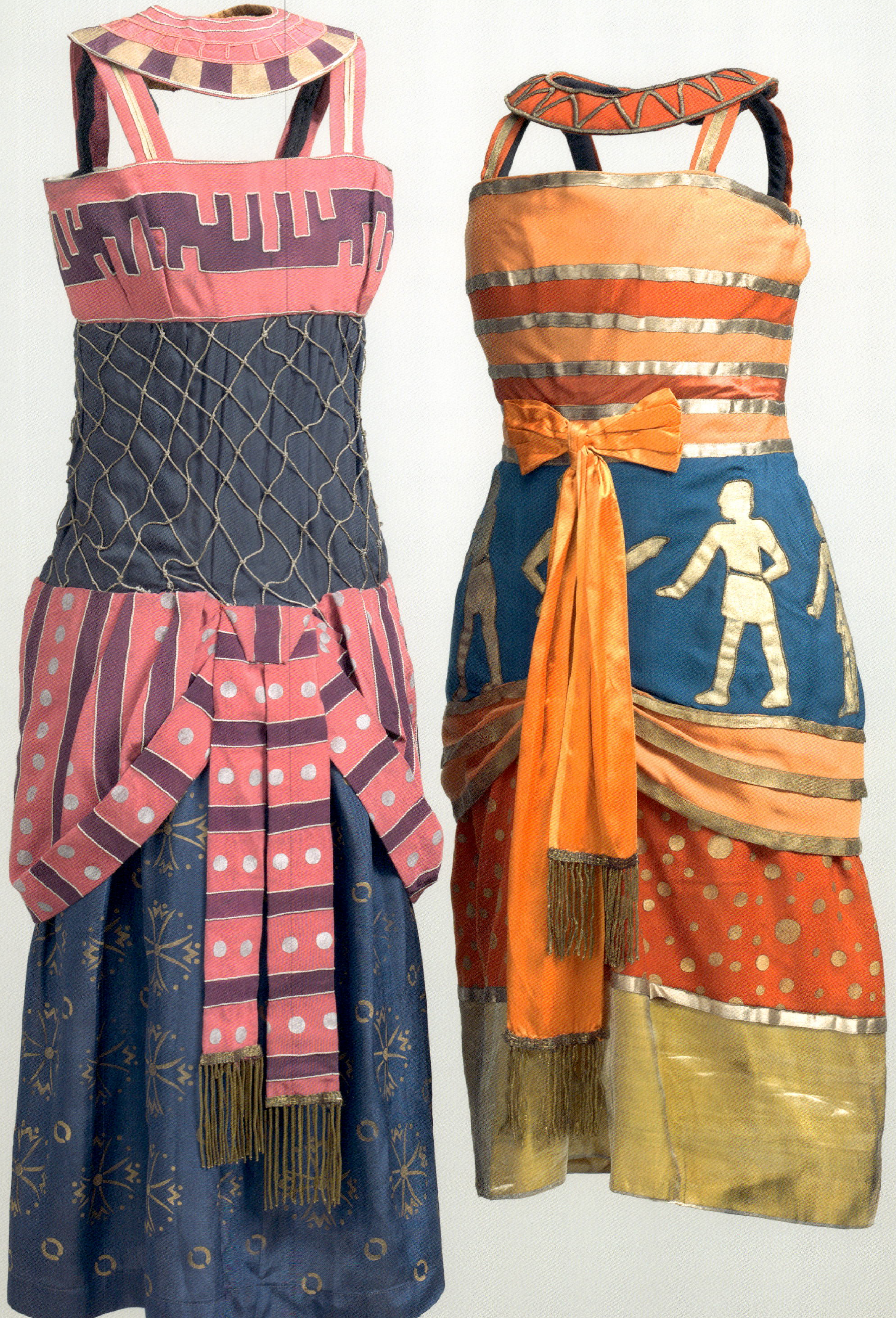

Cléopâtre
Cleopatra

Choreographic drama in one act

Producer:	Les Ballets Russes de Serge Diaghilev
First performed:	As *Une Nuit d'Egypte*, 2 March 1908, Mariinsky Theatre, St Petersburg
Paris premiere:	2 June 1909, Théâtre du Châtelet, Paris
Revival:	5 September 1918, Coliseum Theatre, London
Costume design:	1909 Léon Bakst; 1918 Sonia Delaunay
Scenery design:	1909 Léon Bakst; 1918 Robert Delaunay
Music:	Anton Arensky, Alexander Taneyev, Nikolai Rimsky-Korsakov, Mikhail Glinka, Alexander Glazunov, Modest Mussorgsky, Nicholas Tcherepnin
Choreography:	Michel Fokine
Libretto:	Michel Fokine
Main characters:	Cléopâtre (Cleopatra), Ta-Hor, Amoun, Cleopatra's favourite slave, High Priest of the Temple, Bacchantes, Servants of the Temple, Grecian women, Grecian men, Silenes, Egyptian women, Egyptian men, Jews, Syrian musicians

The ballet is set during the reign of Cleopatra (51–30 BCE), Queen of Egypt, when two young lovers, Ta-Hor and Amoun, meet in the grounds of a temple. Their tryst is interrupted by the high priest of the temple announcing the arrival of Cleopatra and her court. On seeing Cleopatra, Amoun immediately falls in love with her. Ta-Hor attempts to re-engage her lover's affections but to no avail. Amoun sends Cleopatra a message to which she responds that he can spend the night with her but in return he must drink poison in the morning. He agrees to the bargain and Ta-Hor later returns to the temple grounds to find the body of her dead lover.

■

Cléopâtre was the most extraordinary production in the Ballets Russes' 1909 season and signalled Léon Bakst's mastery of sumptuous and exotic design. Against his powerful stage imagery of desert scenery and ancient Egyptian temple architecture and interior design, the dancers' loose and abbreviated costumes glittered like jewels, animated by the physicality of their wearers. Bakst's colour orchestration of gold, lapis blue, malachite green, pink, orange and violet was expressed in imagined Egyptian design motifs on the characters' costumes, jewellery and weaponry. Dancer Ida Rubinstein's dark, angular and unconventional beauty invested her role of Cleopatra with a mesmerising sensuality and, through Fokine's choreographic innovations and Bakst's revealing costumes, she and the other dancers showed that the whole body could be used for expressive effect. While the apparently bare sections of their bodies caused a sensation, the dancers were in fact wearing 'fleshings', flesh-toned silk or jersey inserts that simulated skin (and reduce the necessity and time for body make-up), a costumier's technique used until 1912. These inserts seldom survive, nor are they evident in retouched contemporary stage photography.

(opposite left) **Léon Bakst**
Costume for a slave or dancing girl 1909

(opposite right) **Sonia Delaunay**
Costume for a slave or dancing girl 1918
© L & M Services BV Amsterdam

(above) **E O Hoppé**
Cleopatra—Madame Fedorova 1913
plate 14 from *Studies from the Russian Ballet*

Léon Bakst
(above left) *Costume design for a Syrian dancer* 1909
page 10 in *Souvenir program for
Serge de Diaghileff's Ballet Russes* 1916–17

(above right) *Costume for a Jew* c 1909–20s

(right) *Costume for a Greek* c 1909

(opposite) *Costume for a Syrian woman* 1909 and 1930s
from *Cléopâtre*

90   Ballets Russes: the art of costume

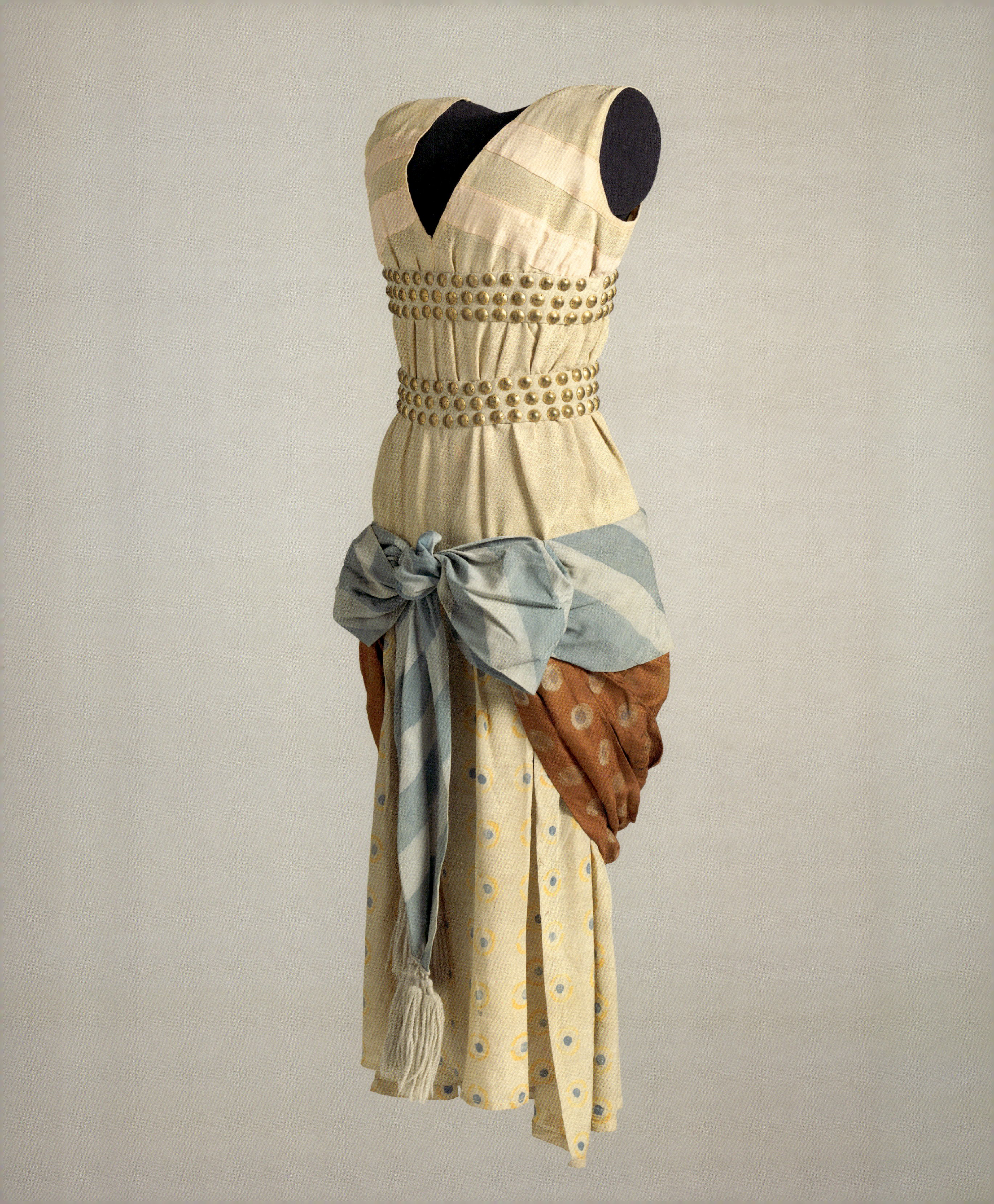

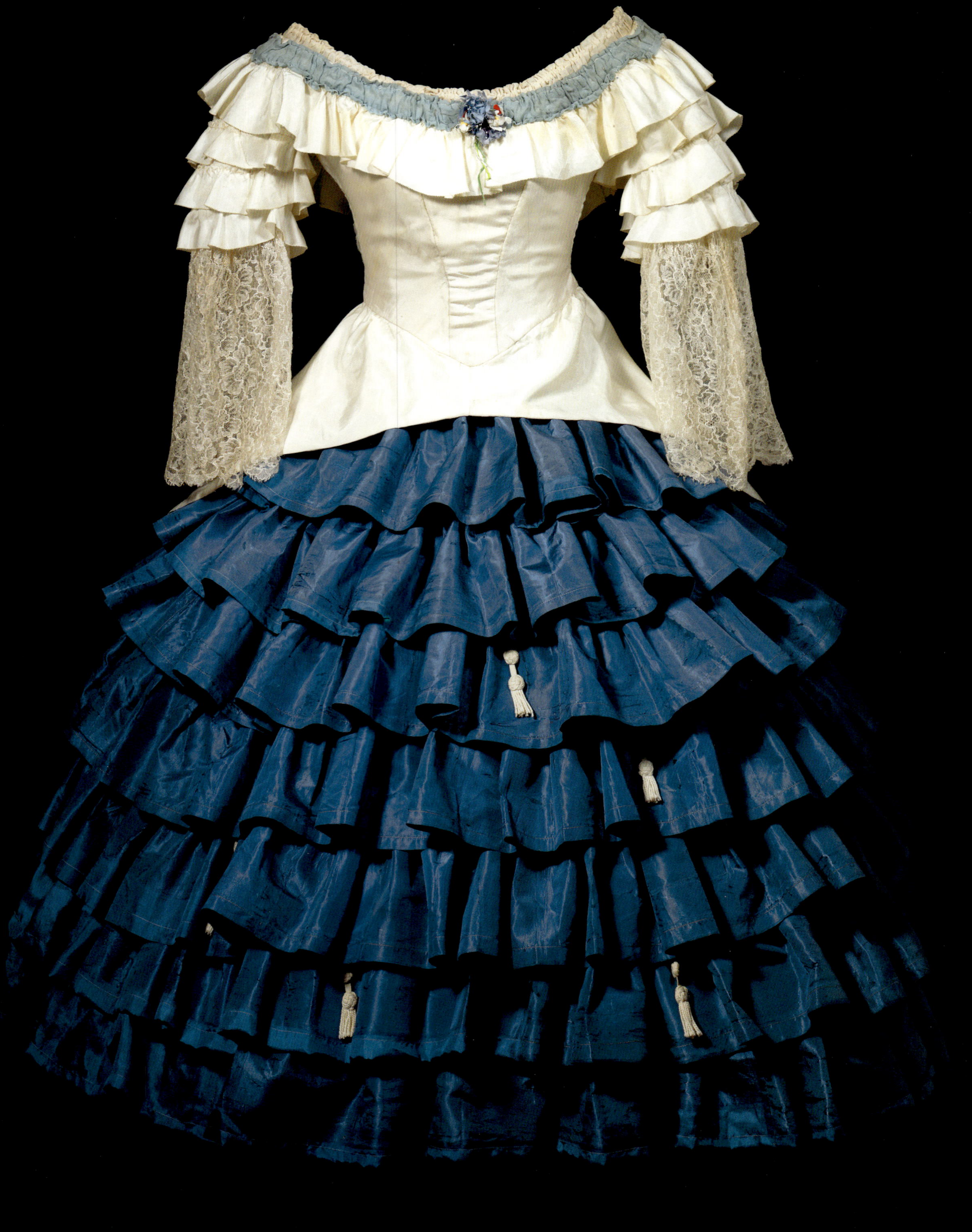

Carnaval
Carnival

Pantomime-ballet in one act

Producer:	Les Ballets Russes de Serge Diaghilev
First performed:	20 February 1910, Pavlov Hall, St Petersburg
Premiere:	20 May 1910, Theater des Westens, Berlin
Costume design:	Léon Bakst
Costumier:	Morris Angel & Son
Scenery design:	Léon Bakst
Music:	Robert Schumann; orchestrated by Nikolai Rimsky-Korsakov, Anatol Liadov, Alexander Glazunov, Nicholas Tcherepnin
Choreography:	Michel Fokine
Libretto:	Léon Bakst and Michel Fokine
Main characters:	Columbine, Estrella, Chiarina, Papillon, Pierrot, Harlequin, Pantalon, Eusebius, Florestan

The ballet takes place during a masked ball, where the melancholy and woebegone Pierrot unsuccessfully pursues Papillon (Butterfly); the fickle Columbine participates in a frivolous flirtation with the sprightly and mischievous Harlequin, both of whom in turn taunt Pierrot; the romantic Eusebius shadows Chiarina; the ardent and impetuous Florestan pursues Estrella and the pompous Pantalon is ridiculed and teased again by Columbine and Harlequin. The ballet ends with the entry of the disruptive Philistines, who unsuccessfully attempt to dampen the atmosphere of light-hearted revelry.

The characters in *Carnaval* were first given musical dimension in Robert Schumann's 1834 work, *Carnaval* (*Scenes mignonnes*) *op 9*, in which twenty-two short piano pieces represent the spirit and character of masked revellers at Carnival. Familiar characters from Italian *commedia dell'arte*, including Papillon, Pierrot, Pantalon, Harlequin and Columbine, join evocative depictions of figures from Schumann's life and characterisations of himself (as Florestan and Eusebius) and his wife Clara (as Chiarina). Bakst's set for the Ballets Russes' 1910 ballet was designed in the early nineteenth-century German Biedermeier style to suggest the anteroom of a ballroom in which the masked characters interact in flirtatious, light-hearted and poignant vignettes. While Bakst based their costumes broadly on the semiotic conventions of *commedia dell'arte*, each character is finely drawn to suggest the light elegance of the period in which Schumann conceived this enduring work.

Léon Bakst
(opposite) *Costume for Chiarina* c 1910

(top) *Costume for Pierrot* c 1910

(above) **George Barbier**
Nijinsky as Harlequin, with Pierrot and Columbine, from Carnaval in *Designs on the dances of Vaslav Nijinsky* 1913
National Gallery of Australia Research Library, Canberra

Léon Bakst
Dress from costume for Columbine c 1942

Léon Bakst
Costume for a lady c 1920

Schéhérazade

Choreographic drama in one act

Producer:	Les Ballets Russes de Serge Diaghilev
Premiere:	14 June 1910, Théâtre national de l'Opéra, Paris
Costume design:	Léon Bakst
Costumier:	Marie Muelle
Scenery design:	Léon Bakst
Music:	Nikolai Rimsky-Korsakov
Choreography:	Michel Fokine
Libretto:	Léon Bakst and Michel Fokine, after the first tale of *A thousand and one nights*
Main characters:	Zoebéide (Zoebeida), Zoebéide's Favourite Slave, Shah Shahriar, King of the Indes, Shah Zeman, the Chief Eunuch, Odalisques, Almées (dancing girls)

The ballet is set in the harem of the Oriental palace of the Persian ruler, Shah Shahriar. Suspecting his wives of infidelity, the Shah and his brother, Shah Zeman, leave the palace on the pretence of a hunting expedition. As soon as the men leave, the women, lead by Shahriar's favourite wife Zoebéide, persuade the Chief Eunuch to release their slave lovers. Shahriar and his brother return unexpectedly and burst in on the ensuing orgy. Enraged at his discovery, Shahriar orders his guards to kill the women and their lovers. Zoebéide pleads for mercy, but finding her husband unrelenting, she stabs herself in the heart and falls dead at his feet.

■

Schéhérazade created a sensation in the Ballets Russes' 1910 season, its design by Bakst building on the powerful visual effects of his earlier *Cléopâtre*. This dance drama was the first production completely devised by Diaghilev and his *miriskusniki* collaborators, bringing together vivid visual spectacle, powerful choreography and a re-orchestrated version of the 1888 symphonic suite that Rimsky-Korsakov had based on tales from *The arabian nights*. Bakst's costumes are an imagined orientalist amalgam of Ottoman and Persian styles, pale and diaphanous silk harem pants for the *almées* contrasting with strongly coloured, embroidered and intricately structured silk and velvet costumes for the lead male characters. Bakst's drawing for Shah Zeman is an earlier, more ornate, version of the Shah's actual costume, accentuating the strong rhythms of the dancer's body by depicting the fabrics and the skirt ornaments as moving and floating. With gold body paint and bejewelled outfit, Nijinsky commanded the stage with his voluptuous and feline performance as Zoebéide's favourite slave. Against the set's emerald green walls and red carpets, the massed costumes of dancers in frenzied motion created a moving spectacle of colour intensifying towards the ballet's orgiastic and violent climax.

(above) **Auguste Bert**
Chief Eunuch from Schéhérazade page 51
in *Official program of the Ballets Russes at the Théâtre du Châtelet, June 1911*

(opposite) **Léon Bakst**
Costume for the Chief Eunuch 1910

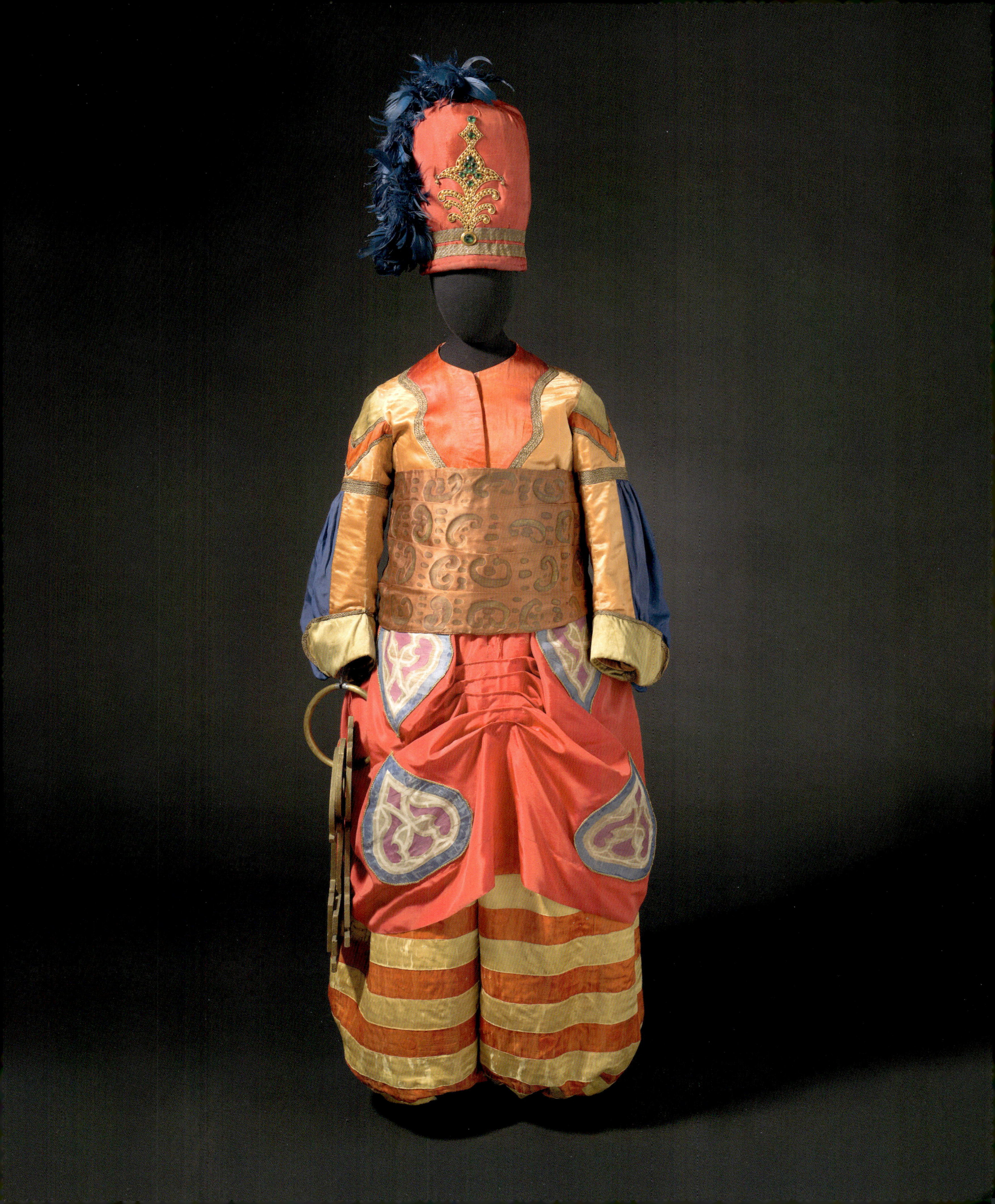

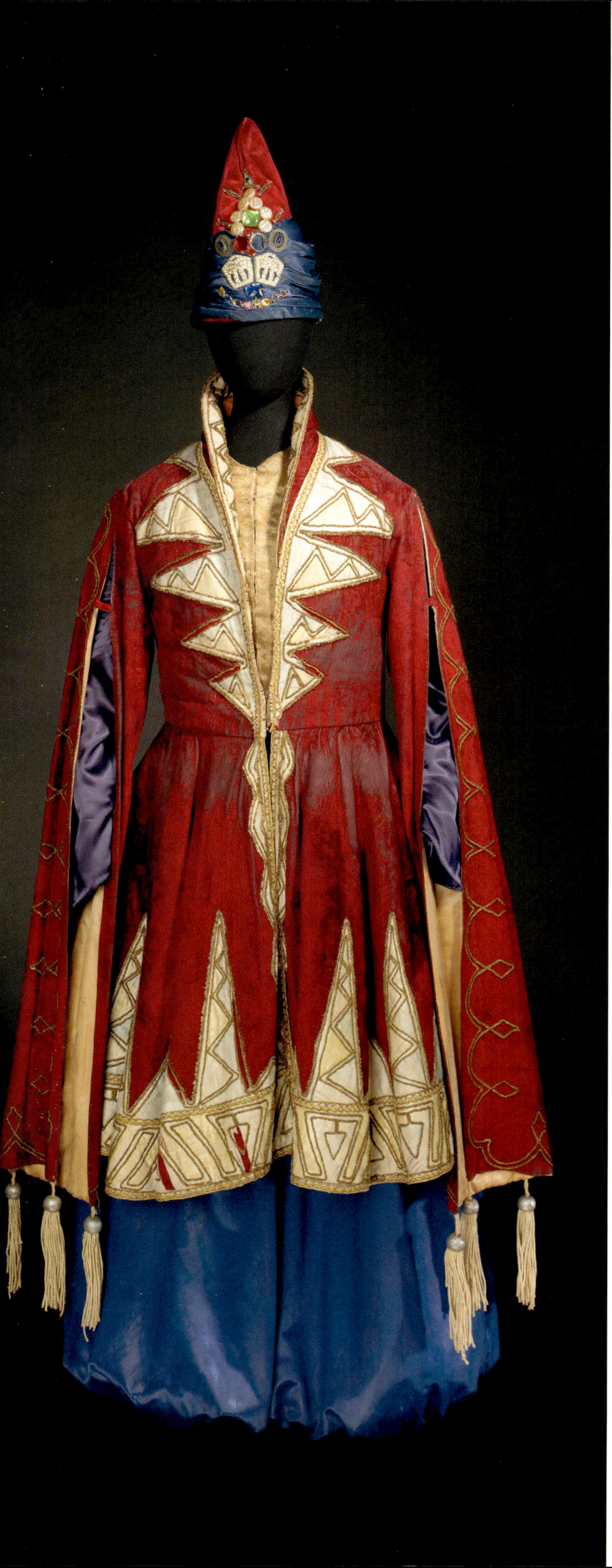
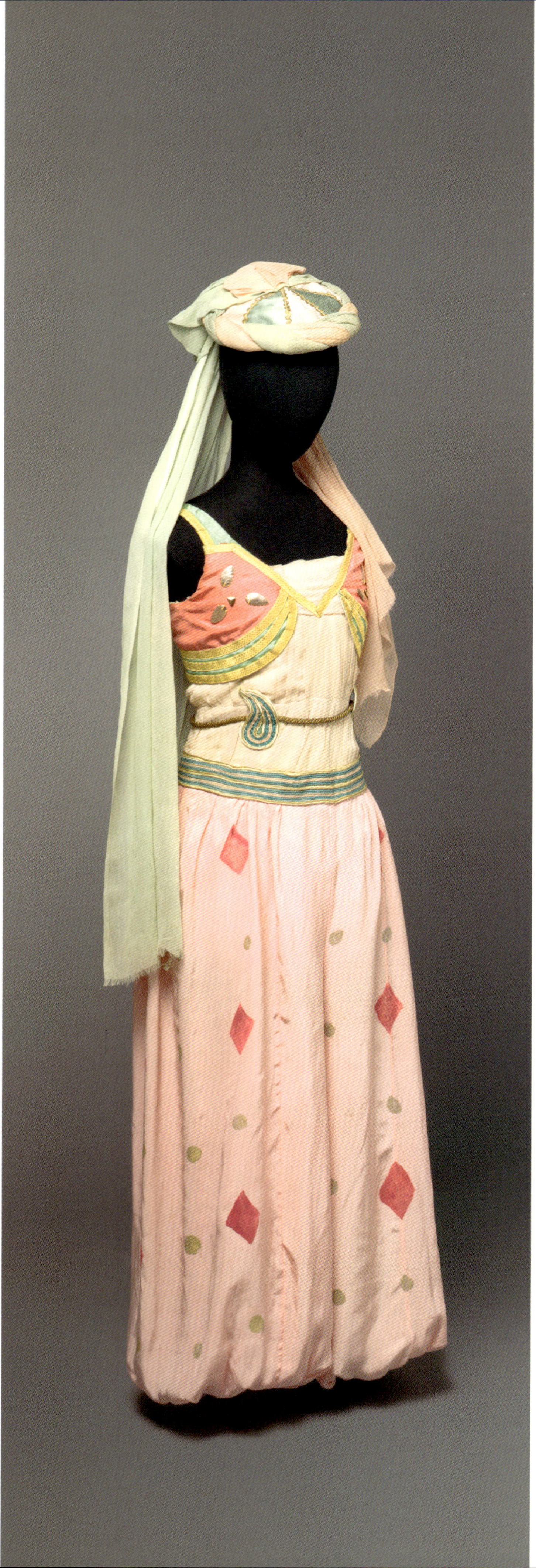

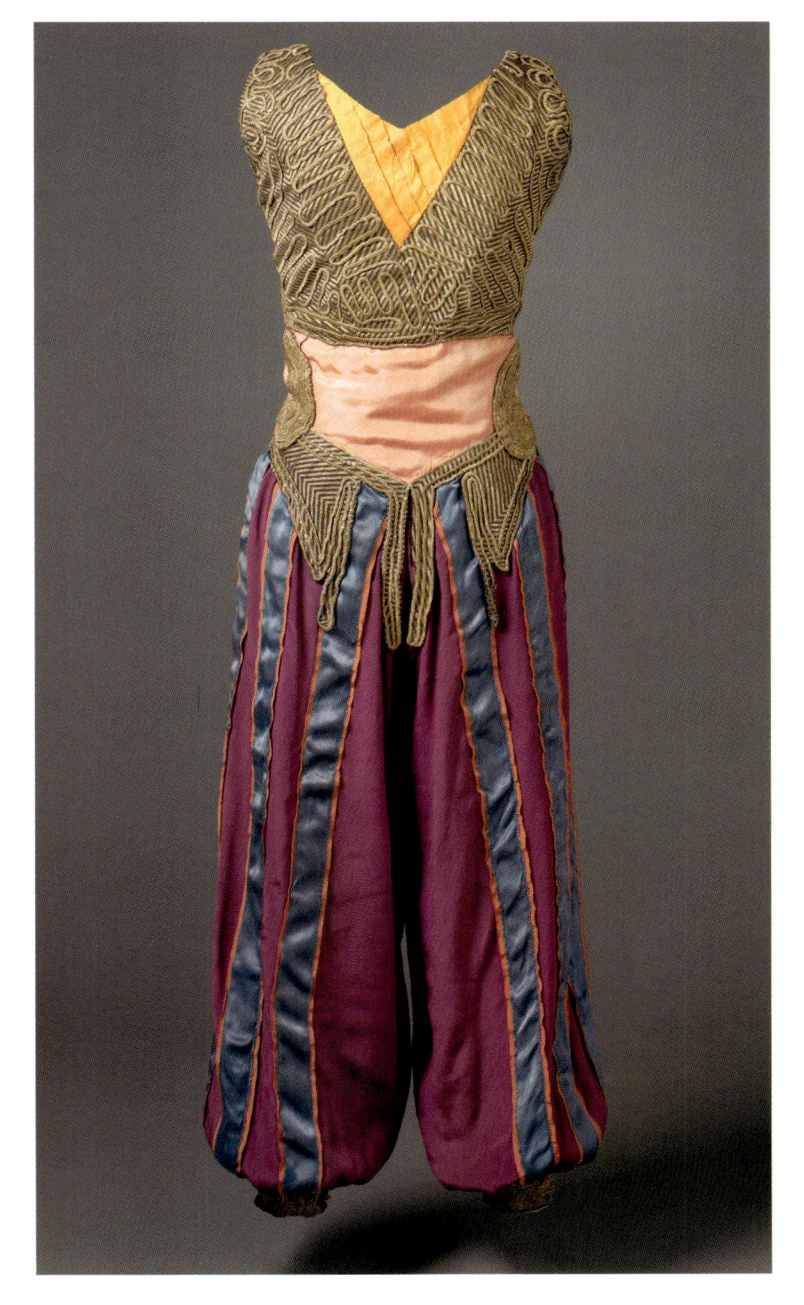

Léon Bakst
(opposite left) *Costume for Shah Shahriar* 1910–30s

(opposite right) *Costume for a dancing girl or odalisque* c 1910

(top left) *Costume designs for Schéhérazade* pages 11 and 12 in *Ballets Russes supplement edition of Comoedia Illustré*, 15 June 1910

(top right) **Unknown photographer**
Scene from Schéhérazade
page 28 in *Souvenir program for Serge de Diaghileff's Ballet Russe* 1916–17

(above) **George Barbier**
Nijinsky as the Golden Slave and Rubinstein as Zoebéide in Schéhérazade
in *Designs on the dances of Vasiav Nijinsky* 1913
National Gallery of Australia Research Library, Canberra

(left) **Léon Bakst**
Costume for a dancing girl or odalisque c 1915–30s

Costumes for Les Ballets Russes de Serge Diaghilev 1909–29

Léon Bakst
(above) *Costume design for an odalisque* 1910

(right) *Costume design for Shah Zeman* 1910

(opposite) *Costume for Shah Zeman* 1910–30s

(opposite inset) **Auguste Bert**
Shah Zeman from Schéhérazade
page 53 in *Official program of the Ballets Russes at the Théâtre du Châtelet*, June 1911

100   Ballets Russes: the art of costume

Costumes for Les Ballets Russes de Serge Diaghilev 1909–29 101

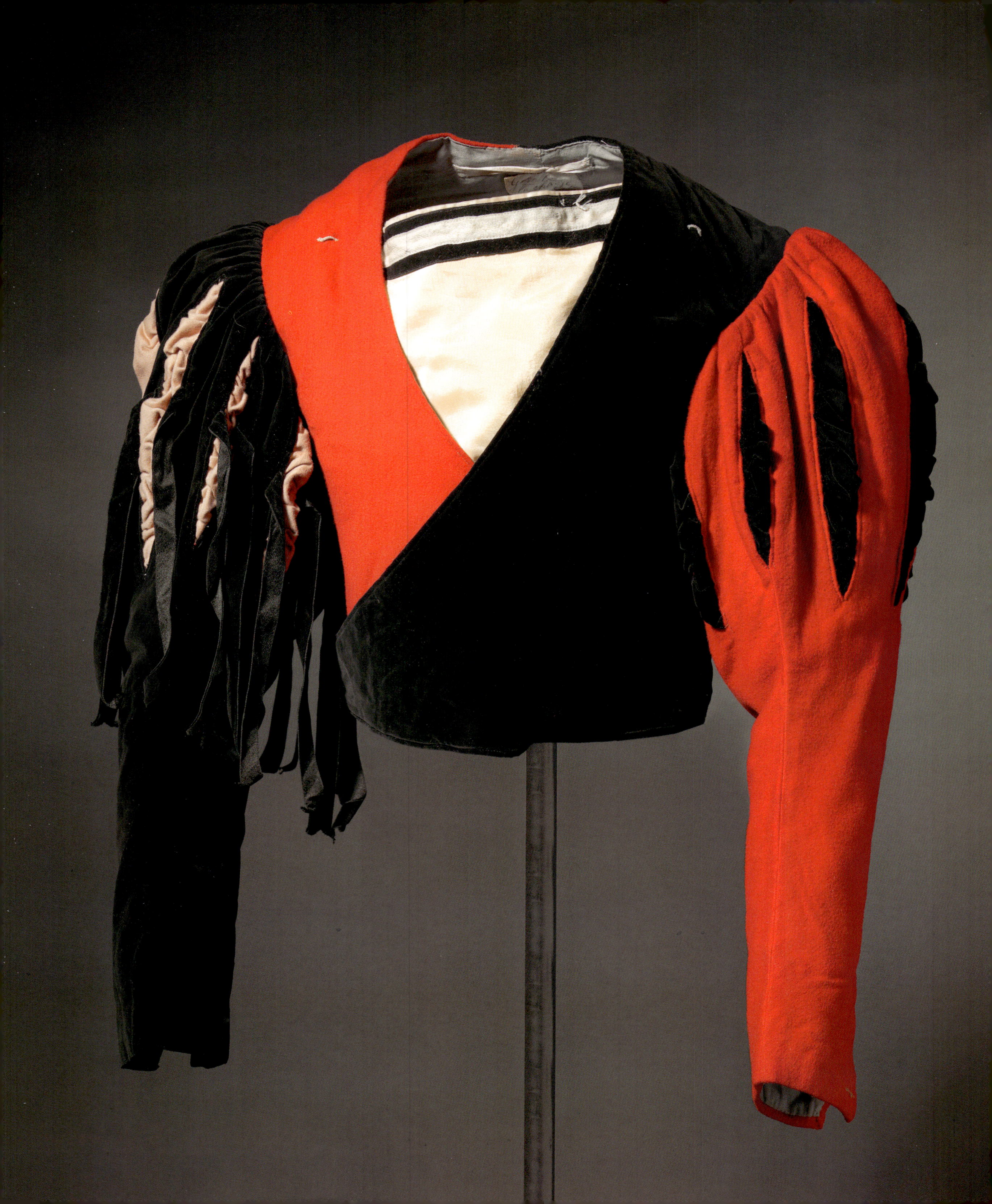

Giselle

Fantastic ballet in two acts

Producer:	Les Ballets Russes de Serge Diaghilev
Premiere:	17 June 1910, Théâtre national de l'Opéra, Paris
Costume design:	Alexandre Benois
Scenery design:	Alexandre Benois
Music:	Adolphe Adam
Choreography:	Michel Fokine, after Jean Coralli and Jules Perrot
Libretto:	Vernoy de Saint-Georges, Théophile Gautier, Jean Coralli
Main characters:	Giselle, Duke Albrecht of Silesia (Loys), Hilarion, Duke of Courland, Princess Bathilde, Bathilde's page, Giselle's mother, Prince of Houston, Peasant girl, Valet, Buffoon, Myrtha, Queen of the Wilis

The ballet is set in a small village in the Rhineland, Germany in the early nineteenth century, where Albrecht, the Duke of Silesia, masquerades as a peasant under the pseudonym of Loys. Although he is already engaged to Bathilde, daughter of the Prince of Courland, he flirts with the mentally unstable Giselle. Hilarion, a local huntsman in love with Giselle, unsuccessfully attempts to dissuade her from forming an attachment with Loys. Following the arrival of Bathilde and her father's hunting party, Giselle discovers Albrecht's deception and, distraught, stabs herself in the heart. In the second act, Giselle haunts the forest with the Wilis, the vengeful ghosts of women who have died before their wedding day. First Hilarion, and then Albrecht, who has realised that he too loved Giselle, enter the forest to pay their respects at her grave. Hilarion is killed by the Wilis, who force him to dance himself to death, but with Giselle's intervention, Albrecht manages to escape. The ballet ends with Giselle returning to the peace of her grave, onto which Albrecht throws himself in despair.

■

Giselle, the best known of the Romantic ballets, was first produced by the Paris Opéra on 28 June 1841. Marius Petipa's 1884 revival for the Imperial Ballet, and Anna Pavlova's 1903 debut in the title role, defined its modern style. Its 1910 production by the Ballets Russes, with Tamara Karsavina's and Nijinsky's commanding presences as Giselle and Albrecht, brought it to the Western stage for the first time. Its light and ethereal costumes for the female dancers, following the long tutu style made fashionable by Marie Taglioni in *La Sylphide* of the 1830s, are set within an overall costume ensemble reflecting the story's historical setting in the Rhineland of the sixteenth century. Albrecht's mourning costume of black, slashed and puffed velvet doublet and trunk hose, over a white square-necked shirt, was designed as a dramatic contrast to Giselle's pale spectre in their final scenes of reconciliation.

Alexandre Benois
(opposite) *Jacket from costume for The hunt in Act 1* c 1910
(top) *Mourning costume for Albrecht* c 1910
(above) *Trunks from costume for Albrecht* c 1910
© Alexandre Benois/ADAGP. Licensed by Viscopy, 2010

Costumes for Les Ballets Russes de Serge Diaghilev 1909–29

L'Oiseau de feu
The firebird

Fantastic ballet in one act

Producer:	Les Ballets Russes de Serge Diaghilev
Premiere:	25 June 1910, Théâtre national de l'Opéra, Paris
Revival:	25 November 1926, Lyceum Theatre, London
Costume design:	1910 Aleksandr Golovin and Léon Bakst; 1926 Natalia Goncharova
Costumier:	Vera Sudeikina (for 1926 revisions)
Scenery design:	1910 Aleksandr Golovin and Léon Bakst; 1926 Natalia Goncharova
Music:	Igor Stravinsky
Choreography:	Michel Fokine
Libretto:	Michel Fokine, from a Russian folk tale
Main characters:	The Firebird, (Prince) Ivan Tsarevitch, Köstchei the Immortal, Tsarevna, the Enchanted Princesses, the Kikimoras

During a night-time hunt near the ancient castle of the evil wizard, Köstchei the Immortal, Prince Ivan captures the enchanted Firebird, half woman and half bird. In exchange for her freedom the Firebird gives Ivan one of her magical feathers and promises to protect him if ever he needs help. Twelve young princesses, enslaved by the sorcerer, approach the castle gates revelling in their one hour of freedom each dawn. During this hour Ivan and Tsarevna, one of the princesses, fall in love. On her return to the castle, the prince attempts to follow her inside. Köstchei and his entourage of monster guards attack him. Prince Ivan brandishes the Firebird's feather which calls her forth, and together they destroy the wizard and his brigade, freeing the princess. The ballet ends with the extravagant wedding party of Ivan and Tsarevna where the prince is crowned king of the realm.

■

Steeped in the Russian folk art and craft revival during his membership of the Abramtsevo and Talashkino groups, the designer Alekandr Golovin became an active participant in the exhibitions and projects of the *miriskusniki* before being commissioned by Diaghilev to design his 1908 opera, *Boris Godunov*. His following commission, *L'Oiseau de feu*, an amalgam of several Russian folk tales developed by Benois and Fokine, was set in the overgrown and sinister garden of Köstchei's palace, stimulating Golovin to design a rich and decorative Symbolist décor. His costumes were influenced by the traditional Slavic festival costumes worn by both men and women, with white belted tunics stencilled in pale colours with patterns simulating the richness of traditional brocades and braids. Hooped overdress hems were layered over tunic underskirts, giving a floating otherworldliness to the costumes. Despite Golovin's completely integrated design schema for this production, Diaghilev was dissatisfied with the costumes for the Firebird, Tsarevna and Ivan Tsarevich, and commissioned Léon Bakst to redesign them. Diaghilev revived the ballet in 1926, commissioning Natalia Goncharova to design new sets and costumes, some of which were modified from the 1910 originals by the addition of different trims and appliqué materials. Golovin's original backdrop was used by the Monte Carlo

(top) **Aleksandr Golovin, Léon Bakst and Natalia Goncharova**
Dress from costume for a member of Köstchei's entourage c 1910 and c 1926

(above) *Costume for a princess* c 1910 and c 1934
© Natalia Goncharova/ADAGP. Licensed by Viscopy, 2010

(opposite) **Aleksandr Golovin and Léon Bakst** *Costume for an attendant of Köstchei* 1910

104 Ballets Russes: the art of costume

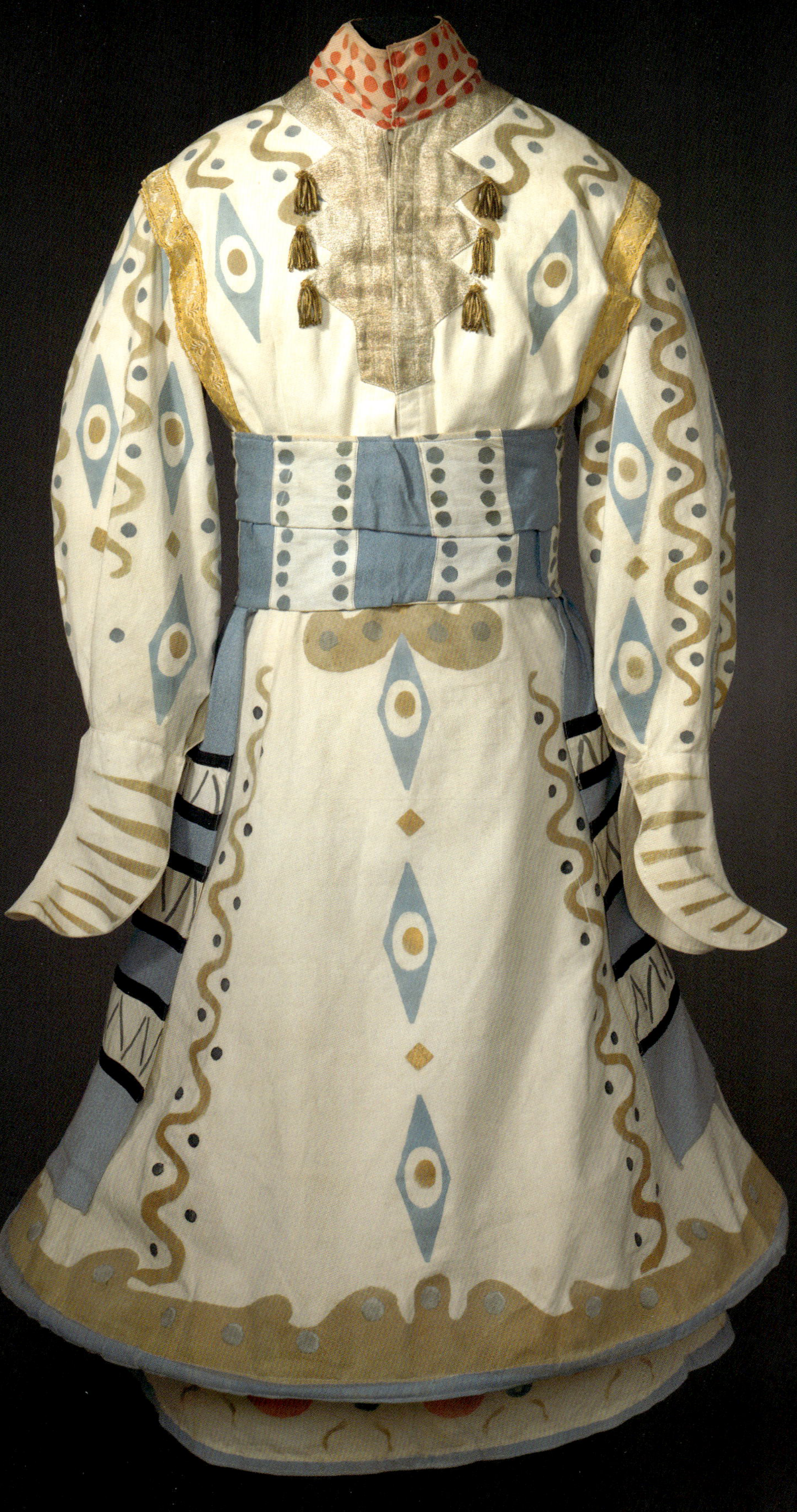

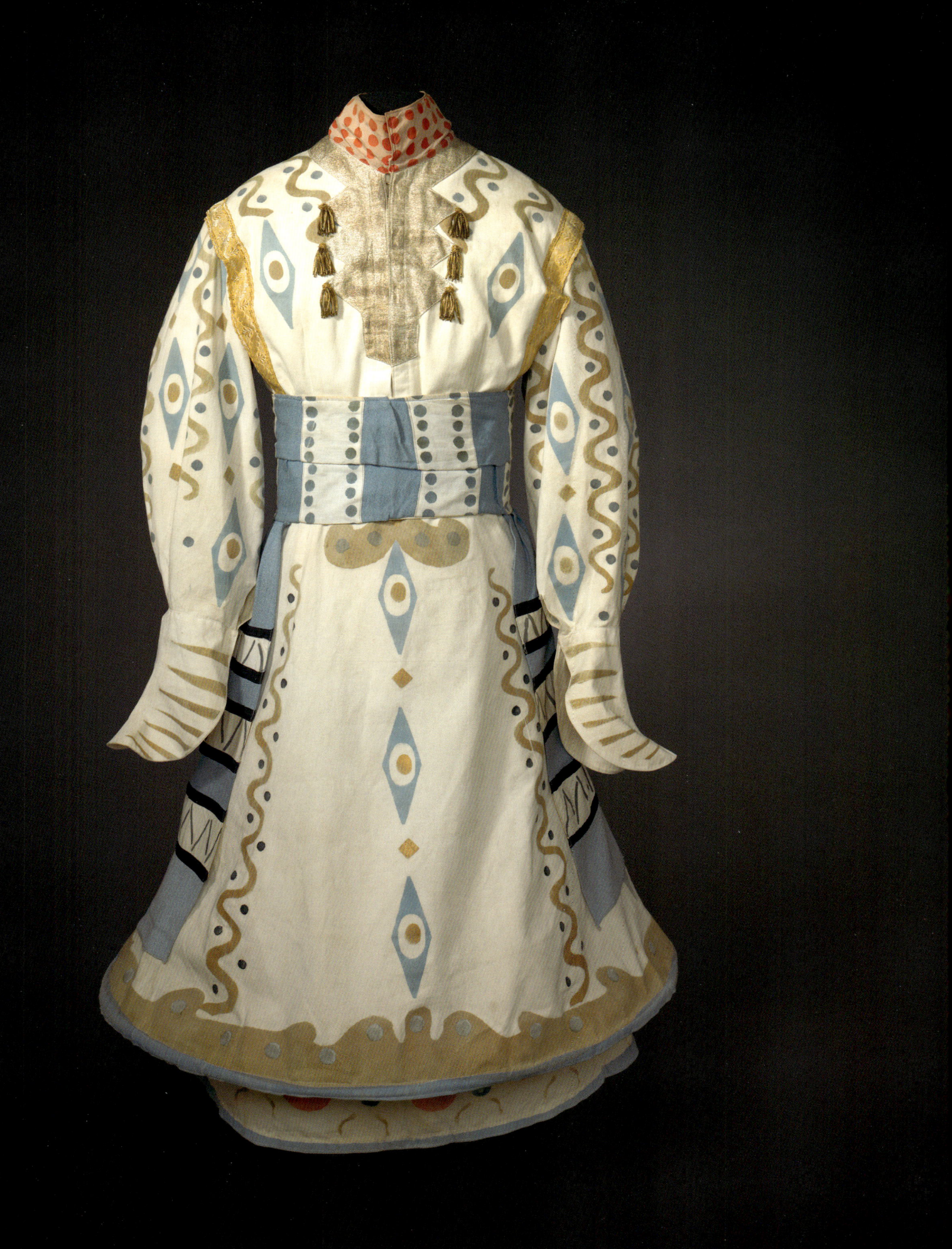

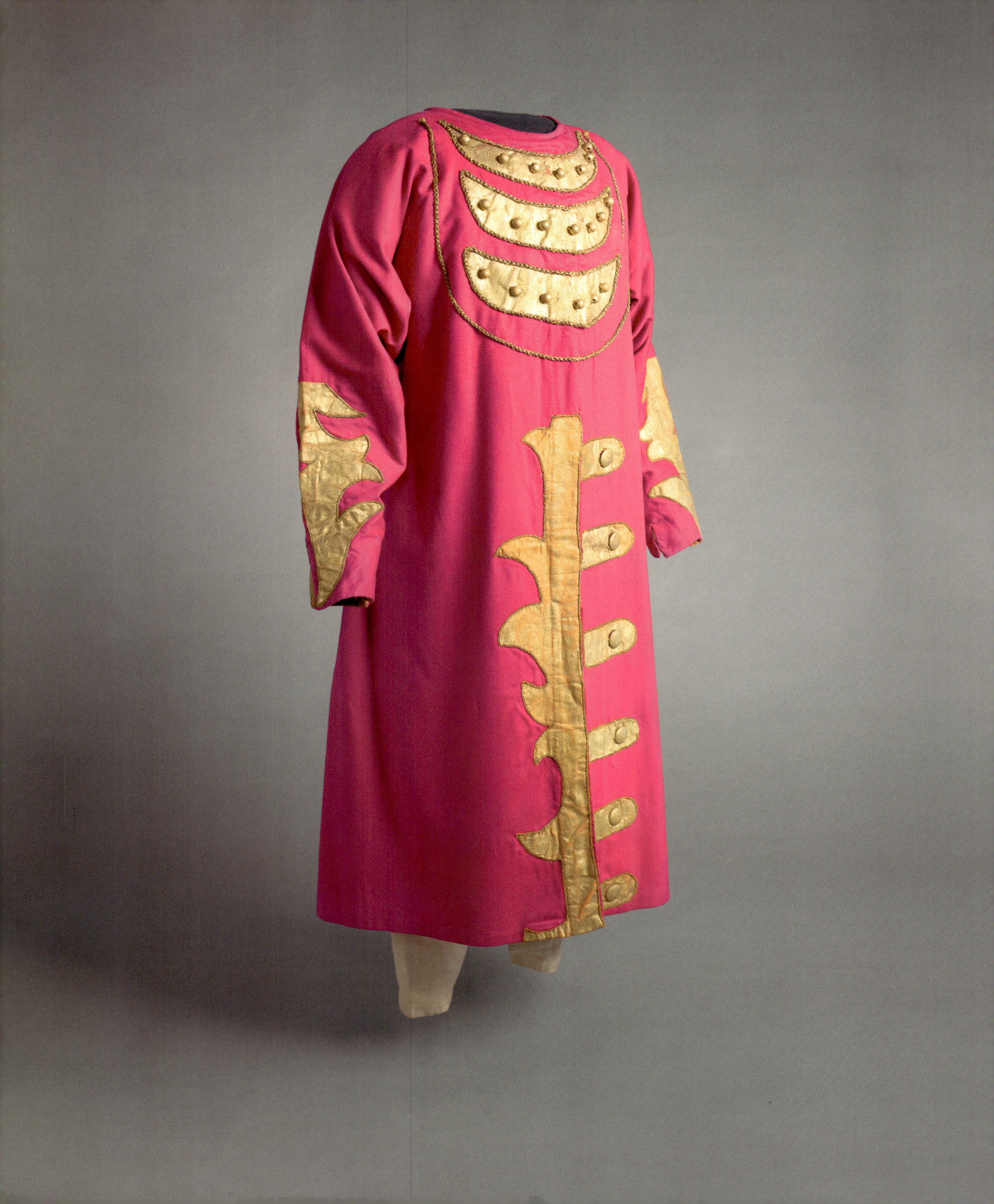

Russian Ballet for its revival production of *The firebird* at His Majesty's Theatre in Melbourne in November 1936.

L'Oiseau de feu entered the canon of twentieth-century music as *The firebird*, Igor Stravinsky's breakthrough ballet score, and the later suites he developed from it. This was the first original score commissioned by Diaghilev for the Ballets Russes and signalled the start of the impresario's lifelong close professional relationship with Stravinsky, and of the composer's career. His extraordinary music for this production was seen as a crucial but equal element of its unique visual, aural and balletic structure, prompting the French critic, Henri Ghéon, to write:

> The old-gold vermiculatino of the fantastic back-cloth seems to have been invented to a formula identical with that of the shimmering web of the orchestra. And as one listens, there issues forth the very sound of the wizard shrieking, of swarming sorcerers and gnomes running amok. When the bird passes, it is truly the music that bears it aloft. Stravinsky, Fokine and Golovin, in my eyes, are but one name.[2]

(opposite) **Natalia Goncharova**
Costume for finale c 1926
© Natalia Goncharova/ADAGP. Licensed by Viscopy, 2010

(above) **Aleksandr Golovin and Léon Bakst**
Costume for a female dancer c 1910

(left) **E O Hoppé**
L'Oiseau de feu—*Madame Thamar Karsavina and M Adolph Bolm*
1913 plate 3 from *Studies from the Russian Ballet*

Costumes for Les Ballets Russes de Serge Diaghilev 1909–29 107

Narcisse
Narcissus

Mythological poem in one act

Producer:	Les Ballets Russes de Serge Diaghilev
Premiere:	26 April 1911, Théâtre de Monte Carlo, Monaco
Costume design:	Léon Bakst
Scenery design:	Léon Bakst
Music:	Nicholas Tcherepnin
Choreography:	Michel Fokine
Libretto:	Léon Bakst
Main characters:	Echo, Narcisse, Bacchantes, Young Boeotian women, Nymphs

Filled with ancient Greek influences, the ballet is set in Boeotia (formally Cadmeis), in the north-eastern part of the Gulf of Corinth, at the shrine of Pomona, the goddess of fruit trees, gardens and orchards. The shrine is in a sylvan glade where a spring feeds into a glassy pool. The ballet tells the myth of Narcissus, a beautiful and self-indulgent youth, who spurns and ridicules the advances of the beautiful mountain-nymph Echo. In anger, Echo applies to Pomona to make Narcissus fall in love in a way that can never be reciprocated. Under Pomona's spell, Narcissus promptly falls in love with his own reflection in the pool. He stands gazing at himself for so long that he sinks into the ground and a narcissus flower grows in his place.

■

Narcisse was the first of a trilogy of Greek-themed ballets designed by Léon Bakst for the Ballets Russes' 1911 and 1912 seasons. His research into the art of ancient Greece had begun in St Petersburg when preparing designs for productions there of the Greek tragedies *Hippolytus*, *Antigone* and *Oedipus and Colonnus* in 1902 and 1904. In 1905 Bakst had met Isadora Duncan, whose Greek dance style inspired his work with Michel Fokine on the Imperial Ballet's production of *Acis and Galatea* later that year. In 1907, with *miriskusniki* colleague, painter Valentin Serov, Bakst travelled in Greece and Crete, visiting the ancient sites of Corfu, Olympia, Delphi and Knossos. His sketches from that trip reveal his fascination with the designs, patterns and colours of the dress he observed in ancient ceramics and sculpture. The soft wool muslin costumes for *Narcisse*—loose, pleated, short and open-necked—revealed the dancers' arms and shoulders and allowed more expressive and fluid movement. The costumes' colours and soft-edged patterns suggest the chalkiness and freshness of ancient fresco painting in a way quite different from the white formalism of the ancient world imagined by the neo-classicists.

(top) **Léon Bakst**
Costume design for Ephebe
page 33 in *Official program of the Ballets Russes at the Théâtre du Châtelet*, June 1911

(above) *Costume design for two bacchantes from Narcisse*
page 9 in *Souvenir program for Serge de Diaghileff's Ballet Russe* 1916–17

(opposite left) *Costume for a Boeotian youth* c 1911

(opposite right) *Dress from costume for a Boeotian girl* c 1911

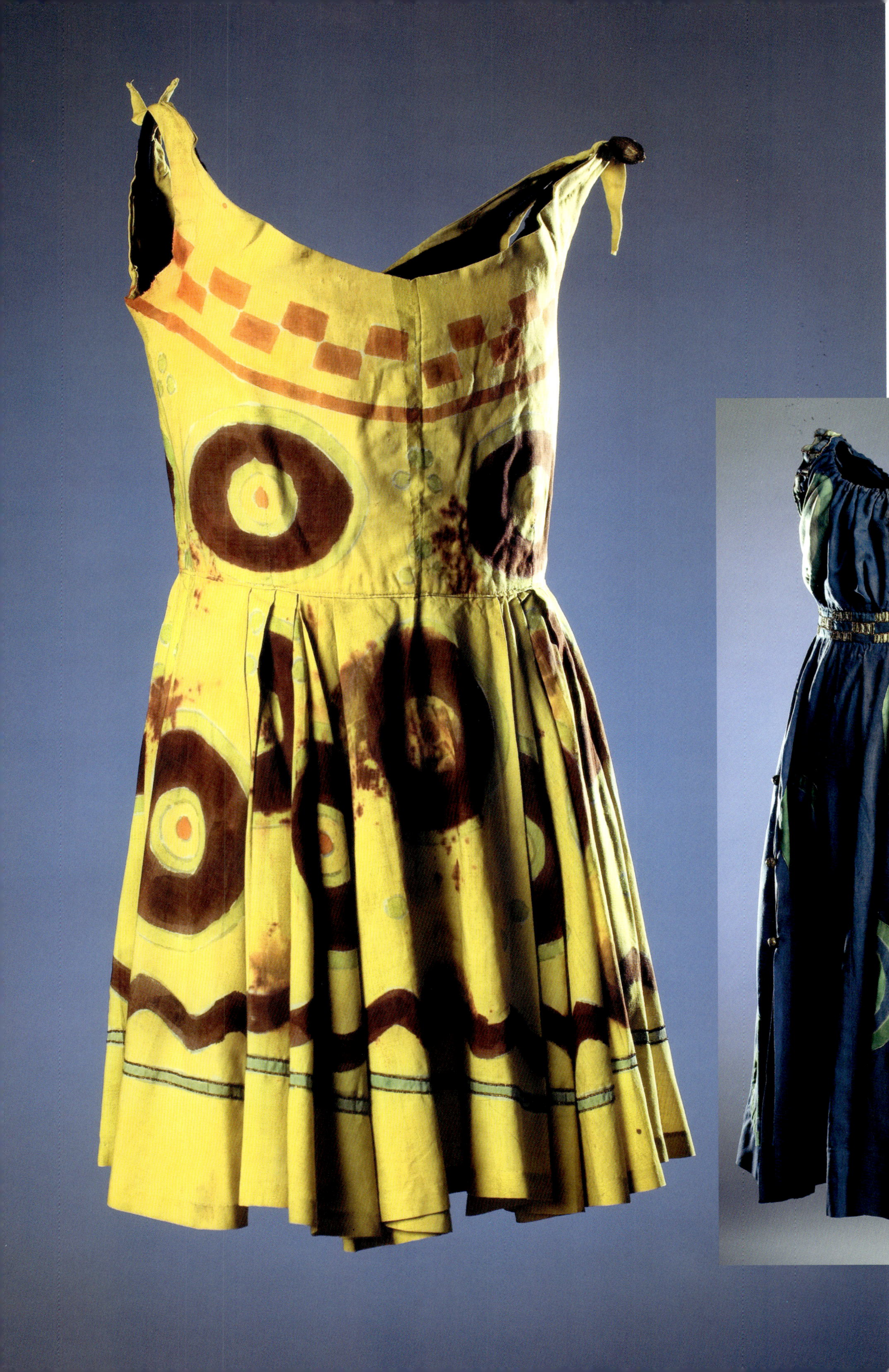
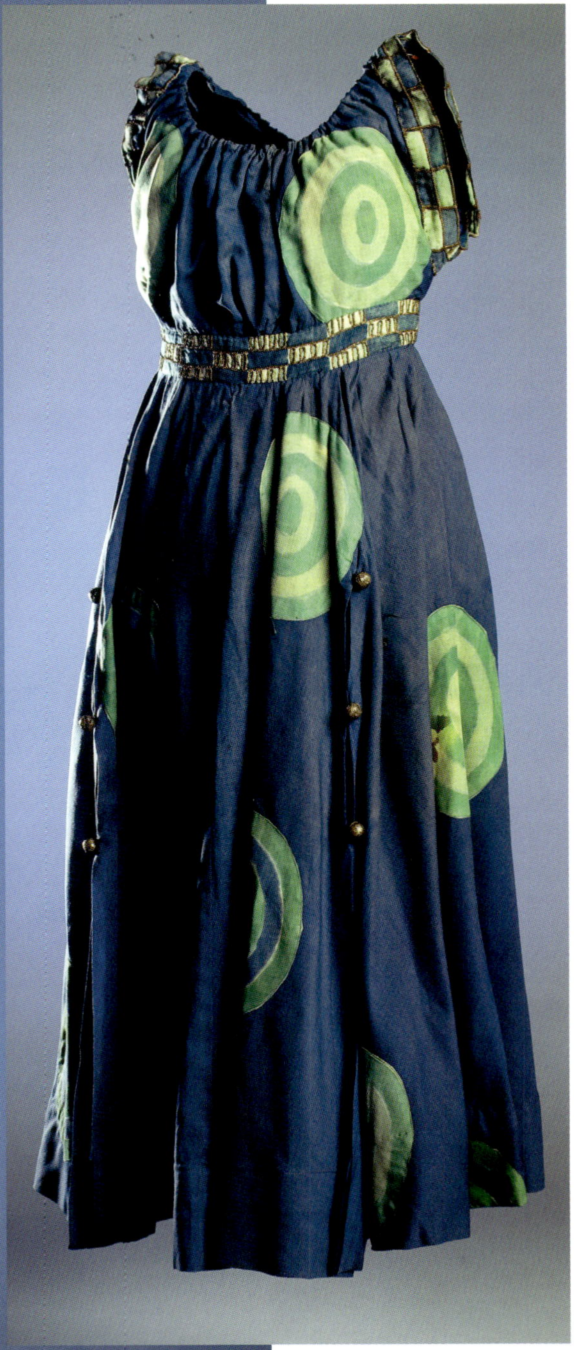

110 Ballets Russes: the art of costume

Petrouchka
Petrushka

Burlesque in four scenes

Producer:	Les Ballets Russes de Serge Diaghilev
Premiere:	13 June 1911, Théâtre du Châtelet, Paris
Costume design:	Alexandre Benois
Costumier:	Ivan Caffi and Vorobier
Scenery design:	Alexandre Benois
Music:	Igor Stravinsky
Choreography:	Michel Fokine
Libretto:	Igor Stravinsky
Main characters:	Petrouchka, the Ballerina, the Moor, the Charlatan, Street dancers, the Chief nursemaid, Nursemaids, Chief coachman, coachmen, masqueraders, peasants

The ballet is set in 1830, just before Lent during the annual Butter Week Festival, in Admiralty Square, St Petersburg. An old and dastardly showman, the Charlatan, demonstrates his lifelike puppets—sad and ugly Petrouchka, a rag doll; the beautiful but vapid Ballerina and the Moor, a brutish exhibitionist—to an eager crowd of boulevardiers, colourful peasantry and other performers. Between their performances the puppets are imprisoned in rooms in the Charlatan's booth. Both Petrouchka and the Moor are in love with the Ballerina. Petrouchka's advances towards her provoke the Moor to attack and kill him with a scimitar. This tragic scenario unfolds in front of the shocked and horrified spectators. The Charlatan hastens to disprove the events by demonstrating that Petrouchka is only a doll filled with sawdust. However, after the crowd leaves the square the ghost of the marionette appears above the booth, menacing the horrified Charlatan.

■

Petrouchka reflects a brilliant fusion of the creativity of Stravinsky, Benois and Nijinsky. Developed from Stravinsky's 1910 piano work, *Petrouchka's cry*, the ballet reflected the interest of the *miriskusniki* in street theatre, mime, puppet shows (*balagani*), and the traditions of *commedia dell'arte*. The use of puppets, particularly in the implicit racism of the depiction of the black Moor and the vapidity of the Ballerina, allowed Stravinsky and Fokine to exploit racial stereotypes within the changing cultural and ethnic landscape of nineteenth-century Russia. In the role of the lifeless Petrouchka, animated and annihilated by love, Nijinsky gave his most memorable and accomplished performance, not least because his grotesque characterisation of the controlled and brutalised puppet was deliberately at odds with his usual feline grace on stage. Benois placed his characters in the evocative setting of *Maslenitsa*, the St Petersburg pre-Lenten Butter Week festivities that he remembered so fondly from his youth. He also moved on from his predilection for eighteenth-century styles to an adventurous exploration of the colour territory that had been mapped by Bakst, particularly in his sets for the Moor's and Petrouchka's rooms with their over-scaled and garish decoration designed to diminish the puppets. Petrouchka's costume is in the stylistic convention of Pierrot, with a white top, a ruff and vandyke braid edging over garish pink and yellow chequered trousers, blue boots, a black and white hat and black mittens.

Alexandre Benois
(opposite, left to right) *Costume design for a merchant* c 1920; *Costume design for a peasant woman* c 1920; *Costume design for a devil* c 1920

(opposite below) *Set design for the Moor's room* c 1920s
© AlexandreBenois/ADAGP Licensed by Viscopy, 2010

(above) **Georges Lepape**
Nijinsky in Petrouchka page 46 in *Official program of the Ballets Russes at the Théâtre du Châtelet May–June 1912*

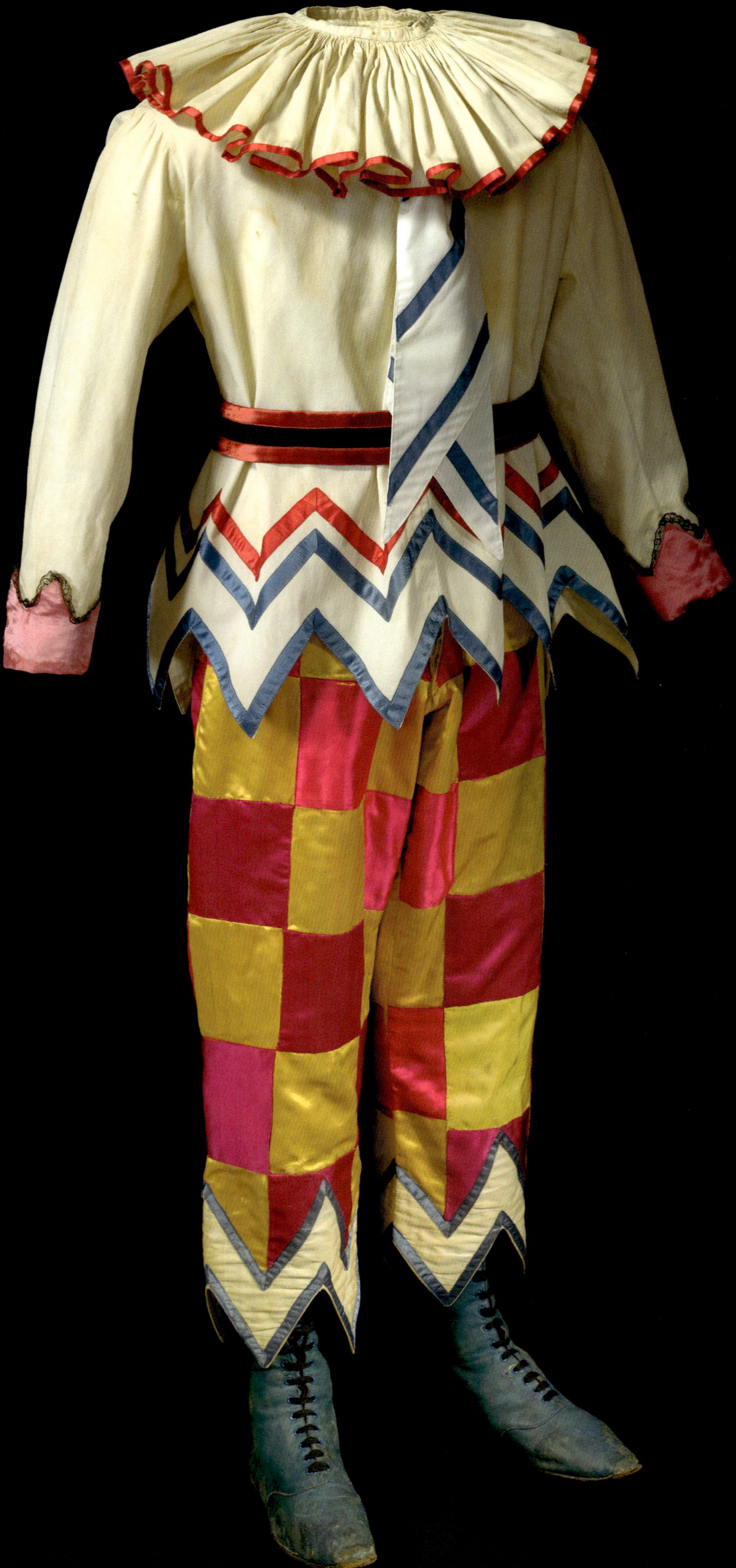

(opposite) **Alexandre Benois**
Costume for Petrouchka c 1911
© Alexandre Benois/ADAGP. Licensed by Viscopy, 2010

(above) **Elliott & Fry**
Nijinsky in the role of Petrouchka c 1913
gelatin silver photograph
14.8 x 11.2 cm
National Gallery of Australia, Canberra

Costumes for Les Ballets Russes de Serge Diaghilev 1909–29 113

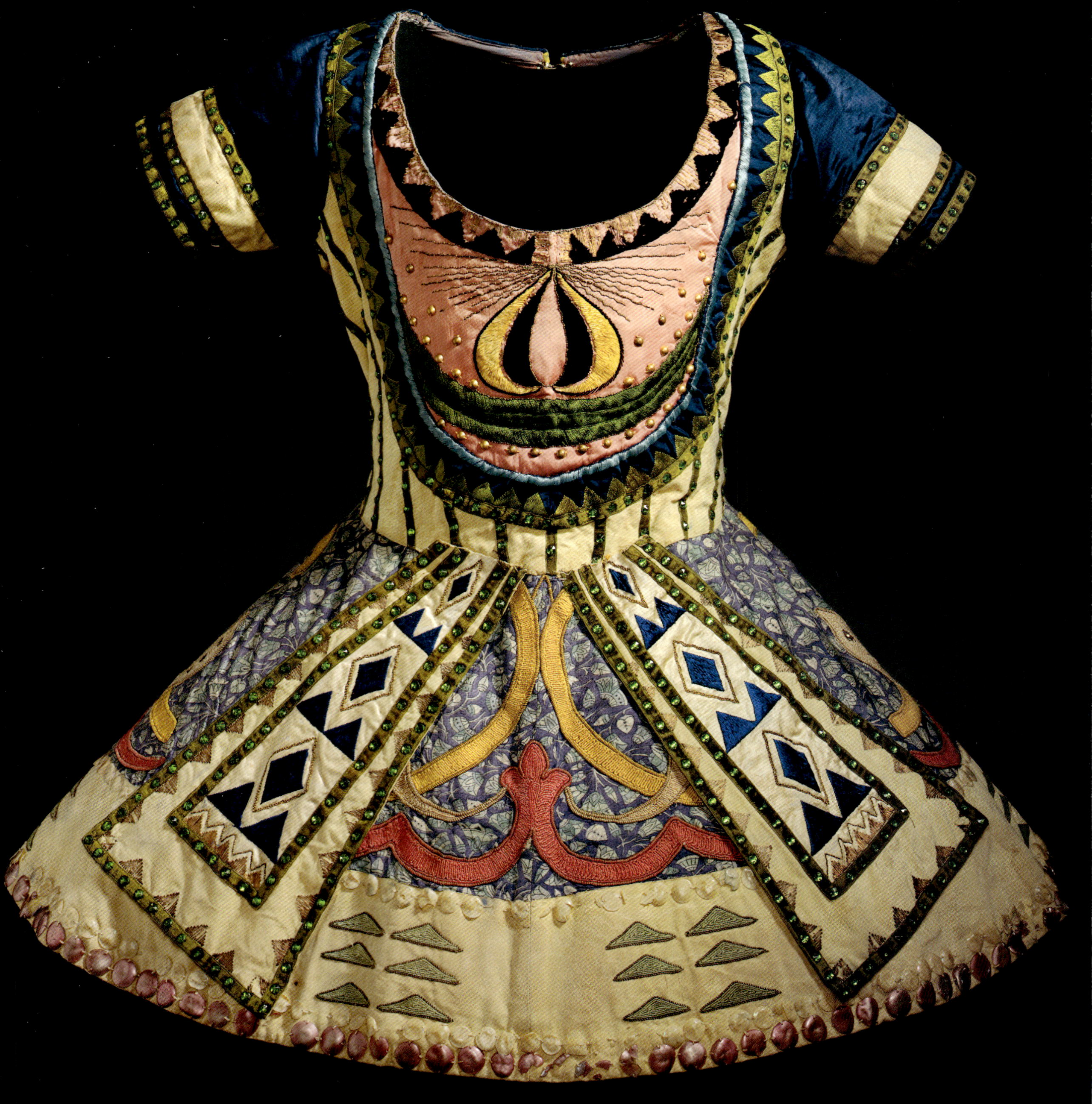

Le Dieu bleu
The blue god

Hindu legend in one act

Producer: Les Ballets Russes de Serge Diaghilev
Premiere: 13 May 1912, Théâtre du Châtelet, Paris
Costume design: Léon Bakst
Costumier: M Landoff and Marie Muelle
Scenery design: Léon Bakst
Music: Reynaldo Hahn
Choreography: Michel Fokine
Libretto: Jean Cocteau and Federico de Madrazo
Main characters: The Blue God, the Bayadere, the Young girl, the Goddess, the Youth, the High Priest, the Peacock bearers

Set in mythical India, the ballet opens at a shrine of the Blue God, which is surrounded by rocks and cliffs with a lotus pond in the centre. Worshippers and a young neophyte, soon to become a priest, gather and wait for the ordination ceremony to commence. After the high priest arrives the ceremony begins but is interrupted by the novice's lover, attempting to rescue him from priesthood. She is captured and imprisoned in the shrine, where she threatened by its resident monsters. While trying to escape she inadvertently lets loose a plethora of monsters. She appeals to the shrine's deity for help and the Blue God and Goddess both rise from the lotus pond. The Blue God subdues the monsters, the lovers are reunited and the gods return to their celestial abodes.

■

The orientalist exoticism of *Cléopâtre* and *Schéhérazade* continued in *Le Dieu bleu*. Bakst's set, with its massive carved faces, showed the influence of those of the Bayon Temple of Angkor Thom in Cambodia, which had been popularised in France through engravings in Louis Delaporte's *Voyage au Cambodge: l'architecture Khmer* (*Voyage to Cambodia: Khmer architecture*), published in Paris in 1880. The French fascination with the cultures of its colonies had given audiences the opportunity to see several troupes of Cambodian court dancers in performance at the 1906 Colonial Exposition in Marseille.[3] Earlier, in 1900 a troupe of Siamese dancers had performed in St Petersburg, forming an impression on Fokine that would take form in his choreographic work on *Le Dieu bleu*. These influences are encapsulated in Bakst's design of the original skirted costume for the Blue God (Krishna) worn by Nijinsky. Made of watered silk and satin, it is embroidered with a closed lotus flower and rays of gold thread and metallic studs. The stiff conical skirt's background fabric is a contemporary printed pattern, overlaid with embroidered arabesques, while its hem is decorated with pearlised pink and white gelatin discs. The intricately decorated bodice was most likely designed to suggest the body jewellery seen in Hindu sculpture, while the stiff formality of the costume was echoed in Nijinsky's performance of sculptural poses rather than active dancing. As Krishna, Nijinsky had worn bright blue make-up in continuance of the tradition of the god's skin being turned blue as a result of being bitten by a poisonous serpent. Traces of this blue make-up are impregnated in the lining of the costume, giving it a particularly intimate connection to Nijinsky.

(opposite) **Léon Bakst**
Tunic from the costume for The Blue God c 1912

(top) **Unknown photographer**
Nijinsky as the Blue God in Le Dieu bleu 1912
Bibliothèque nationale de France, Paris, Fonds Kochno, BN 79 B83515

(above) **Léon Bakst**
Illustration of the Blue God costume page 29 in Official program of the Ballets Russes at the Théâtre du Châtelet, May–June 1912

Costumes for Les Ballets Russes de Serge Diaghilev 1909–29

Thamar

Choreographic drama in one act

Producer:	Les Ballets Russes de Serge Diaghilev
Premiere:	20 May 1912, Théâtre du Châtelet, Paris
Costume design:	Léon Bakst
Costumier:	Marie Muelle
Scenery design:	Léon Bakst
Music:	Mily Alexeyevich Balakirev, 1882
Choreography:	Michel Fokine
Libretto:	Léon Bakst, after a poem by Mikhail Lermontov
Main characters:	Thamar, Queen of Georgia, the Prince, ladies-in-waiting, guards, servants

Set in the castle of Queen Thamar of Georgia, the ballet opens with a scene of daily activity in the court. One of the Queen's ladies-in-waiting notices the approach of a stranger, a prince, through the window. Gesturing with a wave of her blood-red scarf, Thamar indicates that he should be admitted. Following his presentation, Thamar entices him with a series of dances before they retire for lovemaking. When they re-enter, Thamar stabs the unsuspecting prince in the heart and pushes him out through a trapdoor into the flooded river below. Retiring to her couch once more, she invites the arrival of yet another victim with a wave of her scarf.

■

The subject of the life of Thamar, Queen of Georgia from 1184 to 1213, was transformed in the spirit of nineteenth-century Romanticism, becoming a symbol of nationalist pride in the face of growing Russian cultural dominance in the Caucasus. Russian poet Mikhail Lermontov fictionalised Thamar's history within his interpretation of a Georgian legend of a malevolent seductress in his 1841 poem, *Tamara*. It was this version, along with Balakirev's symphonic poem *Tamara*, that inspired Bakst and Fokine for the Ballets Russes production of *Thamar* in 1912. Bakst's looming set dramatised Thamar's isolated court in her castle in the treacherous Terek River and provided a stark background for his sumptuous and richly detailed costumes for the queen, her courtiers, guards and suitors.

The men's costumes are based on the traditional Caucasian *cherkeska* (Circassian coat) or *kaftan* with *beshmet* underdress. They show the traditional small leather pockets (*gazyrnitzas*) for wooden rifle-cartridge tubes sewn in decorative patterns on the chest. The women's costumes are based on the nineteenth-century versions of the traditional southern Russian *poneva* ensembles, with their geometrical and rhomboidal ornamentation of braids and metallic appliqués. Thamar's costume includes the cerise silk scarf with which she lured her hapless suitors.

(top) **Unknown artist**
Mme Karsavina and M Bolm in Thamar *(as Queen Thamar and the Prince, in costumes by Léon Bakst)*
cover of *Comoedia Illustré* June 1912
National Gallery of Australia Research Library, Canberra

(above) **EO Hoppé**
Thamar—Madame Karsavina and M Adolph Bolm 1913
plate 6 from *Studies from the Russian Ballet*

(opposite) **Léon Bakst**
Costume for a friend of Queen Thamar, Costume for Queen Thamar and *Costume for a Lezghin* c 1912

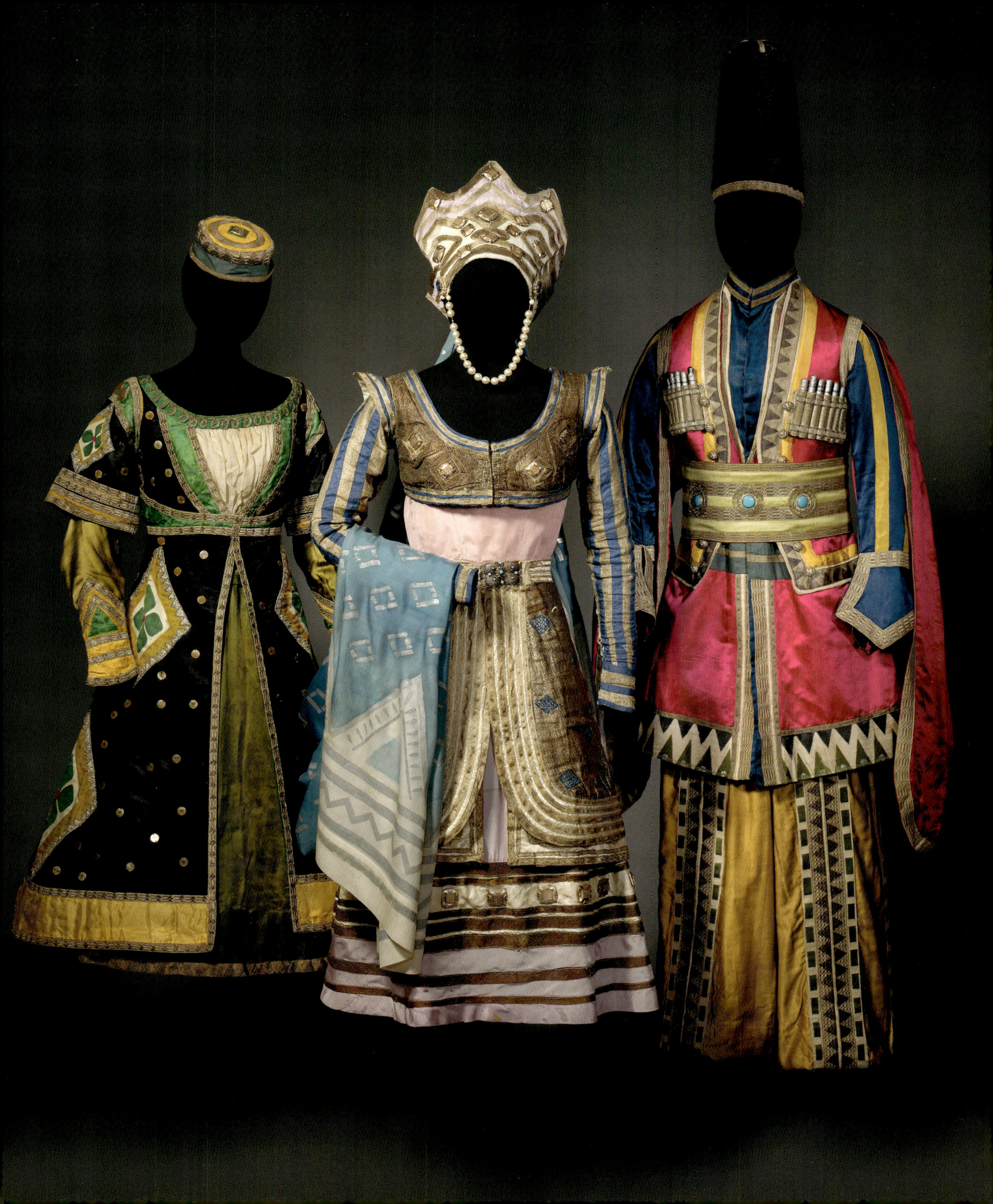

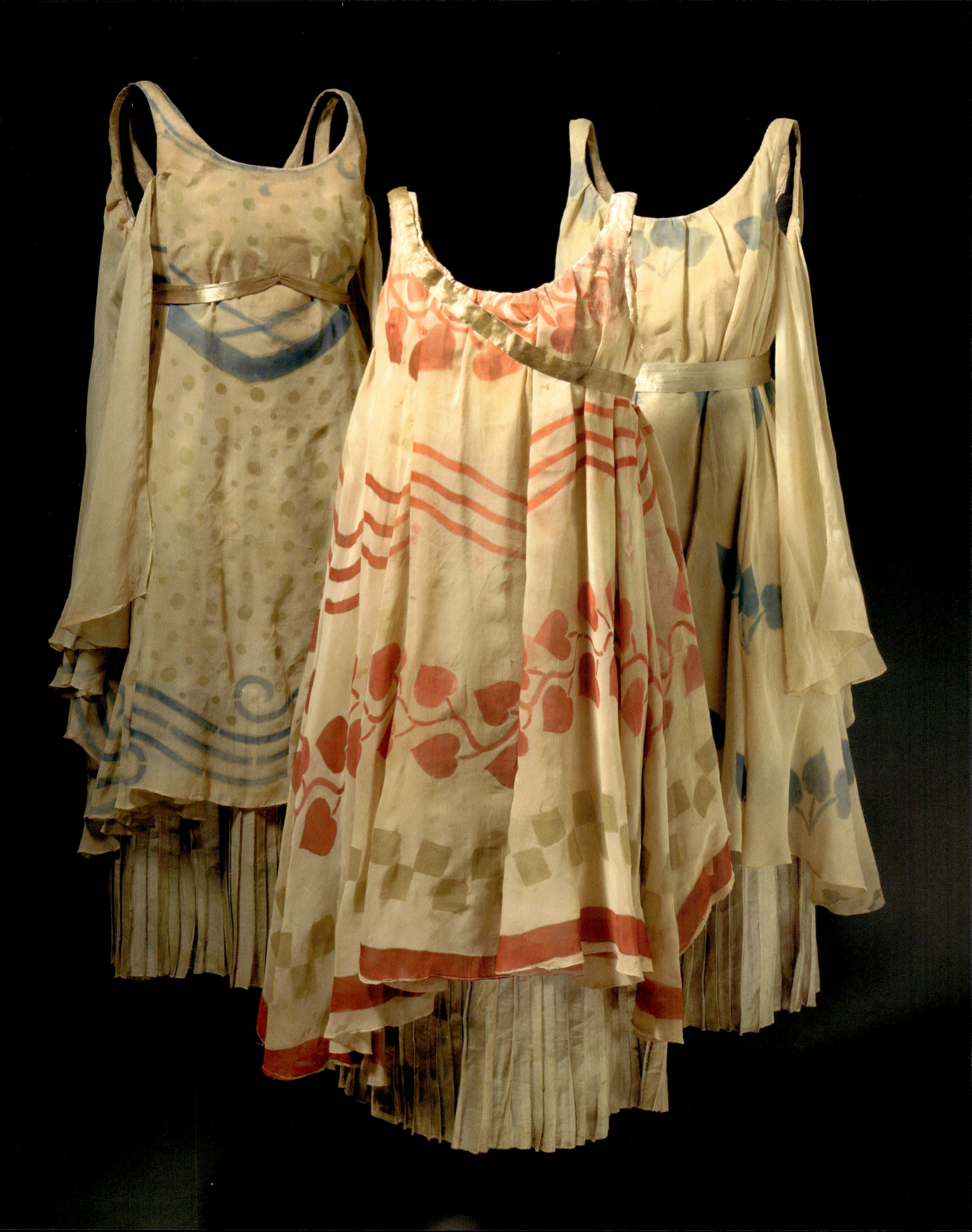

L'Après-midi d'un faune
The afternoon of a faun

Choreographic scene (later choreographic poem)

Producer:	Les Ballets Russes de Serge Diaghilev
Premiere:	29 May 1912, Théâtre du Châtelet, Paris
Costume design:	Léon Bakst
Scenery design:	Léon Bakst
Music:	Claude Debussy, after the poem by Stéphane Mallarmé
Choreography:	Vaslav Nijinsky
Main characters:	The Faun, nymphs

Opening this ballet, a faun lies on a hillock, idling the afternoon away playing the flute and eating grapes. Seven nymphs, or naiads, approach The Faun's domain on their way to bathe in a nearby lake. Enchanted by them the faun approaches, causing them to run away. Upon their return The Faun tries again to ingratiate himself with them, causing all but one to flee in fright. The remaining nymph and The Faun flirt with one another until she too leaves in fright, dropping her scarf. The saddened Faun picks it up and returns to the hillock and falls into a reverie over it, 'consummating' his desire for the nymph in an orgasmic final gesture.

∎

In his second Greek-themed ballet, Léon Bakst worked closely with choreographer Vaslav Nijinsky to achieve the frozen attitudes of Greek dancers seen in Attic art. He also produced an appropriately layered, darkly glowing Symbolist set design, against which the dancers would posture in their frieze-like positions. The geometric patterns of his earlier costumes for *Narcisse* are developed and further energised as the dancers create a moving and rippling pattern across the stage. Nijinsky's choreography exploited this two-dimensionality, eliminating references to traditional ballet technique. The nymphs' flowing costumes are anchored by almost architectural underskirts in metallic pleated fabric, in deliberate contrast to the sinuous, revealing and animal-like costume worn by Nijinsky as The Faun. The languorous and celebrated musical score for this short ballet was written by Debussy in 1894 and chosen by Diaghilev for the shimmering quality that it laid over Nijinsky's and Bakst's visual composition.

(opposite) **Léon Bakst**
Costumes for nymphs c 1912

(left) **George Barbier** *Nijinsky as the Faun from* L'Après-midi d'un faune in *Designs on the dances of Vaslav Nijinsky,* 1913
National Gallery of Australia Research Library, Canberra

Costumes for Les Ballets Russes de Serge Diaghilev 1909–29 **119**

120 Ballets Russes: the art of costume

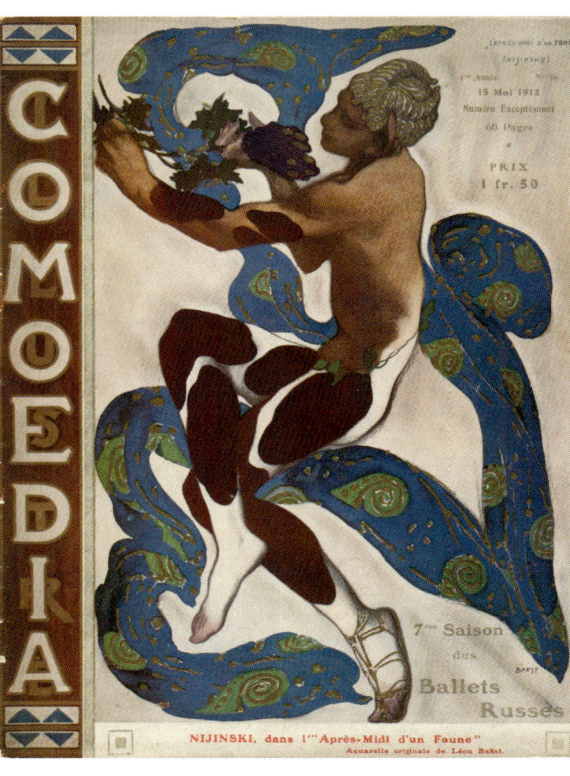

(opposite) **Léon Bakst**
Costume design for a nymph from L'Après-midi d'un faune
page 40 in *Official program of the Ballets Russes at the Théâtre du Châtelet, May–June 1912*

(above) **Unknown photographer**
Scene from L'Après-midi d'un faune—*Mesdames Boniecka, Sokolova, Pflanz, Wassilewska and others*
page 36 in *Souvenir program for Serge de Diaghileff's Ballet Russe* 1916–17

(left) **Léon Bakst**
Nijinsky as the Faun from L'Après-midi d'un faune
cover of *Comoedia Illustré*, special edition, no 16, 15 May 1912

(far left) **Unknown photographer**
Nijinsky and Nijinska in L'Après-midi d'un faune
page 765 in *Comœdia Illustré*, no 8, 15 June 1912
National Gallery of Australia Research Library, Canberra

Costumes for Les Ballets Russes de Serge Diaghilev 1909–29   121

Daphnis et Chloé
Daphnis and Chloë

Choreographic symphony in three scenes

Producer: Les Ballets Russes de Serge Diaghilev
Premiere: 8 June 1912, Théâtre du Châtelet, Paris
Costume design: Léon Bakst
Costumier: Marie Muelle
Scenery design: Léon Bakst
Music: Maurice Ravel
Choreography: Michel Fokine
Libretto: Michel Fokine, 1904, after a story by Longus, 200 CE
Main characters: Chloé (Chloë), Daphnis, Darkon, Lisinion, Lyceion, Briaxis, Lammon, Pan, nymphs, brigands

The ballet takes place on a Mediterranean island, where the shepherd Daphnis and his lover Chloë gather in a grotto with other young people to celebrate the god Pan and his nymphs. Another shepherd, Darkon, and the temptress Lisinion each try to disrupt the pair, to no avail. However, a band of brigands (pirates), led by their chief Briaxis, abduct Chloë. The distraught Daphnis applies to Pan for assistance and the god reunites the pair of lovers by scaring the brigands away. The ballet concludes with celebratory dances by the reunited Daphnis and Chloë.

■

Daphnis and Chloë, a pastoral novel by the second-century Greek writer Longus, published in Florence in 1598, had sparked Fokine's imagination as early as 1904, and piqued Bakst's interest following his 1907 research tour in Greece.[4] It was the last of the Ballets Russes' Greek-themed ballets and shared much of the décor and costume styles of its predecessors *Narcisse* and *L'Après-midi d'un faune*. The National Gallery's costumes are those designed for the ballet's brigand characters, their simple and abstracted tunic shapes and bold patterning showing a divergence from Bakst's more familiar decorative Orientalism. Their chequerboard and chevron motifs, stencilled onto woollen fabrics, show the influence of Greek black-figure ceramics on Bakst's pattern organisation. His close creative collaboration with Fokine meant that these patterns, in vivid colour combinations, would intensify with the asymmetric and angular choreography cutting across his Arcadian setting. Bakst developed some of his *Daphnis and Chloë* costume designs into a series of 'fantasies of modern dress' fashion designs, commissioned in 1912 by the French couturier Jeanne Paquin (1869–1936).

(top) **Léon Bakst**
Set design for Daphnis et Chloé
page 44 in *Official program of the Ballets Russes at the Théâtre du Châtelet*, May–June 1912

(above) *Dioné*
plate 73 from *Journal des Dames et des Modes*, no 34, 1913

(opposite) *Costumes for three brigands* c 1912

(opposite inset) **Unknown photographer**
Mm. Kremnew and Woronzow—M. Goudin—M.Oumanski—M. Kremnew—Daphnis et Chloé page 754 in *Comoedia Illustrè*, no 8, 15 June 1912

122 Ballets Russes: the art of costume

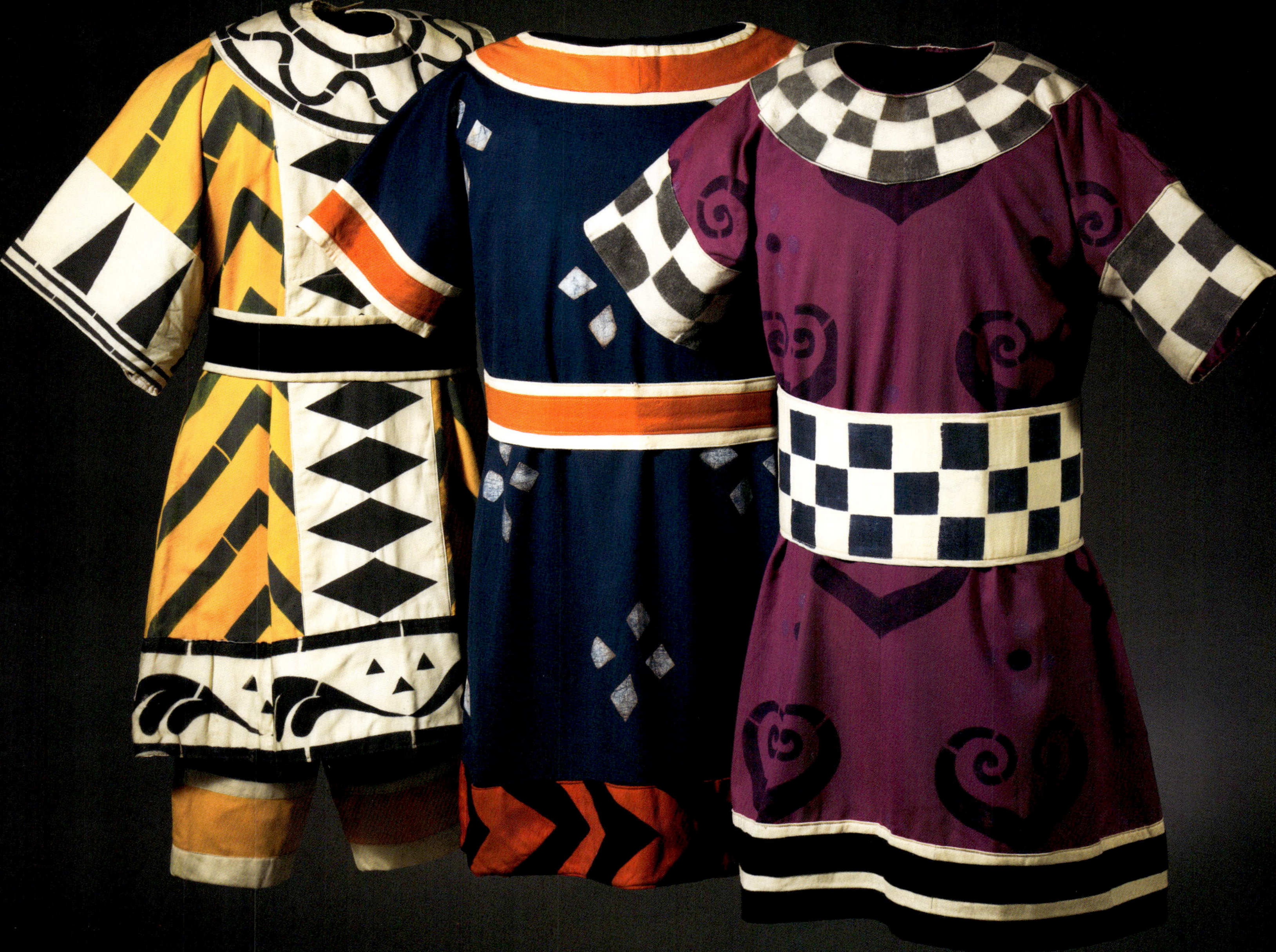

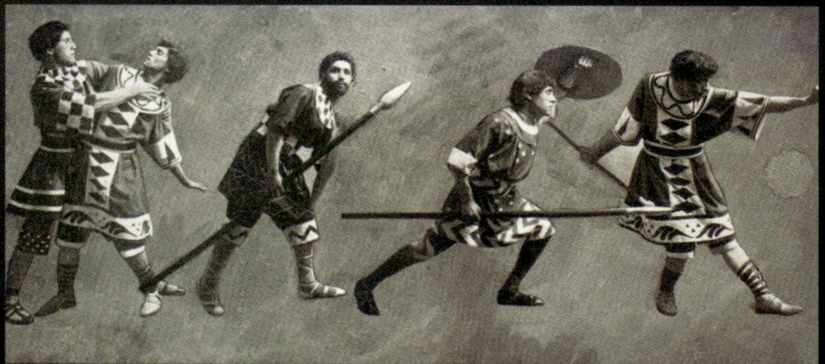

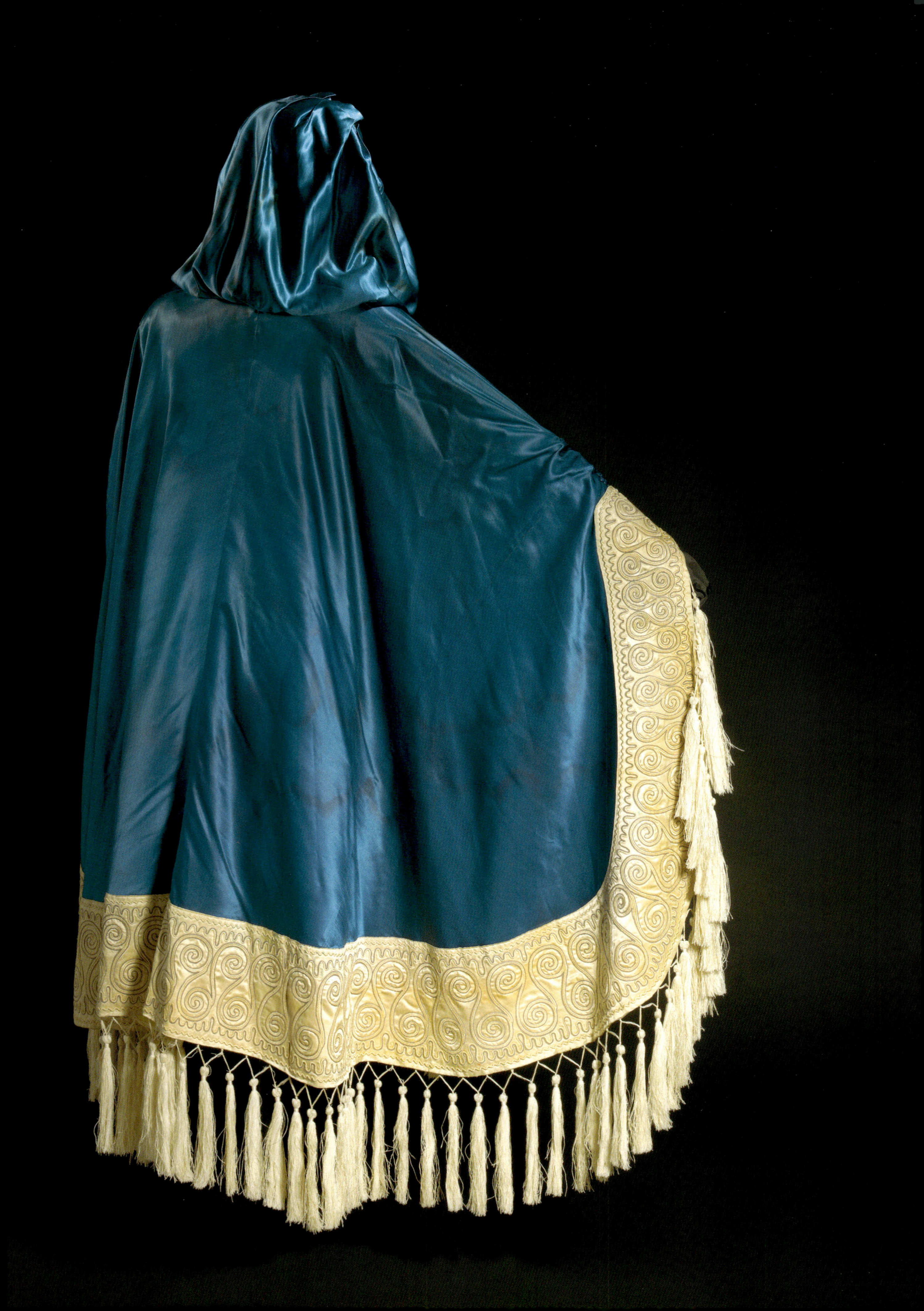

Papillons
Butterflies
Ballet in one act

Producer:	Les Ballets Russes de Serge Diaghilev
First performed:	1912, Mariinsky Theatre, St Petersburg
Premiere:	16 April 1914, Théâtre de Monte Carlo, Monaco
Revival:	17 December 1936, Chicago
Revival producer:	Monte Carlo Ballet Russe
Costume design:	Léon Bakst
Scenery design:	Mstislav Dobujinsky
Music:	Robert Schumann, arranged by Nicholas Tcherepnin
Choreography:	Michel Fokine
Libretto:	Michel Fokine
Main characters:	Pierrot, young girls, butterflies, the Lady, the Valet, Chaperones

The ballet resurrects the character of Pierrot, who appears in the earlier ballet, *Carnaval*. Similarly, *Papillons* is also set on the night of the Carnival Ball and follows the progress of Pierrot as he discovers and courts a group of young women dressed as butterflies. The foolish-minded protagonist lures and captures the prettiest of the group. Following an extended interplay, in which at one stage he damages her wings through rough treatment, the butterflies transform back into women and are escorted from the ball by their chaperones, much to Pierrot's dismay.

■

This airy and festival-like ballet of twelve short dance pieces was choreographed by Fokine to Schumann's Romantic piano work, *Papillons* (1829–31), itself inspired by the novel *Die Flegeljahre* (*The years of indiscretion*) by German writer Jean-Paul Richter (Johann Paul Friedrich Richter, 1763–1825). Bakst's costumes follow his earlier nineteenth-century historicist recreations for *Carnaval* with an ensemble of outfits in the later mid-century early Victorian style.

Léon Bakst
(opposite) *Cape from costume for a lady* c 1914

(above) *Costume design for a lady* in Papillons
page 33 in *Souvenir program for Serge Diaghilev's Ballet Russe, Metropolitan Opera, New York 1916*

Le Coq d'or
The golden cockerel

Producer:	1914 Les Ballets Russes de Serge Diaghilev
	1937 Ballets Russes de Col W de Basil
Premiere:	24 May 1914, Théâtre national de l'Opéra, Paris
Revival:	23 September 1937, Covent Garden, London
Costume design:	Natalia Goncharova
Costumier:	1937 Barbara Karinska
Scenery design:	Natalia Goncharova
Music:	Nikolai Rimsky-Korsakov, adapted by Nicholas Tcherepnin
Choreography:	Michel Fokine
Libretto:	Vladimir Belsky, after Aleksandr Pushkin, revised by Alexandre Benois
Main characters:	The Queen of Shemakhan, King Dodon, the Golden Cockerel, Astrologer, General Polkan, Amelfa, Prince Aphron, Prince Guidon

Set in ancient Azerbaijan, this moral tale tells of an astrologer who has caught and enchanted a golden cockerel which he presents to King Dodon. The king, unsure of how to properly govern his kingdom, requests the advice of his two sons. Prince Guidon encourages a life of frivolity, while Prince Aphron advocates war with their neighbouring kingdom. However, the astrologer's gift of the golden bird means that the lazy king can instead sleep, while the cockerel watches over the city. The king promises the astrologer a gift of anything he desires. The cockerel wakes Dodon to alert him of danger and in response he sends both his sons to war before falling back asleep. The cockerel wakes Dodon again and this time the king himself goes to war, where he finds both his sons dead on the battlefield. However, his grief is short-lived as he comes across the tent of the Queen of Shemakhan, with whom he promptly falls in love. He returns to his kingdom with her as his bride but the astrologer asks for her as his promised gift. Dodon refuses and beats the astrologer to death for his impertinence. The cockerel then swoops down and strikes the king on the head, killing him, and magically the queen and the cockerel disappear. The astrologer then comes back to life to explain the moral of his tale.

Natalia Goncharova, already an extraordinary modern painter, drew her complex neo-primitivist fantasy of a traditional Russian city for the stage set of *Le Coq d'or* in 1914. Layers of onion domes, striations of red, pink and yellow, bold square blocks and perfectly geometrical buildings made up the backdrop for this Russian fairy tale. Although designed by a modernist artist, with modern music by Stravinsky, this production looked to a world already disappearing, soon to be imagined only outside Russia. Goncharova's interpretation of the conventions, patterns and colours of traditional Russian folk dress, popular *lubok* prints and crafts, deliberately linked the high-key colours and abstracted shapes of the costumes to the backdrops, creating an overall spectacle of Byzantine richness and complexity.

(top) **Natalia Goncharova**
Set design for Scene 1 from Le Coq d'or
page 24 in *Program for the Original Ballet Russe, Canadian Tour, September 19th – October 18th, 1941*
National Gallery of Australia Research Library, Canberra

(above) *Costume design for a peasant woman* c 1914

© Natalia Goncharova/ADAGP. Licensed by Viscopy, 2010

126 Ballets Russes: the art of costume

Textiles were used in a symbolic way, with the simple light appliquéd cotton for the peasants' dresses contrasting with the heavy embroidered velvet richness of the king's costume, complete with ermine tails as decoration. Its weight and bulk emphasised the dancer's awkward movements as a representation of the king's diminishing authority in the midst of an energised and vital peasantry returned to life like highly coloured painted mechanical peasant toys. The ballet's evident symbolism at the brink of the First World War was given further impact as the vehicle for Diaghilev's first engagement with Modernism, and an enduring professional artistic relationship with Goncharova. The designer had the opportunity to reconstruct and revise her costumes for the ballet's 1937 revival, the originals having been mostly lost by then.

(above left and right) **Natalia Goncharova**
Costume design for a peasant woman c 1914 (front and back)
© Natalia Goncharova/ADAGP. Licensed by Viscopy, 2010

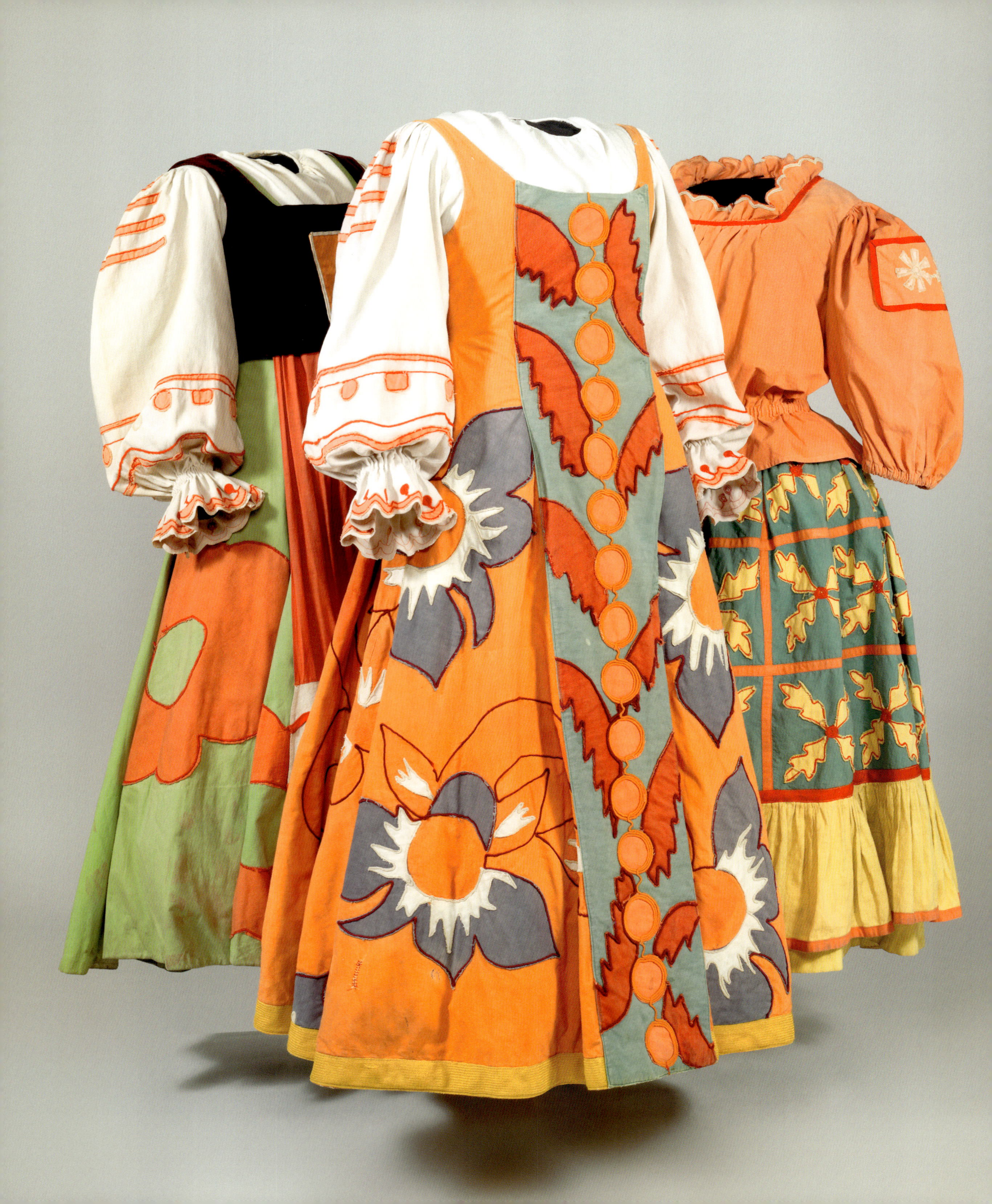

Natalia Goncharova
(opposite left to right) *Costume for a female subject of King Dodon; Costume for a peasant woman;* and *Costume for a nursemaid to King Dodon* c 1937

(left) *Robe from costume for King Dodon* c 1937

(inset) *Mantle from costume for King Dodon* c 1937
© Natalia Goncharova/ADAGP.
Licensed by Viscopy, 2010

Costumes for Les Ballets Russes de Serge Diaghilev 1909–29   129

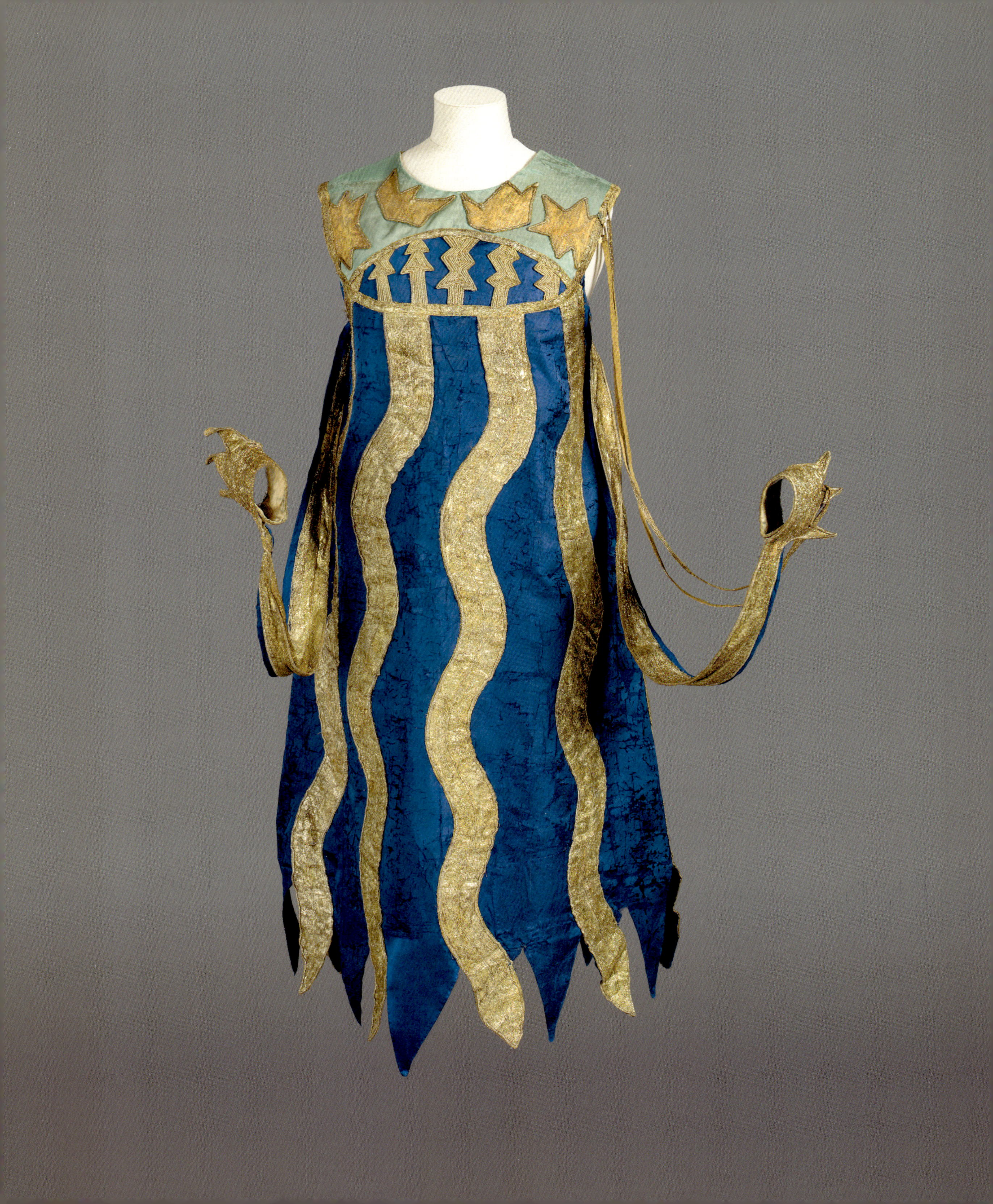

Sadko—in the underwater kingdom
Scene 6 from the opera

Producer: 1898 Les Ballets Russes de Serge Diaghilev
1916 Serge de Diaghileff's Ballet Russe
First performed: January 1898, as the full opera
Premiere: 16 June 1911, Théâtre du Châtelet, Paris
Revival: 9 October 1916, Manhattan Opera House, New York
Costume design: 1911 Boris Anisfeld and Léon Bakst
1916 Natalia Goncharova
Scenery design: 1911 Boris Anisfeld and Léon Bakst
1916 Natalia Goncharova (with 1911 set by Boris Anisfeld)
Music: Nikolai Rimsky-Korsakov
Choreography: 1911 Michel Fokine
1916 Adolph Bohm
Libretto: Nikolai Rimsky-Korsakov and Vladimir Belsky
Main characters: Sadko, Princess Volkova, the King of the Sea, princesses, the Pilgrim, the Golden Fish, the Riverlet, Rusalkas, streams, naiads, goldfish, squid, sea monsters, seahorses

The full opera version of this ballet is taken from an epic Russian folk poem set in Novgorod, Russia, where Sadko, an impoverished musician, leaves his wife in search of his fortune. He plays his *gusli* (a traditional stringed instrument) by the shores of Lake Ilmen, captivating Princess Volkova, the youngest daughter of the King of the Sea. She makes the minstrel a wealthy seaman. However, after travelling the oceans for many years Sadko becomes stranded in calm water and is forced to dive into the sea, where he is reunited with, and marries, Volkova. Following the wild revelry of the wedding, attended by monsters of the deep and fantastic sea creatures, Sadko returns to his wife in Novgorod and the princess becomes the Volkova River. The Ballets Russes only ever produced the sixth scene of the opera, *The kingdom under the sea*, as a ballet, focusing of the festivities of Sadko and Volkova's wedding, attended by the monsters, fish and sea creatures.

■

In 1911 Anisfeld produced his extremely elegant, rich and self-contained drawings for characters in the underwater ballet segment of Rimsky-Korsakov's fairytale opera *Sadko*. His designs show the continuing influence of the Art Nouveau and Secession styles which dominated European art at the turn of the century. There is a dramatic contrast with Goncharova's more robust realisations of the same ballet made only five years later, in the midst of the First World War. Instead of Golovin's delicate *fin-de-siècle* designs, she presented vivid marine creatures such as the golden seahorse and the squid. Goncharova's knowledge and love of Russian folk dress can be seen in the design of the costumes and in the shape of the headdresses for the Fish characters. The seahorse's dappled patterns and the squid costume's undulating tentacles outlined in metallic lamé over ultramarine silk allowed the dancers to interpret Fokine's choreography, suggesting the fluid movement of water and the shimmer and iridescence of marine creatures.

Natalia Goncharova
(opposite) *Costume for a squid* c 1916)
(top) *Costume for a seahorse* c 1916 (also see p 258)
(above) *Headdress from costume for a fish* c 1916
© Natalia Goncharova/ADAGP. Licensed by Viscopy, 2010

La Boutique fantasque
The magical toyshop

Ballet in one act

Producer:	Les Ballets Russes de Serge Diaghilev
Premiere:	5 June 1919, Alhambra Theatre, London
Costume design:	André Derain
Scenery design:	André Derain
Music:	Gioacchino Rossini, arranged and orchestrated by Ottorino Respighi
Choreography:	Léonide Massine
Libretto:	Serge Diaghilev, Léonide Massine, Serge Grigoriev, André Derain, after *Puppenfee* (*The fairy doll*) by Josef Bayer
Main characters:	The Shopkeeper, the Shopkeeper's Assistant, Cancan dancers, the Tarantella dancers, the Brown Poodle and the White Poodle, the Russian Merchant Family, the American and his Wife, the English ladies, the Queen of Clubs, the Queen of Hearts, the King of Spades, the King of Diamonds, the cossacks

This ballet is set in a toyshop. As it opens, an English lady, an American family and a Russian family enter to peruse its wares. The many mechanical toys and dolls—Tarantella dancers, street vendors, kings and queens from a pack of playing cards, poodles, Cossacks and two cancan dancers—are demonstrated to the customers by the owner of the shop. As the shop shuts for the day, many of the dolls are purchased by the various shoppers. The toys then come to life and lament the fate of the two cancan dancers, who are lovers and who will be sent to different families the next day. The toys devise a plan to allow the dancers to escape together. The next day the owner is confronted by the angry customers who claim that their parcels of toys have not been delivered as promised and are now only empty boxes. A ruckus ensues among the angry customers and the remaining toys return to life, with the cossacks chasing the customers from the shop and all celebrating with the Shopkeeper at this outcome.

■

Set in the period of the 1860s, this ballet is a re-working of a popular Viennese ballet, *Die Puppenfee* (*The fairy doll*) of 1888, which had been revived by Serge and Nicholas Legat in St Petersburg early in the twentieth century.[5] Diaghilev, stimulated by Respighi's discovery of *Les Riens* (*Trifles*), a suite of piano pieces by Rossini, was inspired to commission Respighi to arrange these works for *La Boutique fantasque*.[6] Bakst had expected to be commissioned by Diaghilev to design the ballet but a misunderstanding led to Diaghilev instead commissioning André Derain who, despite having no theatre experience, brought the freshness of his Fauvist painting to the task and a new connection for Diaghilev to the world of contemporary painters. Derain's light and elegant painterly approach to the set and the costumes for a variety of engaging characters brought the stage to life and enhanced Massine's staccato choreography for the mechanical toys. Derain's designs were presented as oil sketches, showing little concern for the technical details of the costumes. The popular comedic figures of the dancing poodles were costumed to resemble actual toys, a triumph of the costumiers' skills in interpreting Derain's sketches. Like worn teddy bears today, they retain their tattered charm.

(top) **André Derain**
Costume design for the Can-Can Dancer c 1919

(above) **Unknown photographer**
Vera Nelidova and Serge Lipatoff (as the Brown Poodle and the White Poodle from La Boutique fantasque*)*
page 67 in *Program for Col. W. de Basil's Ballets Russes, Jubilee Season, Royal Opera House Covent Garden*
National Gallery of Australia Research Library, Canberra

(opposite) **André Derain**
Costume for the White Poodle c 1919

132   Ballets Russes: the art of costume

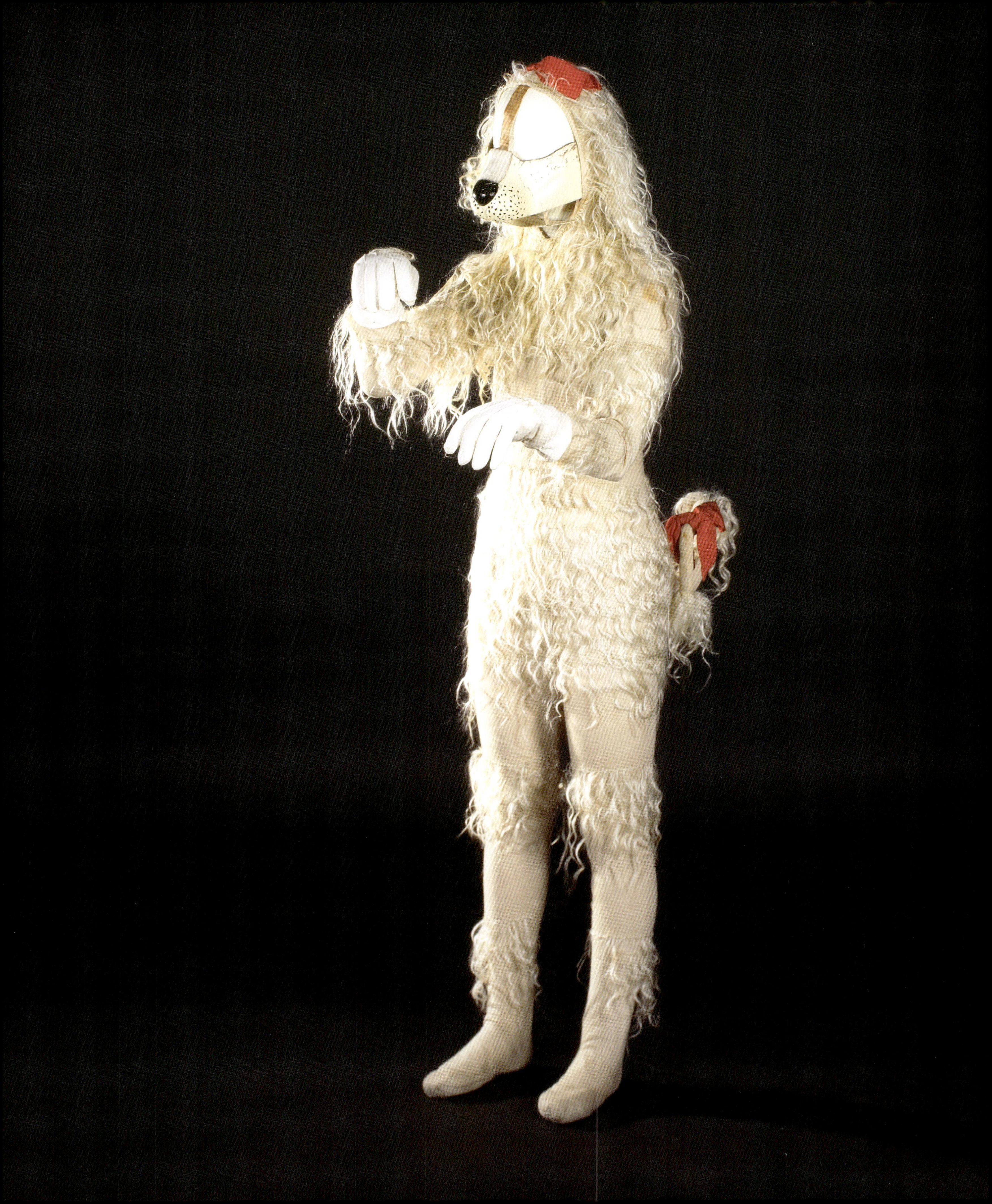

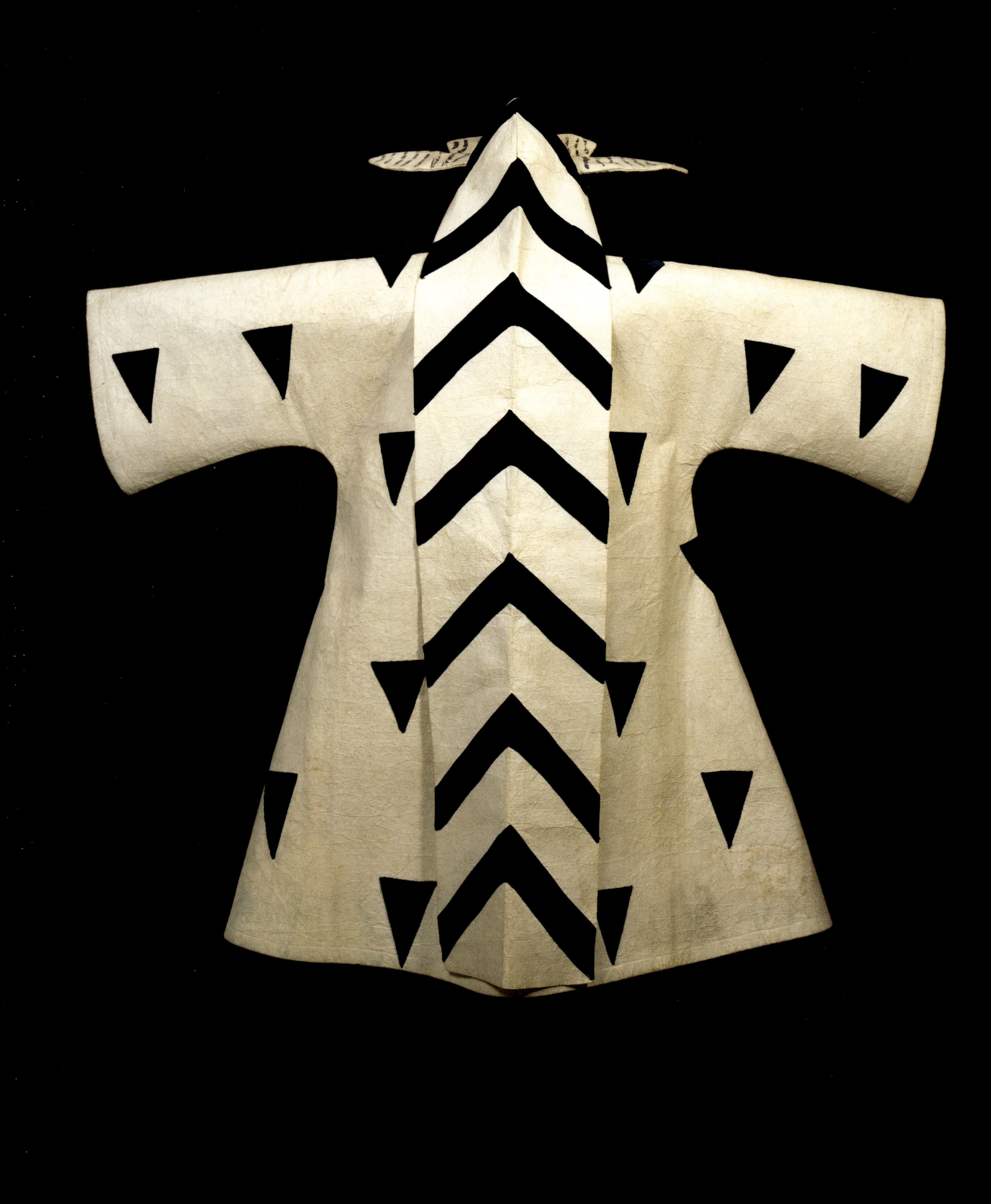

Le Chant du rossignol
The song of the nightingale

Choreographic poem in one act

Producer:	Les Ballets Russes de Serge Diaghilev
Premiere:	2 February 1920, Théâtre national de l'Opéra, Paris
Costume design:	Henri Matisse
Costumier:	Marie Muelle
Scenery design:	Henri Matisse
Music:	Igor Stravinsky
Choreography:	Léonide Massine
Libretto:	After the story by Hans Christian Andersen
Main characters:	The Nightingale, the Emperor of China, the Mechanical Nightingale, the Japanese Maestro, Death, Mandarins, chamberlains, mourners

The setting is the court of the Chinese Emperor, who owns a nightingale that sings for the court's entertainment. However, the Japanese Emperor arrives for a visit, bearing a gift of a mechanical nightingale. The Chinese Emperor and his court are overjoyed with the new toy and soon the real nightingale leaves, neglected. Later, the Chinese Emperor becomes ill and on his death bed requests music be played. Just as he is about to die, the real nightingale returns to the palace and begins to sing, promising to continue if Death relents. The bargain is kept, the Emperor recovers and the Nightingale is restored to its former position in his court.

■

Based on a Hans Christian Andersen fairytale of the same name, this production was adapted from Stravinsky's opera, *Le Rossignol*, produced by Diaghilev in 1914. The original opulent orientalist set and costumes by Benois were destroyed during the First World War, a loss that stimulated Diaghilev to commission a new ballet version which, following his successful engagements with Picasso and Derain, he hoped would be designed by another major artist. In 1919, he visited Henri Matisse to persuade him to design his new production, and was delighted to discover Matisse's collection of exotic birds and his admiration of Massine's choreography. Matisse had no theatre experience but took the commission with enthusiasm, determined to produce a design that was different from the high-keyed exoticism associated with the Ballets Russes. Using light colours against a porcelain-white backdrop, his refined costumes were based on traditional Chinese Ming court dress in colour orchestrations derived from Chinese ceramics and lacquer. The courtiers' costumes were elaborately tailored in silk, with loose decorations painted and directed by Matisse. Their massing on stage created the impression of a continuous pattern, as if on a scroll painting. The final unfurling of the recovered Emperor's long vermilion cloak was a calligraphic gesture, contrasting with the massed graphic of the black and white clad mourners at his feet. Their animal-like cloaks, among the most breathtaking of Matisse's designs, were made from a white felt-like curtain lining material with appliquéd triangles and chevrons of navy blue velvet, inspired by the markings on Chinese deer.

Henri Matisse
(opposite) *Costume for a mourner* c 1920

(top) *Headress for costume for a mourner* c 1920 (detail)
© Succession H Matisse/Visccpy, 2010

(above) **Henry Manuel**
Performance of Le Chant du rossignol
Bibliothèque nationale de France, Paris, Fonds Kochno, BN 79, C92682

Henri Matisse
(above) *Costume for a Mandarin* c 1920

(left) *Hat for costume for a courtier* 1920
© Succession H Matisse/Viscopy, 2010

(above) **Henri Matisse**
Robe for costume for a chamberlain c 1920
© Succession H Matisse/Viscopy, 2010

(left) **Enriett**
Group of dancers from Le Chant du rossignol
page 15 in *Souvenir program for the Ballets Russes at l'Opéra, May–June 1920*

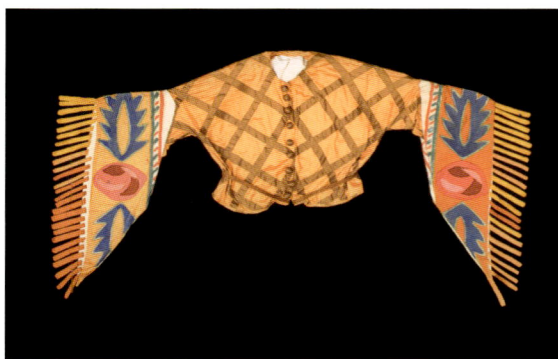

Chout
The buffoon

Russian legend in six scenes

Producer:	Les Ballets Russes de Serge Diaghilev
Premiere:	17 May 1921, Théâtre de la Gaîté-Lyrique, Paris
Costume design:	Mikhail Larionov
Costumier:	Germaine Bongard (Maison Jove)
Scenery design:	Mikhail Larionov
Music:	Serge Prokofiev
Choreography:	Mikhail Larionov and Thadée Slavinsky
Libretto:	Serge Diaghilev
Main characters:	The Buffoon, the Old Buffoons, the Merchant, the Buffoon's Wife, bridesmaids

Wielding a 'magic' whip, a young village buffoon tricks his elders into believing that he has killed his wife and then brought her back to life. Convinced by the stunt, seven old buffoons each buys a 'magic' whip and kills his wife, only to find that they cannot be brought back to life as promised. In order to escape the wrath of the older men, the young buffoon disguises himself as a cook. Meanwhile, a merchant who has been invited to select his bride from one of the seven old buffoons' daughters mistakenly chooses the 'cook', who escapes but leaves in his place a goat, which the merchant kills. The young buffoon returns, dressed as himself and accompanied by soldiers, to request that the non-existent cook be brought forward or that he be compensated by the merchant. The ballet ends with the young buffoon and his wife celebrating their extorted prosperity as the soldiers woo the seven old buffoons' daughters.

Chout was based on an old Russian folk tale and as a ballet had a particularly long artistic gestation, having been originally conceived by Diaghilev in 1915, when he commissioned Prokofiev to write the score. The same year, Larionov (with his partner, Natalia Goncharova) joined Diaghilev's circle in Lausanne and began work on the stage and costume design for *Chout*, as well as taking a leading role in developing its choreography with Diaghilev's new and inexperienced Polish choreographer, Thadée Slavinsky. The result, finally presented in 1921, was a particularly vivid expression of the Cubo-Futurism that came to be associated with Larionov and Goncharova. Echoing the vividly coloured Cubist scenery graphics, the costumes' abstracted angular shapes and patterns and flattened, almost deconstructed, forms made the dancers a moveable part of an overall scenario. Although based on the conventions of peasant clothing, some of the costumes were visually extended with stiffened buckram, felt, rubberised cloth and heavy cane structures, hindering movement to the extent that the dancers feared that they could not carry out the planned choreography, and causing Diaghilev to enforce their contracts in the face of a strike.

Mikhail Larionov
(top) *Costume for a soldier* c 1921
(above) *Bodice from costume for a bridesmaid* c 1921
(opposite) *Costume for the Buffoon's Wife* c 1921
© Mikhail Larionov/ADAGP. Licensed by Viscopy, 2010

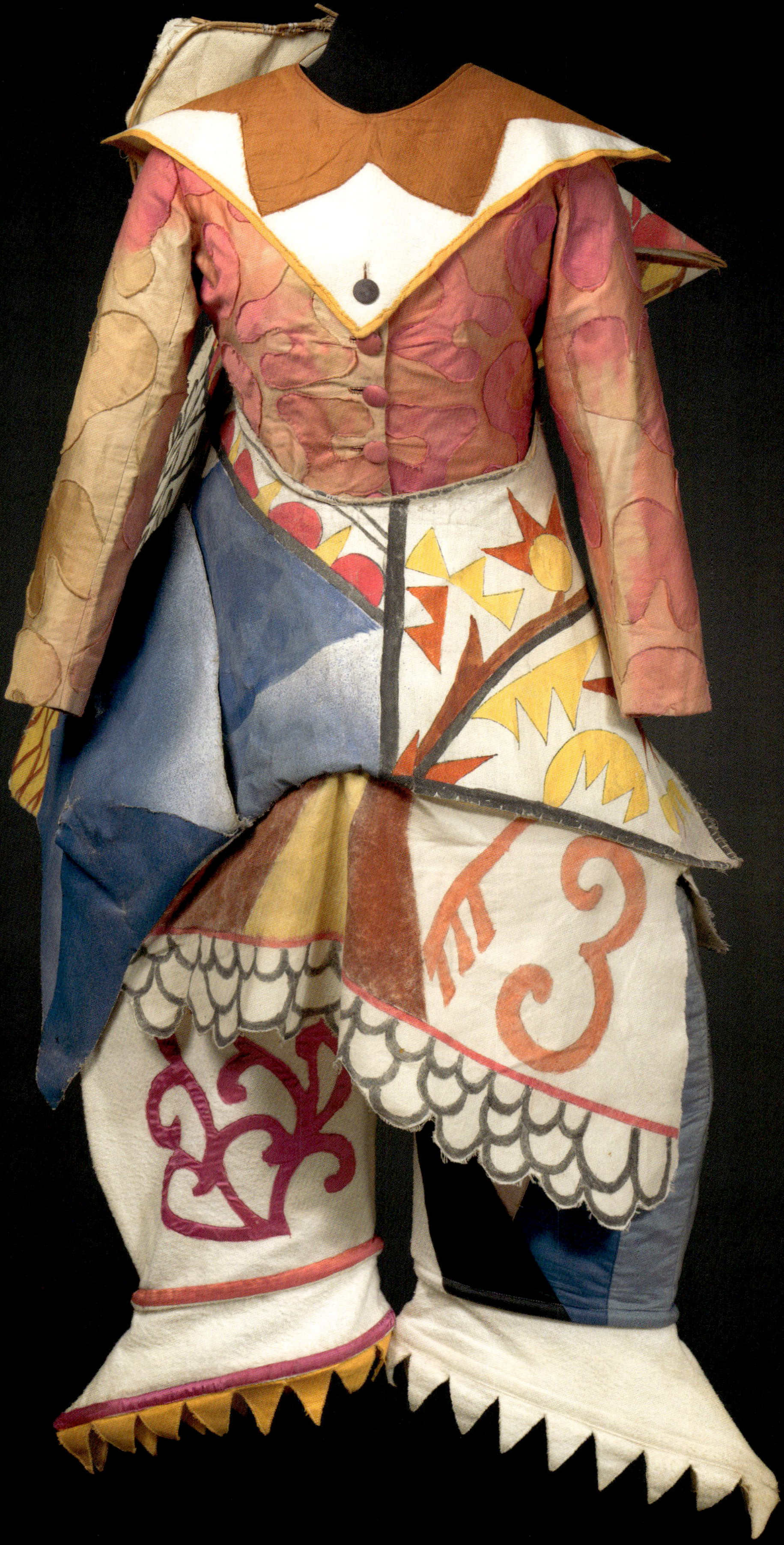

The sleeping princess

Ballet in three acts and five scenes

Producer:	Les Ballets Russes de Serge Diaghilev
First performed:	by Marius Petipa as *Sleeping beauty*, 1890, Mariinsky Theatre, St Petersburg
Premiere:	2 November 1921, Alhambra Theatre, London
Costume design:	Léon Bakst
Costumiers:	Pierre Pitoeff, Lovat Fraser, Miss Norman, Maison Muelle Rossignol
Scenery design:	Léon Bakst
Music:	Pyotr Il'yich Tchaikovsky, partly reorchestrated by Igor Stravinsky
Choreography:	Marius Petipa (reproduced by Nicholas Sergeyev), Bronislava Nijinska (after Petipa)
Libretto:	Marius Petipa and I Vsevolozhsky, after Charles Perreault
Main characters:	Princess Aurora, Prince Florimund, the Lilac Fairy, the Enchanted Princess, Carabosse, the Wicked Fairy, King Florestan XXIV, Queen, Catalabutte, the Fairy of the Pine Woods, Sister Anne, the Cherry Blossom Fairy, Red Riding Hood, the Fairy of the Humming Birds, Pierrette, the Fairy of the Song Birds, the Carnation Fairy, Columbine, the Fairy of the Mountain Ash, Ariana, the Spanish Prince, Harlequin, the Indian Prince, the Italian Prince, the English Prince, Puss in Boots, Pierrot, the White Cat, the Bluebird, Shéhérazade, the Shah, the Shah's Brother, the Porcelain Princesses, the Mandarin, Innocent Ivan and his brothers

This ballet is adapted from the classic fairytale *Sleeping beauty*. At the birth of his daughter, King Florestan XXIV and his queen invite all the fairies of the land to be godmothers to the baby Princess Aurora at her christening at the palace. All the fairies arrive and bestow a magic wish on the young princess. However, the ceremony is interrupted by the wicked fairy Carabosse who, angry that she has been left off the invitation list, curses Aurora, promising that one day she will prick her finger and die. Although she cannot break the curse, the Lilac Fairy frustrates Carabosse by exchanging Aurora's imminent death with a long slumber, from which Aurora can only be woken by the kiss of a prince. Aurora's awakening by Florimund a hundred years later is followed by their spectacular marriage.

◼

This ballet had its genesis as *Sleeping beauty*, presented in 1890 by Marius Petipa for the Mariinsky Theatre and celebrated for its lavish production quality and for the commissioning of Tchaikovsky for its musical score. The young Bakst, Benois and Diaghilev saw this production, and were enthralled by its fusion of historical art, design and contemporary music. The ballet was given a number of times outside Russia, including a version for Anna Pavlova's company in New York in 1916, with costume designs by Bakst. While the Ballets Russes had reached the end of the decade as the acknowledged leader in modern ballet, Diaghilev's decision to stage this ballet in 1921 was driven by the company's weak financial position and the

Léon Bakst
cover of *Souvenir program for* The sleeping princess *at the Alhambra Theatre* 1921

hope that such a classic might secure for the Ballets Russes a long-running season in the conservative, but lucrative, London theatre world. He reconciled with Bakst, offering him the design work, secure in the knowledge of Bakst's previous experience with this production and his sketches prepared for the earlier Pavlova commission. Diaghilev secured the backing of Sir Oswald Stoll, the director of the Alhambra Theatre, to fund the production, renamed in English *The sleeping princess*, but soon ran over budget. The costs of Bakst's costumes for a huge cast spiralled due to their lavish use of expensive materials and couture-like construction and detailing, with the final detail of every costume personally overseen and approved by Diaghilev. The National Gallery's costume for a lady-in-waiting is an indication of the extravagance, as a costume provided for a relatively minor character. Bakst's six elaborate sets, inspired by the Baroque work of the seventeenth-century theatre designer Ferdinando Galli Bibiena (1656–1743) and the eighteenth-century work of Bérain and Boquet (for the later period of Aurora's awakening), also drained the budget.

The demanding, lengthy performance of a single ballet did not appeal to audiences used to a more varied repertoire, and crucial audience numbers did not eventuate, forcing the production to close after 114 performances and leaving Diaghilev with crippling debt. As security, Stoll impounded the valuable costumes and properties at his Coliseum Theatre until Diaghilev was able to repay the debt, something he did not achieve until 1926. Having fled London before the production finished, without his properties and unable to return to Britain due to the risk of legal action and penalty, Diaghilev was again forced to change direction and focus. An unplanned future benefit of this episode was that the sturdily crafted costumes remained in relatively good condition, having been worn lightly and stored for a long period. By the time they were released, Diaghilev had moved on from such historical spectacles and the costumes, like Aurora, entered another long period of slumber and obscurity.

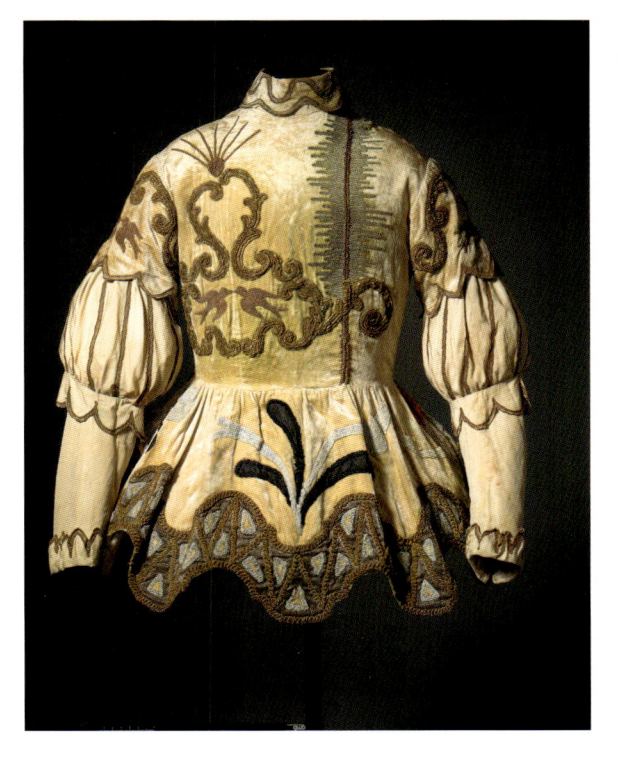

Léon Bakst
(above) *Costume for the Bluebird* c 1921

(left) *Costume for the page to the Hummingbird Fairy* (front and back) c 1921

Léon Bakst

(above) *Costume for a court lady* (front and back) c 1921

(opposite) *Costume for a lady-in-waiting* c 1921

142   Ballets Russes: the art of costume

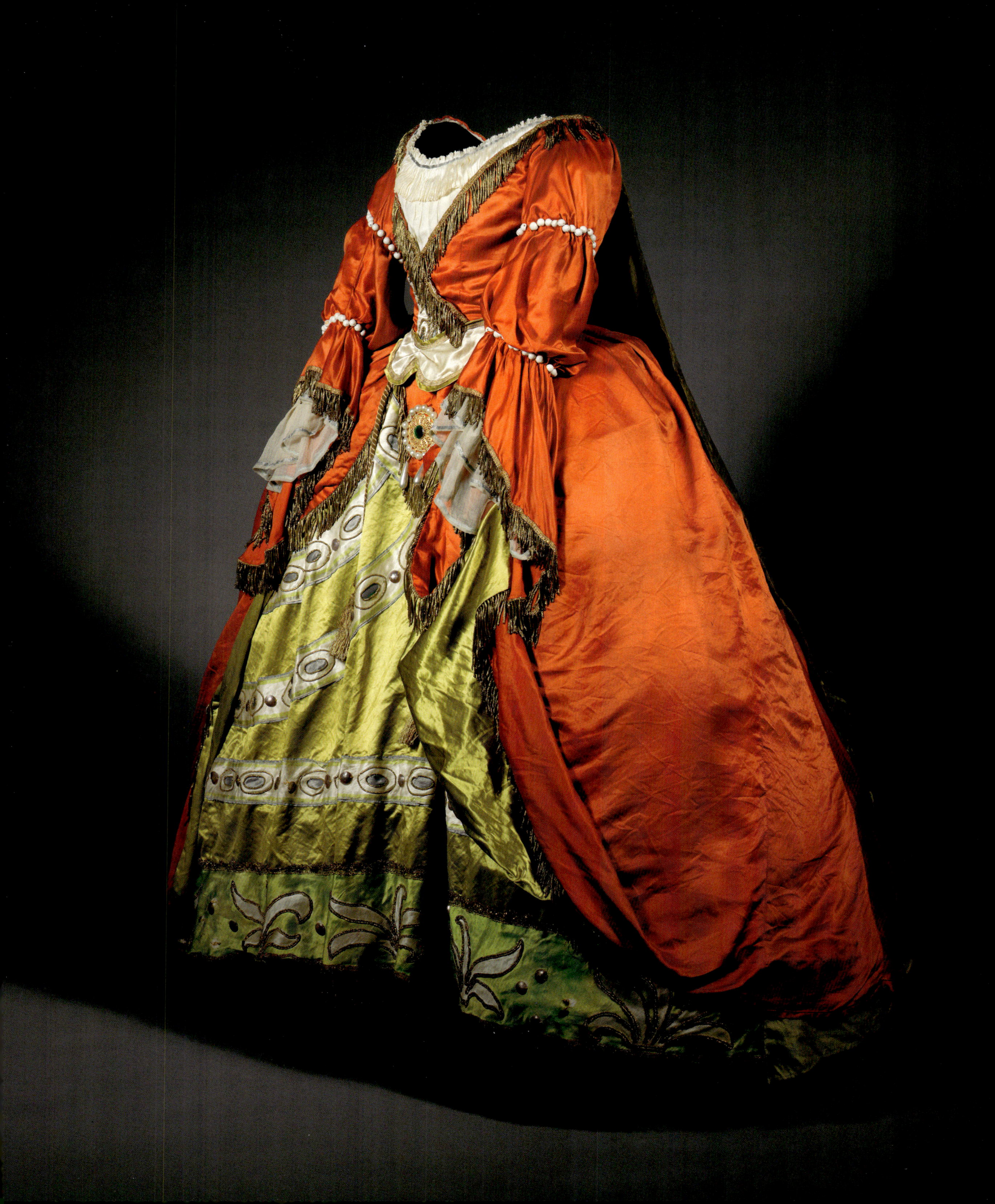

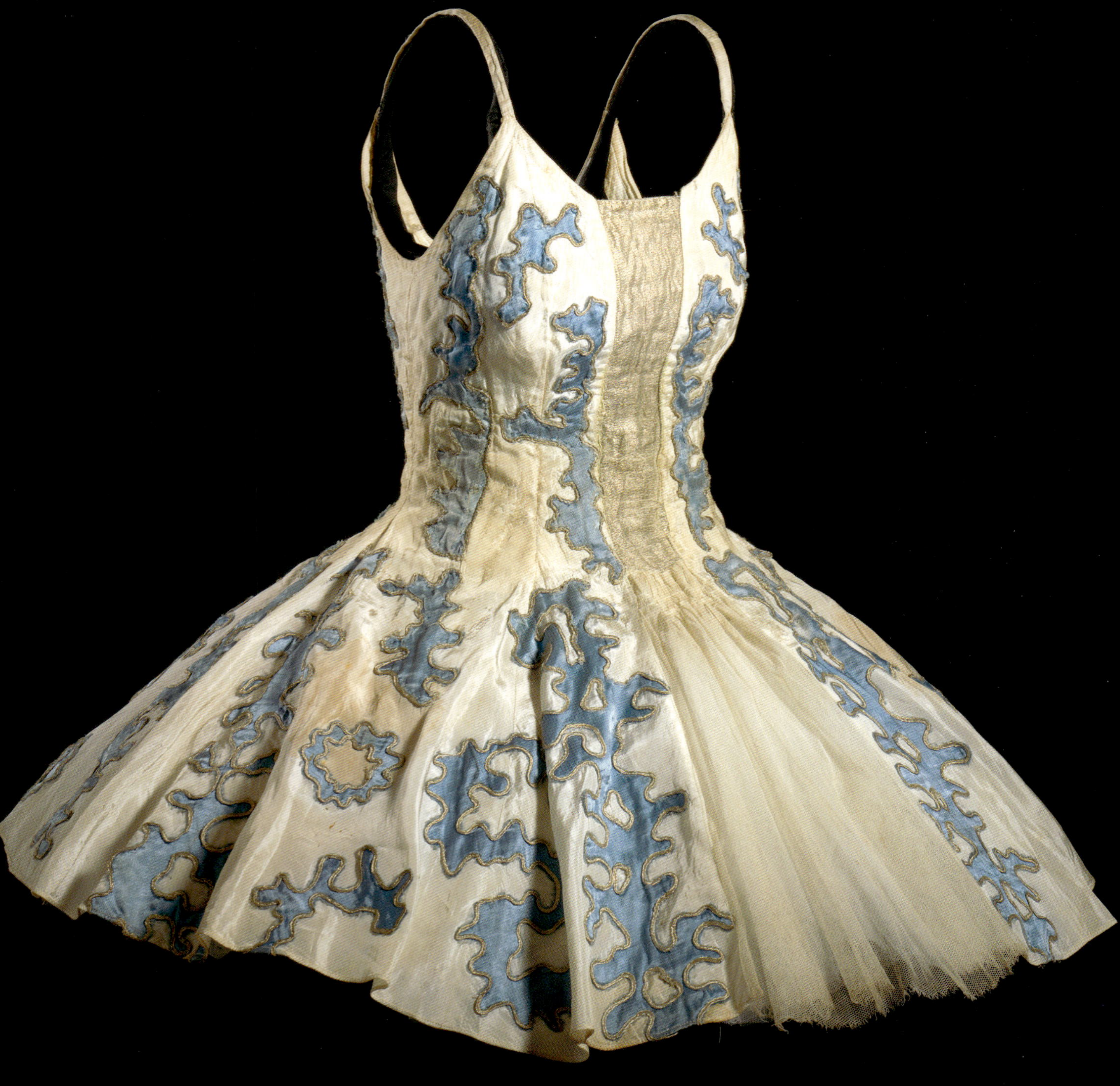

Le Mariage d'Aurore
Aurora's wedding
Ballet in one act

Producer:	Les Ballets Russes de Serge Diaghilev
Premiere:	18 May 1922, Théâtre national de l'Opéra, Paris
Costume design:	Alexandre Benois (from *Le Pavillon d'Armide*) with new costumes by Natalia Goncharova
Costumier:	Ivan Caffi (Imperial Theatres, St Petersburg) for re-used costumes from *Le Pavillon d'Armide*
Scenery design:	Alexandre Benois (from *Le Pavillon d'Armide*)
Music:	Pyotr Il'yich Tchaikovsky, partly re-orchestrated by Igor Stravinsky
Choreography:	after Marius Petipa
Libretto:	Marius Petipa and I Vsevolozhsky, after Charles Perreault's fairytale
Main characters:	Princess Aurora, Prince Florestan, Shéhérazade, Bluebird, Little Red Riding Hood, Blue Beard, Buffoons, Ivan and his brothers

This ballet confines itself to the final part of the ballet *Sleeping beauty*, the marriage feast of Aurora and her prince. It consists of a series of novelty character dances performed by the wedding guests, among which are nobles, a retinue of fairies (from the earlier production of *The sleeping princess*), the Bluebird and Little Red Riding Hood, who join the awakened Princess Aurora dancing with her new groom Prince Florestan in an enchanted setting.

■

After the financial failure of *The sleeping princess*, Diaghilev returned to Paris in very reduced circumstances, unable to bring the production to the city as he had planned. With little money to create entirely new works, but with a loyal cohort of experienced dancers looking to him for employment, he decided to stage the final act of *The sleeping princess* as *Le Mariage d'Aurore* using the music score that he had retained. He decided to re-use a mélange of costumes from his stock, including a number of key eighteenth-century style outfits from his 1909 production of *Le Pavillon d'Armide*. Premiered with the new work, *Le Renard* (*The fox*), developed by Stravinsky and designed by Larionov, *Le Mariage d'Aurore* proved to be a popular, if artistically compromised, production that would remain in the repertoire of Diaghilev's Ballets Russes successors during the 1930s.

(opposite) **Alexandre Benois**
Overdress from costume for Aurora c 1922
© Alexandre Benois/ADAGP. Licensed by Viscopy, 2010

(above) **Unknown photographer**
Dancer wearing costume for Aurora from Aurora's wedding
page 20 in *Program for Col W de Basil's Ballets Russes, Jubilee Season, Royal Opera House Covent Garden*
National Gallery of Australia Research Library, Canberra

(top) **Unknown photographer**
Stage performance of Aurora's wedding
page 44 in *Program for Col. W. de Basil's Ballets Russes de Monte-Carlo, Royal Opera House Covent Garden, June–September 1936, third season*
National Gallery of Australia Research Library, Canberra

(above) **Unknown photographer**
Roland Guerard as the Bluebird from Aurora's wedding
page 50 in *Program for Col. W. de Basil's Ballets Russes, Jubilee Season, Royal Opera House Covent Garden*
National Gallery of Australia Research Library, Canberra

Natalia Goncharova

(above) *Costume design for the Wolf from Aurora's wedding*
page 36 in *Program for Col W de Basil's Ballets Russes de Monte-Carlo, 1936–1937 October–April, 4th American season*
National Gallery of Australia Research Library, Canberra

(opposite) *Costume for an Ivan* c 1922
© Natalia Goncharova/ADAGP. Licensed by Viscopy, 2010

146   Ballets Russes: the art of costume

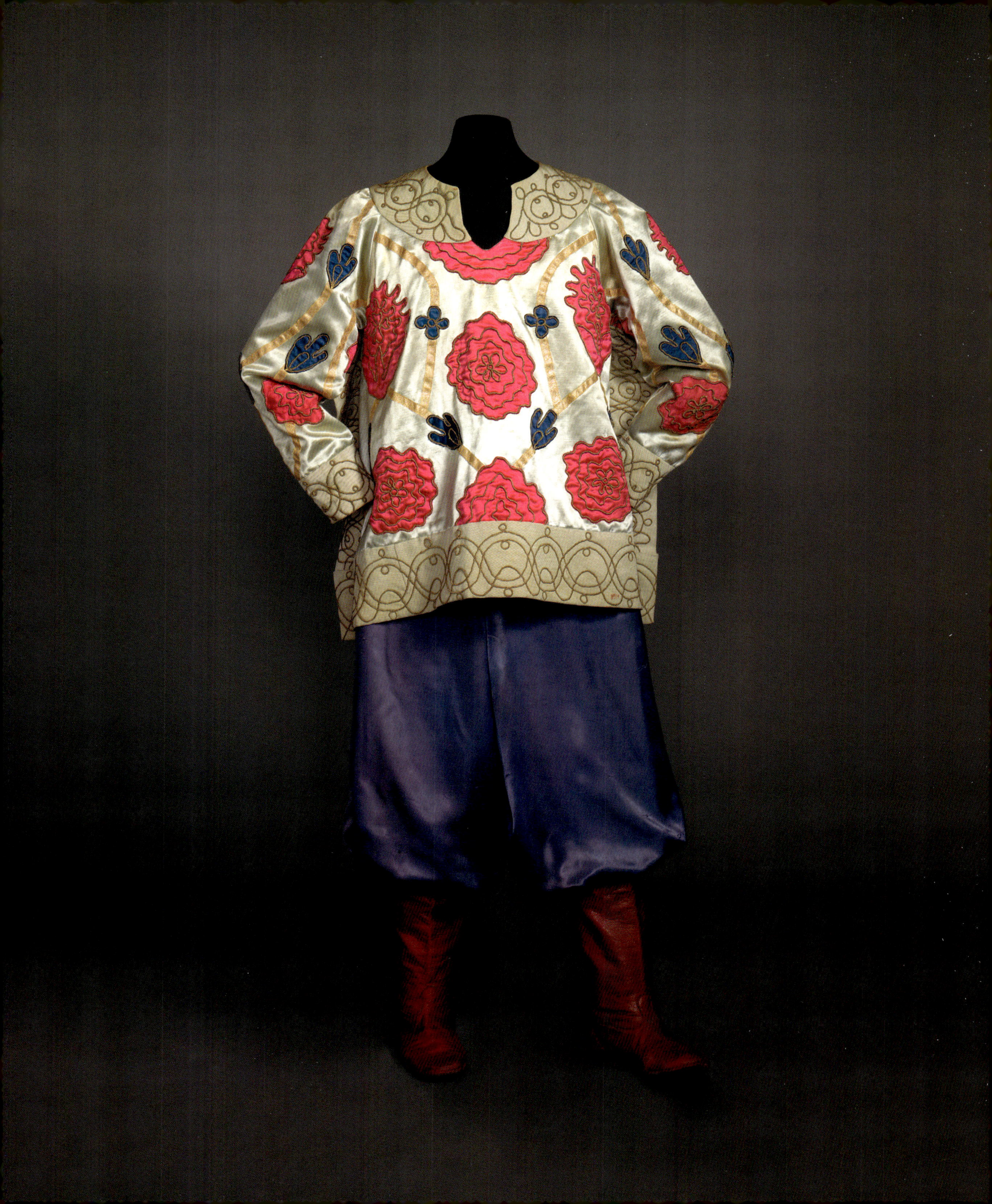

Les Tentations de la bergère (or L'Amour vainqueur)

The temptations of the shepherdess

Ballet in one act

Producer: Les Ballets Russes de Serge Diaghilev
Premiere: 3 January 1924, Théâtre de Monte Carlo, Monaco
Costume design: Juan Gris
Costumier: possibly Marie Muelle
Scenery design: Juan Gris
Music: Michel de Montéclair, arranged by Henri Casadesus
Choreography: Bronislava Nijinska
Main characters: Shepherdess, Shepherd, Marquis, Counts, Countesses, King

A shepherdess is courted by a lord. However, she prefers the attentions of the local shepherd to the nobleman. The ballet ends with the king agreeing to the Shepherdess and Shepherd's marriage union.

■

Les Tentations de la bergère, developed from an earlier interest by Diaghilev and the *miriskusniki* circle in the neoclassical and Renaissance music that was popular in Russia during the 1890s and early 1900s, particularly the dance of Michel Pignolet de Montéclair (1667–1737) which had been rearranged as *Les Plaisirs champêtres* by Henri Casadesus (1897–1947) for his Society of Ancient Instruments.[7] After hearing it, Benois proposed it as a ballet. The young Stravinsky also was impressed with the 'bucolic pleasures' of the music, and the interest shown by these two men may have persuaded Diaghilev to develop it, with Gris, into a ballet in 1924, along with the similarly eighteenth-century themed *Ballet de l'Astuce féminine / Cimarosiana* of the same season. The National Gallery's costume for the Countess from this production, with its splendid appliquéd regal *fleur-de-lys* design, may have been used for one of Diaghilev's private Fêtes Mervilleuses held in the Hall of Mirrors at the Palace of Versailles in 1923.

(top) Juan Gris
Costume design for the Marquis 1923
(above) *Costume design for Barons* 1923
(opposite) *Costume for the Countess* c 1924

148   Ballets Russes: the art of costume

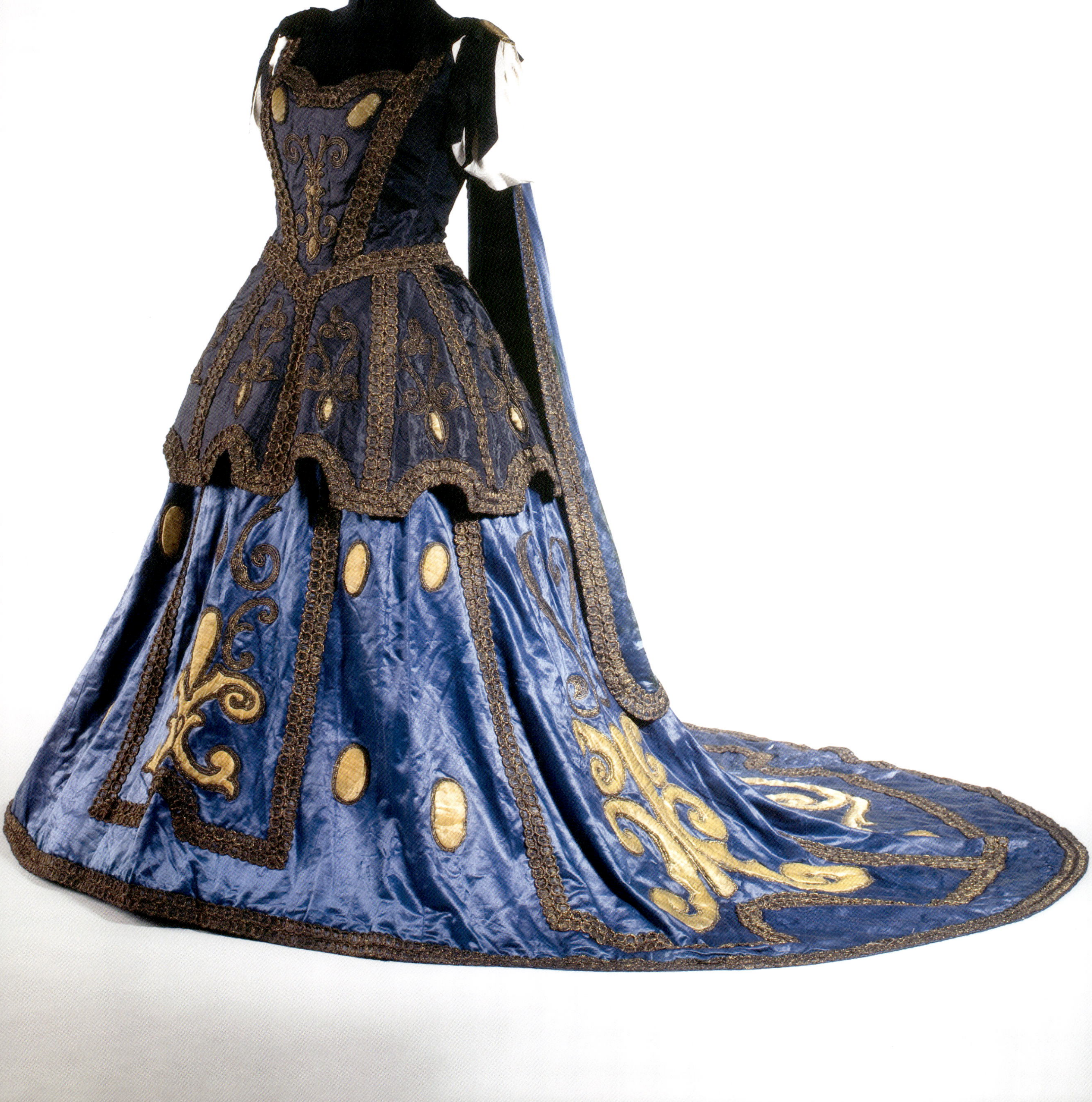

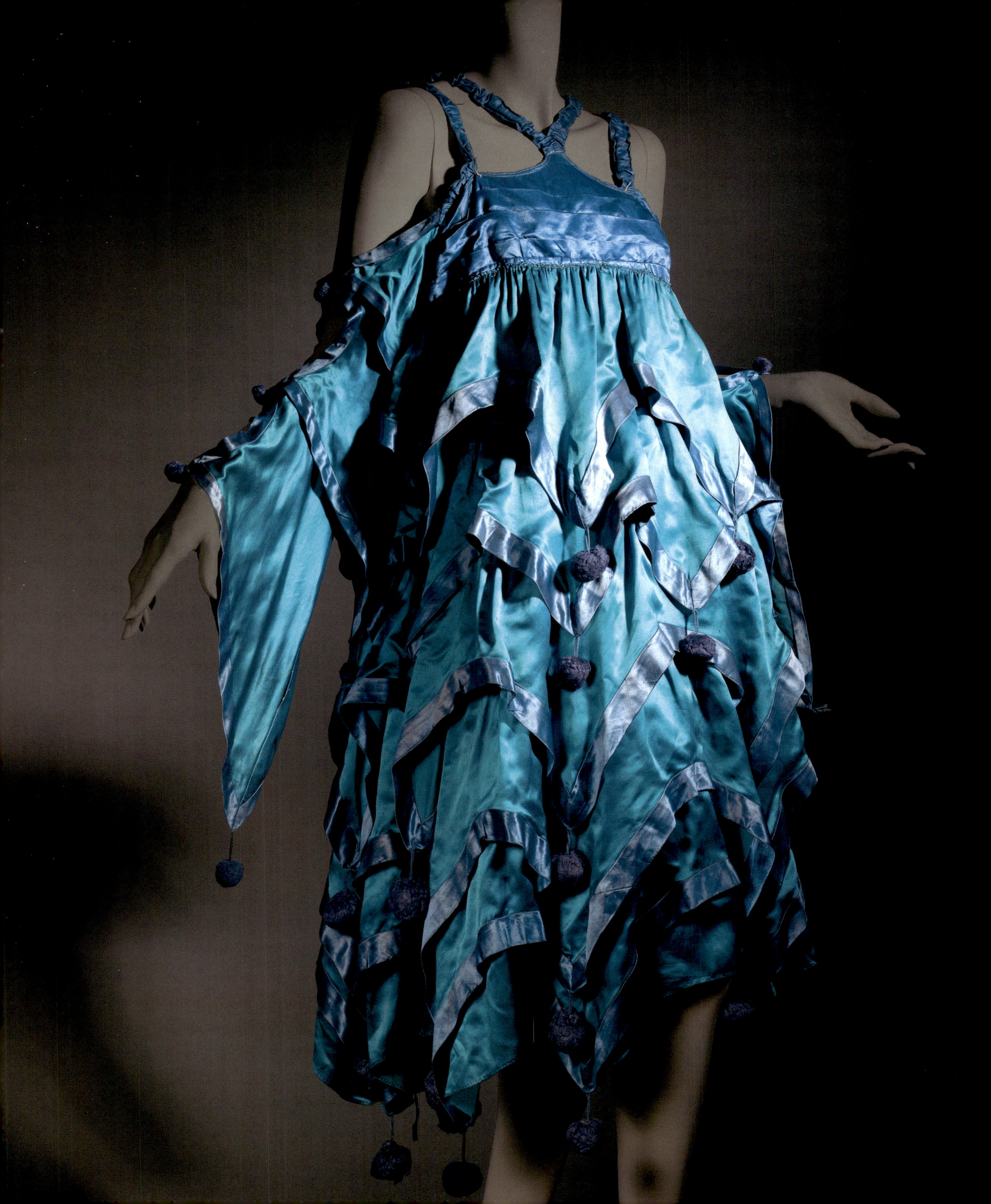

Ballet de l'Astuce féminine (Cimarosiana)
Women's wiles
Opera-ballet in three scenes

Producer: Les Ballets Russes de Serge Diaghilev
Opera premiere: 27 May 1920, Théâtre national de l'Opéra, Paris
Ballet premiere: 8 January 1924, Théâtre de l'Opéra, Monte Carlo
Costume design: José-María Sert
Costumier: Marie Muelle
Scenery design: José-María Sert
Music: Domenico Cimarosa, orchestrated by Ottorino Respighi
Choreography: Léonide Massine, with Bronislava Nijinska
Libretto: Guiseppe Palomba
Main characters: Bellina, Giampaolo, Doctor Romualdo, Leonora, Filandro

Ballet de l'Astuce féminine is set in eighteenth-century Italy, where Bellina, a wealthy Roman heiress, in accordance with her father's will must marry Giampaolo, an elderly Bergamo merchant. Her tutor, the elderly Doctor Romualdo, would like to marry her as well, although he is engaged to Bellina's governess, Leonora. Bellina likes neither one; she loves Filandro. After running away and returning, both dressed as Cossacks, the pair eventually wed.

■

The ballet was included as a choreographic divertissement in Diaghilev's 1920 opera production of the Domenico Cimarosa (1749–1801) opera *Le Astuzie femminili*, and later presented as an independent production, *Ballet de l'Astuce féminine*, in 1924, following which, in Barcelona on 24 April 1924 it was presented, and from then on known as, *Cimarosiana*. José-María Sert's scenery and costumes brought rich and humorous Surrealist elements to an overall structure of Baroque design. The ballet consists of several different folk-based dances such as a tarantella and a contre-danse in a combination of peasant Greek, opera-bouffe, *commedia dell'arte* and Sicilian styles.

José-María Sert
(opposite) *Dress* 1920–24
(above) *Costume for Pierrot* 1920–24

Costumes for Les Ballets Russes de Serge Diaghilev 1909–29

José-María Sert
(above) *Set design for Act 1 of* Ballet de l'Astuce féminine
page 23 in *Souvenir program for the Ballets Russes at L'Opéra, May–June 1920*

(right) *Costume designs for Dr Romualdo from* Ballet de l'Astuce féminine
page 27 in *Souvenir program for the Ballets Russes at L'Opéra, May–June 1920*

(opposite) *Costume for Dr Romualdo* 1920–24

152 Ballets Russes: the art of costume

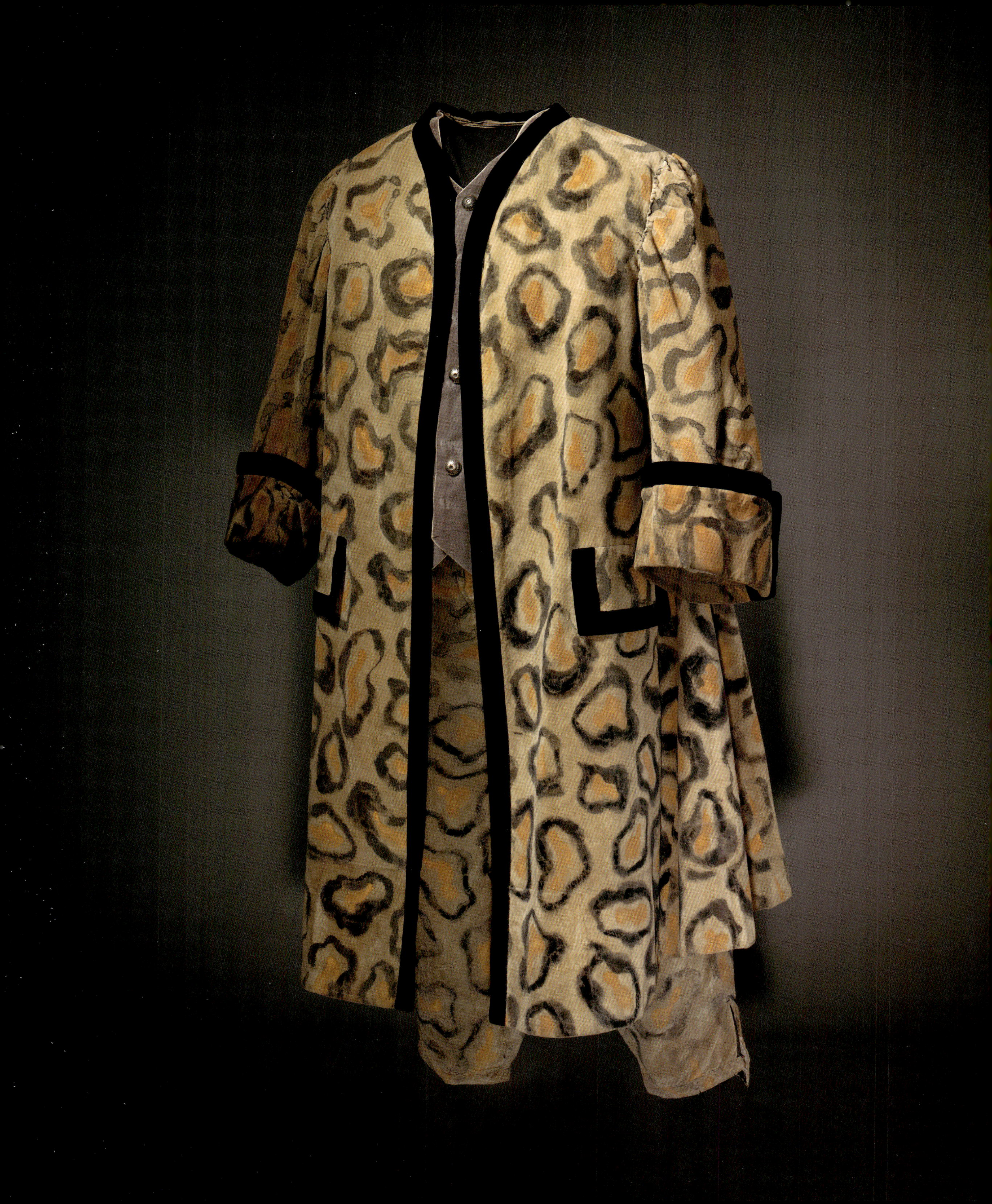

Zéphire et Flore
(Zephyr and Flora)

Ballet in three scenes

Producer:	Les Ballets Russes de Serge Diaghilev
Premiere:	28 April 1925, Théâtre de Monte Carlo, Monaco
Costume design:	Georges Braque (with additional masks by Oliver Messel in London in November 1925)
Scenery design:	Georges Braque
Music:	Vladimir Dukelsky
Choreography:	Léonide Massine
Libretto:	Boris Kochno
Main characters:	Flora, Zephyr, Boreas, Cupid, muses

This ballet is set on Greece's Mount Olympus, where Boreas, the north wind, is plotting to abduct Flora, the wife of Zephyr, the west wind. Boreas initiates a game of blind man's bluff to separate the pair and leads Zephyr off, killing him with an arrow. After he takes Flora off to his cave, she swoons from fright. Meanwhile nine mourning muses bring Zephyr's body to Olympus, where he revives after his funeral procession. The muses then tie Flora tightly to Zephyr's wrist so that she will not be lost again, and Boreas is punished.

■

Flore et Zéphire was first produced by Charles-Louis Didelot (1767–1836) in London in 1796, becoming a popular part of the ballet repertoire throughout the nineteenth century. The original ballet became famous for its introduction of technical innovations such stage machinery and strung wires to support dancers as if in flight, as well as pointe work for the female dancers. As a pre-Romantic ballet, its exploration of Anacreontic classicism found favour again during the neoclassical design revival of the 1920s.[8] Its theme of lightness, characterising Zephyr's role, also appealed to mid-1920s designers and audiences enthralled with the idea of speed and flight. The principal dancers' brief costumes allowed for enough skin exposure to emphasise the sensual athleticism of their roles, while the short, sequinned, flapper-style shifts for the muses gave them a fashionable, if unflattering, modernity. Oliver Messel's bronzed papier-mâché masks de-emphasised the dancers' personalities, adding to the pared-back classicism of the production.

Georges Braque
(top) *Overskirt from costume for Zephyr* c 1925

(centre) *Cap from costume for Zephyr* c 1925

(above) *Helmet from costume for Boreas* c 1925
© Georges Braque/ADAGP. Licensed by Viscopy, 2010

(opposite) **Eileen Mayo**
Serge Lifar as Boreas in Zéphire et Flore *plate 1 from* Serge Lifar *1928*
National Gallery of Australia Research Library, Canberra, Feint Collection

Costumes for Les Ballets Russes de Serge Diaghilev 1909–29

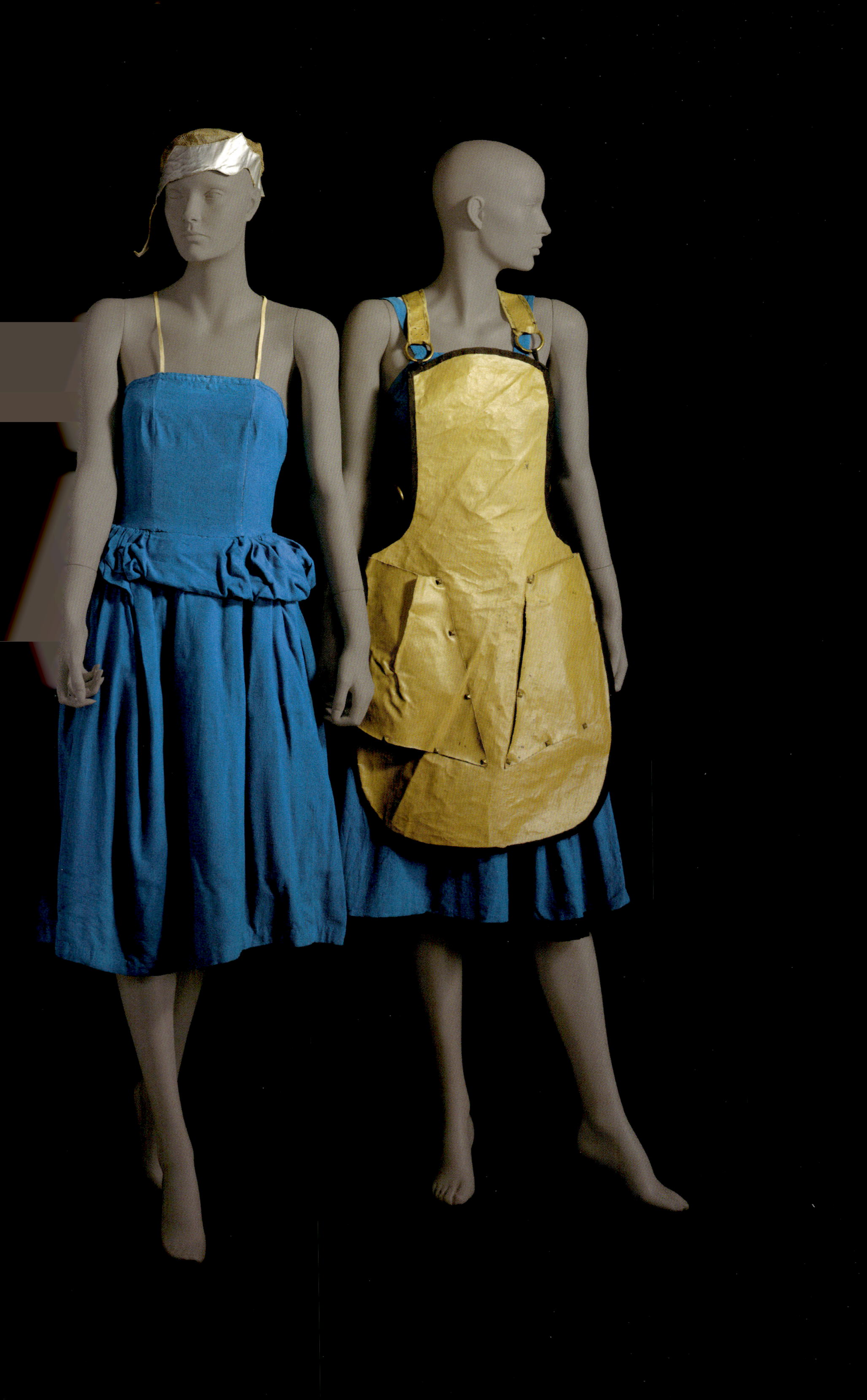

Le Pas d'acier
Step of steel
Ballet in two scenes

Producer:	Les Ballets Russes de Serge Diaghilev
Premiere:	7 June 1927, Théâtre Sarah Bernhardt, Paris
Costume design:	Georgy Yakulov
Costumier:	A Youkine
Scenery design:	Georgy Yakulov
Music:	Serge Prokofiev
Choreography:	Léonide Massine
Libretto:	Serge Prokofiev, Georgy Yakulov
Main characters:	The Sailor, the Worker Girl, male and female workers, peasants

The first act is set in a train station during the Russian famine. The train station was a common representation of change, transition and progress in early Soviet art. This first section introduces the hero and heroine, the Sailor and the Worker Girl, as a pair of lovers. The second act is set in a multi-level factory where the lovers are separated. The second half of the ballet revolves around the pair trying to reconnect. Eventually they are set to work together and their love is celebrated by the other workers.

■

The ballet scenario is a metaphor for the transformation of the Soviet Union into an industrialised nation. It was the only Ballets Russes production to have both a Soviet revolutionary theme and a Constructivist design and was originally titled *Ursignol*, the combination of 'URSS' (French for USSR) and 'gnol' from the end of *rossignol* (nightingale)—a reference to Diaghilev's 1914 production of Stravinsky's opera *Le Rossignol* (*The nightingale*). Its title has been variously translated as 'Steel dance', 'Step of steel' and 'The steel leap'. While the ballet celebrated the ideal of the Bolshevik state and the supposed nobility of an industrialised society in transition from rural poverty to collective wealth, in the rich Western context in which it was received it represented a soulless, exploitative and grim future. The costumes are asymmetrically-cut workers' clothes in synthetic ponyskin and coarse, plain, rust, grey and blue fabrics, overlaid with aprons in the industrial imitation leather fabric known as in the 1920s as 'American cloth'. The ballet was not popular with its anti-Bolshevik émigré Russian Paris audience and also suffered against the film *Metropolis*, by German director Fritz Lang, which had premiered in Berlin five months earlier (although with wider release not until 1928). The film's depiction of the harshness of an industrial future for society, clothed in a stylistic extension of fashionable Art Deco design, had the advantage of powerful and emotional visual narrative in a period where the cinema was capturing the attention of audiences from all classes of society.

(opposite) **Georgy Yakulov**
Two costumes for female workers c 1927

(top) **Eileen Mayo**
Serge Lifar in Le Pas d'acier, plate 12 from *Serge Lifar* 1928

(above) **Unknown photographer**
Model of set of Le Pas d'acier
page 6 in *Souvenir program XXI Saison des Ballets Russes de Serge Diaghilev* 1928
National Gallery of Australia Research Library, Canberra, Feint Collection

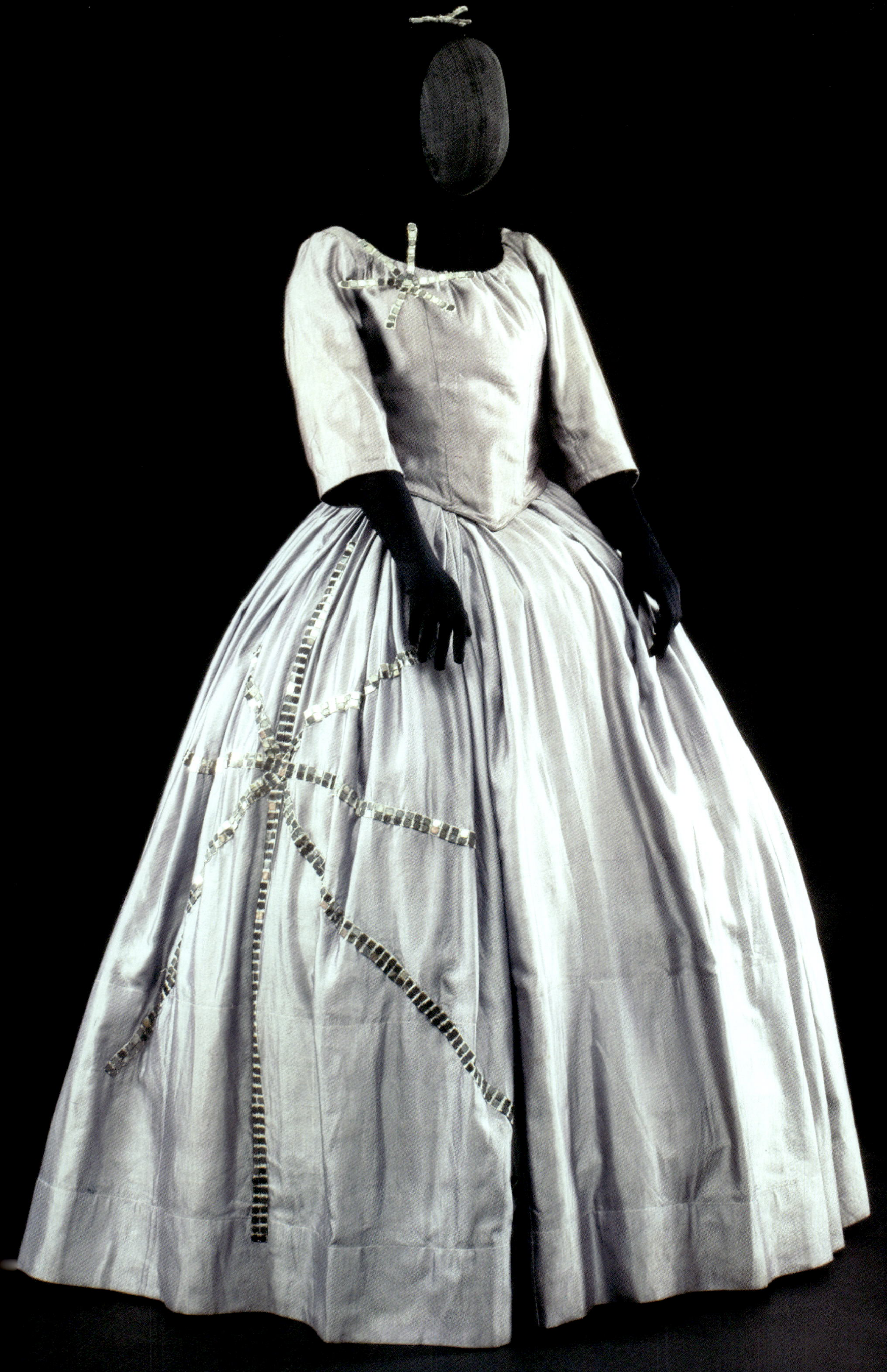

Ode

Spectacle in three acts

Producer:	Les Ballets Russes de Serge Diaghilev
Premiere:	6 June 1928, Théâtre Sarah Bernhardt, Paris
Costume design:	Pavel Tchelitchew and Pierre Charbonnier
Costumier:	A Youkine
Scenery design:	Pavel Tchelitchew and Pierre Charbonnier
Music:	Nikolai Nabokov
Choreography:	Léonide Massine
Libretto:	Boris Kochno, after *Spiritual odes* by Mikhail Lomonosov
Main characters:	Nature, the Pupil, constellations, stars, rivers

Nature, originally presented as a statue on a pedestal, comes to life and descends in answer to a student's questions. He asks Nature to display her power over the constellations, the rivers, planets and humankind. However, after these displays the student is not satisfied and begs Nature for a glimpse of her festival—the Aurora Borealis. Mesmerised by the beauty and wonder of this display, the student attempts to enter the Aurora Borealis, only to destroy it. The ballet ends with Nature returning to her statue form.

■

Billed as 'an evening meditation on the majesty of God on the occasion of an apparition of the Aurora Borealis', this ballet is based on Mikhail Lomonosov's eighteenth-century hymn of the same name dedicated to the Russian Empress Elizabeth. Diaghilev's original brief for this ballet was that it be presented in the manner of an eighteenth-century court spectacular as homage to the empress, from whom he claimed he was descended. However, his commissioning of Tchelitchew, an innovative young artist who had studied with the stage designer Alexandra Exter, drove the design in the distinctly different direction of radical Constructivism. Tchelitchew's stage design placed the dancers in formations among three-dimensional geometric delineations of the stage area formed by white cords, along which miniaturised puppet versions of the dancers were placed to simulate perspective. The costumes, crinoline-skirted dresses with mesh masks or fitted bodysuits in black, white, grey and blue gauzy fabrics, were appliquéd with geometric designs of mirrored paillettes or painted with phosphorescent paint in angular designs. The balletic action was set before a cinema screen on which projected moving images and rear-projected lighting provided a changing and visually dynamic spectacle for the audience. The overall effect was a celebration of the projected, reflected, diffused and sparkling qualities of light itself in a revolutionary piece of theatre design, although as a choreographic performance its rigidity did not endear it to audiences already used to the more dynamic entertainment they were seeing in movie theatres.

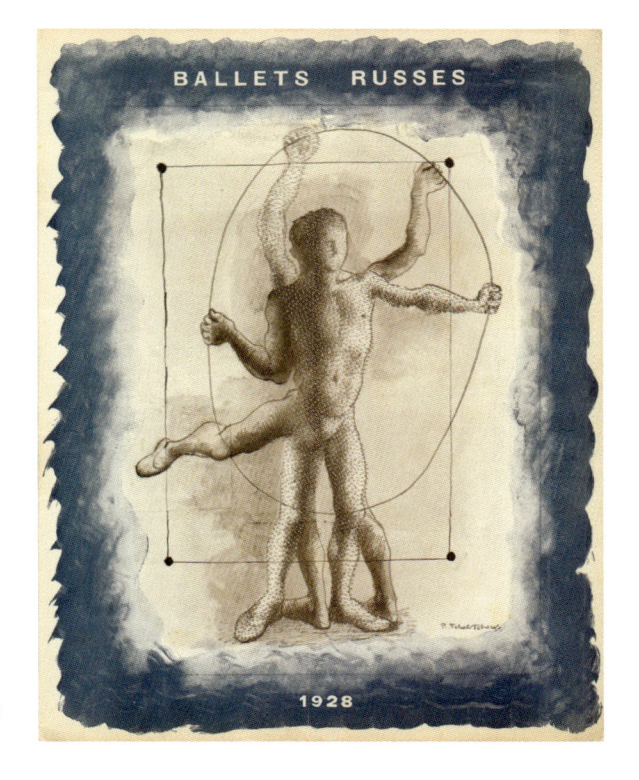

(opposite) **Pavel Tchelitchew**
Costume for a star c 1928

(above) cover of *Souvenir program XXI Saison des Ballets Russes de Serge Diaghilev* 1928

(above) **Boris Lipnitzki**
Scene from Ode 1928
SAEML Parisienne de Photographie
© Boris Lipnitzki/Roger Viollet

(far right) *Drawing for* Ode
page 28 in *Souvenir program
XXI Saison des Ballets Russes
de Serge Diaghilev* 1928

(right) **Eileen Mayo**
Serge Lifar in Ode
plate 14 from *Serge Lifar* 1928
National Gallery of Australia
Research Library, Canberra

(opposite) **Pavel Tchelitchew**
Costume for a constellation
c 1928

160 Ballets Russes: the art of costume

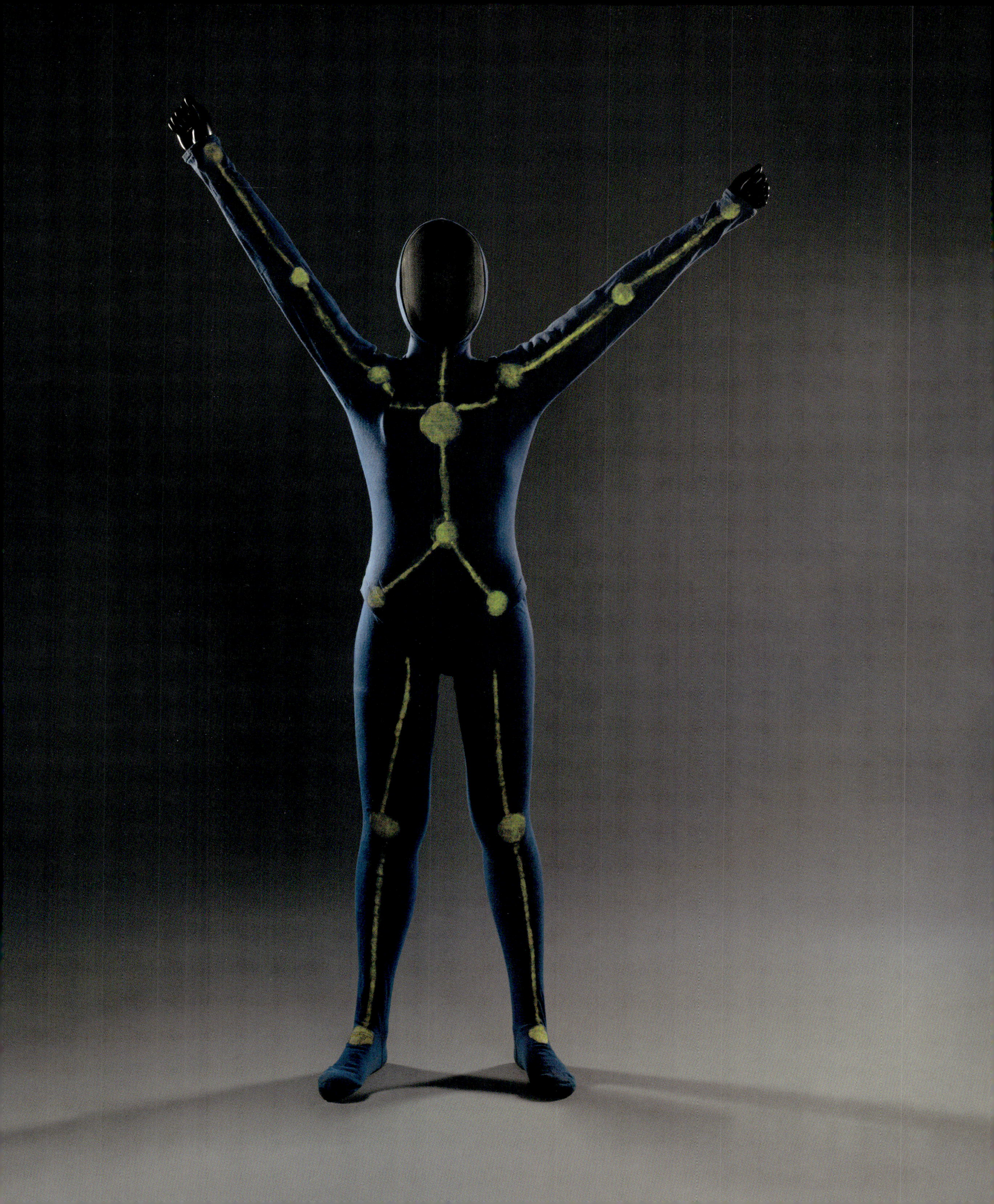

Le Bal
The ball

Ballet in one act and two scenes

Producer:	Les Ballets Russes de Serge Diaghilev
Premiere:	7 May 1929, Théâtre de Monte Carlo, Monaco
Costume design:	Giorgio de Chirico
Costumier:	A Youkine
Scenery design:	Giorgio de Chirico
Music:	Vittorio Rieti
Choreography:	George Balanchine
Libretto:	Boris Kochno, after a novel by Count Vladimir Sollogub
Main characters:	The Lady, the Young Man, the Astrologer, the Sylphides, the Italian guests, the Spanish guests, the Statue

A young man, dressed as a military officer, attends a masked ball where he meets a beautiful masked lady accompanied by an old astrologer, and falls in love with her, even as she flirts with his rival, a young Italian man. While overseen by the ballroom's giant classical statue, which is possessed of magical powers, the sylphides mischievously dress to imitate the couple in order to confuse their suitors. The young man finally persuades the lady to remove her mask and is dismayed to see her as an old woman. He tries to leave but she pursues him, and as the ball ends the old woman leaves on the arm of the astrologer. As she passes the young officer she and the astrologer both remove further masks, revealing them as a beautiful young couple. Attempting to follow them, the dazed young officer is held back by the statue to contemplate his behaviour.

■

While the Italian Surrealist painter, Giorgio de Chirico, had worked in theatre design since 1924, his commission from Diaghilev for *Le Bal* gave him his most public success. As a version of the popular theme of the masked ball, the story's dreamlike quality explored the nature of duplicity, ambiguity and deception. De Chirico drew upon his interest in desolate, unpeopled built spaces for his design of the ballroom, an austere room with exaggerated cornices, strangely proportioned openings and scattered with fragments of classical architecture. This theme is echoed in the guests' costumes, rendering each performer a moveable element of an architectural ensemble. Jackets and trousers became pilasters and columns, shirts and dresses roughly sketched examples of the classical orders. Their complexity and weight was further laden with stuccoed wigs for the dancers, adding to an air of ossified antiquity even though Balanchine's choreography was light and acrobatic. While the radicalism of rational modernism was taking hold in the late 1920s in Europe, de Chirico's work for *Le Bal* is a vivid example of the Italian Novecento design movement that returned classicism to mainstream taste during the 1920s. It also echoed Diaghilev's lifelong admiration for Italian history, and gained particular poignancy as his last production before his death in Venice one month after the closure of the ballet's London season.

(top) **Giorgio de Chirico**
Jacket from costume for the Young Man c 1929
© Giorgio de Chirico/SIAE. Licensed by Viscopy, 2010

(above) **Numa Blanc Fils**
Anton Dolin and Alexandra Danilova in Le Bal
page 23 in *Souvenir program XXIIe Saison des Ballets Russes de Serge Diaghilev* 1929

(opposite) **Giorgio de Chirico**
Costume for a male guest c 1929
© Giorgio de Chirico/SIAE. Licensed by Viscopy, 2010

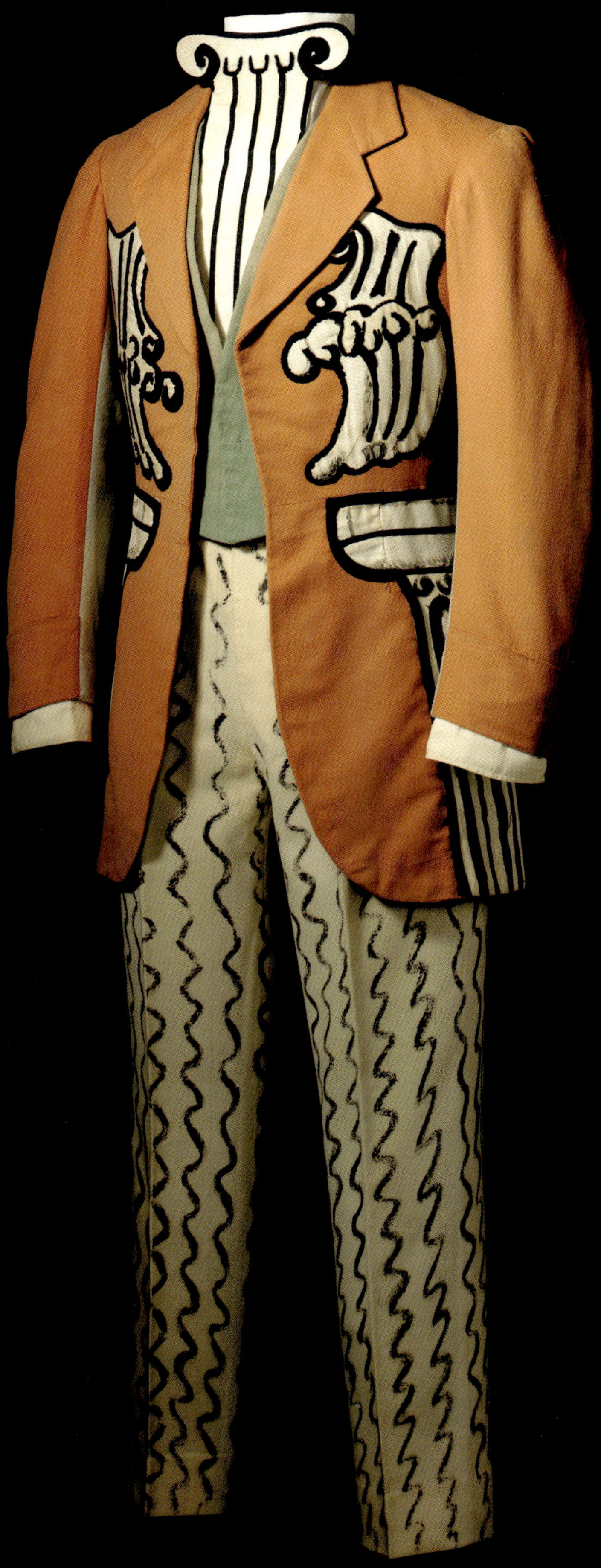

COSTUMES OF COLONEL DE BASIL'S BALLETS RUSSES
DE MONTE CARLO 1932–39

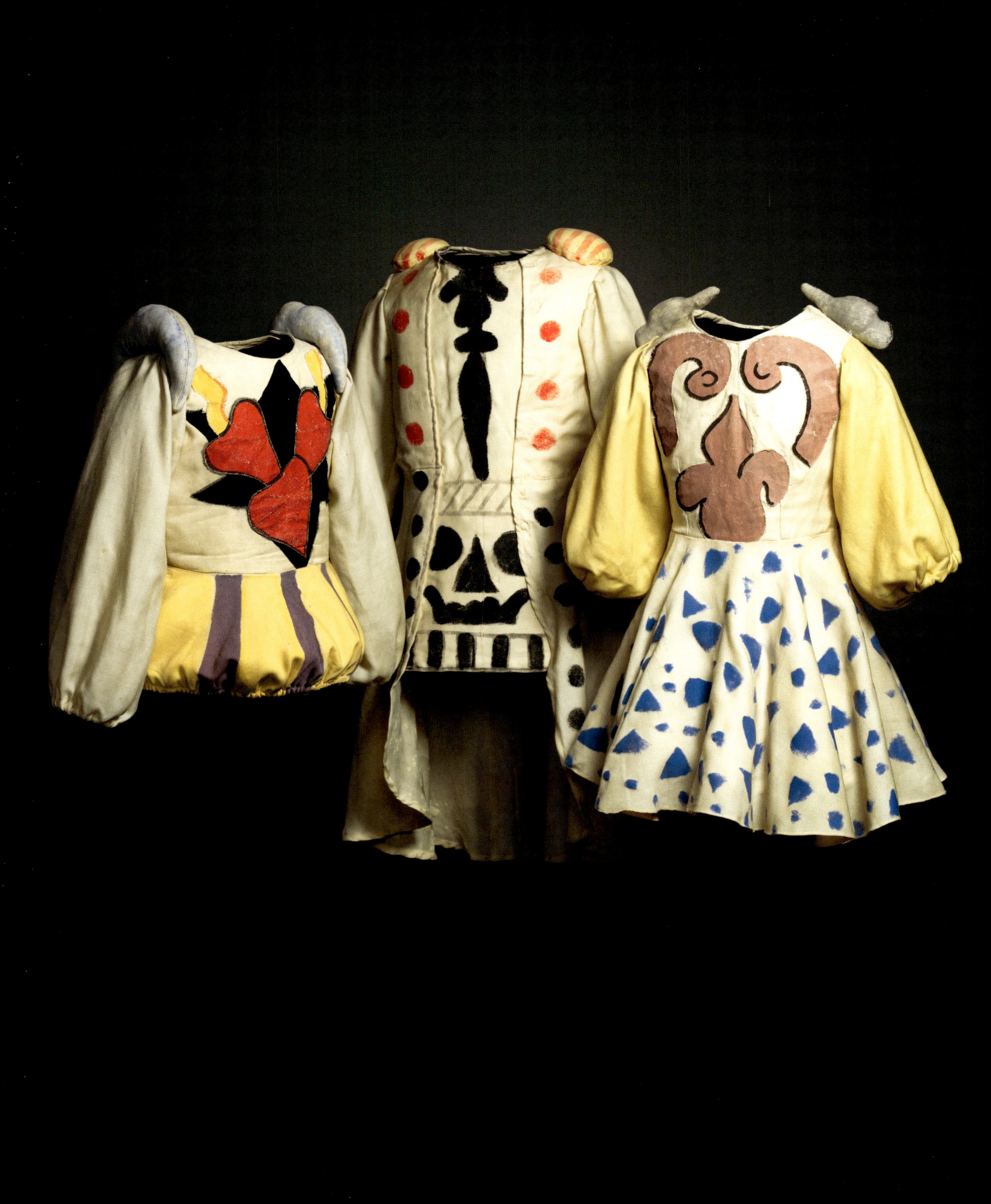

Pulcinella

Ballet in one act

Original producer: Les Ballets Russes de Serge Diaghilev
Premiere: 15 May 1920, Théâtre national de l'Opéra, Paris
Revival producer: Ballet de l'Opéra Russe à Paris
Premiere: April 1931, Théâtre national de l'Opéra, Paris
Revival producer: Ballets Russes de Monte Carlo
Premiere: 1932, Théâtre de Monte Carlo, Monaco
Costume design: Giorgio de Chirico
Scenery design: Giorgio de Chirico
Music: Igor Stravinsky, after Giovanni Battista Pergolesi
Choreography: Boris Romanov
Libretto: Igor Stravinsky
Main characters: Pulcinella, Pimpinella

All the young ladies of the country are in love with Pulcinella. Their suitors are extremely jealous and attempt to kill him but are deceived by his double, pretending to lie dead. Believing to have made a success of their plan, all the young men disguise themselves as Pulcinella and come to woo the young girls. The real Pulcinella, disguised as a magician, 'revives' the corpse, reveals the joke and blesses their all marriages. He is then married to the prettiest, his mistress, Pimpinella.

■

This ballet was originally conceived by Diaghilev following his research into eighteenth-century Italian composers during his frequent visits to Italy during the First World War. He persuaded Stravinsky to develop the ballet story and Pergolesi's music, stimulating a neoclassical phase in the composer's work. Picasso was the designer for Diaghilev's 1920 production, but for the 1931 revival the Italian Surrealist painter, Giorgio de Chirico, was commissioned by the Ballet de l'Opéra Russe à Paris as set and costume designer. Invoking the overdrawn character stereotypes of traditional Italian *commedia dell'arte*, de Chirico's costume designs were simplified eighteenth-century models decorated with cartoonish painted and appliquéd designs. The National Gallery of Australia's costumes, for Death and several other unspecified characters, are most likely from the 1931 and 1932 productions, of which few details are recorded.

Giorgio de Chirico
(opposite left to right) *Tunic, coat for Death and dress* 1932

(above) *Back of coat for Death* 1932
© Giorgio de Chirico/SIAE. Licensed by Viscopy, 2010

Costumes of Colonel de Basil's Ballets Russes de Monte Carlo 1931–40

Les Présages
Destiny

Choreographic symphony in four scenes

Producer:	Les Ballets Russes de Monte Carlo
Premiere:	13 April 1933, Théâtre de Monte Carlo, Monaco
Costume design:	André Masson
Costumier:	Barbara Karinska
Scenery design:	André Masson
Music:	Pyotr Il'yich Tchaikovsky (*Fifth symphony in E minor*)
Choreography:	Léonide Massine
Libretto:	Léonide Massine
Main characters:	First movement: Action, Temptation, Movement
	Second movement: Passion, Fate, Destinies
	Third movement: Frivolity, Variation
	Fourth movement: Passion, Frivolity, Action, Fate, The Hero, Destinies

Humanity's struggle with destiny is represented in the four scenes of this ballet. The first scene, Action, is devoted to life's diversions, desires and temptation. The second scene, Passion, explores the contest between the base emotion of passion and the purity of love, which triumphs after an extensive battle. In the third scene, Frivolity, destiny is momentarily forgotten with the distractions of frivolity. Lastly, in War, heroes are eventually victorious and triumph over the evils of war.

■

Masson is celebrated as an avant-garde artist, and prominent in the Surrealist movement after the First World War. His innovative designs for the radical production *Les Présages* were made in 1932 and 1933 in a first attempt at giving visual structure to a symphonic ballet. Instead of narrative, Massine and Masson presented ideas and allegorical characters which reflected primordial gestures and movements. It was conceived to represent no particular time or place, rather an expression of universal emotions, driven by the controversial use of Tchaikovsky's *Fifth symphony in E minor* as its score. The backdrop of Masson's expressionist set was painted in flickering and swirling flame-like images, almost as a diagram for Massine's handling of the dancers as a single organism. While the costume designs are locked into 1930s Futurism (H G Wells's *The shape of things to come* was published in the same year), their jagged patterns and sometimes bitter colour orchestrations in the massed and undulating structures of Massine's choreography brought an almost architectural energy to the stage. This production was seen in Australia only three years after its European premiere, providing audiences with a direct and visceral experience of Modernism in ballet that was being constructed on Diaghilev's legacy.

(above) **Unknown photographer**
Scene from Les Présages *page 48 in* Souvenir program for Col. W. de Basil's Ballet, Australia–New Zealand 1939–40
National Gallery of Australia Research Library, Canberra

(opposite left to right) **André Masson**
Jacket for costume for a male (Scene 1); *Dress for costume for a female (in Scene 1)*; *Dress from costume for Action*; *Dress from costume for a female (in Scene 2)*; and *Jacket for costume for a male (Scene 1)* 1933
© André Masson/ADAGP. Licensed by Viscopy, 2010

168 Ballets Russes: the art of costume

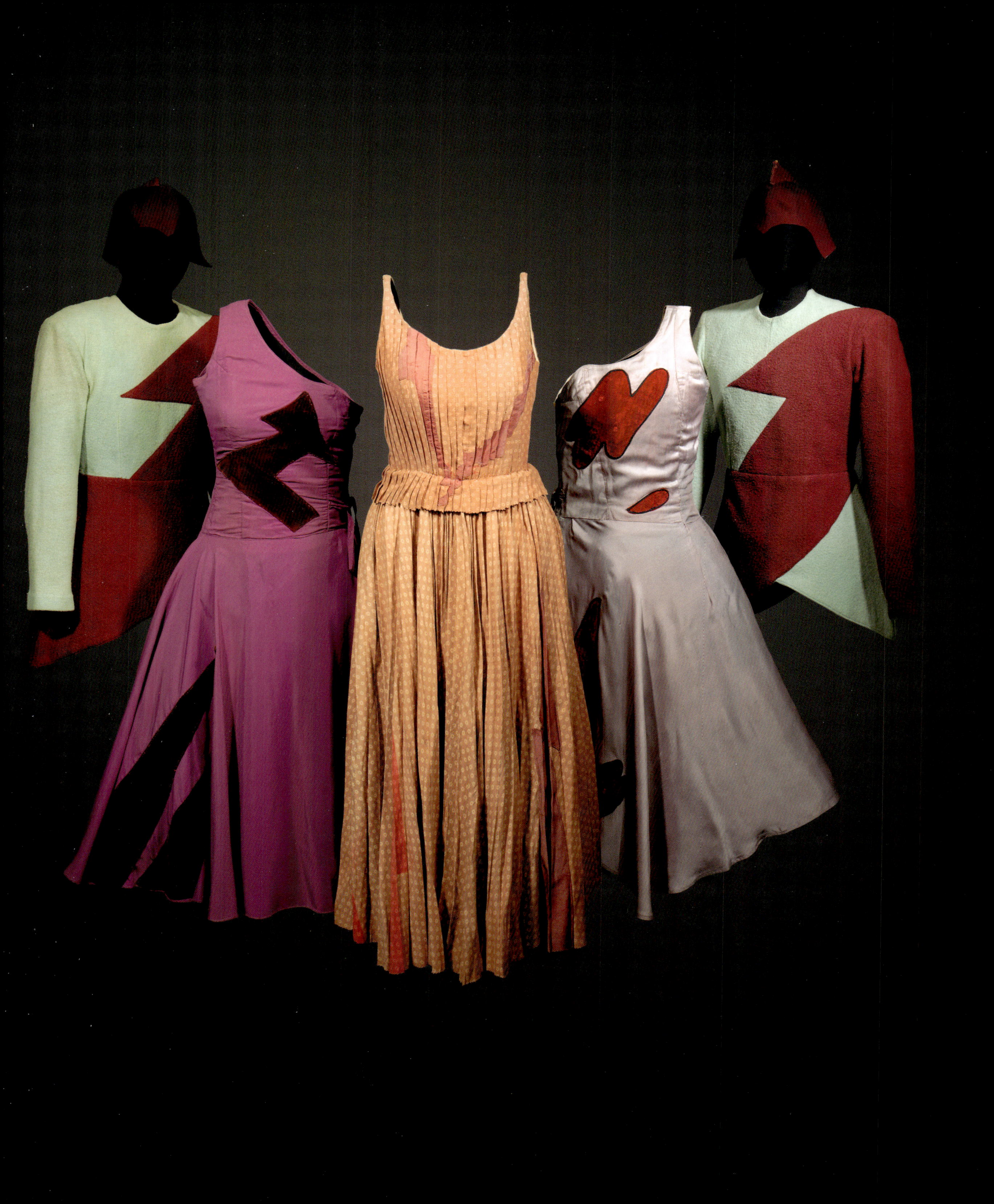

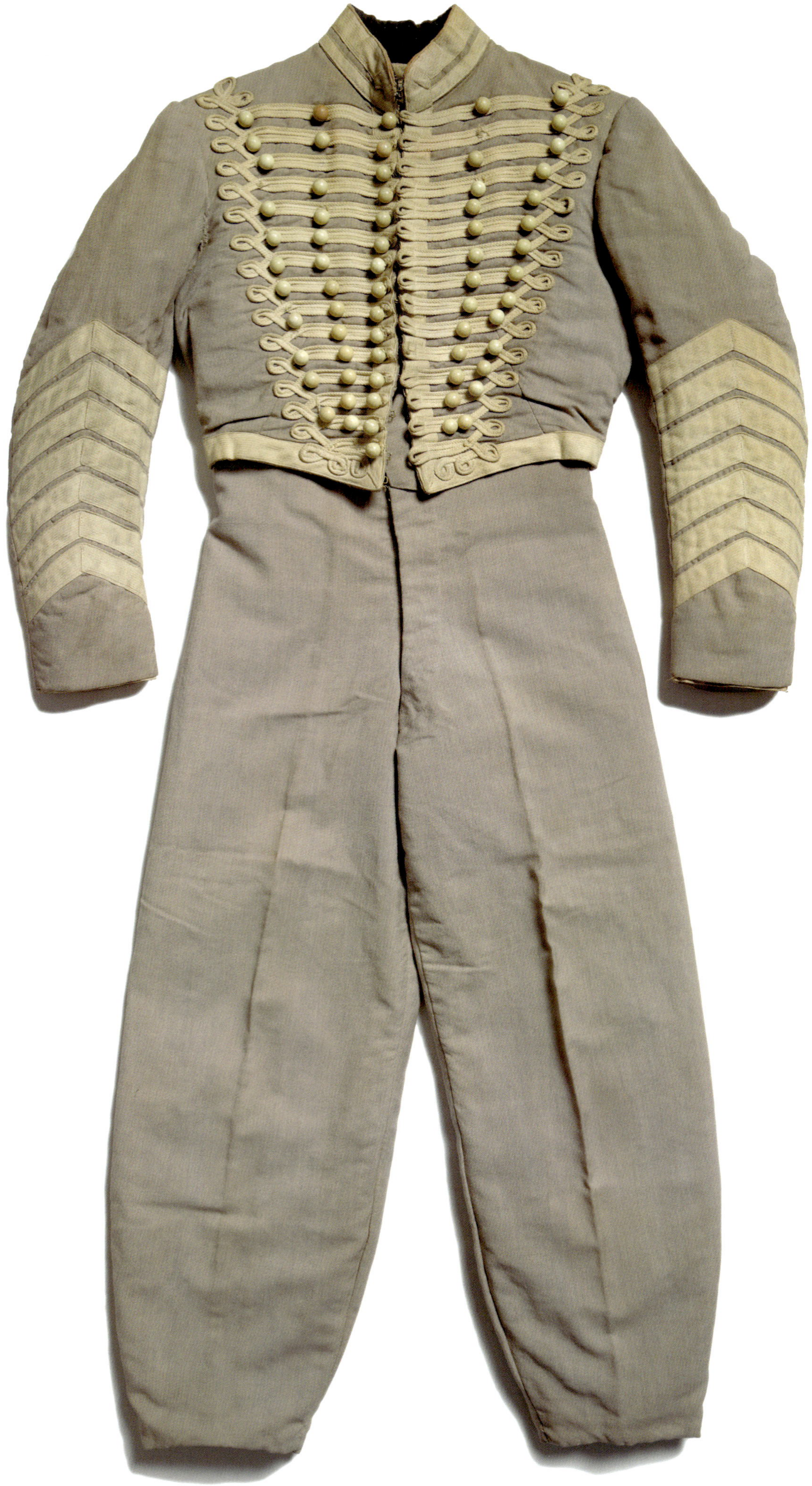

Le Beau Danube
The beautiful Danube

Ballet in one act and two scenes

Producer:	Ballets Russes de Monte Carlo
Premiere:	15 April 1933
Venue:	Théâtre de Monte Carlo, Monaco
Costume design:	Count Etienne de Beaumont
Scenery design:	Vladimir and Elisabeth Polunin, after Constantin Guys
Music:	Johan Strauss, arranged by Roger Désormière
Choreography:	Léonide Massine
Libretto:	Léonide Massine
Main characters:	The Mother, the Father, the Street Dancer, the Eldest Daughter, younger daughters, the Hussar, the Athlete, the Manager, the Artist, the First Hand, the Gardener, dandies, seamstresses, needlewomen, ladies of the town, salesmen

Set in the summer of 1860, the ballet opens in the Wiener Prater, a large public park in Vienna. A variety of Viennese citizens are out enjoying the sunshine—included in the crowd are artists, dandies, street performers, and a young hussar who meets and courts a beautiful young girl who is in the park with her aristocratic parents. One of the street performers, a young female dancer, recognises the hussar as a former lover and interrupts the courtship. The young girl faints from the emotional shock and is led away by her parents, while the dancer and hussar renew their acquaintance. The young girl returns and fights the dancer for the hussar's affection. Finally the dancer retreats and all is forgiven between the hussar and the girl. The ballet ends with all the park-goers dancing in celebration, including the young dancer who has accepted the situation.

■

This work, with choreography and libretto both by Massine, was based on the ballet *Le Beau Danube bleu*, created by Massine in 1924 for Count Etienne de Beaumont's *Les Soirées de Paris*. The Ballet Russe de Monte Carlo revived it in 1933 and it was included in the Monte Carlo Russian Ballet Australian tour of 1936 and again in 1940, when it was re-named *Le Danube bleu*.[1] De Beaumont's costume design reflected his knowledge and understanding of mid nineteenth-century Viennese fashion and manners, with light and elegant outfits for the main characters contrasting with earthier traditional dress for the street characters, all set against the open expanses of his interpretation of the Prater's formal elegance.

Etienne de Beaumont
(opposite) *Costume for the Huzzar* c 1933

(top) *Costume for a lady* c 1933

(above) **Sasha**
Tatiana Riabouchinska and Léonide Massine (in costumes designed by Etienne de Beaumont for Le Beau Danube) page 37 in *Program for Ballets Russes du Col. W. de Basil, Royal Opera House Covent Garden*
National Gallery of Australia Research Library, Canberra

Le Tricorne
The three-cornered hat

Ballet in one act

Original producer:	Les Ballets Russes de Serge Diaghilev
Premiere:	22 July 1919, Alhambra Theatre, London
Revival producer:	Les Ballets Russes de Monte Carlo
Revival premiere:	20 February 1934, Auditorium Theatre, Chicago
Costume design:	Pablo Picasso
Scenery design:	Pablo Picasso
Music:	Manuel de Falla
Choreography:	Léonide Massine
Libretto:	Gregorio Martínez Sierra, after a novella by Pedro Alarcón
Main characters:	The Miller, the Miller's Wife, the Corregidor, the Corregidor's Wife, the Dandy, Alguacile

This ballet is a love story set in the eighteenth century in a small Spanish village, where a miller and his wife, although very much in love, flirt with passers-by in order to test each other's affection. One of these passers-by is the Corregidor, governor of the province, who is travelling with his entourage. Attracted by the miller's wife, he begins to court her. Although she initially leads him on, once her husband returns she makes fun of him as being old and ridiculous. The angry Corregidor leaves, promising revenge on the couple for this humiliation. He returns with his officers, who arrest the miller. After they have left, the Corregidor attempts to grab the miller's wife, who runs away. Although he chases after her she eludes him, trips him into a stream and runs off, frightened. Drenched, the Corregidor enters the mill, undresses and hangs his clothes out to dry before retiring to the miller's bed for a nap. The miller returns and, seeing the Corregidor's clothes, steals them, replacing them with his own and a note. The Corregidor is forced to leave in the miller's clothes to the taunts of the villagers.

■

Pedro Antonio de Alarcón y Ariza's (1833–1891) Andalusian story, *El sombrero de tres picos* (*The three-cornered hat* 1874), inspired Diaghilev and Massine's 1919 Ballets Russes production of this classic tale. Having immersed themselves in Spanish dance and music during their sojourn in Spain, and with their successful collaboration with Pablo Picasso, the production was a critical and enduring success. Massine's revival in 1934, using the sets and costumes from Diaghilev's 1919 production, placed the ballet in the heightened international consciousness of Spain at the time of its bitter civil war. The National Gallery's *Le Tricorne* works are elements of costumes for unspecified male dancers, most likely in the corps de ballet, and are probably from the 1934 revivals, as it is known that almost no original costumes survive from the 1919 production. Based on Picasso's original designs, they still retain something of the character, pattern and colour organisation of his original vision for this landmark production.

(top) **Pablo Picasso**
Breeches 1919–c 33
© Pablo Picasso/Succession Picasso. Licensed by Viscopy, 2010

(above) **Lachmann**
Pablo Picasso working on the curtain for Le Tricorne *1917*
page 35 in *Program of the Ballets Russes de Serge de Diaghilev, December 1920, Théâtre des Champs-Élysées*

Pablo Picasso
(opposite top) *Bolero jacket* 1919–c 33

(opposite) *Vest and shorts* 1919–c 33
© Pablo Picasso/Succession Picasso. Licensed by Viscopy, 2010

Costumes of Colonel de Basil's Ballets Russes de Monte Carlo 1931–40 173

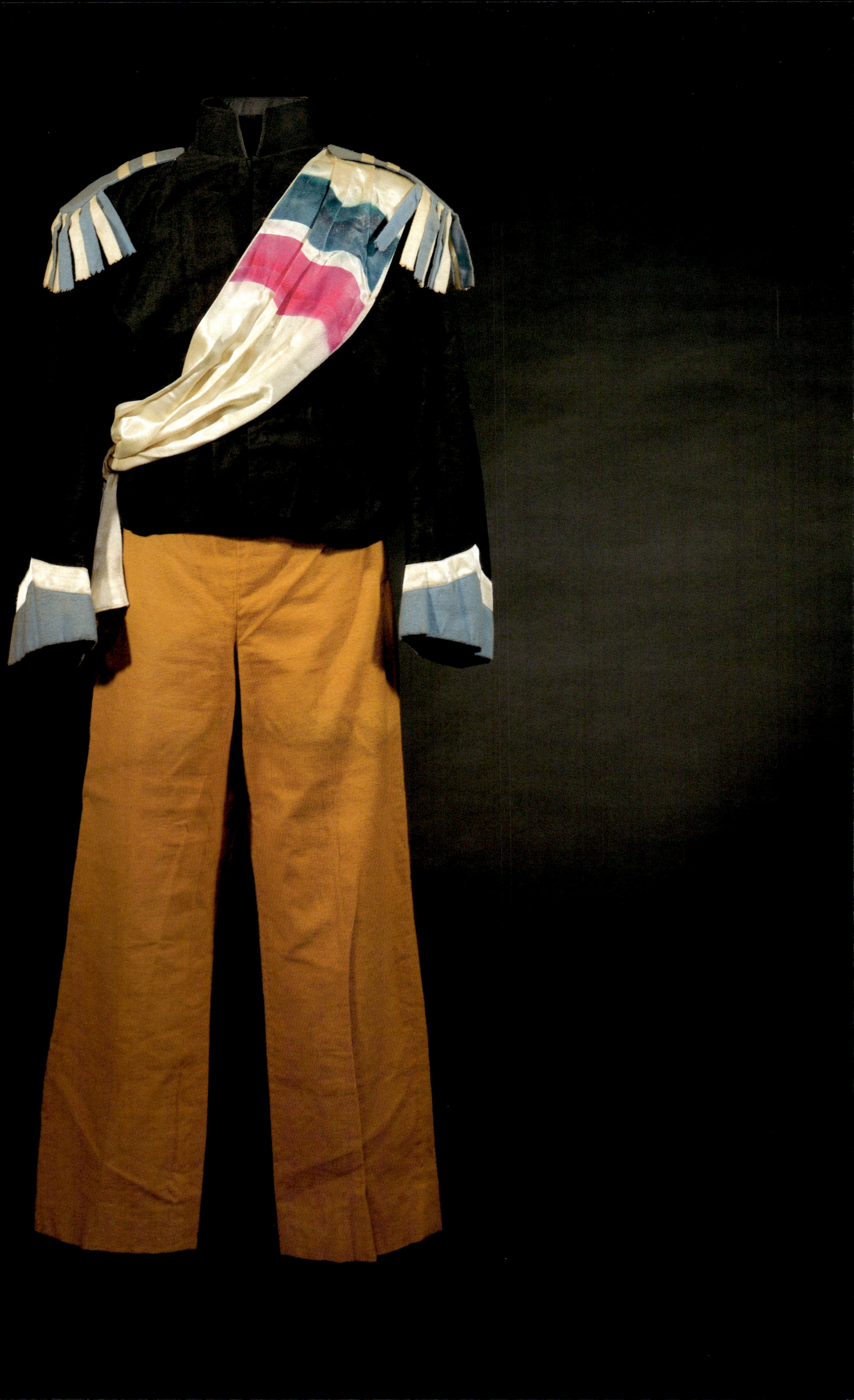

Jardin public
The public gardens

Producer:	Monte Carlo Ballet Russe
Premiere:	8 March 1935
Venue:	Auditorium Theatre, Chicago
Costume design:	Jean Lurçat, with Alice Halicka re-design in 1936
Costumier:	Helen Pons
Scenery design:	Jean Lurçat
Music:	Vladimir Dukelsky
Choreography:	Léonide Massine
Libretto:	Vladimir Dukelsky and Léonide Massine, from a fragment of *The counterfeiters* by André Gide
Main characters:	The Statue, the Old Roué, the Poet, the Suicidal Man, the Old Couple, the Poor Couple, the Rich Couple, the Chair Vendor, the Vision, sweepers, nurses, schoolboys, workmen

The ballet, set in a public park, opens in the early morning as the park is opened for the day by the sweeper. The ballet traces the interaction of the people who frequent the park over the course of the day. Several nurses with small children enter, pursued by an elderly rake. A large group of schoolboys precede a poet who is analysing the park surroundings in search of inspiration. Workers also gather to eat their lunch. A suicidal man enters along with two pairs of lovers, one rich and one poor. The rich lovers dance with the poet and the suicidal man, ending with the latter shooting himself in the head. Before dusk an elderly couple enter to reminisce on their love affair. The poor lovers snatch the elderly woman's purse. A military band heralds the park's evening festivities. The characters continue to interact—the rich and the poor couples fight and the workers join with the poor couple. In the finale the poor couple return the stolen purse and all are reconciled.

■

This ballet is based on a fragment of the novel, *The counterfeiters*, by André Gide, giving dancers the roles of alienated park visitors. Jean Lurçat's surrealist scenery for this ballet presented the park as sombre and dark, with the silhouettes of deep purple trees and human figures providing a desolate but unifying backdrop for the parade of disconnected and contrasting characters as they play out both dark and frivolous emotions in the course of a day. His costumes were based on everyday dress, from military uniforms and formal town fashions, to the overalls of street sweepers, giving the audience a spectacle of movement and fragile human interaction against the grim unchanging architecture of his urban park setting. Its attenuated graphics prefigured Lurçat's design style for the later modern tapestries that provided his most enduring artistic impact.

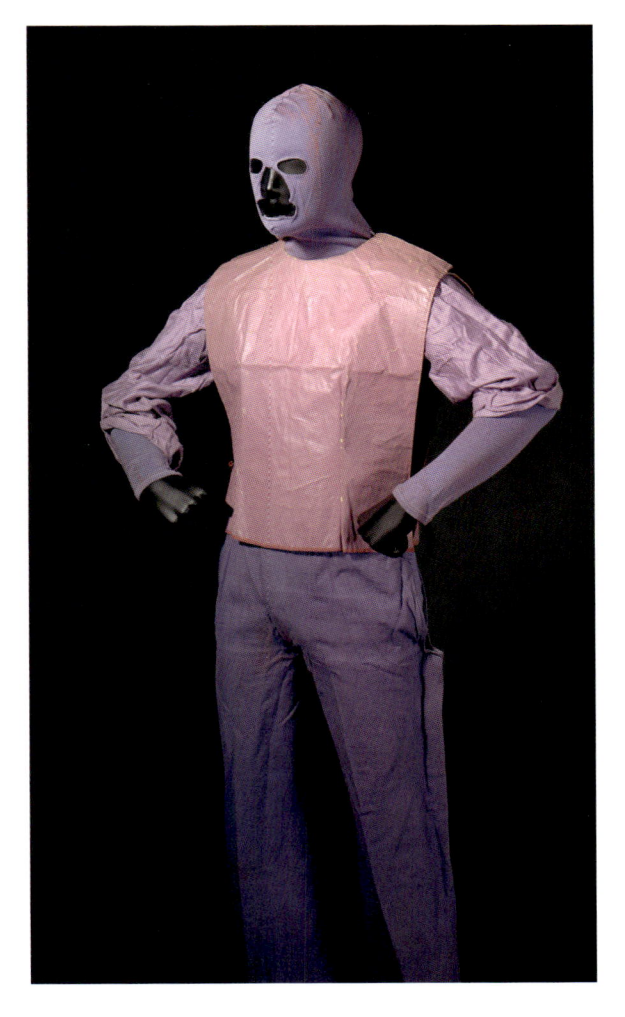

Jean Lurçat
(opposite) *Costume for a military musician* c 1935
(top) *Costume for a street sweeper* c 1935
© Jean Lurçat/ADAGP. Licensed by Viscopy, 2010

(above) **Unknown photographer**
Stage performance of Jardin public
page 26 in *Program for Col. W. de Basil's Ballet Russe, Théâtre national du Palais de Chaillot, 7–8–10–12–13–14–16–17 October 1947*

Costumes of Colonel de Basil's Ballets Russes de Monte Carlo 1931–40   **175**

Francesca da Rimini

Ballet in two scenes

Producer: Ballets Russes de Col W de Basil
Premiere: 15 July 1937, Royal Opera House, Covent Garden, London
Costume design: Oliver Messel
Costumier: Barbara Karinska
Scenery design: Oliver Messel
Music: Pyotr Il'yich Tchaikovsky
Choreography: David Lichine
Libretto: David Lichine and Henry Clifford
Main characters: Francesca, Gianciotto Malatesta, Paolo Malatesta, Chiara, Girolamo, Domenico, the Signori of Rimini, Francesca's ladies, the Angeleic Apparition, Guinevere, Lancelot, soldiers, servants, dwarfs, townspeople

The Lord of Ravenna attempts to establish a peace with the neighbouring province of Rimini by offering his daughter, Francesca, to the future Lord of Rimini, Gianciotto Malatesta. Malatesta is worried that his physical deformity will disgust his future bride and so sends his brother Paolo as a proxy to marry Francesca. During the journey back to Rimini, Francesca and Paolo fall deeply in love. When the lovers arrive, Malatesta's spy, Girolamo, alerts his master to the situation, causing the enraged Malatesta to carry Francesca off, to the distress of Paolo. The second scene opens with the lovers reading the story of Lancelot and Guinevere, who come to life and dance before the couple as they kiss. The arrival of Malatesta and his entourage interrupts the tryst. Paolo is found hiding on the terrace and is killed in a fight with his brother. The distraught Francesca then fatally throws herself on her husband's sword.

■

This ballet is set in the period of the early Renaissance and is partly taken from the tragedy of Paolo and Francesca from Canto V of Dante's *Inferno*. It was based on the 1853 play by the American playwright George Henry Boker (1823–1890). Mikhail Fokine had created a version of the story as a ballet for the Mariinsky Theatre in St Petersburg in 1915 but it was not produced by a Ballets Russes company until its 1937 production in London. With his well-established credentials as a historicist designer, Messel was an appropriate choice to bring authenticity to *Francesca da Rimini*'s Italian setting and its tragic characters.

(top) **Oliver Messel**
Jacket from costume for a courtier c 1937

(above) **Unknown photographer**
Scene from the powerful ballet Francesca da Rimini
page 46 in *Souvenir program for Col. W. de Basil's Ballets, Australia–New Zealand 1939–40*
National Gallery of Australia Research Library, Canberra

(right) **Oliver Messel**
Costume for a court lady c 1937

176 Ballets Russes: the art of costume

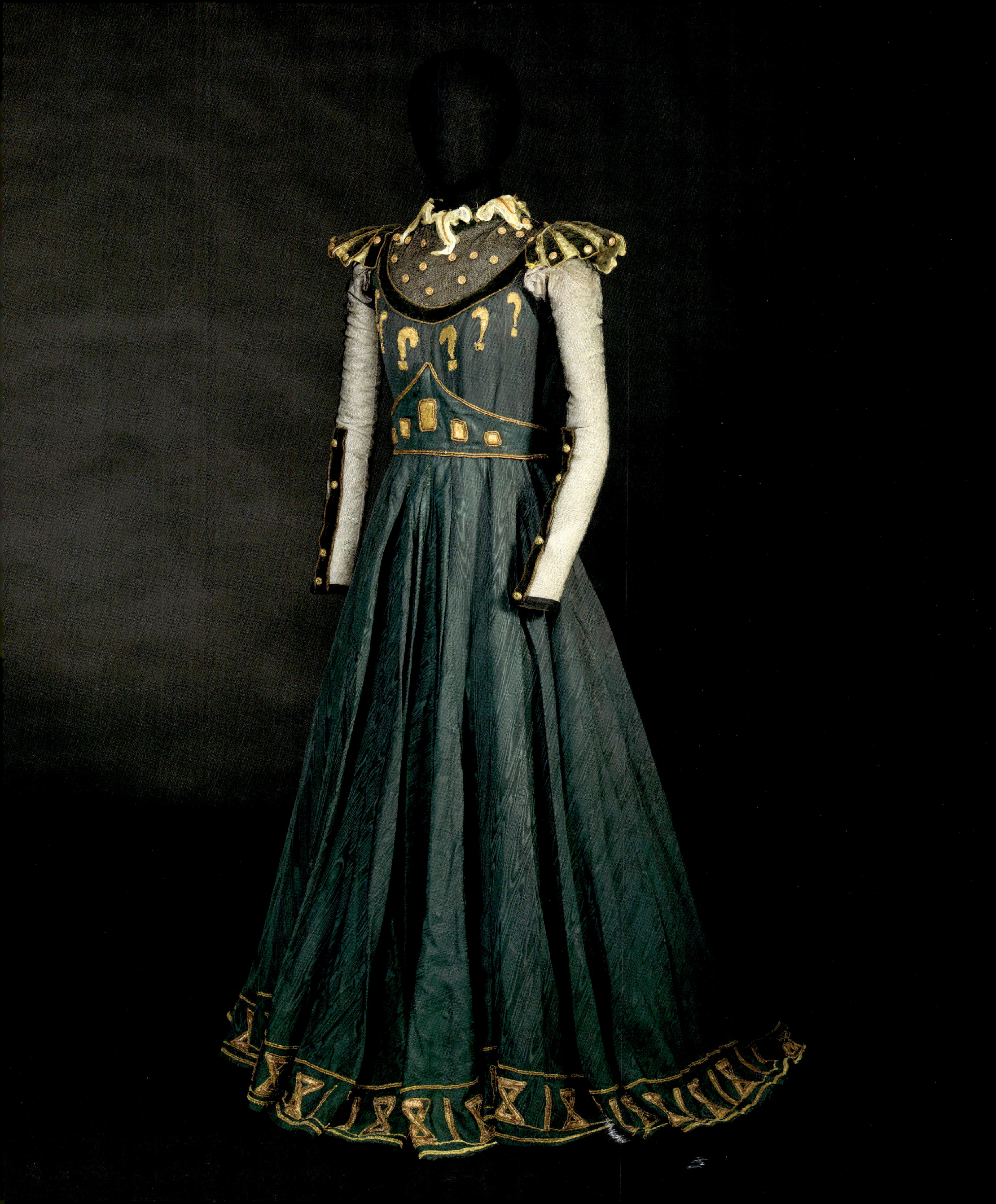

178 Ballets Russes: the art of costume

La Lutte éternelle
The eternal struggle
Ballet in one act

Producer: Original Ballet Russe Ltd's Col W de Basil's Ballet Company
Premiere: 29 July 1940, Theatre Royal, Sydney
Costume design: Kathleen and Florence Martin
Costumier: Olga Larose
Scenery design: Kathleen and Florence Martin
Music: Robert Schumann, arranged by Antal Donati
Choreography: Igor Schwezov
Libretto: Igor Schwezov
Main characters: Man, Woman, Beauty, Illusion, Truth, Will, Obsessions

The ballet is a danced allegory of humanity's progress and struggles against the pitfalls and temptations of life. Man is distracted in turn by Illusion and Obsession. However, with the help of Beauty and Truth he finds his Will and the ballet ends with him victorious.

■

La Lutte éternelle is the reworking of *Elkerlyc*, a 1936 ballet by choreographer Igor Schwezoff, based on a fifteenth-century Dutch morality play. Schwezoff had joined de Basil's Ballets Russes company as a dancer in 1939, and the production of *La Lutte éternelle* was his first for the company. Its structure, with its use of symphonic music (Schumann's 1837 *Etudes symphoniques*), showed the influence of *Les Présages*, particularly in its theme of 'man's progress towards an ideal beyond worldly things'. The allegorical roles of Truth, Illusion, Beauty and Will anchored characters depicting such qualities as obsession.

The backcloth, decorated with symbolic line drawings suggesting 'beseeching hands', as a Sydney reviewer put it, was lit to give the illusion of a tunnel through which light streamed. Of the costumes, those for the four Obsessions were particularly striking. On one level they elaborated on a standard item of ballet costuming— the familiar long, romantic tutu, usually white, with its flowing skirt and delicate bodice. But the Martin sisters produced a startling variation on this form of costuming with their striking use of reds, golds and blacks, and in the close-fitting, long-sleeved, high-necked bodice. The skull caps with their flame-like decorative elements were perhaps modelled on headdresses such as that worn by the Rose in *Le Spectre de la rose*, but again the design moved in a different and bold direction.[2]

La Lutte éternelle received only seven performances in Australia, all in Sydney, but Schwezoff continued to stage the work for de Basil's Ballets Russes in North and South America in the 1940s.

(opposite) **Kathleen and Florence Martin**
Costume design for Obsessions 1940

(above) **Unknown photographer**
Stage performance of La Lutte éternelle c 1940
National Gallery of Australia Research Library, Canberra, papers of Kathleen and Florence Martin

Costumes of Colonel de Basil's Ballets Russes de Monte Carlo 1931–40 179

PEOPLE, PATRONAGE AND PROMOTION:
THE BALLETS RUSSES TOURS TO AUSTRALIA, 1936–40

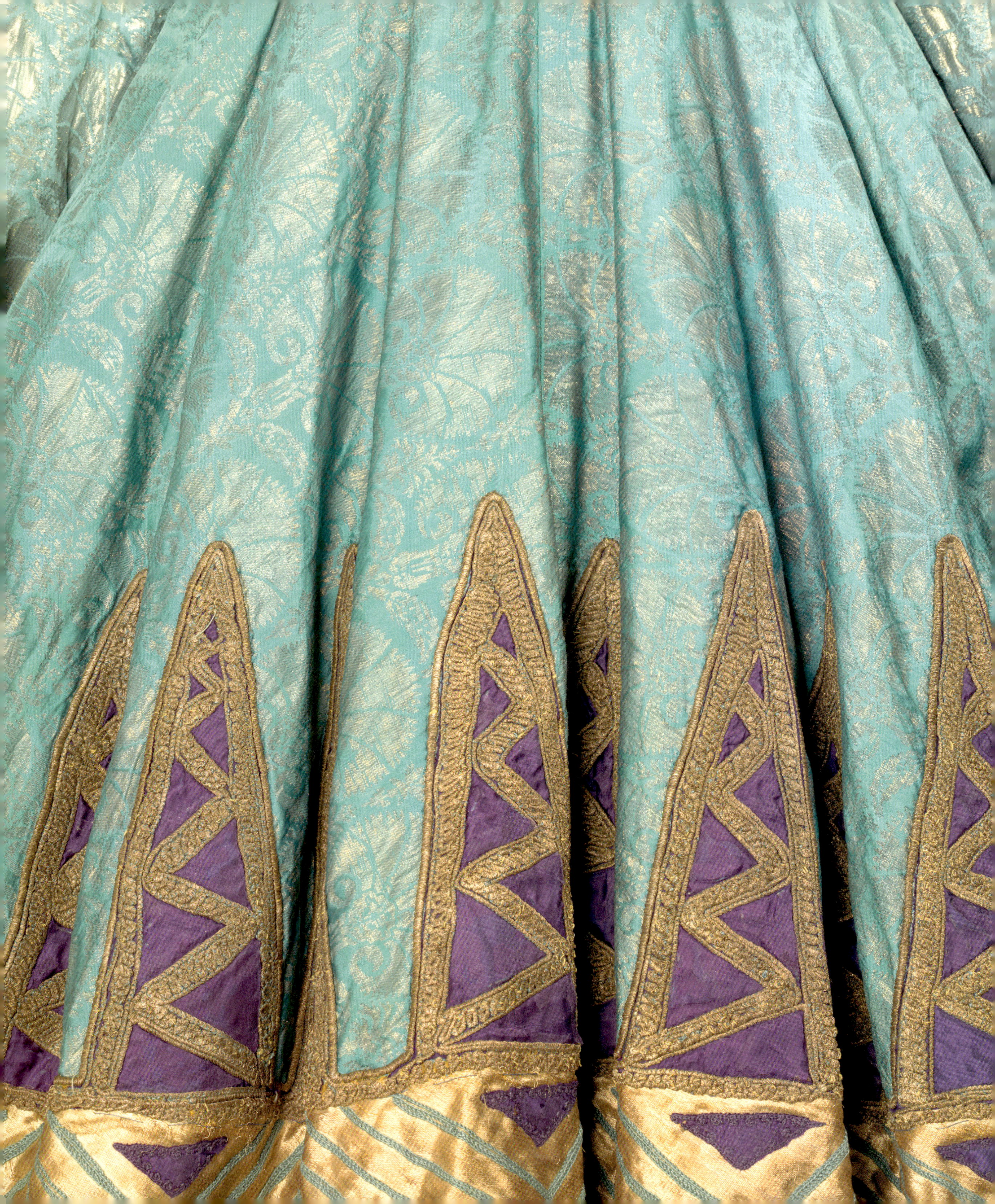

PEOPLE, PATRONAGE AND PROMOTION: THE BALLETS RUSSES TOURS TO AUSTRALIA, 1936–40

Michelle Potter

When Serge Diaghilev and the acclaimed Ballets Russes made a series of momentous tours to America in 1915, 1916 and 1917, publicity and promotion was managed by Edward L Bernays. Bernays is now an acknowledged pioneer of the concept of public relations and a man more recently described as the father of spin.[1] For the Diaghilev tours he developed a highly successful publicity campaign, flooding American newspapers and magazines with images and stories about the company. He specifically promoted the company as one that was bringing disparate arts together, whose work and personnel could have an impact on the American way. His campaign was not without its flamboyant moments—in one enlightened move he promoted the largely unknown dancer Flora Revalles by having her photographed in her costume as Zobéide in *Schéhérazade* with a live snake from the Brooklyn zoo draped around her neck.[2]

Bernays found the experience of dealing with Diaghilev and his company fascinating, as he recalled in his autobiography:

> I had never imagined that the interpersonal relations of the members of a group could be so involved and complex, full of medieval intrigue, illicit love, misdirected passion and aggression. But while it happened I took it all for granted as part of a stimulating job. Nevertheless, my experience had a life long effect on me for it prepared me to understand and cope with the vagaries of men and women who lived in special worlds of their own.[3]

In many respects the three tours to Australia between 1936 and 1940 by Ballets Russes companies under the direction, if sometimes from afar, of Colonel Wassily de Basil, revealed similar complexities in interpersonal relations. The Ballets Russes dancers led a peripatetic life at a time when travel was largely by ship or train, when communications were not the instant experience of the twenty-first century. They lived, worked and travelled in close proximity, supporting each other in a profession that centred on physical activity, on relentlessly pushing an often exhausted body to its limits to achieve a vision of exoticism, glamour and fantasy. A number of the female dancers were so young that they travelled with their mothers as chaperones. Many of the personnel were stateless, travelling on Nansen passports, which made many aspects of their lives insecure and the prospect of long-term citizenship of a welcoming country very uncertain. The Ballets Russes lifestyle and background fascinated Australian audiences, as many would go on to record.[4]

Letters from the dancers to friends and family on the other side of the world indicate that there was a mutual fascination on the part of these glamorous stars and Australians from all walks of life. The letters recount personal successes and failures, company gossip, and comments about the strange new country in which they found themselves, not to mention the manners of the people who inhabited it. They also reveal that the dancers enjoyed socialising with their Australian hosts, who enthusiastically provided all kinds of activities on performance-free days—picnics, trips to wildlife sanctuaries, barbecues, dinners, weekends at the beach, were all on the social calendar. The letters make intriguing reading.[5]

Léon Bakst
Costume for Shah Zeman
1910–30s (detail) from
Schéhérazade

Studio Iris
Stage performance of Les Présages *page 28 in* Program for Col. W. de Basil's Ballets Russes de Monte-Carlo, Royal Opera House Covent Garden, June–September 1936, third season
National Gallery of Australia Research Library, Canberra

As inheritors of the legacy of Diaghilev, with its defining aesthetic of collaborating with the most forward-thinking choreographers, artists and composers of the day, the Ballets Russes companies had a remarkable impact on the development of and thinking about the arts in Australia. Many of the works they performed generated public debate, often advanced through 'Letters to the editor' columns in metropolitan newspapers. Issues surrounding the designs for *Les Présages* (*Destiny*) by André Masson created discussion in the pages of *The Argus*, for example. After the ballet was presented in Melbourne in 1940, the reviewer for *The Argus*, Geoffrey Hutton, was less than enthusiastic about Masson's work, calling it pretentiously modern. A flurry of letters ensued, some from anonymous writers, others from high-profile members of the Melbourne arts community. In Masson's defence, art patron and champion of contemporary art, John Reed, wrote that the designer's striking work contributed to the success of the ballet, noting that 'the component elements—dance, music and decor—are particularly harmonious'.[6] In total disagreement, Hutton's subsequent response included the suggestion that *Les Présages* would look better without Masson's costumes: 'One critic has described as perfect a performance of "Les Présages" in practice costume. It would make an interesting comparison.'[7]

Unlike Reed, artist and designer William Constable commended Hutton on his courage in not accepting Masson's work as 'good just because it is the work of a great artist'. Constable wrote:

> I have no quarrel with what is called 'modern' art and I consider Masson a great designer, but every artist meets a 'low' at some time and this is Masson's, if ever he had one. This decor and foolish costumes are completely foreign to Tschaikowsky's symphony and do nothing but distract and detract from the vivid music and dancing of this ballet.[8]

In addition to debates over the value of costumes and scenery, at a time when ballet aroused strong opinions about artistic issues, throughout the duration of the three tours other debates surfaced over choreography and music.

On a practical level, some Australian artists received a boost to their emerging careers as a result of Ballets Russes commissions. Sidney Nolan's design commission for *Icare* for the Original Ballet Russe in Sydney in 1940 is well known as the first in a series of works he made for the theatre.[9] Loudon Sainthill also received a commission for the 1939–40 tour to design *Etude*, a new work by company dancer Nina Verchinina. Although his designs were not used in the final production, they were exhibited in Melbourne and Sydney in the exhibition Art for theatre and ballet and were publicised in Australia and England.[10] Sainthill's mature theatrical work was made largely in England in the 1950s and 1960s. The engagement to design *Etude*, and the subsequent work Sainthill did for the Kirsova Ballet, established in Sydney in 1941 by former principal with the Monte Carlo Russian Ballet, Hélène Kirsova, were significant early steps in his international career as a stage designer.[11]

Other Australians, among them critic and art historian Bernard Smith, were inspired by the Ballets Russes visits to examine theoretical issues. In the unpublished typescript '"Paganini", notes after attending the Monte Carlo Diaghilev Ballet [sic] in Sydney', 1940, Smith, then in the early stages of his long career, makes an analysis in Marxist terms of Paganini, a work first seen in Australia in December 1939[12] , that includes the following:

> The second scene is a feudalist-bourgeois conception of the people, of lovers in an ideal pastoral world, where there are no class barriers. This conception of the people

184 Ballets Russes: the art of costume

cannot be art because it is totally false. It cannot be justified on the grounds that the limitations of Balletic art demand a romanticised conception of the people. Dancing was perhaps the first means whereby man projected the production patterns evolved through his active contact with the world in work into the realm of fantasy. It arose therefore before classes, as a method of developing the group consciousness; before the need for looking backwards, before romanticism. The 'people' of the second scene are not the mass of the people at all, they are only the idealised conception of what the bourgeois would look like if they could forget that their own freedom depended upon the slavery of others.[13]

Interest in the Ballets Russes was not confined to the more serious matters of art, of its creation, history and theory. The Ballets Russes and some of its artists became an intrinsic part of advertising and graphic design. Irina Baronova became the face of Paul Duval cosmetics during the 1938–39 tour of the Covent Garden Russian Ballet, for example. As perhaps the most popular star of that tour her name was a powerful drawcard; she advertised a range of other items as well, including De Reszke cigarettes. Advertisements for the products she sponsored regularly featured in magazine programs and newspapers of the time.

One the firms most actively using the Ballets Russes as a feature in its advertising was the Melbourne-based menswear store Henry Buck's. The directors of the company and their children, especially the grand-daughter of Henry Buck himself, Suzanne Cecil, were lovers of the arts and counted among their friends many of the dancers and several well-respected Australian artists, including Frederick McCubbin and Donald Friend.[14] Their graphic designer in the 1930s was the young, aspiring artist Alan McCulloch. He designed and wrote the text for the Henry Buck's advertisements that appeared in Ballets Russes programs as well as for the store's 1938 Christmas

Vene Beck
Stage performance of Icare (Icarus falls to the ground) 1940
gelatin silver photograph
16.6 × 24.6 cm
National Gallery of Australia, Canberra, gift of Mrs Haydn Beck and her daughter Mrs Norman Johnstone, 1982

People, patronage and promotion: the Ballets Russes tours to Australia, 1936–40   185

Léon Bakst
Set design for Thamar 1912
watercolour on paper
Musée des Arts décoratifs, Paris
Photograph: Giraudon/Bridgeman
Art Library

catalogue—*Xmas 1938: a few ballet ideas from Henry Buck's*.[15] The catalogue includes two brief stories, 'The vanquished vamp' and 'Interlude orientale', which combine allusions to the ballet, items sold by Henry Buck's, and occasional Melbourne icons, including the tramway system. 'The vanquished vamp' clearly references the storyline of *Thamar*, a work that had been extremely popular during the Monte Carlo Russian Ballet tour of 1936–37, in which Thamar, the Georgian princess, waves a scarf from the tower window of her castle to seduce passers-by. 'The vanquished vamp' says of its heroine:

> In a high tower overlooking the tram-stop, sits the fair and fatal Candelabra. Each day, she takes toll of the young men who pass on their way to business. Luring them to her tower, she devours their lunches to the last crumb, saving the butter to grease the palm of the policemen on the beat.

> Candelabra goes to the window and waves a tie of surpassing elegance. It is thus that she lures her victims to their fate.

'Interlude orientale' does not make such obvious reference to a particular work, but its cartoon-like illustrations refer to many of the Ballets Russes costumes with which McCulloch would have been familiar, such as the harem costumes from *Schéhérazade*, the Astrologer's costume from *Le Coq d'or* and the generously cut pantaloon-style trousers with their simple but powerful design motifs worn by the Chief Eunuch in *Schéhérazade*.

The book *Ballet bogies*, published in 1938 in Melbourne by Lionel Smalley, and written and illustrated by Alan McCulloch and his brother Wilfred, is similar to the Christmas catalogue in tone, text and

186 Ballets Russes: the art of costume

illustrations.¹⁶ It includes advertisements promoting MacRobertson's chocolates and the Henry Buck's store. Wilfred McCulloch's illustration for the chocolate advertisement is in the style of the Russian Primitivist designs of Mikhail Larionov for *Soleil de minuit* (*Midnight sun*), first seen in Australia in December 1936, while the Henry Buck's advertisement, 'Spectre de la shirt', prefigures a prank performance at a Red Cross fundraiser in the Melbourne Town Hall in 1940 at which Wilfred and Alan, with their close friend Arthur Boyd (who became one of Australia's most admired and respected artists), dressed as ballerinas and 'frantically threw themselves about in wild antic movements, impersonating the members of the Ballets Russes in a parody of *Le Spectre de la Rose*'.¹⁷

The patronage of the Buck family, and the popular direction in which the McCullochs took their design commissions, make clear that the impact of the Ballets Russes was widespread, entering Australian life and the Australian psyche at many levels. In fact, the emphasis that has so often been placed on artists whose careers were advanced as a result of commissions to design for the Ballets Russes (which was obviously significant), has to a large extent obscured the fact that behind the performances and commissions the tours were being publicised and promoted in a wide range of styles. And while promoters of Australian products drew upon the widespread popularity of the Ballets Russes to help their sales, behind the scenes there was also in operation a major campaign to promote a particular set of messages about the touring companies.

The Ballets Russes visits were managed as a shrewd and resolute business endeavour. At the heart of the venture was J C Williamson Ltd, for decades Australia's leading theatrical entrepreneurial organisation and under whose banner the Russian companies toured Australia and New Zealand. Much of the business activity surrounding the ballet tours is recorded in books of cables assembled by the Williamson organisation, which was led during the time of the

Léon Bakst
(above left) *Costume design for a dancing girl or odalisque* c 1910 from *Schéhérazade* page 19 in *Souvenir program for Serge Diaghilev's Ballet Russe, Metropolitan Opera, New York 1916*

(above right) *Costume for a dancing girl or odalisque* c 1910 (detail) from *Schéhérazade*

Ballets Russes visits by the Tait family.[18] Exchanged largely between Williamson representatives in London and the organisation back home in Australia, the cables initially discuss in detail which company would be brought to Australia. Many cables later, in which transportation, salaries, repertoire, dancers, casting and many other issues had been debated, Nevin Tait, Williamson's London representative, informed Australia that the ballet option negotiated with Colonel de Basil and his Monte Carlo Russian Ballet had been exercised.[19]

During the exchange of cables it was clear, not surprisingly, that the Williamson organisation was keen to broker the best possible financial deal for their own company, and to ensure that the best dancers and most popular works were brought to Australia. And once the ballet had arrived, the organisation showed a constant interest in box office takings. Regular cables setting out weekly figures were sent to London and New York, keeping Williamson representatives and Colonel de Basil fully informed. The ballet seasons were financially more than successful and takings regularly outstripped those of other Williamson shows, often by more than 100 per cent:

```
TO COLONEL DE BASIL IN NEW YORK FROM
E J TAIT
FIRST WEEK MELB £3350.[20]
TO JANTATE NEW YORK
BALLET 3225 GILBERTS 1430 WIDOW
ADELAIDE 1515.[21]

TO MANOAH LONDON
WEEK: OVERGOES 1450, MONCRIEFF 1760,
BALLET ADELAIDE 2800.[22]
```

As purposeful businesspeople, the Taits were astute enough to realise that the artistic issues that had been discussed in the cables prior to the arrival of the Monte Carlo Russian Ballet in Australia would need to be managed by publicity and promotional activities in Australia. One of the most pressing of the artistic problems centred on whether any of the dancers could be legitimately promoted as a star. The 1913 Australian tour of Danish ballerina Adeline Genée, billed as 'The world's greatest dancer', along with tours by Anna Pavlova in 1926 and 1929, and Olga Spessivtseva in 1934, had given Australians a taste of the star system—hence the concern that was expressed in a number of cables when well-known names began to drop off

(above left) **Mikhail Larionov**
Costume design for
Soleil de nuit
page 33 in *Program for Col. W. de Basil's Ballets Russes de Monte-Carlo, Royal Opera House Covent Garden, June–September 1936, third season*
© Mikhail Larionov/ADAGP. Licensed by Viscopy, 2010
National Gallery of Australia Research Library

(above right)
Wilfred McCulloch
MacRobertson chocolate advertisement inner cover of *Ballets bogies* 1938

the proposed list of performers. At one stage, a cable reported that Tamara Toumanova, Alexandra Danilova and Bronislava Nijinska, all exceptional names, would be coming in 1936.[23] A little later, however, these names disappeared from the cast lists, with various excuses being offered by London. From Australia came the cable:

```
CONSIDERABLE PUBLIC DISAPPOINTMENT
TUAMANOVAS [SIC] ABSENCE ENDEAVOUR
INCLUDE HER.[24]
```

The reply from London:
```
BLINOVA EQUALLY GOOD STANDING
TOUMANOVA ESPECIALLY AS LATTER
SHOWING SIGNS OF WEIGHT.[25]
```

There was also concern that the first tour to Australia was to be made by a company assembled from dancers who were not going to the United States with the main de Basil company. In many respects it was a scratch company, made up of those artists from de Basil's Ballets Russes de Monte-Carlo who could be persuaded or harangued into coming, and artists from Les Ballets de Léon Woizikowsky, which had been appearing in Paris, London and other European cities in 1935 and 1936. The company that eventually came to Australia was often referred to as 'Woizikowsky's company' and its mixed composition, which resulted in a dual management structure, created many tensions and divided loyalties.[26] In the eyes of the Williamson management, the idea that this was a second company—in other words, second best—needed to be strongly countered.

Another troubling issue was the quality of what would be seen in Australia, in particular the scenery and costumes. In cable transmissions the Williamson organisation had been assured of spectacular productions[27], but at the opening of the Monte Carlo Russian Ballet season in Adelaide on 13 October 1936, Williamson management complained that the decor was in fact less than they had expected. A cable from Australia to London calls the decor for *Les Sylphides* unsatisfactory[28], and British dance writer Arnold Haskell records a conversation in which E J Tait was less than happy with what he had seen.[29] These issues would be the specific focus of an ongoing promotional campaign in the style of Bernays.

Just who was officially charged with the responsibility of assuring Australians they were getting the best is unclear. Williamson Theatres had their own publicity manager, but a Ballets Russes press representative or publicity manager is not mentioned in programs and other publicity material. Olga Philipoff, who travelled to Australia as secretary to her father Alexander Philipoff, executive manager for de Basil, was a frequent contributor to newspapers and magazines over all three tours. But as one newspaper reported, her role was 'arranging for interviews and photographs, putting inquirers in touch with their friends among the ballet, planning publicity and advertisements'.[30] Her own writings confirm her interests were confined to day-to-day media issues rather than serious promotion of a corporate ideal.[31]

But in terms of promoting an image of the Russian Ballet as a company of outstanding practitioners whose lineage was impeccable—that is, in terms of addressing the concerns expressed by the Taits—the names of Arnold Haskell and the Australian publisher, artist and patron Sydney Ure Smith are conspicuously to the fore. They, more than anyone else, manipulated public perceptions about the worth of the Ballets Russes. Drawing on their influential network of businessmen, artists, publishers, editors and society figures, they mounted a major campaign to promote Ballets Russes productions as significant art and the dancers as exceptional artists.

Arnold Haskell appears on programs for the 1936–37 season as 'liaison officer'. In his autobiographies and his other writings about Australia he is never really specific about this role. In fact he seems happiest when skirting around the issue, initially couching his joining the Monte Carlo Russian Ballet for the Australian tour as a response to his desire to see Ceylon on the way out and Honolulu on the way home.[32] Several decades later, however, he would admit that he had been asked by de Basil to travel with the company in order to act in an advisory capacity.[33] Haskell returned during the 1938–39 tour by the Covent Garden Russian Ballet, noting that the purpose of this visit was 'an attempt to study the continent and provide a background for my enchantment'.[34] Once again, however, he was extremely active as a writer, public speaker and advocate for the ballet and the Australian arts in general.

The articles Haskell wrote while in Australia clearly indicate that his aim was to promote the Ballets Russes as a company of outstanding dancers, and he was more than eager to emphasise that many of the younger dancers had real star potential. In 'Some reasons for the popularity of ballet', published in February 1937, he discussed the significance of the Ballets Russes companies as ensembles of dancers of great individuality rather than companies with 'one blazing star and a background of mechanical dancers' and noted that this kind of company structure had great merit: 'The ensemble of small personalities gives a far greater artistic result than the major personality'.[35] In other articles he lauded de Basil's perspicacity in fostering young dancers who might not have an instantly recognisable name but who had considerable future promise.[36]

Haskell had a staunch ally in Basil Burdett, art critic for the Melbourne newspaper *The Herald*. Haskell maintains that Burdett became his closest friend and, in the slightly patronising manner that characterises much of his writing from Australia, intimates that he had acted as an adviser to Burdett on some issues.[37] Burdett wrote prolifically about the tours in both reviews and feature articles, a number of which promoted the links he observed between what Australians were seeing on stage and the legacy of Diaghilev. He took pains to note that audiences really had no grounds for complaint, and clearly supported Haskell's views:

> The latest season of ballet in Australia under the auspices of Colonel de Basil, who is doing his gallant best to continue the great work of Diaghileff interrupted by Death in Venice some years ago, has upset a good many people's idea of ballet. There is no Pavlova. There is not even the Toumanova we were promised when the season was first announced.

> But despite the absence of a world-famous ballerina from the company, it is likely to prove I think a more authentic introduction to ballet as Diaghileff understood and conceived it than any previous visitation … For the first time in Australia we are seeing in Australia ballets with the original décor and costumes designed for Diaghileff by Bakst, Benois and other collaborators.[38]

Haskell and his colleagues needed outlets beyond the daily press. Their writing was wider in scope than could be accommodated by newspapers, whose business was to run reviews and brief news items of the kind provided by Olga Philipoff. It was Sydney Ure Smith who constantly provided editorial space in publications such as *The Home*, *Art in Australia* and *Australia: National Journal*, publications which he either published or edited, or with which he was otherwise closely involved.[39]

Ure Smith and Haskell shared a close friendship over a number of years and moved in a socially influential circle that included artists, businessmen and the cream of society. Ure Smith was also an aficionado of the ballet, with his interest going back at least to the tours to Australia by Anna Pavlova in the 1920s; Pavlova had sent him a telegram saying 'Very much touched by your constant friendly appreciation …'[40] His collected letters indicate that he socialised with the Ballets Russes dancers when they were in Australia and that they remembered him fondly and continued to correspond with him after they had left the country.[41]

Ure Smith and Haskell also shared an interest in the power of the print medium as both an instructive and aesthetic tool. In 1906, when Ure Smith was just

(above) **Léon Bakst**
Costume design for a reveller in a pig mask c 1920
from *Petrouchka*

(opposite) **Max Dupain**
Arnold Haskell 1937
gelatin silver photograph
37.7 x 29.9 cm
National Gallery of Australia, Canberra

People, patronage and promotion: the Ballets Russes tours to Australia, 1936–40

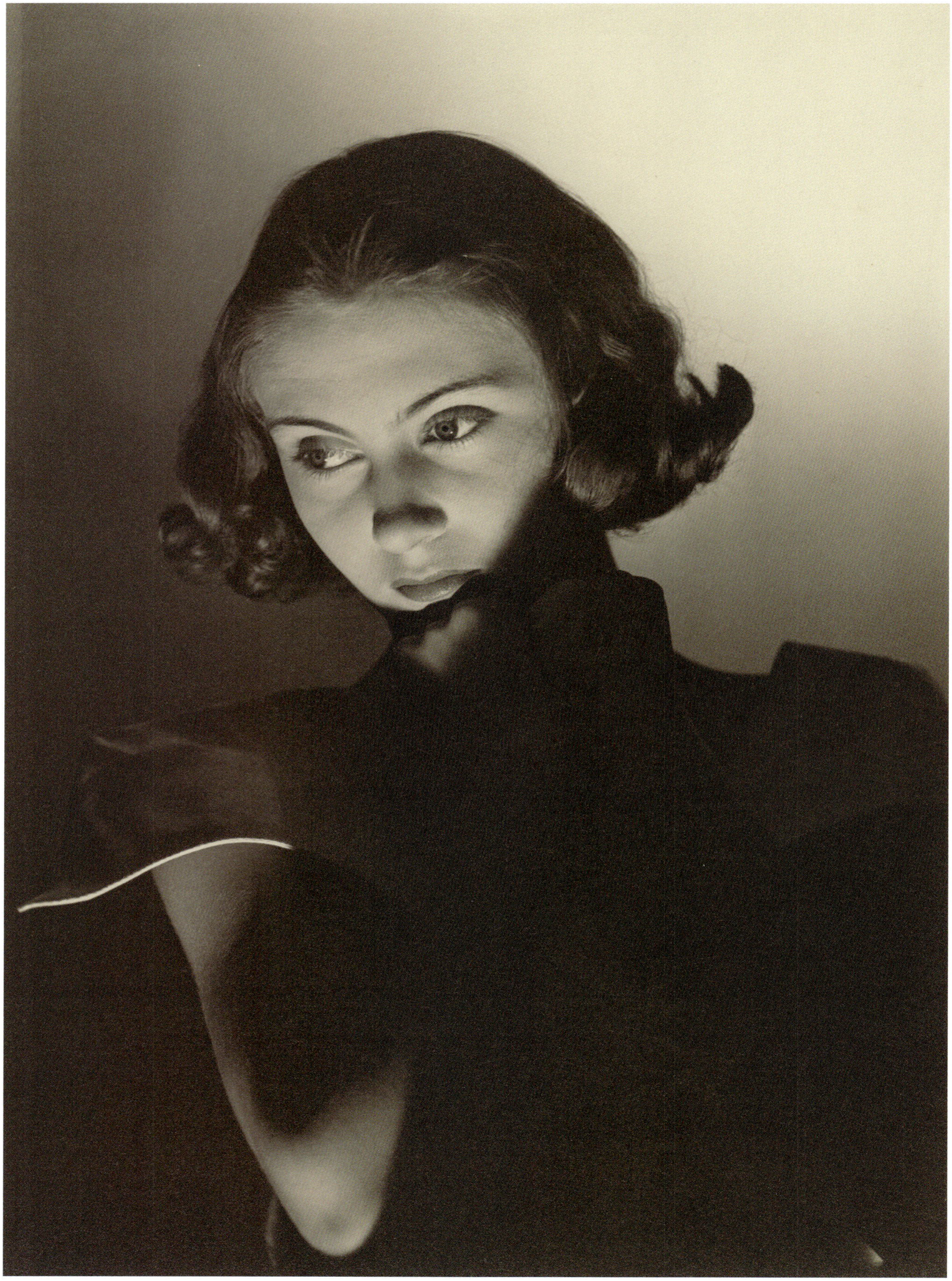

nineteen years old, he and cartoonist Harry Julius had established an advertising agency named Smith & Julius Studios. Ure Smith's biographer maintains that the agency 'set high standards in Australian advertising and became the country's first such agency to feature such quality for professional artwork'.[42] It quickly became a hub for Sydney's art community and established Ure Smith's reputation as a patron of high art. Haskell clearly admired Ure Smith's engagement with high quality publishing and glowingly referred to him as 'in aim and accomplishment Australia's Diaghileff, the Diaghileff of the "World of Art" (Mir Isskustva) days'[43], referring to the radical art journal that Diaghilev edited.[44] Ure Smith also firmly believed that publicising art by modern methods was essential. In 1933 he commissioned a study from the advertising agency Catts-Patterson to research methods used in the United States to achieve the best results in production, circulation, editorial and advertising.[45]

Ure Smith took up promotion of the Ballets Russes as part of his editorial strategy and aesthetic aims. He and his colleagues and successors on the various journals with which he had connections published a barrage of articles about the work of the Ballets Russes. With one exception, in which the author suggested that the standard of dancing was poor by comparison with what an audience could see in a musical comedy or on film[46], the articles were always laudatory and didactic in tone. Ure Smith also actively promoted and published photographic portraits of the dancers and production shots from the most popular works. Especially notable was a series of luminous portraits commissioned from Max Dupain who, while he never placed much store on what he called his 'ballet series', acknowledged Ure Smith's influence and his indebtedness to him as a patron.[47]

Many questions emerge relating to the activities in which Haskell and Ure Smith were engaged, in particular the contractual arrangements behind their campaign. Bernays was employed by the Musical Bureau of the Metropolitan Opera in New York[48], but what of Haskell and Ure Smith? Haskell and de Basil had been good friends for a number of years, and both Ure Smith and Haskell engaged with the Taits on a number of levels. Did either Haskell or Ure Smith take a salary or a cut in the profits from de Basil or the Taits? Did Ure Smith promote the Ballets Russes so prolifically simply as part of his editorial strategy, or did he have other motives? These and similar questions remain largely unanswered.

The reasons for the success of the Australian Ballet Russes tours are complex. They are consistently regarded as presenting a panorama of dance, music and design of a kind not seen here before, and of providing the impetus for dance to flourish in Australia. At the same time they created a fascinating glimpse of a glamorous and exotic people living in a very different world. But as much as the tours offered these kinds of kinaesthetic, visual, aural and personal experiences, and a host of opportunities for home-grown developments, they must also be acknowledged as a successful business enterprise. Sound business acumen on the part of the Williamson organisation meant that the tours made money at a time when revenue had to come largely, if not completely, from box-office takings. Alongside this business model was a powerful promotional campaign spearheaded by Haskell and Ure Smith. Working with a strongly focused set of ideas in support of management, they, as Bernays had done in America two decades earlier, bombarded Australians with stories and articles promoting the company as inheritors of a great tradition and as an ideal to follow in their own endeavours. It was an exercise, supported by a number of smaller ventures, in what might be referred to in the twenty-first century as 'branding'.

Max Dupain
Lelia Roussova 1937
gelatin silver photograph
46.8 x 34 cm
National Gallery of Australia, Canberra

SIGHTS UNSEEN: TAGS, STAMPS AND STAINS

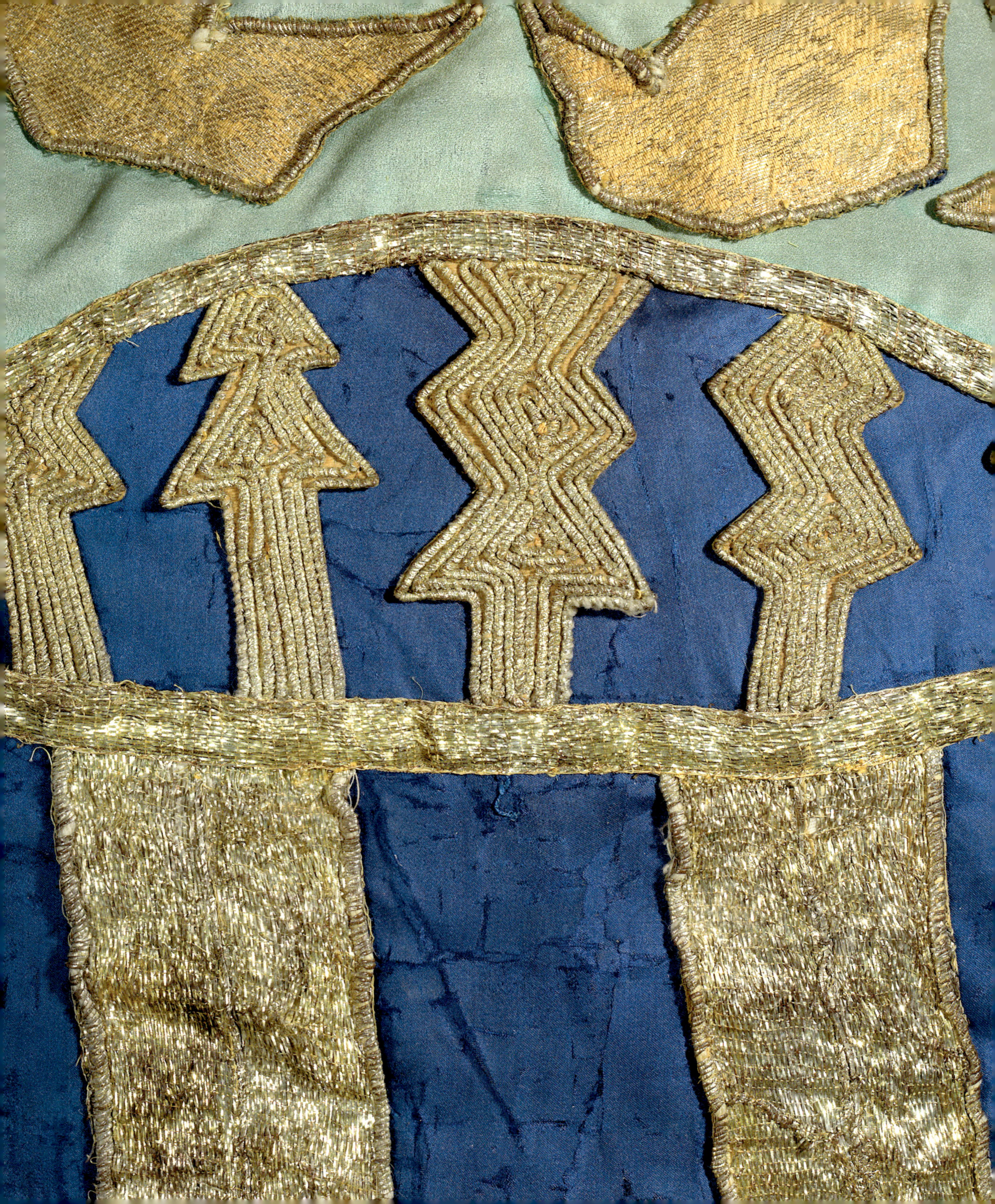

SIGHTS UNSEEN: TAGS, STAMPS AND STAINS

Debbie Ward

More than six thousand fibres have been identified, hundreds of metres of fabric have been dyed to undertake repairs, and fifty thousand hours have been devoted to restoring the National Gallery of Australia's significant collection of costumes from the productions of the Ballets Russes.[1] These costumes, unique in their construction, ornamentation and history, have presented a range of challenges for the Gallery's conservation team.[2] In return for their time, skills and patience, conservators develop an especially intimate knowledge of the costumes. Sights never intended to be seen by the ballet public become their focus. As a result of the conservators' endeavours, the Gallery's Ballets Russes costumes can been seen free of the contaminating effects of performance and time—sweat, mould, insect damage, rips, deteriorated fabrics and innumerable alterations.

There is a sense of excitement as a costume is brought from the store to the laboratory for investigation and treatment, which can take up to six months. Determining a suitable treatment is not possible without an extensive knowledge of the costume. Every fabric and thread is identified by the textile conservator, details of stains and damage are recorded, and all aspects of construction documented. If further research is required, conservators sometimes study photographs, film and programs from the time to assist with dating, to identify dancers or other aspects of the costumes' history and use.

The inscriptions most costumes carry are among the first things to be noted by the conservator.[3] The several types of inscriptions that are unique to the costumes of the Ballets Russes, and an integral part of their history, can reveal the date a costume was constructed, its manufacturer and the dancer who wore it. On rare occasions an inscription identifies the ballet for which the costume was designed. But the designs for each production were so distinctive that it seems there was little need for such inscriptions, and costumes for only eight of the 34 ballets conserved in the Gallery's collection carry such identification. Handwritten in ink onto white cotton fabric and neatly sewn to the costume linings, the rarity of these labels suggests that they were not a requirement of the designer or the company, merely a practical measure by the manufacturer. In the face of tight deadlines and large numbers of similar costumes, these labels allowed the manufactures to track all costumes ordered.

Conservators greatly admire costumiers' technical skills and their ability to interpret designers' drawings. While a designer would regularly monitor the costumes as work progressed[4], the costumier often contributed a significant creative element as well. Such creative intervention was seldom acknowledged in the performance programs and rarely identified on the costumes themselves.[5] Where machine-embroidered or stamped labels are present, they usually identify companies that were in their infancy during their involvement with the Ballet Russes—a collaboration that would help to establish them in their fields.

About 1910 Morris Angel & Son—now called Angels, and London's longest established costumier, famous for their film and theatrical work—created the costume for Pierrot in the Ballets Russes production of *Carnaval*. Shoemakers Anello & Davide, shortly after commencing operations in London in 1922, made

Natalia Goncharova
Costume for a squid c 1916
(detail) from *Sadko*
© Natalia Goncharova/ADAGP.
Licensed by Viscopy, 2010

(left to right)
German customs stamp on the lining of the bodice of the costume for a friend of Queen Thamar, from *Thamar*, designed by Léon Bakst c 1912

Costumier Maison Muelle Rossignol's label for the costume of a court lady, from *The sleeping princess*, designed by Léon Bakst c 1921 'Mos Muelle Rossignol Sr, Costumier de L'Opera, 12 Rue delLa Victoire, PARIS'

Label in the jacket of the costume for *The hunt* from *Giselle*, designed by Alexandre Benois c 1910

the boots for the two Ivans from *Le Mariage d'Aurore*, each with 'ANELLO & DAVIDE/LONDON WC/NEW COMPTON' embossed on their leather soles. This firm went on to great success, specialising in performance footwear and bespoke handmade shoes for their many celebrated clients, including royalty. Marie Muelle, a leading costumier for the stage in Paris, considered her involvement with the Ballets Russes prior to 1915 as the greatest 'feather in her cap'. She continued to receive commissions for costumes for later Ballets Russes productions (such as *Le Chant du rossignol* in 1920 and *The sleeping princess* in 1921), but only two costumes in the Gallery's collection bear her label.[6] While costumier labels were a well-established practice in contemporary fashion houses such as Worth, Lanvin, Paquin and Vionnet, they remain a scarcity in the earlier theatre costumes. Labels were a sign of haute couture which, in the early decades of the twentieth century, had very strict rules for inclusion, such as the designing house must have at least fifteen employees and hold twice yearly fashion shows of their own designs. Costumiers may not have been able to meet these criteria while completing orders for the Ballets Russes.

A very different and invaluable resource is the inscriptions that identify the wearers of the costumes. The dancers' names—which are predominantly Anglicised Russian names—are written, often scribbled, in ink or pencil and later with fibre-tipped pens, usually on the lining of bodices. It is common for several names to appear on the one costume, with some crossed through indicating that those dancers were replaced in later productions. The costume for a Lezghin from *Thamar* carries more than 12 entries[7], and 10 names appear inside the costume for a *genie des heures* from *Le Pavillon d'Armide*. However, the costumes for the Blue God in *Le Dieu bleu*, and Petrouchka, are inscribed with just one name—Nijinski (Vaslav Nijinsky). Overall, the linings of the costumes conserved from the collection carry 174 inscribed names of various degrees of legibility.

The most significant inscriptions for the conservator are the presence of two types of customs stamps. One stamp (Douane Centrale Paris Exportation) was secured as the Ballets Russes departed France and another (Direktion des Russichen Balletts * Sergiei von Diaghilews) as the company crossed the German border.[8] Their use is irregular, as some productions have all items including undergarments stamped and others only one or two items. These stamps only appear on costumes from the 1909–12 seasons so despite their sporadic use, their presence plays a defining role in dating costumes from the early productions. Such stamps are most clearly evident on costumes from the productions of *Cléopâtre*, *Petrouchka*, *Schéhérazade*, *Daphnis et Chloé* and *Pavillon D'Armide*.

After details of inscriptions have been documented, fabrics and fibres are analysed. This enables the textile conservator to develop an appropriate treatment plan. This is not an easy task. As many as 20 different

198 Ballets Russes: the art of costume

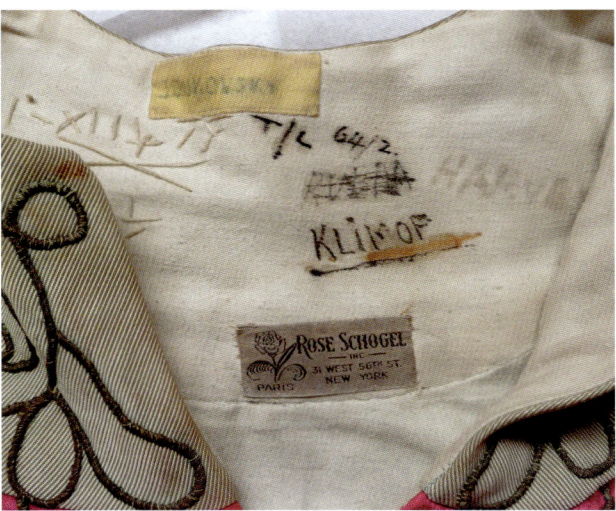

fabrics and fibres, and an equally varied and numerous selection of threads, may have been employed in the construction and decoration, as well as repairs, of a Ballets Russes costume. The conservator becomes acquainted with the opulence associated with Diaghilev's productions: brightly hand-dyed silks, fine satins with over 80 threads to a centimetre, gold braids, pearls and genuine fur trim. But the richness of fabric lies more in reputation than reality, as the dancers predominantly performed their roles wearing felt, cotton flannelette, wool or calico, with less than half the costumes in the Gallery's collection having a silk component. With the plain fabrics, decoration was paramount to capturing and conveying the characters of each performance. These costumes are highly decorated with appliqué, stencilled patterns and painted designs; sequins, feathers and beads also adorn many of them.

The variety and unusual assortment of fabrics used in the Ballets Russes costumes leads to questions about the underlying rationale for their selection. For instance, the fabric chosen for the frockcoat for Shah Zeman from *Schéhérazade* implies a requirement for authenticity. Ten metres of luscious turquoise silk and gold thread brocade bearing Persian motifs clearly reflect the cultural setting for the ballet. But silk was not chosen for the players of the court in *Le Pavillon d'Armide*, where felt and flannelette were dyed, painted and decorated to become visual representations of seventeenth-century French court attire, rather than actual replicas.

It appears that consideration for the movement and comfort of the dancers was not always a prime concern for the designer. As King Dodon made his grand entrance on stage in *Le Coq d'or*, robed in silk velvet, gold braid and ermine tails, he undoubtedly dazzled the audience, but his steps were perhaps laboured under the weight of up to eight layers of fabric. In *Daphnis et Chloé*—at almost an hour, one of the longest of the Ballets Russes' Paris productions, and which premiered in the summer of 1912—the Brigand characters danced in thick, coarse, unlined woollen tunics, with belts and capes, costumes that would have been extremely hot and uncomfortable.

The availability of funds did not always play a critical role in the types of fabrics used in a production. Despite the company facing severe financial pressure for the 1921 London production of *The sleeping princess*, the costume for a Court Lady uses over 20 metres of dyed silk in the skirt and bodice, with 8 metres of hand-painted decoration and feather trim adorning the edges of the skirt. Silk ribbons and metal beads decorate the bodice, and the cuffs are trimmed with pleated organza: no expense was spared in replicating the opulence of the eighteenth-century court.[9]

A primary influence in the selection of fabrics was their availability—and this is clearly demonstrated by the frequent use of artificial fibres in the transformation from design to costume. Expensive silks and satins do not withstand vigorous dance

(left to right)
Costumier Morris Angel & Son Ltd's label in the jacket for the Huzzar, from *Le Beau Danube*, designed by Etienne de Beaumont 1935. The label also identifies the costume as for the dancer Léonide Massine. 'Morris Angel & Son Ltd, 119 Shaftesbury Avenue, LONDON WC, DATE 16/9/35, Massine'

Inscription and costumier's label in the lining of the tunic for an Ivan, from *Le Mariage d'Aurore*, designed by Natalia Goncharova c 1920s. 'Rose Schogeli, Paris, 31 West 56th St, New York'

Label identifying this costume for a Jew, from *Cléopâtre*, designed by Léon Baskt c 1909. There is also a label identifying the dancer Constantin Kobeleff and a German customs stamp.

Sights unseen: tags, stamps and stains 199

Costume for a squid, from *Sadko—in the underwater kingdom*, designed by Natalia Goncharova 1916, prior to conservation treatment.

(left) The blue silk of the costume was completely shattered with several areas of fabric lost before restoration.

(right) The green silk front yoke was extensively damaged around the shoulders. The garment was washed and aligned before being repaired.

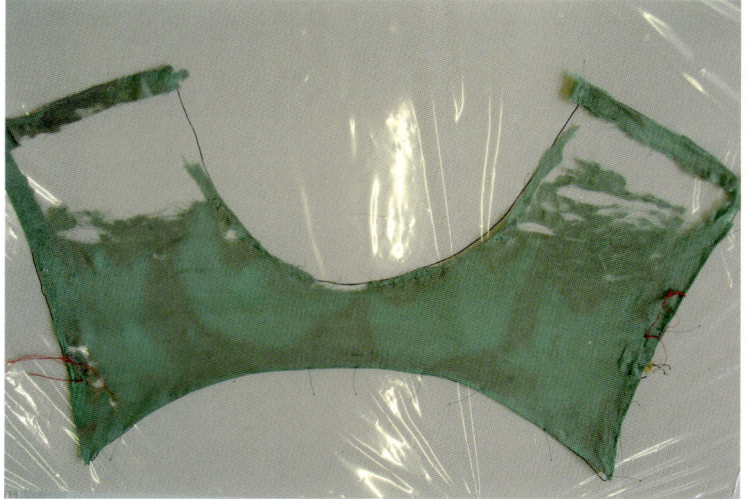

movements well, and most costumes with a silk component attest to this in repeated repairs and patches. In the early decades of the twentieth century, there was no alternative to silk if sheen and richness was desired. As soon as artificial fabrics became available, however, they appeared in theatre wardrobes and today play a critical role in helping to date not only entire costumes, but also when costumes were revamped or repaired. 'Artificial silk' has specific production dates, with rayon, first commercially produced in England in 1905, becoming popular after the First World War, and cellulose acetate from 1924.[10] The earliest example of artificial fibres in the Gallery's Ballets Russes collection is a hand-painted rayon ribbon from the edges of the jacket for a Polovtsian warrior from the 1909 production of *Danses polovtsiennes du Prince Igor*. By the mid 1920s artificial fabrics were readily embraced due to their unique qualities of visually resembling silk with increased strength.

While artificial fibres, with their specific production dates, provide a valuable means of dating, this is not always a straightforward process. Textile conservators spent many hours assessing the Gallery's costume for Queen Thamar against photographs from the first production of *Thamar* in 1912, with Tamara Karsavina dancing the principal role. The metallic fabrics used in the overskirt and vest were visually identical, and proved to be very similar in detail to other fabrics used in the costumes for this production. But the dress itself is made from acetate, placing its manufacture more than a decade after 1912. The original dress, which would have been made from silk, may have become severely damaged due to constant contact with the metallic thread of the vest and overskirt. The dress itself was probably remade sometime after the mid 1920s, utilising the original trim and over-garments.

Following identification of the components of the costumes, the conservator details their construction— a process that reveals the technical excellence of a bygone era of costume manufacture. All but a few of the costumes in the Gallery's collection are fully lined with cotton, and created to the very high standards that manufacturers considered essential in the early twentieth century. Although full linings with panelled bodices have machine-stitched seams, they were secured by hand-stitched French seams. Bone stays were employed in shaping bodices, each sewn by hand into perfectly fitted casings. Buttonholes were sewn by hand, so finely that they appear machine made. Perfectly cut fabric facings and placards hide the fastening mechanisms, which at that time were large metal press-studs or hooks and eyes (zippers did not appear on costumes until 1919). The costume for Shah Zeman in *Schéhérazade* reveals how complex construction could be, with over 80 fabric pieces contributing to the completed outfit. While the high level of technical accuracy in construction has contributed significantly to the longevity of many costumes, paradoxically this can complicate the restoration process, especially if seams need to be undone to facilitate repair.

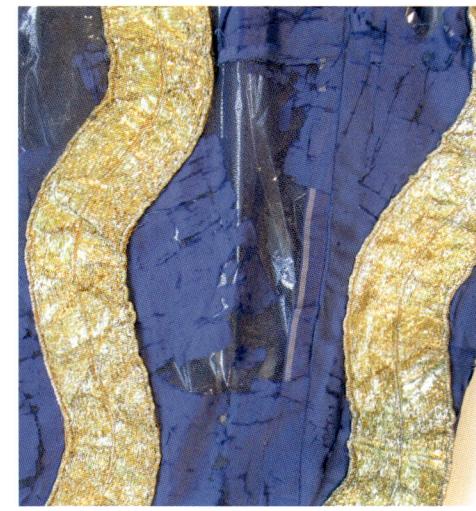

It is highly unlikely that the costumes of the Ballets Russes were ever cleaned. Even if it was desirable, cleaning would have been difficult due to the unstable dyes and decorative elements. Dry-cleaning did not become an easily accessible option until the 1930s, so most costumes carry a chronological assortment of stains. Hemlines and the soles of thick cotton-knit tights are black from the dust of the stage floor. Metallic thread and braids tarnish; metal fasteners corrode; and the repeated lines of rust staining the shoulders of many costumes demonstrate that they were stored on the newly invented wire coathanger. Transferred or dislodged dyes and areas of mould attest to a costume having become wet at some time during storage.

One stain that has a severe impact on the condition of a costume is perspiration. As the dancers performed without the many personal hygiene products available today, such as anti-perspirants, the linings of the costumes bear witness to their vigorous physical activity. The cotton linings of tightly fitted garments are discoloured from perspiration to a deep brown and the affected fabric is extremely brittle. If silk is present in this area it is darkened and generally rotted, with large areas of loss. In the few costumes where 'sweat pads' were used they were of cotton backed with an early synthetic coating, but by now these pads have totally disintegrated. Fortunately Vaslav Nijinsky appears to have perspired only moderately, compared to many of the other members of the corps de ballet, allowing his costumes to be only minimally affected by this form of damage. The personal nature of some of the stains the textile conservator is required to remove would perhaps horrify many people, but for the conservator this is part of the care of the collection.

Most costumes are heavily stained with greasepaint makeup. The blended greasepaints provide unique insights into the appearance of the dancers in an era prior to colour imaging. Although there may have been slight discoloration over time, the fact that the costumes were always stored in the dark and have not been cleaned has allowed the makeup colours to remain very close to the original. Léon Bakst's design drawing for the Blue God depicts a figure with exposed skin of a very dark hue verging on deep navy blue.[11] The evidence of makeup on the costume worn by Nijinsky in the 1912 production of *Le Dieu bleu* indicates that a much lighter and brighter blue was deemed appropriate for the stage. Queen Thamar in *Thamar* wore makeup with such a pink tone it was almost a peach colour. A similar peach-coloured makeup was worn by the Chief Eunuch in *Schéhérazade*—although Bakst's design drawing for this character portrays him as African in origin.[12]

To clean a costume the conservators first vacuum it to remove loose dirt particles. This is undertaken with micro vacuum nozzles through a fine screen so that the fibres are held in place during suction to reduce damage but still allow the removal of loose dirt. All dirt samples are kept as part of the documentation of the costume's conservation. Then follows extensive

(left) The bodice lining viewed under ultra violet radiation revealing faded inscriptions; the orange areas are perspiration stains.

(centre) When acquired, the damaged silk had been backed by coarse nylon net adhered to the inner face. The net had to be removed to avoid further damage to the fragile silk, a process which took hundreds of hours.

(right) Costume for a squid, from *Sadko* after conservation treatment (also see p130).
© Natalia Goncharova/ADAGP. Licensed by Viscopy, 2010.

(following pages) **Léon Bakst** *Costume for a friend of Queen Thamar* c 1912 (detail) from *Thamar*, after conservation treatment (also see p 117).

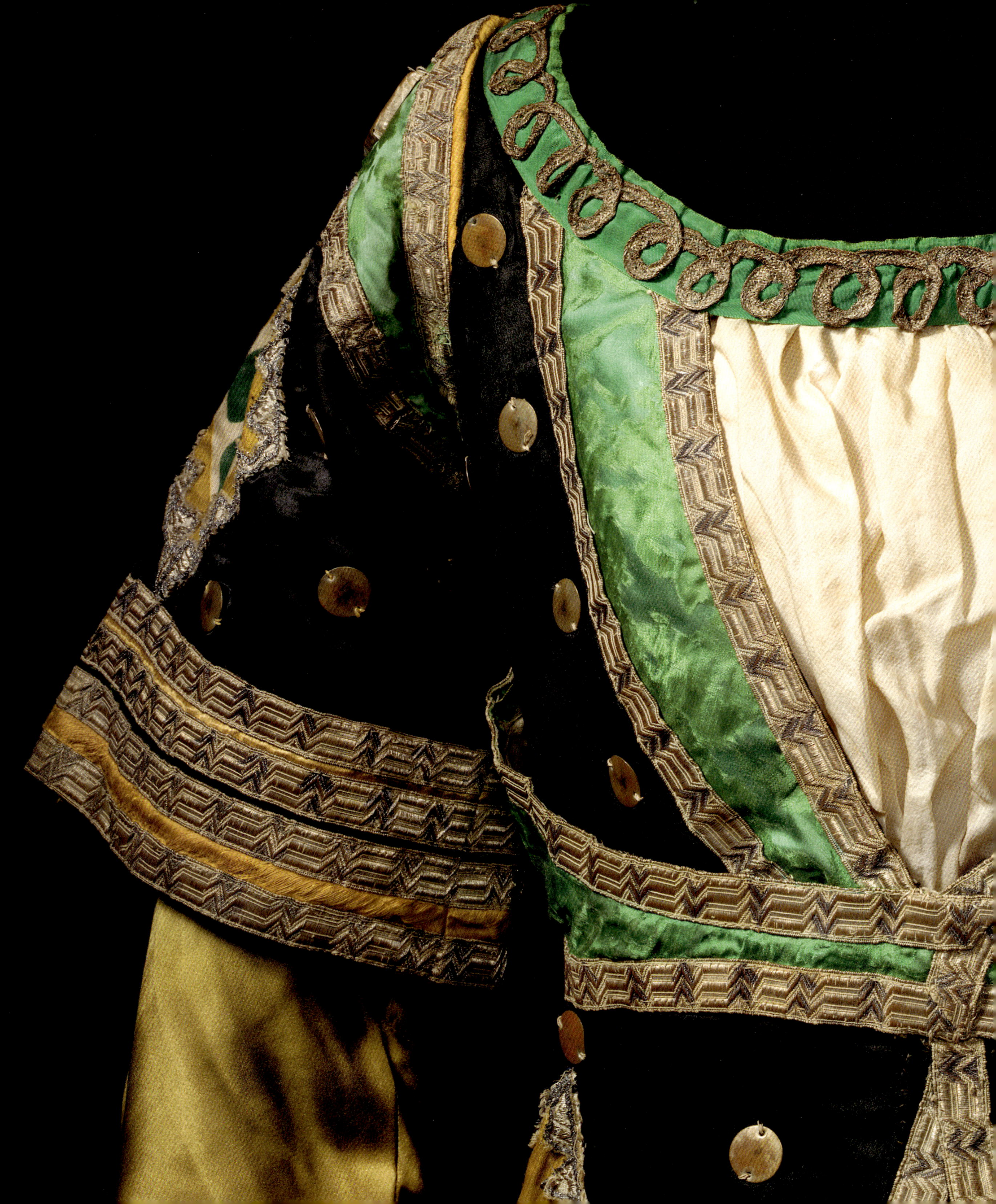

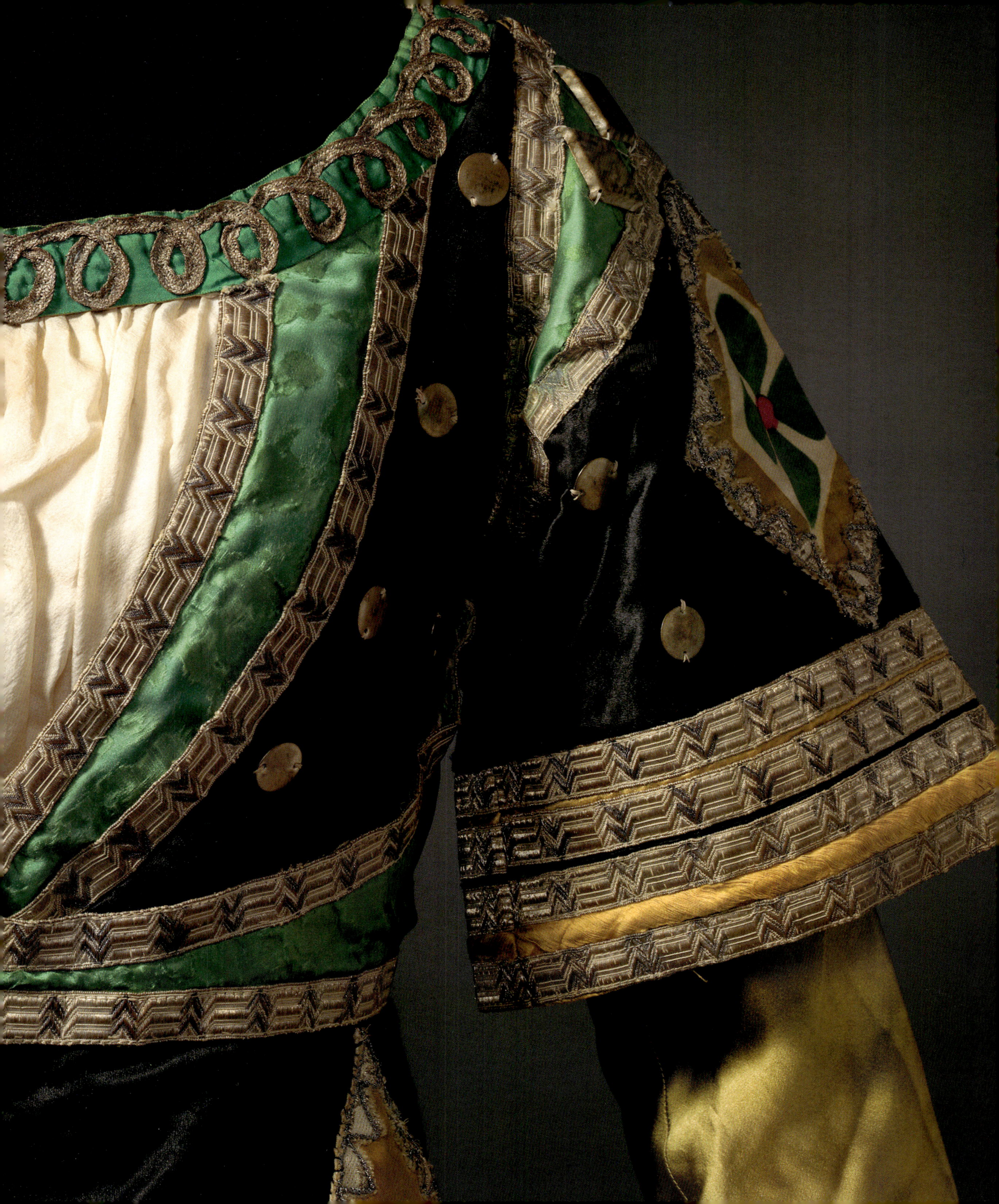

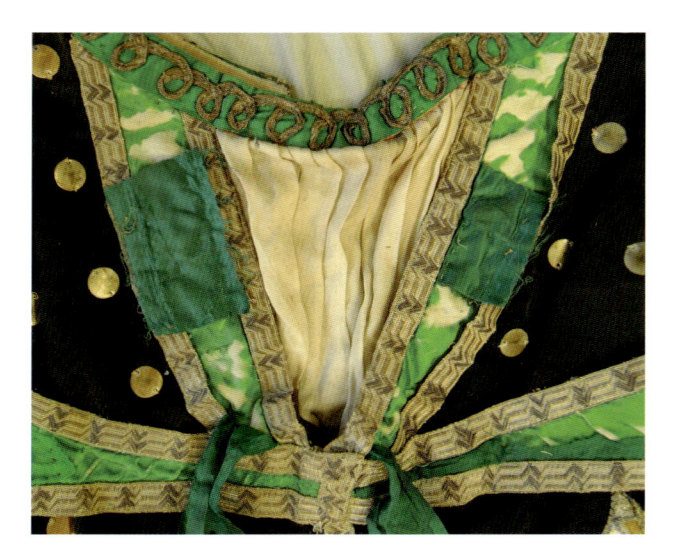

Costume for a friend of Queen Thamar, from *Thamar*, designed by Léon Bakst c1912, prior to conservation treatment.

(left) Front bodice showing extensive damage; repairs are evident in the areas of design with green silk.

(centre) Damage to the satin-weave fabric at the back of the bodice.

(right) Part of the lining showing the seams and gathers have yellowed with age and large areas were damaged with rust stains.

testing of every component, including testing the stains for solubility. Due to the presence of inscriptions and unstable dyes, and the composite materials used, it is rare that a costume can be totally cleaned. Stains are treated with specially developed cleaning agents applied with cotton tips, or using micro suction plates that direct the agent through the stain, isolating it and preventing transfer to other areas of the costume. Rusted fasteners are removed after every stitch is documented, and cleaned and stabilised before being reattached.

Stains can cause deterioration and potentially distract from the original design, but the greatest threat is physical damage. Ballets Russes costumes originally constructed for the dancers who performed at the premiere of a specific ballet could be worn by other dancers in later performances. If these dancers were smaller than the original wearers, seams had to be taken in and hems shortened—rarely with the same attention to detail as the original costumier had applied. To accommodate larger figures, side panels were inserted; but seams put under pressure could split and tear. Satin-weave fabric with fine floating silk threads could not withstand energetic dance movements, and the metallic braid so often preferred as a form of decoration easily cut through the threads.

Posing the greatest problem to the conservator are fabrics that were manufactured with unstable components, such as the early synthetic material used in the jacket of the costume for a soldier from *Chout* in 1921 and the apron from the costume for a worker in *Le Pas d'acier* in 1927. These materials have deteriorated considerably over time and their exact chemical composition is very difficult to determine. Without detailed information a successful treatment cannot be developed, so the conservator must focus on stabilising such costumes rather than undertaking a full restoration. Similarly in the late nineteenth and early twentieth century, fine silks were often treated with metallic mordants to increase lustre and add body to the fabric (a process known as weighting the silk). Over time these chemicals cause the silk to deteriorate, making it so brittle that the slightest movement can bring about disintegration. Extensive damage of this type was found on the costume for a squid from *Sadko* and the skirt of the costume for Chiarina from *Carnaval*.

Silk shatters into small fragments in a similar way to a sheet of glass. For silk that has shattered, sewing restoration is not an option as the movement of the needle through the fabric leads to further damage. Instead, fine silk gauze is dyed to match the original fabric and painted with a very thin layer of heat-sensitive adhesive, then attached to the reverse side of the damaged fabric using an iron the size of a little fingernail. Every thread of the silk must be perfectly aligned before the backing is attached. This was the only method suitable for the treatment of the squid costume, and required the total deconstruction of the tunic—a task made considerably more difficult by the fact that the silk had previously been crudely stuck to nylon netting. During the restoration of this costume, which lasted over five months, the previous repairs were removed, all components of the costume were supported with new silk backing and it was completely reconstructed.

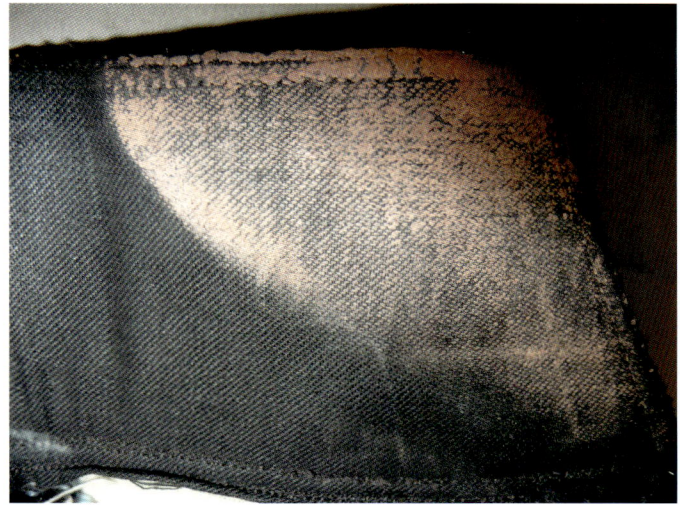

The total backing of fabrics is an extremely time-consuming process, and the most difficult restoration tasks are encountered when the damaged areas are surrounded by brocades and design motifs that do not allow simple backing of the affected areas. The bodice of the costume for a friend of Thamar in *Thamar* is highly decorated with stencils and rows of gold braid and medallions. Between the braid were bands of green silk that were completely shattered, with large areas lost. It was not possible to remove the silk to back it with a support silk, as the braid could not be removed. Instead, the conservator inserted patches beneath the remnants of the original silk and applied adhesive before sewing them into place. This type of treatment requires exceptional skill, not only to avoid damaging the remaining original fabric, but in keeping the patch perfectly aligned.

Even the simplest treatments can reveal unexpected insights into the history of a costume. The voluminous orange harem pants from the costume of the Chief Eunuch from *Schéhérazade* were in very good condition, with only the elastic at the ankles requiring attention. The stitches of the seams at the ankles were documented and then carefully removed to place new elastic. Once the seams were opened the conservator discovered several other layers of silk rather than just the cotton lining. After investigation the curious history of the repair of the costume was revealed.

The original pants from the 1912 production were of fine orange silk decorated with yellow silk stripes adorned with small oval metallic medallions, and backed by a white cotton lining. The silk had been damaged and several patches applied to conceal this. Sometime later the appearance of the pants was deemed no longer suitable and so they were repaired again. This last repair, however, was in the form of a totally new pair of pants sewn over and completely obscuring the original striped pants. Textile conservators were able to remove all past repairs and conserve the original costume: its location would have remained a mystery without the process of conservation.

The work of the textile conservator takes one on a journey of discovery of a garment's construction secrets and its history of use and repair. The painstaking and detailed work undertaken by the Gallery's conservators has revealed more information about the lives of these costumes that can be gathered from contemporary photographs or written accounts of Ballets Russes productions. The work that develops from the privileged view of the conservator is not intended to compete with the costume's overall visual impact when on display but provides an unseen but vital new structural foundation for the continuing preservation of these artefacts.

(left) Rich pink make-up on the lining of the bodice from the costume of Chiarina, from *Carnaval*, designed by Léon Bakst c 1910. The inscription is for the dancer L Tchernicheva.

(right) Make-up on the inner collar of the costume for a military musician, from *Jardin public*, designed by Jean Lurçat c 1935.

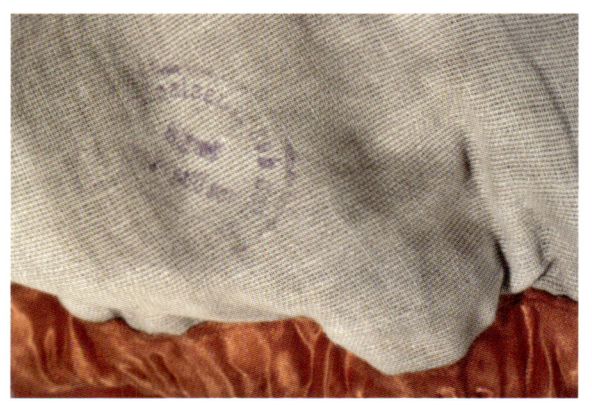

Costume for the Chief Eunuch, from *Schéhérazade*, designed by Leon Bakst c 1910, prior to conservation treatment.

(clockwise from left)
Original pants showing several stages of repair. In the centre a small section of the original orange silk with yellow stripes is revealed beneath cotton repair stripes. These are all encased in a new pair or pants pulled back and visible on the left.

The original pants with patches over damaged silk were completely encased within a new pair of satin pants.

One of the original silk stripes of the pants, damaged from contact with the decorative medallions.

A very faded customs stamp on the lining of the pants, identifying it was from one of the earlier productions of the ballet.

Extensive damage to the original stencilled appliqué design of the heart on the overskirt

(opposite) **Léon Bakst**
Costume for the Chief Eunuch c 1910 (detail) from *Schéhérazade*, after conservation treatment.

206   Ballets Russes: the art of costume

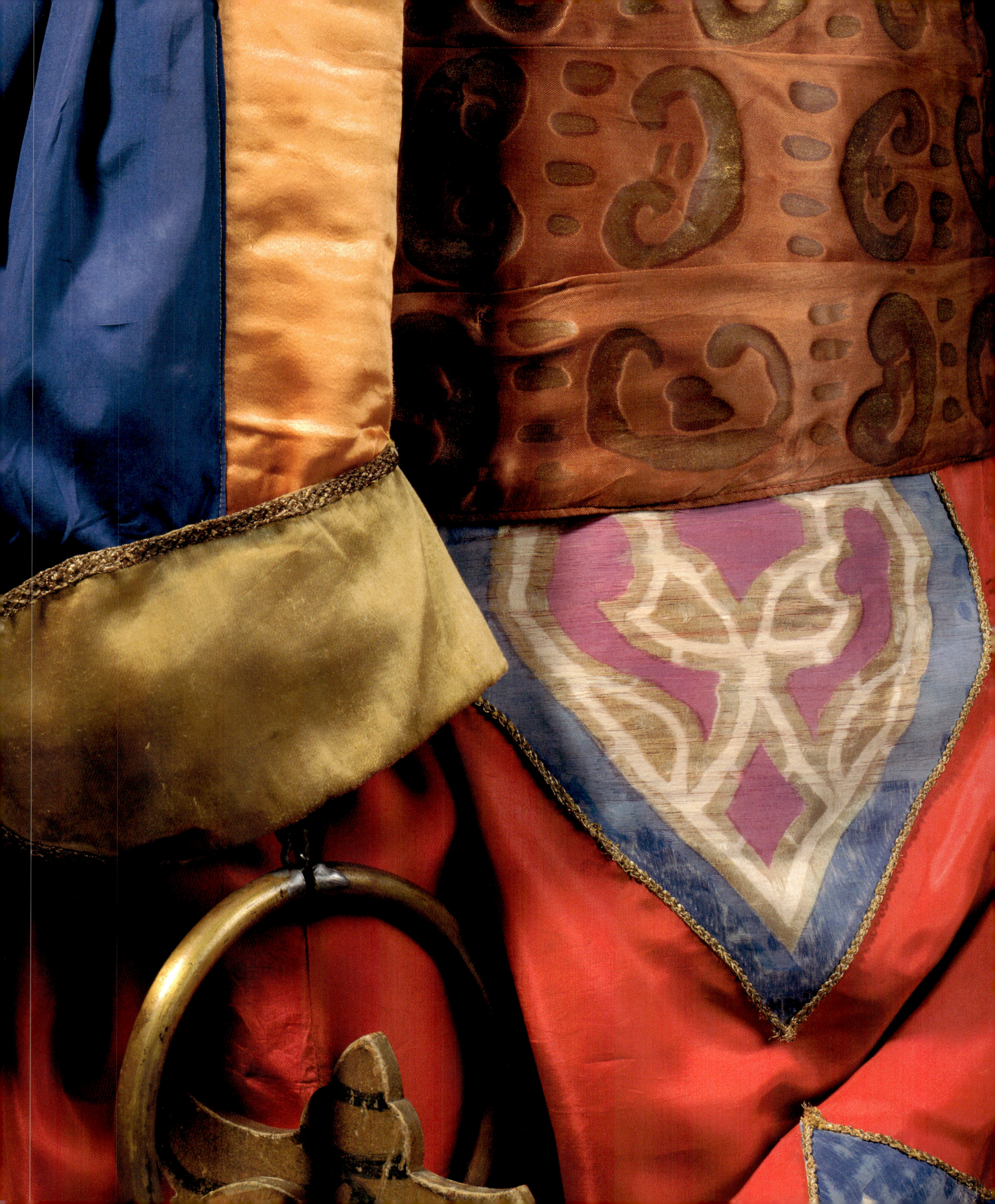

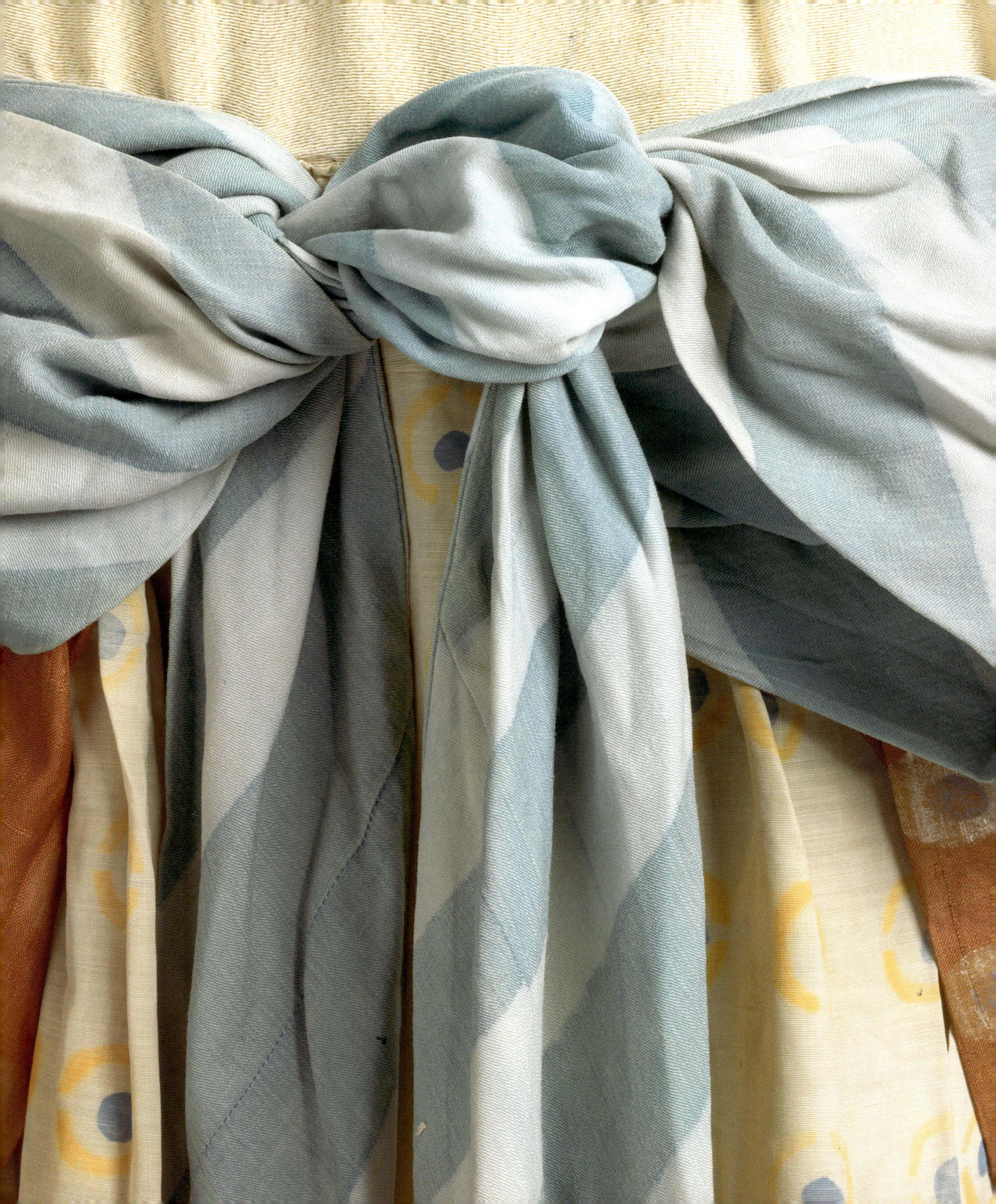

NOTES

The Ballets Russes costume legacy Robert Bell (pp19–21)

1. The National Gallery of Australia's collection of Ballets Russes costumes comprises complete costumes, parts of costumes and accessories such as hats, boots and jewellery.
2. García-Márquez, *The Ballets Russes: Colonel de Basil's Ballets Russes de Monte Carlo 1932–1952*, Alfred A Knopf, New York, 1990, p 315. See also E Näslund (ed), *Ballets Russes: the Stockholm collection*, Dansmuseet Stockholm and Bokförlaget Langenskiöld, Stockholm, 2009, pp 11–13.
3. See Debbie Ward's account of the conservation process in this publication, 'Sights unseen', pp 197–206, and J Carter, 'Conserving costumes from Les Ballets Russes de Serge Diaghilev', in R Healy & M Lloyd, *From studio to stage: costumes and designs from the Russian Ballet in the Australian National Gallery*, Australian National Gallery, Canberra, 1990, pp 60–3.
4. *From studio to stage: painters of the Russian Ballet 1909–1929*, curated by Robyn Healy and Michael Lloyd, was held at the Australian National Gallery from 8 December 1990 to 3 February 1991. *From Russia with love: costumes for the Ballets Russes 1909–1933*, curated by Roger Leong and Christine Dixon, was held at the Art Gallery of Western Australia from 6 February to 5 April 1999 and at the National Gallery of Australia from 15 May to 1 August 1999.
5. *Working for Diaghilev* was held from 11 December 2004 to 28 March 2005. The National Gallery of Australia's costumes are illustrated in S Scheijen (ed), *Working for Diaghilev*, BAI and Groninger Museum, Schoten, Netherlands, 2004, pp 228–34, 238–9, 243–4, 249–50.

Wild dream: imagining the Ballets Russes Robert Bell (pp 23–47)

1. Théophile Gautier, 'Omphale', *One of Cleopatra's nights*, trans Lafcadio Hearn, Wildside Press, Gillette, NJ, 1999, p 221.
2. For a fuller discussion of the development of the *ballet de cour*, see R Strong, 'Dress as hieroglyph: costume in the ballet de cour', *Designing for the dancer*, Elron Press, London, 1981, pp 9–32.
3. Louis XIV established the ballet school, l'Académie royale de Danse, in 1661 and l'Académie d'Opéra in 1669. Opera and ballet came together in 1713 as the state institution, the Ballet de l'Opéra.
4. Major figures who developed *ballet d'action* were Jean-Georges Noverre (1727–1810) in Stuttgart, Franz Hilverding (1710–1768) in Vienna and St Petersburg, and Gasparo Angiolini (1731–1803) in Vienna.
5. *La Sylphide* was choreographed by Filippo Taglioni (1777–1871) as a showcase for his daughter, Marie Taglioni (1804–1884), as the Sylph. Music was by Jean Madeleine Marie Schneitzhoeffer and libretto by Adolphe Nourrit.

Léon Bakst
Costume for a Syrian woman c 1909–30s (detail) from *Cléopâtre*

6. For a fuller discussion of the development of nineteenth-century costume design, see I Guest, 'Costume and the nineteenth century dancer', *Designing for the dancer*, Elron Press, London, 1981, pp 33–64.
7. Biographical details of Benois, Bakst and Roerich are included with those of other Ballets Russes designers later in this publication.
8. Finland's status as a semi-autonomous Grand Duchy within the Russian empire had allowed its artists a freedom of expression envied by progressive Russians, but by the 1890s its neo-nationalist character began to be officially repressed. Leading Finnish artists, such as the painter Akseli Gallen-Kallela and the architect Eliel Saarinen, gained international attention (including articles in *Mir Iskusstva*) for their expressions of National Romanticism in their work and its role in promoting the cause of Finnish separatism.
9. Talashkino and Abramtsevo remain as museums of late nineteenth-century and early twentieth-century Russian folk and applied arts.
10. A complete set of *Mir Iskusstva* is held in the National Library of Australia. See Michelle Potter, '*Mir iskusstva*: Serge Diaghilev's art journal', *National Library of Australia News*, July 2005, pp 3–6.
11. Mamontov's business dealings resulted in legal proceedings against him in 1900, with subsequent financial ruin. Tenisheva withdrew her support on the basis of objections to *Mir Iskusstva*'s editorial directions, under Alexandre Benois, which she felt were moving away from her preference for neo-nationalism.
12. Léo Delibes's French ballet *Sylvia* (1876) had never been performed in Russia. Diaghilev proposed to stage it at the Mariinsky Theatre.
13. Diaghilev's homosexuality is discussed in S Scheijen, 'The "homosexual clique" 1906–1907', *Diaghilev: a life*, Profile Books, London, 2009, pp 140–52.
14. Proper names used in this publication are given in their most commonly used and accepted European or English variants, with original birth names following at first mention. To maintain a Russian identity with their increasingly multinational troupes, it was the practice of Diaghilev's and other Ballets Russes companies to change their English dancers' names to fictitious 'Russianised' versions; these are used in this publication, with original names in parentheses. Sergei (or Sergey) Diaghilev styled himself as Serge de Diaghileff in France and America, but is commonly referred to by the French variant of his name, Serge Diaghilev. Among family and friends he was known by the diminutive Serioja (or Seriozha).
15. After the split with Diaghilev, Fokine worked as ballet master with the Stockholm Opera during 1913 and toured Sweden again during 1918, forming a close association with the wealthy impresario Rolf de Maré (1888–1964), who would go on to found the avant-garde touring ballet company, the Ballets Suédois (1920–1925).
16. In Fokine's letter to *The Times*, published on 6 July 1914, he outlines his five principles for choreography, by which dance movement should: respond to the character of the music, be an expression of dramatic action, use the whole body for expression, use groups of dancers to build dramatic expressiveness and be an equal partner to music and stage design.

17   Isadora Duncan (1877–1927) was born in Oakland, California and moved to Europe in 1898. She met Diaghilev in 1904 during her first season of performances in St Petersburg. A proponent of free movement and costuming based on the culture of ancient Greece, Duncan had a strong influence on the emergent contemporary dance movement in Russia. Loïe (Marie Louise) Fuller (1862–1928) was born in Chicago, Illinois and first performed in Paris at the Folies Bergère in 1892, becoming well known for her interpretive dancing, voluminous costume drapery and innovative lighting techniques. She performed in her own pavilion at the Exposition Universelle and depictions of her dancing were popularised through the Art Nouveau movement.

18   *L'Exposition de l'art russe* was curated by Serge Diaghilev, designed by Léon Bakst and later toured, in a reduced version, to Berlin and Venice. It included the work of Bakst, Somov, Benois, Lanceray, Larionov and Goncharova.

19   The 1907 concerts, held on 16, 19, 23, 26 and 30 May, included works by Modest Mussorgsky, Pyotr Il'yich Tchaikovsky, Alexander Borodin, Mily Balakirev, Mikhail Glinka, Nikolai Rimsky-Korsakov, Sergei Rachmaninov, Alexander Scriabin, Sergei Lyapunov and Alexander Taneyev.

20   *Boris Godunov*, revised by Nikolai Rimsky-Korsakov in 1896, was designed by Alexandre Benois, Aleksandr Golovin, Konstantin Yuon and Ivan Bilibin, and staged on 19, 21, 24, 26 and 31 May 1908.

21   Production details and costumes from this and other Ballets Russes productions from which the National Gallery of Australia holds costumes are listed and illustrated elsewhere in this publication.

22   Anna Pavlovna Pavlova (1881–1931); Ida Rubinstein (1885–1960); Vera Fokina (1886–1958, married Mikhail Fokin 1905); Tamara Platonovna Karsavina (1885–1978); Ludmila Schollar (1888–1978).

23   Vaslav Nijinsky (Wacław Niżyński, 1890–1950); Adolph Rudolphovich Bolm (1884–1951); Michel Fokine (Mikhail Mikhailovich Fokin, 1880–1942); Mikhail Mordkin (1880–1944).

24   For a discussion on the prominence of male dancers in the Ballets Russes, see Lynn Garafola, 'Reconfiguring the sexes' in L Garafola & N Van Norman Baer (eds), *The Ballets Russes and its world*, Yale University Press, New Haven, 1999, pp 244–68.

25   See L Garafola, 'The sexual iconography of the Ballets Russes', in R Leong & C Dixon, *From Russia with love: costumes for the Ballets Russes 1909–1933*, National Gallery of Australia, Canberra, 1998, pp 56–65.

26   Paul Poiret (France, 1879–1944) opened his Paris fashion house in 1902 and established the Atelier Martine school of decorative art in 1911. Diaghilev maintained a friendship with the Venice-based Spanish textile and dress designer, Mariano Fortuny (1871–1949) and also with the French couturier, Gabrielle 'Coco' Chanel (1883–1971), whom he commissioned to design the costumes for the Ballets Russes 1924 production, *Le Train bleu*. Léon Bakst also designed dresses for an influential private clientele.

27   Stravinsky created scores for the Diaghilev opera productions *Le Rossignol* (1914), *Mavra* (1922), *Oedipus Rex* (1927); and the ballets *L'Oiseau de feu* (1910), *Petrouchka* (1911), *Le Sacre du printemps* (1913), *Le Rossignol* (1914), *Feu d'artifice* (1917), *Le Chant du rossignol* (1920), *Pulcinella* (1920), *Le Renard* (1922), *Les Noces* (1923) and *Apollon musagète* (1928).

28   Enrico Cecchetti trained as a dancer in Florence and taught at the Imperial School of Ballet in St Petersburg from 1887 to 1902, followed by directorship of the Imperial School of Ballet in Warsaw, Poland until 1906.

29   See Serge Grigoriev (Vera Bowen, trans & ed), *The Diaghilev ballet 1909–1929*, Constable, London, 1953. Walter Nouvel joined Grigoriev in managing the company from 1920.

30   Diaghilev's Ballets Russes toured the United States of America from 17 January to 6 May 1916, playing sixteen towns and cities. The second tour, as the Ballets Russes and under the direction of Vaslav Nijinsky and Adolph Bolm, played 53 towns and cities in the United States and Canada from 9 October 1916 to 24 February 1917.3

31   Misia Sert (Maria Zofia Olga Zenajda Godebska 1872–1950) was an émigré Polish pianist who hosted an influential artistic salon in Paris from 1903. José-María Sert was her third husband.

32   *Parade* premiered at the Théâtre du Châtelet in Paris on 18 May 1917.

33   See H Hammond, 'Spectacular histories: the Ballets Russes, the past and the classical tradition', this publication, pp 51–67.

34   The American-born Winnaretta Singer (1865–1943), the heir to the Singer sewing machine fortune, married Prince Edmond de Polignac in 1893. After his death in 1901 she used her fortune to support contemporary music and arts.

35   For an account of Balanchine's work see R Buckle & J Taras, *George Balanchine, ballet master*, Random House, New York, 1988.

36   Serge Lifar trained with Bronislava Nijinska and joined the Ballets Russes in 1923. Diaghilev sent him to Turin to study technique under Enrico Cecchetti, before making him his premier dancer in 1925.

37   See C Dixon, 'Modern art, modern ballet', this publication, pp 71–81.

38   See I Baronova, *Irina: ballet, life and love*, Penguin Group, Melbourne, 2005.

39   Barbara Karinska operated a couture business in Moscow from 1921 to 1924. Her third husband, Vladimir Mamontov, was the son of Savva Mamontov.

40   The outcome of the legal case in London in February 1938 was that Massine would retain the copyrights to *Le beau Danube*, *La Boutique fantasque*, *Le Tricorne* and *Les Matelots*.

41   K Sorley Walker, *De Basil's Ballets Russes*, Hutchinson, London, 1982, p 28.

42   The author drew upon the recollections of his family members, Joyce Orchard and Elsie Stewart, who attended every performance of the Ballets Russes in Sydney.

43   The Hugh P Hall Collection is held by the National Library of Australia, Canberra. See also Hugh P Hall, *Ballet in Australia from Pavlova to Rambert*, Georgian House, Melbourne, 1948. Anderson's and Murray-Will's films are held by the National Film and Sound Archive, Canberra.

44   See M Potter, 'People, patronage and promotion: the Ballets Russes tours to Australia, 1936–1940', this publication, pp183–193.

45   Nolan's work for *Icare* is discussed in M Potter, 'Spatial boundaries: Sidney Nolan's ballet designs', *Brolga*, 3, December 1995, pp 53–67.

46   '*Lutte éternelle*', *Australia Dancing*, National Library of Australia, Canberra, http://www.australiadancing.org/subjects/5101.html, accessed 5/5/2010.

47   See M Potter, 'A strong personality and a gift for leadership: Hélène Kirsova in Australia', *Dance Research* (Oxford), XIII, No 2, Autumn 1995, pp 62–76.

48   The project's website, http://www.nla.gov.au/balletsrusses/resources.html, includes extensive details of events and performances that celebrate the tours, as well as listing resources relating to the tours and their impact on Australian culture.

Spectacular histories: the Ballets Russes, the past and the classical tradition
Helena Hammond (pp 51–67)

1   Diaghilev quoted in Ann Kodicek (ed), *Diaghilev: creator of the Ballets Russes*, exhibition book, Barbican Art Gallery and Lund Humphries, London, 1996, p 38.

2   On the representation of history in *The sleeping beauty* see Helena Hammond, 'Cecchetti, Carabosse and beauty', *Dancing Times*, May 2007, pp 32–5.

3   Hanna Järvinen, '"The Russian Barnum": Russian opinions on Diaghilev's Ballets Russes, 1909–14', *Dance Research*, vol 26.1, Summer 2008, p 35.

4   Alexandre Benois, *Reminiscences of the Russian Ballet*, trans Mary Britineva, Putnam, London, 1941, p 127.

5   Ibid, p 121.

6   Prince Peter Lieven, *The birth of the Ballets-Russes*, trans L Zarine, George Allen & Unwin Ltd, London, 1936, p 28.

7   Benois, *Reminiscences of the Russian Ballet*, p 124.

8   Charles Spencer, *Léon Bakst and the Ballets Russes*, Academy Books, London, 1995, p 45.

9   Léon Bakst, 'Tchaikovsky and the Russian Ballet' in *Souvenir Programme: The Sleeping Princess* (Alhambra Theatre, Leicester Square), 1921, London.

10   Benois, *Reminiscences of the Russian Ballet*, p 124.

11   Benois quoted in Lieven, *The birth of the Ballets-Russes*, p 269.

12   Benois, *Reminiscences of the Russian Ballet*, pp 130, 129.

13   Benois quoted in John Roland Wiley, *A century of Russian ballet: documents and eyewitness accounts 1810–1910*, Oxford University Press, Oxford, 1990, pp 387, 391, 388.

14 Joan Acocella & Lynn Garafola, *André Levinson on dance: writings from Paris in the twenties*, Wesleyan University Press and University Press of New England, Hanover, NH, 1991, p 16.
15 André Levinson, *The story of Léon Bakst's life*, Alexander Kogan Publishing Company 'Russian Art', Berlin, 1922, p 66.
16 Ibid.
17 Ibid.
18 Alexandre Benois, 'The origins of the Ballets Russes', in Boris Kochno, *Diaghilev and the Ballets Russes*, trans Adrienne Foulke, Harper & Row, New York/Evanston, 1970, p 4.
19 Kodicek, *Diaghilev: creator of the Ballets Russes*, p 34.
20 Ibid, p 16.
21 Lieven, *The birth of the Ballets-Russes*, pp 37, 270.
22 Kodicek, *Diaghilev: creator of the Ballets Russes*, p 26.
23 Benois, *Reminiscences of the Russian Ballet*, p 233.
24 Ibid.
25 Ibid.
26 Levinson, *The story of Léon Bakst's life*, p 134.
27 Ibid.
28 Ibid.
29 Alexandre Benois, *Memoirs*, vol II, trans Moura Budberg, Chatto & Windus, London, 1964, p 247.
30 Järvinen, '"The Russian Barnum"', p 22.
31 Metelitsa in R Healy & M Lloyd, *From studio to stage: costumes and designs from the Russian Ballet in the Australian National Gallery*, Australian National Gallery, Canberra, 1990, p 31.
32 Diaghilev quoted in Arnold Haskell, *Diaghileff*, Victor Gollancz, London, 1955, p 28.
33 Lieven, *The birth of the Ballets-Russes*, p 96.
34 Benois in Lieven, *The birth of the Ballets-Russes*, p 100.
35 Diaghilev quoted in Alexander Schouvaloff, *The art of Ballets Russes: the Serge Lifar Collection of theater designs, costumes and paintings at the Wadsworth Atheneum, Hartford, Connecticut*, Yale University Press, New Haven, CT, 1997, p 109.
36 Elizabeth Emery & Laura Morowitz, *Consuming the past: the medieval revival in fin-de-siècle France*, Ashgate, Aldershot, UK and Burlington, VT, 2003, pp 86, 87.
37 Ibid, pp 107, 87.
38 Marcel Proust, 'The captive and the fugitive', *In search of lost time*, vol V, trans C K Scott Moncrieff & Terence Kilmartin, revised D J Enright, Vintage Books, London, 2000, pp 421–2.
39 Ibid, p 742.
40 Ibid, p 422.
41 Massine quoted in John Drummond, *Speaking of Diaghilev*, Faber & Faber, London and Boston, 1997, p 167.
42 Stephen Bann, *Romanticism and the rise of history*, Twayne Publishers, New York, 1995, p xiii.
43 Emery & Morowitz, *Consuming the past*, pp 4, 67.
53 Alain Erlande-Brandenburg, Pierre-Yves Le Pogam & Dany Sandron, *Musée national du Moyen Age Thermes de Cluny*, Réunion des Musées Nationaux, Paris, 1993, p 11; Emery & Morowitz, *Consuming the past*, p 67.
46 Lieven, *The birth of the Ballets-Russes*, pp 100–1.
47 Levinson, *The story of Léon Bakst's life*, p 99.
48 Benois, *Reminiscences of the Russian Ballet*, p 236.
49 Schouvaloff, *The art of Ballets Russes*, pp 35, 133.
50 Lieven, *The birth of the Ballets-Russes*, p 278.
51 Ibid, p 92.
52 Ibid, p 269.
53 Proust, *In search of lost time*, vol V, pp 267–8.
54 Emery & Morowitz, *Consuming the past*, p 4.
55 Kochno, *Diaghilev and the Ballets Russes*, p 37.
56 Lieven, *The birth of the Ballets-Russes*, p 79.
57 Benois quoted in Charles Spencer, *Léon Bakst and the Ballets Russes*, Academy Books, London, 1995, p 64.
58 Benois in Kochno, *Diaghilev and the Ballets Russes*, p 11.
59 Lieven, *The birth of the Ballets-Russes*, p 270.
60 Ibid, p 101.
61 Ibid, pp 270, 271.
62 Ibid, pp 270, 190.
63 Levinson quoted in Acocella & Garafola, *André Levinson on dance*, p 38.
64 Ibid, p 41.
65 Schouvaloff, *The art of Ballets Russes*, p 217.
66 Maribeth Clark, 'The role of *Gustave, ou Le bal masqué* in restraining the body of the July Monarchy', *Music and Culture* 88, 2006, p 205.
67 Karin von Maur, 'Music and theatre in the work of Juan Gris' in Christopher Green (with contributions by Christian Derouet & Karin von Maur), *Juan Gris*, Whitechapel Art Gallery, London, 1992, pp 275.
68 Schouvaloff, *The art of Ballets Russes*, p 218.
69 Quoted in Schouvaloff, *The art of Ballets Russes*, p 218.
70 Jane Fulcher, *French grand opera as politics and as politicized art*, Cambridge University Press, Cambridge, 1987, p 52.
71 Clark, 'The role of *Gustave*', p 221.
72 Stephen Walsh, *Igor Stravinsky: a creative spring: Russia and France 1882–1934*, Jonathan Cape, London, 2000, p 328.
73 Benois, *Reminiscences of the Russian Ballet*, p 130.
74 Walsh, *Igor Stravinsky: a creative spring*, p 328.
75 Stravinsky in *Souvenir Programme: The Sleeping Princess*, no page numbers given.
76 Bakst in *Souvenir Programme: The Sleeping Princess*, no page numbers given.
77 Schouvaloff, *The art of Ballets Russes*, p 87.
78 Benois, *Reminiscences of the Russian Ballet*, pp 132, 124.
79 Alexandre Benois, *Memoirs*, vol II p 60.
80 Levinson, *The story of Léon Bakst's life*, p 10.
81 Benois in *Souvenir Programme: The Sleeping Princess*, no page numbers given.
82 Benois, *Reminiscences of the Russian Ballet*, 124.
83 Richard Taruskin, *Defining Russia musically: historical and hermeneutical essays*, Princeton University Press, Princeton, NJ, 1997, p 253.
84 See Mark Franko, *Dance as text: ideologies of the Baroque body*, Cambridge University Press, Cambridge, 1993.
85 *The Times* 3 November 1921, quoted in Nesta Macdonald, *Diaghilev observed by critics in England and the United States 1911–1929*, New York Dance Books Ltd, London and New York, 1975, p 275.
86 Sacheverell Sitwell, '*The sleeping beauty* at the London Alhambra, 1921', *Ballet—to Poland*, ed Arnold Haskell, London, 1940, p 17.
87 Ibid, p 18.
88 André Levinson, *The designs of Léon Bakst for 'The sleeping princess', a ballet in five acts after Perrault, music by Tchaikovsky, preface by André Levinson*, Benn Brothers Ltd, London, 1923, p 13.
89 Deborah Howard, 'A sumptuous revival: Bakst's designs for Diaghilev's *Sleeping princess*', *Apollo* 91, April 1970, p 307.
90 Diana Souhami, *Bakst: The Rothschild panels of 'The sleeping beauty'*, Philip Wilson, London, 1992, p 11.
91 Selma Schwartz, *The Waddesdon companion guide*, The National Trust, Waddesdon Manor, Bucks, UK, 2003, p 78.
92 Souhami, *Bakst: The Rothschild panels of 'The sleeping beauty'*, p 11.
93 Schouvaloff, *The art of Ballets Russes*, p 88.
94 Walsh, *Igor Stravinsky: a creative spring*, p 328; Walter Propert, *The Russian ballet 1921–1929*, Bodley Head, London, 1931, p 11.
95 Beaumont quoted in Lynn Garafola, *Diaghilev's Ballets Russes*, Oxford University Press, London, 1989, p 222.

96 *Daily Mail* 3 November 1921, quoted in MacDonald, *Diaghilev observed by critics*, p 275.

97 Lieven quoted in Charles Spencer, *Léon Bakst and the Ballets Russes*, Academy Books, London, 1995, p 190.

98 Emery & Morowitz, *Consuming the past*, p 69

99 Howard, 'A sumptuous revival', p 305; Benois quoted in Howard, p 305.

100 Cyril Beaumont, *Bookseller at the Ballet: Memoirs 1891–1929*, C W Beaumont, London, 1975, p 286.

101 Consecutive performances: Garafola, *Diaghilev's Ballets Russes*, 1989, p 223; Paris Opera: Schouvaloff, *The art of Ballets Russes*, p 89.

102 Acocella & Garafola, *André Levinson on dance*, p 63.

103 Sitwell, '*The sleeping beauty* at the London Alhambra, 1921', p 19.

104 Bann, *Romanticism and the rise of history*, pp 6–7.

Modern art, modern ballet Christine Dixon (pp 71–81)

1 Quoted by Léonide Massine in *My life in ballet*, MacMillan & Co, London, 1968, p 85.

2 Quoted in Mary Chamot, *Goncharova, stage designs and paintings*, Oresko, London, 1979, p 15.

3 For example, the critic Michel Georges-Michel wrote, 'I don't believe any spectacle has ever given such an impression of splendour as did the first performance of *Coq d'or*', quoted in Robyn Healy and Michael Lloyd, *From studio to stage: costumes and designs from the Russian Ballet in the Australian National Gallery*, Australian National Gallery, Canberra, 1990, p 38.

4 Nancy Van Norman Baer, 'Design and choreography', in *From Russia with love*, National Gallery of Australia, Canberra, 1998, p 48.

5 The painting was later renamed by Malevich *Suprematist composition: white on white* 1918, oil on canvas. 78.7 x 78.7 cm. The Museum of Modern Art, New York.

6 John E Bowlt, 'From studio to stage: the painters of the Ballets Russes' in Nancy Van Norman Baer, *The art of enchantment*, The Fine Arts Museums of San Francisco and Universe Books, San Francisco, 1988, p 56.

7 Massine, p 147.

8 Nicholas Watkins, *Matisse*, Phaidon Press, Oxford, 1984, pp 173–4.

9 Lesley-Anne Sayers, 'Re-discovering Diaghilev's *Pas d'acier*', in *Dance Research: The Journal of the Society for Dance Research*, vol 18, no 2, Winter 2000, p 164. http://www.jstor.org accessed 12/04/2010.

10 Massine pp 171–2.

11 See Sayers note 9, pp 163–185. http://www.jstor.org accessed 12/04/2010.

12 'Les Matelots', *New Statesman*, 4 July 1925, p 338, quoted in Lynn Garafola, *Diaghilev's Ballets Russes*, Oxford University Press, New York & Oxford, 1909, p 367, note 124.

Costumes for Les Ballets Russes de Serge Diaghilev 1909–29
Robert Bell and Simeran Maxwell (pp 85–162)

1 The spelling of characters' names and titles (for all productions listed in this catalogue) are generally written as they were given in the programs of the original performances, with descriptions of characters and roles in English. Some French versions of Russian names and titles were used in 1909–48 productions in English-speaking countries and have become standardised in English-language Ballets Russes literature. Plot descriptions are based on synopses given in contemporary program notes and those used for later Ballets Russes performances in Australian venues during the tours of the 1930s.

2 Henri Ghéon, *Nouvelle revue française* (1910), in Richard Taruskin, *Stravinsky and the Russian traditions*, Oxford University Press, Oxford, 1996, p 638.

3 For a discussion of Cambodian dance see Hideo Sasagawa, 'Post/colonial discourses on the Cambodian court dance', *Southeast Asian Studies*, vol 42, no 4, March 2005, pp 418–41.

4 Fokine had written a libretto for *Daphnis and Chloë* and proposed to stage it at the Imperial Theatre in 1904, but the project was unrealised.

5 Nikolai Gustavovich Legat (1869–1937) was a dancer with the Russian Imperial Ballet from 1888 to 1914, along with his brother, Sergei Legat (d 1905) from 1894.

6 Respighi developed Rossini's *Les Riens* into an orchestral suite titled *Rossiniana* in 1925.

7 The Société des Instruments Anciens was founded by Henri Casadesus in 1901 with the sponsorship of the French composer Charles-Camille Saint-Saëns (1835–1921).

8 Inspired by the surviving poetry of the Greek poet Anacreon (c 582–c 485).

Costumes of Colonel de Basil's Ballets Russes de Monte Carlo 1932–39
Robert Bell and Simeran Maxwell (pp 167–179)

1 *Le Danube bleu* premiered in Sydney on 9 February 1940. Its name change resulted from a 1938 legal case brought by Léonide Massine against Wassily de Basil over his copyright of *Le Beau Danube*. Copyright was retained by Massine and attribution of his choreography for the ballet was removed from its program, which instead credited Serge Lifar with the arrangement of its dances and scenes.

2 This commentary from Australian ballet historian Michelle Potter in correspondence with Robert Bell, April 2009.

People, patronage and promotion: the Ballets Russes tours to Australia, 1936–40
Michelle Potter (pp 183–193)

1 Larry Tye, *The father of spin: Edward L Bernays and the birth of public relations*, Crown Publishers, New York, 1998.

2 Lynn Garafola, *Diaghilev's Ballets Russes*, Oxford University Press, New York, 1989, p 204.

3 Edward L Bernays, *Biography of an idea: memoirs of public relations counsel*, Simon & Schuster, New York, 1965, p 102.

4 See for example a variety of diaries, autobiographies, amateur film footage, oral histories, photographs and scrapbooks, many of which are listed as resources on the National Library of Australia's Ballets Russes website: http://www.nla.gov.au/balletsrusses/resources.html. In addition see in particular Arthur Wigram Allen: Diaries 1891–1941, Mitchell Library, MSMSS 1317 and the Chesterman Collection of Ballets Russes films, especially 'Ballets Russes beach scenes', National Film and Sound Archive, title no: 326073

5 Two significant, publicly available collections of letters are the Maroussia Richardson Collection, National Library of Australia, MS 9915: http://www.nla.gov.au/apps/cdview?pi=nla.ms-ms9915-1, and Papers of Harcourt Algeranoff, National Library of Australia, MS 2376: http://www.nla.gov.au/cdview/nla.ms-ms2376-1.1.14, especially items 574–596.

6 'Letters to the editor', *Argus*, 4 April 1940, p 7.

7 Ibid.

8 'Letters to the editor', *Argus*, 8 April 1940, p 2.

9 Sidney Nolan's theatrical commissions are listed in Brian Adams, *Sidney Nolan: such is life* (Hutchinson, Melbourne, 1987), p 264. In addition to the works listed by Adams, when he died in 1992 Nolan was working on designs for Richard Wagner's cycle of operas, *Der Ring des Nibelungen*, for the Victorian State Opera. For more about the *Icare* commission see Michelle Potter, 'Spatial boundaries: Sidney Nolan's ballet designs', *Brolga*, 3 (December 1995), 53–67; and Frank Hinder, 'Memories of Icarus', unpublished manuscript in the archives of the Art Gallery of New South Wales, quoted in Lesley Hardin (ed) *Creating a scene: Australian artists and stage designers 1940–1965*, Victorian Arts Centre, Melbourne, 2004, pp 39–40.

10 H Tatlock Miller, *An exhibition of art for theatre and ballet: Australia 1940* (British Council, London, 1939?). The catalogue has an insert of items by Sainthill offered for sale at the exhibition and, although *Etude* is not mentioned by name on the list, Basil Burdett mentions items 510 and 513 as being for *Etude*: Basil Burdett, 'Theatre and ballet in striking art display', *Herald* (Melbourne), 17 April 1940, p 8. Sainthill's work for *Etude* is also mentioned in 'De Basil in Australia', *Dancing Times* (London), no 356 (May 1940), p 473.

11 For more on Sainthill's designs for Kirsova see Michelle Potter, 'A strong personality and a gift for leadership: Helene Kirsova in Australia', *Dance Research* (Oxford), XIII, No 2, Autumn 1995, pp 62–76.

12 Bernard Smith, '"Paganini", notes after attending the Monte Carlo Diaghilev Ballet [sic] in Sydney', 1940. Unpublished typescript, Papers of Bernard Smith, MS 8680, National Library of Australia, Box 1, Folder 5. Smith erroneously refers to the company he saw as the Monte Carlo Diaghilev Ballet. None of the companies that performed in Australia ever had the word 'Diaghilev' in its name.

13 Ibid, p [2].
14 Tim Cecil, Managing Director, Henry Buck Pty Ltd, email communication with the author, 21 December 2008.
15 *Xmas 1938: a few ballet ideas from Henry Buck's*, Henry Buck Pty Ltd, Melbourne, 1938, unpaginated.
16 Lionel Smalley & Alan McCulloch, *Ballet bogies*, Lionel Smalley, Melbourne, 1938.
17 Darleen Bungey, *Arthur Boyd: a life*, Allen & Unwin, Sydney, 2007, p 100.
18 *Records of J C Williamson 1874–1976*, MS 5783, National Library of Australia, 'Cables 1931–1937', 'Cables 1937–1945'. The story of the Tait family is told in Viola Tait, *A family of brothers: the Taits and J C Williamson*, Heinemann, Melbourne, 1971.
19 'Cables 1931–1937': cable dated 1/7/36.
20 Ibid: cable dated 9/11/36.
21 Ibid: cable dated 27/11/36.
22 Ibid: cable dated 19/7/37.
23 Ibid: cable dated 7/7/36.
24 Ibid: cable dated 25/8/36.
25 Ibid: cable dated 27/8/36.
26 For a further exploration of the tensions of this dual structure see Michelle Potter, 'Arnold Haskell in Australia: did connoisseurship or politics determine his role?', *Dance Research* (Edinburgh), 24, no 1, Summer 2006, especially pp 45–48; and Tamara Finch, 'My dancing years, part three', *Dance Chronicle*, 27, no. 3, 2004, p 391.
27 'Cables 1931–1937': cable dated 29/6/36.
28 Ibid: cable dated 17/10/36.
29 Arnold Haskell, *Dancing round the world: memoirs of an attempted escape from ballet*, Victor Gollancz, London, 1937, p 77.
30 'Australians now ballet-conscious', *Courier Mail* (Brisbane), 25 June 1940, p 9.
31 Olga Philipoff, 'Ballet business', *Australia: National Journal*, Autumn issue, no 4, March–May 1940, pp 40–46; 94.
32 Arnold Haskell, *Waltzing Matilda: a background to Australia*, Adam & Charles Black, London, 1944, p xvii. In addition to *Waltzing Matilda* and *Dancing round the world*, both of which relate largely to his Australian visits, Haskell wrote two volumes of autobiography: *In his true centre: an interim autobiography*, Adam & Charles Black, London, 1951, and *Balletomane at large: an autobiography*, Heinemann, London, 1972.
33 Haskell, *Balletomane at large*, p 93.
34 Haskell, *Waltzing Matilda*, p xvii.
35 Arnold Haskell, 'Some reasons for the popularity of ballet', *The Home*, February 1937, p 24.
36 See in particular Arnold Haskell, 'The dancer's influence on ballet', *Art in Australia*, February 1937, pp 39–51; and 'Colonel de Basil', *The Home*, February 1937, p 58, as well as Haskell's program notes on de Basil published in Australian programs for the Ballets Russes between 1936 and 1940.
37 Haskell, *Dancing round the world*, p 116.
38 Basil Burdett, 'Notes on the ballet', *The Home*, January 1937, pp 28–9. See also Basil Burdett, 'The Russian Ballet', *The Home*, February 1937, p 41.
39 For more about Sydney Ure Smith see Nancy D H Underhill, *Making Australian art 1916-49: Sydney Ure Smith patron and publisher*, Oxford University Press, Oxford, 1991.
40 Telegram to Sydney Ure Smith from Anna Pavlova dated 23 May 1929, Papers of Sydney Ure Smith, ML MSS 31/7, State Library of New South Wales, Letters received 1905–1949, LIN–PRO.
41 Various letters to Sydney Ure Smith. Ibid., Letters received, 1905–1949: LIN–PRO; and Papers of Sydney Ure Smith, ML MSS 31/9, State Library of New South Wales, Miscellaneous letters received 1925–1947.
42 Underhill, pp 35–6.
43 Haskell, *Dancing round the world*, p 158.
44 For more on *Mir Iskusstva* see Janet Kennedy, *The 'Mir Iskusstva' group and Russian art, 1989–1912*, Garland, New York, 1977. The National Library of Australia's holdings of the journal are discussed in Michelle Potter 'Mir Iskusstva: Serge Diaghilev's art journal', *National Library of Australia News*, July 2005, pp 3–6; http://www.nla.gov.au/pub/nlanews/2005/jul05/article1.html
45 'Report for Art in Australia Limited regarding investigations in U.S.A'. Report for Sydney Ure Smith prepared by Catts-Patterson Company Ltd, 1933. Papers of Sydney Ure Smith, State Library of New South Wales, ML MSS 1042.
46 E J Francis, 'Fits for Mr Haskell', *The Home*, March 1937, p 32.
47 Max Dupain, oral history interview recorded by Michelle Potter, 11 September 1990, Esso Performing Arts and Oral History Archive Project, National Library of Australia, TRC 2360: http://nla.gov.au/nla.oh-vn1276615
48 Garafola, p 204.

Sights unseen: tags, stamps and stains Debbie Ward (pp 197–206)

1   For an account of Diaghilev's and subsequent Ballets Russes companies see Robert Bell, 'Wild dream: imagining the Ballets Russes', this publication, pp 23–47.
2   Primary conservation treatments have been undertaken on the NGA Ballets Russes collection since 1980 by Josephine Carter, Carol Cains, Debbie Ward, Micheline Ford, Sue Ride-Garbo, Carmela Mollica, Jane Wild, Chandra Obie, Sarah Clayton, Stefanie Woodruff, Charis Tyrell, Hannah Barrett and Debra Sphoer.
3   Labels of several types are present on 78 per cent of the costumes on display in the current exhibition.
4   For example, Henry Matisse, who was actively involved with Marie Muelle in the production of his costume designs for *Le Chant du rossignol* 1920, had a confrontation with Paul Poiret, who was commissioned to manufacture the Emperor's robe. Poiret insisted the costume would take months to make due to the extent of embroidery required in the motifs: Matisse insisted the designs should just be appliquéd. See Robyn Healy & Michael Lloyd, *From studio to stage: costumes and designs from the Russian Ballet in the Australian National Gallery*, Australian National Gallery, Canberra, 1990, p 50.
5   In the current exhibition only eight costumiers are identified by their labels as manufacturers of the garments on display: Roza Schogel (New York), Anello & Davide (London), Barbara Karinska (Paris), Reynolds House (London, New York), Helene Pons (New York), A & L Corne (London), Marie Muelle (Paris), Morris Angel & Son Ltd (London) and A Ingrao (Monte Carlo).
6   One of the two Muelle labels on costumes in the NGA collection reads 'Mos Muelle Rossignal SR/Costumier de l'Opera/12 Rue de la Victoire, Paris'; see Marjorie Howard, 'Muelle—Known to every singer … who wants a distinctive Paris costume in which to create a new role', *New York Times*, 25 April 1915.
7   VLADIM, Maligine, Burns, Daman, L---rai, WZ, Stephens, [illegible], IRM/RM, Fisher. Aleks, FROMAN, DN/533, ALEXAN, SCH YA.
8   Twenty-one costumes on display in the current exhibition carry the German customs imprint, relating to the 1912 Berlin season of nine ballets: *L'Oiseau de feu, Daphnis et Chloé, Cléopâtre, Narcisse, Thamar, Schéhérazade, Danses polovtsiennes du Prince Igor, Le Dieu bleu* and *Le Pavillon d'Armide*.
9   Healy & Lloyd, p 29; see also Bell, this publication, p 43.
10 The term 'artificial silk' has been used for both rayon and cellulose acetate fabrics. Rayon was first commercially produced in England by the Courtald company, Coventry, in 1905. Production in the USA dates from 1911, and in Japan from 1915; see John Singleton, *The world textile industry*, Routledge, London, 1997, p 88.
11 Drawing in the collection of the San Francisco Performing Arts Library and Museum.
12 Designs for *Schéhérazade* from *Les Ballets Russes' Official Program*, published by *Comœdia Illustré*, National Gallery of Australia Research Library, Canberra.

THE DESIGNERS

Léon Bakst

Léon Bakst (b Grodno, Russia/Lithuania border (now Belarus) 10 May 1866 – d Rueil-Malmaison, France 27 December 1924) attended the Academy of Fine Arts in St Petersburg from 1883 until he was expelled in 1887. Art school exposed him to the influence of the Russian Realist group, the Wanderers.

Bakst started his career as a book illustrator and painter, achieving only moderate success as a portraitist. In 1890 he met Alexandre Benois and joined the Nevsky Pickwickians, through whom he also met Diaghilev.

From 1893–97 he lived in Paris on and off, studying at the Académie Julian under the Academist painter, Jean-Léon Gérome, whose interest in Orientalism and Greek mythology were relayed to Bakst. He visited Spain, Germany, Tunisia, Algeria and Greece, settling permanently in Paris in 1912 after being exiled from Russia.

From 1898–1904, Bakst was Diaghilev's art assistant for *Mir Iskusstva*. In 1901 he designed his first theatre work for Diaghilev—Léo Delibes's ballet, *Sylvia*. Although this production was never realised, from that time Bakst concentrated on designing both sets and costumes for various theatres in St Petersburg.

In 1909, Bakst was invited to design productions for the first Saison Russe in Paris. He continued working with the Ballets Russes, becoming the artistic director in 1911, until 1919. Bakst designed more of Diaghilev's Ballets Russes productions than any other artist associated with the company, while also working as a freelance dress and costume designer for select clients. Bakst designed for several productions in London and Paris and returned to the Ballets Russes to design *The sleeping princess* in 1921.

E O Hoppé
Léon Bakst 1916
Collection of Curatorial Assistance, Pasadena, California

Etienne de Beaumont

Comte Etienne de Beaumont (b Paris, 8 March 1883 – d Paris 1956), a leading figure in Parisian society, was famous for his elaborate and extravagant parties and masquerade balls. He hired many of the leading avant-garde artists to decorate his apartment and garden for these events, and designed many of the masquerade outfits himself. Entrances were orchestrated and music and dances were composed and choreographed specifically for each evening.

Beaumont was a generous patron and passionate about the arts. In 1918, he staged Paris's first jazz performances using black American soldiers. In 1920, he assisted Jean Cocteau to stage *Le Boeuf sur le toit*, a theatrical event that incorporated circus elements. Before the First World War Beaumont and his wife Edith financed avant-garde films and ballets and later founded L'Association Franco-Américaine. In 1924, the writer Raymond Radiguet based the main character in his second novel, *Le Bal du Comte d'Orgel* (*The ball of the Count d'Orgel*), on Beaumont.

With the assistance of Cocteau and Léonide Massine, Beaumont presented the *Soirées de Paris* at the Théâtre de la Cigale in Montmartre, Paris. The season, from 17 May to 30 June 1924, combined ballet performances with poetry and theatre. Beaumont designed for one of these ballets, *Le Beau Danube*. Following this Beaumont went on to produce designs for Colonel de Basil's ballet productions *Scuola di Ballo* (1934) and *Les Imaginaires* (1934), and for the re-staging of *Le Beau Danube* in 1940.

Man Ray
Comte de Beaumont 1925
Man Ray Trust
© Man Ray Trust/ADAGP. Licensed by Viscopy, 2010/Telimage, 2010

Alexandre Benois

Aleksandr Nikolaevich Benois (b St Petersburg, 4 May 1870 – d Paris, 9 February 1960) studied at the Imperial Academy of Fine Arts in St Petersburg from 1887–88.

Benois began to exhibit in 1891 with the Society for the Encouragement of the Arts. He became a founding member of Mir Iskusstva, exhibiting with them from 1899–1904; and with the Union of Russian Artists from 1903–10. His work was included in Diaghilev's exhibition of Russian art at the 1905 Salon d'Automne.

Benois first visited Paris in 1896 with Léon Bakst, living at Versailles. During this time he produced paintings based on the court of King Louis XIV, a historical period that became an intrinsic theme of his career. His first theatre design, in 1895, was for the unrealised production of Christoph Willibald von Gluck's opera *Orpheus and Eurydice*; he also designed costumes for Act I of another unrealised production, Léo Delibes's ballet *Sylvia*, in 1901. In 1900 he created stage designs for Aleksandr Taneev's opera *Cupid's vengeance* (1902) at the Hermitage Theatre in St Petersburg, followed by countless designs for stage productions in Russia and Europe, and was the artistic director of the Moscow Arts Theatre from 1909–14.

Beginning with the Ballets Russe' *Le Pavillon d'Armide* in 1907, Benois became one of Diaghilev's chief theatre designers for a total of nine productions. Following his split with the company in 1924, Benois worked in theatre design in Russia and Europe for many years. From 1950–59 he worked for La Scala theatre in Milan and in 1955 his memoirs were published in two volumes.

Georges Braque

Georges Braque (b Argenteuil-sur-Seine, Seine-et-Oise, France, 13 May 1882 – d Paris, 31 August 1963) studied at night-school at the Ecole des Beaux-Arts in Le Havre and later in Paris in 1900. Influenced by Impressionism, Neo-Impressionism and Fauvism, Braque later focused on his own explorations of geometric forms and space. Another important interest throughout Braque's career was ancient Greek and Etruscan art.

Braque collaborated with his friend Pablo Picasso to forge the new style of Cubism in 1909, developing it through four stages: Cézannesque, analytic, hermetic and synthetic. Braque passed through these four stages and then began to drift away from the movement. Mobilised for the First World War, he suffered a serious head injury that caused the loss of his sight for a significant period, preventing him from painting again until 1917. By 1920 Braque had become interested in neoclassical aesthetics and by the 1930s his style had totally changed.

In 1923 Braque received his first commission from Diaghilev to produce set designs for the Ballets Russes production of *Les Fâcheux* (*The bores*). He collaborated with the Ballets Russes again in 1925 for the production of *Zéphyre et Flore* and in 1926 for *Les Sylphides*. As well as his work with the Ballets Russes, Braque designed scenery and costumes for Darius Milhaud's *Salade*, which was choreographed by Léonide Massine and performed at the Théâtre de la Cigale in Paris in 1924. In 1950 he designed for Louis Jouvet's production of Molière's play *Tartuffe* at the Théâtre de l'Athénée in Paris.

Marcovitch
Alexandre Benois
Bibliothèque nationale de France, Paris, Fonds Kochno, BN 79

Man Ray
Georges Braque 1922
Man Ray Trust
© Man Ray Trust/ADAGP. Licensed by Viscopy, 2010/Telimage, 2010

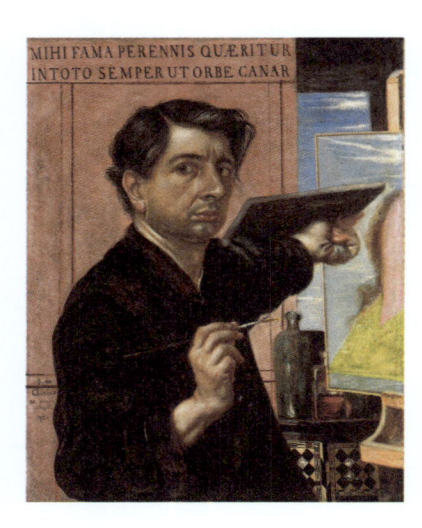

Giorgio de Chirico

Giorgio de Chirico (b Volo, Greece, 10 July 1888 – d Rome 1978) studied art in Athens and then Florence before moving to Germany in 1906, where he attended the Academy of Fine Arts, Munich. Returning to Italy in 1909 he painted enigmatic works, with empty spaces, shadows and strange perspectives. From 1914 he began to use tailors' dummies—painted, with plaster heads and rubber gloves—which foreshadowed much of his Surrealist imagery.

Conscripted into the Italian armed forces in 1915, de Chirico suffered a mental breakdown after being assigned to the military hospital in Ferrara. Here he met Futurist painter Carlo Carrà and together they founded the Scuola Metafisica. Following the group's break-up around 1920, de Chirico began to take a serious interest in the Italian classical painting tradition. By 1925 he had moved to France and become part of the arisian Surrealist movement.

De Chirico designed for many ballets during his career. He provided designs for the Ballets Suédois's *La Jarre* (*The jar*) in 1924, before designing costumes and sets for Diaghilev's Ballets Russes 1929 production of *Le Bal*. Between the end of Diaghilev's Ballets Russes and the redevelopment of the company under de Basil, de Chirico worked for the Paris Opera. De Basil commissioned him to provide costumes for *Pulcinella* (1931) and *Protée* (*Proteus*) (1938). Following his involvement with the Ballets Russes, de Chirico designed for productions by Italian ballet companies, including *La Légende de Joseph* (*The story of Joseph*) for La Scala in Milan in 1951, and for the Maggio Musicale Fiorentino festival.

Giorgio de Chirico
Self-portrait 1924
tempera on canvas
Kunstmuseum Winterthur
© Giorgio de Chirico/SIAE. Licensed by Viscopy, 2010

Sonia Delaunay

Sonia Delaunay (b Gradižsk, Ukraine, 14 November 1885 – d Paris, 5 December 1979) studied at the Akademie der Bildenden Künste in Karlsruhe from 1903–05 before moving to Paris to study at the Académie de la Palette. In 1910 she married her second husband, fellow artist Robert Delaunay.

In 1911 she began to experiment with abstract patterns, producing fabrics known as 'simultaneous contrasts' to make collages, book bindings and clothes. She spent the rest of her career exploring how forms and colours interact, particularly in fabric.

The Delaunays travelled to Berlin to exhibit at the first German Salon d'Automne at Der Strum Gallery, and at the outbreak of war in 1914 moved to Madrid and Portugal. Sonia had studied dances such as flamenco and tango before meeting Diaghilev, who helped her launch a career in design, particularly fashion. In 1917 he asked her to create costumes for the Ballets Russes revival of *Cléopâtre* (1918). She opened a clothes shop in Madrid in 1918 and designed costumes for the opera *Aida* at the Liceo Theatre, Barcelona.

Returning to Paris in 1921, Sonia received her first order for her 'simultaneous' textiles and by 1925 was showing her designs in her Boutique Simultanée at the Exposition Internationale des Arts Décoratifs.

She continued in theatre in collaboration with her husband until his death in 1941. Sonia also began to produce costumes for film, beginning with Marcel L'Herbier's *Le Vertige* in 1927. She worked in costume design until 1968, when she produced costumes and stage sets for the Ballet Théâtre d'Amiens performances of Igor Stravinsky's *Danses concertantes*.

Unknown photographer
Sonia Delaunay in her design studio, Paris 1920s
unknown collection

André Derain

André Derain (b Chatou, near Paris, 10 June 1880 – d Garches, France, 8 September 1954) studied at l'Académie Camillo, Paris from 1898. With Henri Matisse, Derain began to explore the decorative qualities of colour and became one of the main proponents of Fauvism, exhibiting at famous Fauve exhibition at the Salon d'Automne in 1906. After staying with Pablo Picasso, Derain became attracted by some of the Cubist philosophy and interested in African and Roman sculpture. In 1911 Derain, influenced by early Renaissance art, embarked on his Gothic period, which lasted for ten years. The rest of his career was devoted to Classical Realism, drawing inspiration from nineteenth-century French masters such as Jean-Baptiste-Camille Corot.

In 1918 Derain began to design for the theatre, with a commission for the Duvoc Theatre Company's production of *L'Annonce faite à Marie*. A year later he began work with Diaghilev on the Ballets Russes productions of *La Boutique fantasque* (1919) and *Jack-in-the-box* (1926). He designed the scenery for the ballet *Concurrence* (1932), produced by the Ballets Russes de Monte Carlo, and for George Balanchine's ballets *Fastes and Les Songes*, performed at the Théâtre Champs-Elysées in 1933. In 1936 he again worked with the Ballets Russes de Monte Carlo on *L'Epreuve d'amour*. He wrote the books for the last three ballets himself.

At the end of the Second World War, Derain returned to theatre with décor designs for *Que le Diable l'emporte* (Ballets Roland Petit) and *Mam'zelle Angot* (Sadler's Wells Theatre, London). He completed two more ballet projects, *Il Seraglio* in 1951 and *The barber of Seville* in 1953, for the Festival d'Aix-en-Provence.

Pablo Picasso
André Derain 1917
page 33 in *Official program for the Ballets Russes at the Opéra, December 1919 – January 1920*
National Gallery of Australia, Canberra
© Pablo Picasso/Succession Picasso. Licensed by Viscopy, 2010

Aleksandr Golovin

Aleksandr Yakovlevich Golovin (b Moscow, 17 February 1863 – d Pushkin (then Detskoe Selo), 17 April 1930) studied architecture at the Moscow Institute of Painting, Sculpture and Architecture before switching to painting. In 1899 he moved to Paris, studying at the Académie de Filippo Colarossi and the Académie Witti.

He worked in the Art Nouveau style during the 1890s. From 1899–1907 Golovin contributed to *Mir Iskusstva* exhibitions and designed several covers for the journal. He co-designed the interior of the craft section of the Russian Pavilion for the Exposition Universelle in Paris in 1900. In 1906 Diaghilev included Golovin's work in his Russian art exhibition at the Salon d'Automne in Paris.

Golovin began producing designs for the theatre in 1897. In 1899 and 1900 he designed productions for Savva Mamontov's Private Russian Opera, and in 1901 for *The maid of Pskov* for the Bolshoi Theatre. He became an advisor for the Imperial Theatres in 1902 and principal designer in 1908, working with the company until 1917.

Diaghilev collaborated with Golovin on the Saisons Russes from 1908–13: the opera *Boris Godunov* (1908); *The maid of Pskov* (1908, with Nicholas Roerich and Sergi Stelletsky); *L'Oiseau de feu* (1910); *Swan lake* (1911, a collaboration with Konstantin Korovin); and the opera *Ivan the Terrible* (1913). Back in Russia he designed for a production of *Masquerade* (1917) at the Alexandrinsky Theatre in St Petersburg. From then until his death he worked mainly as a stage designer in Russia (from 1927 as designer for the Moscow Art Theatre) and Europe.

Unknown photographer
Golovin c 1910–17 (detail)
St Petersburg State Museum of Theatre and Music, St Petersburg
© St Petersburg State Museum of Theatre and Music Arts

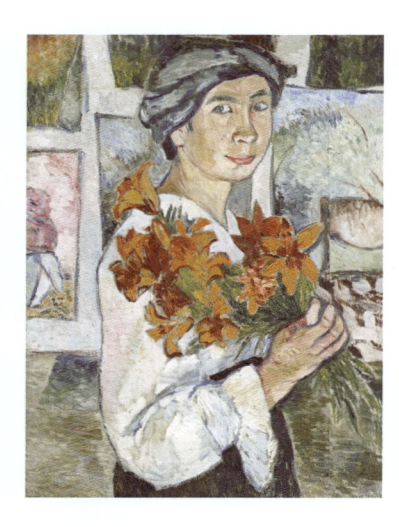

Natalia Goncharova

Natalia Sergeevna Goncharova (b Nagayevo, Tula province, Russia, 4 June 1881 – d Paris, 17 October 1962) began studying sculpture at the Moscow Institute of Painting, Sculpture and Architecture in 1898—where she met Mikhail Larionov, who was to become her lifelong partner—before taking up painting. While there she focused on Eastern and Byzantine art, Russian folk art—particularly *lubok* prints and icon paintings—as well as embroidery and fabric design, all important influences on her Neo-Primitive style.

Included in Diaghilev's 1906 Russian exhibition at the Salon d'Automne in Paris, she exhibited with many important Russian modernist movements—the Union of Youth, St Petersburg (1910), as co-organiser of the *Knave of Diamonds* exhibition, Moscow (1910); and the *Target* exhibition, Moscow (1913).

Goncharova was first commissioned by Diaghilev for the Ballets Russes production of *Le Coq d'or* in 1913. She later joined the company in Lausanne, Switzerland in 1915, designing for *Liturgie*. She also redesigned several ballets for Diaghilev—reforming her own Russian folk style to a starkly Futurist style for *Les Noces* (1923) at the request of Bronislava Nijinska and also changing the 1910 *L'Oiseau de feu* designs for the 1926 revival.

After de Basil's reformation of the Ballets Russes, Goncharova was commissioned to create new designs for the 1937 Covent Garden London revival of *Le Coq d'or*, and costumes and set designs for *Cinderella* (1938). During the Second World War, Goncharova designed ten ballets for Boris Kniaseff that were shown in South America, and afterward designed for opera and ballet productions in London and Paris.

Juan Gris

José Victoriano Carmelo Carlos González Pérez (b Madrid, 23 March 1887 –d Boulogne-sur-Seine, France, 24 January 1927) studied at Madrid's Escuela de Artes y Manufacturas but left to work under Spanish academic painter, José Moreno Carbonero. From 1905 he began to identify himself as a *modernista* or modern artist working in the international Art Nouveau style, and called himself Juan Gris.

In 1906 he left Spain permanently, moving to Paris where he associated with artists such as Pablo Picasso and Georges Braque. From 1912 he exhibited with the Salon des Indépendants and contributed to Cubist exhibitions, becoming a leading collagist, particularly with paper collage from 1913.

Through Picasso, Gris was introduced to Diaghilev and the Ballets Russes and watched the rehearsals of *Parade*. However, it was not until 1922 that he began to design for the company, with costumes and sets for *Les Tentations de la bergère* (1924). He also was commissioned by Diaghilev to design costumes and sets for the receptions and balls known as Fêtes Mervilleuses, held in the Hall of Mirrors at Versailles (1923). In 1924 he also provided designs for the comic opera *La Colombe* (*The dove*) and the one-act operetta *Une Education manqué* (*An incomplete education*). Both these productions were staged in Monte Carlo. In May 1924 Gris produced his final collaboration with Diaghilev, a Red Cross gala held at Les Grands Magasins du Printemps in Paris.

Natalia Goncharova
Self-portrait with yellow lilies 1907
oil on canvas
77 x 58.2 cm
State Tretyakov Gallery, Moscow
© Natalia Goncharova/ADAGP. Licensed by Viscopy, 2010

Man Ray
Juan Gris 1924
Man Ray Trust
© Man Ray Trust/ADAGP. Licensed by Viscopy, 2010/Telimage, 2010

Mikhail Larionov

Mikhail Feodorovich Larionov (b Tiraspol, Moldova, Russia, 3 June 1881 – d Fontenay-aux-Roses, France, 10 May 1964) studied from 1898–1908 at the Moscow Institute of Painting, Sculpture and Architecture, meeting artistic collaborator and partner Natalia Goncharova.

Larionov was one of the leading Futurists, exhibiting in all the leading avant-garde exhibitions in Russia, as well as many abroad, including Diaghilev's *Exposition de l'art russe* at the Salon d'Automne, Paris, and with Der blaue Reiter (The Blue Rider group) in Munich (1912). He and Goncharova launched their Futurist-inspired Rayonnist style at the *Target* exhibition, Moscow (1913).

Before his move to Paris in 1916, Larionov (with Goncharova) had joined Diaghilev in Lausanne in 1915, becoming a close and frequent collaborator. Larionov became Diaghilev's art consultant and occasional choreographer, and wrote several ballet scenarios. He was commissioned to design for *Soleil de minuit* (*Midnight sun*) (1915); the unrealised *Histoires naturelles* (1916); *Contes russes* (1917); *Chout* (1921); and finally *Le Renard* (1922).

As well as working with the Ballets Russes, Larionov worked on many other theatre projects: a series of sketches for the ballet *Karagoz* (*Karaguez, gardien de l'honneur de son ami*) staged by Adolph Bolm in Chicago in 1924 with Goncharova; *The little Catherine* at Antoine's Theatre, Paris (1930); *Symphonie classique* (*Classical symphony*) at the Théâtre Pigalle; *Sur le Borysthène* (*On the Dnieper*) at the Grand Opera (1932). When de Basil reformed the Ballets Russes he commissioned Larionov to design for its production of *Port Said* (1936) at the London Coliseum.

Man Ray
Mikhail Larionov c 1925
gelatin silver photograph
Man Ray Trust
© Man Ray Trust/ADAGP. Licensed by Viscopy, 2010

Jean Lurçat

Jean Lurçat (b Bruyères, France, 1 July 1892 – d Saint-Paul de Vence, France, 6 January 1966) began painting under Victor Prouvé at the Ecole de Nancy, in 1912. He subsequently moved to Paris to study at the Ecole des Beaux-Arts and later at the Académie Colarossi. At the beginning of the First World War, Lurçat enlisted in the French army but was discharged after being wounded, recovering at his parents' home in Sens where, with his mother's guidance he completed his first canvas stitched tapestry. He moved to Geneva and in 1921 received his first theatre commission, to design scenery and costumes for *Celui qui reçoit des gifles* for the Pitoeff company.

Between 1923 and 1925 Lurçat travelled in Spain, North Africa, Greece and Asia. During this time he worked in a Cubist and Surrealist style. But on seeing the fourteenth-century Gothic tapestry *La tapisserie de l'Apocalypse* at Château d'Angers in the early 1930s, Lurçat decided to devote himself exclusively to the design of tapestries. The first of these was made in 1933 on a high-warp loom at the internationally renowned Gobelins factory in Aubusson, France. In the same year he was commissioned by de Basil to produce designs for the set and costumes for the George Balanchine ballet *Jardin public*.

Lurçat worked tirelessly on modernising the ailing French tapestry industry. To this end, in 1939 the French government commissioned him to create a series of tapestries. In 1940 he wove twenty tapestries in the Tabard and Gobelins factories with the collaboration of André Derain and Raoul Dufy.

Unknown photographer
Jean Lurçat in his studio Villa Seurat, Paris 1926
unknown collection

Florence and Kathleen Martin

The Australian sisters Florence Beresford Martin (b Ballarat, Victoria, 28 August 1908 – d Sydney, 20 December 1984) and Emily Kathleen Martin (b 4 September 1903 – d ?) collaborated on art and theatre design projects. In 1935 Florence and Kathleen began exhibiting together. They first collaborated on theatre design in Melbourne—*The lower depths* (1936), *Murder in the cathedral* (1937) and *The cherry orchard* (1938).

In 1940, they entered de Basil's competition to design costumes for an Australian themed ballet during the Ballets Russes tour. The first prize went to artist Donald Friend, but their entry was highly commended and de Basil commissioned them to design costumes for *La Lutte éternelle* (1940).

Kathleen and Florence then designed for a production of *Midsummer night's dream* (1941), and for the Borovansky Company's *Fantasy* (1941), performed at Melbourne's Princess Theatre. In 1942 they moved to New York, where Kathleen worked for leading theatrical costumier Edith Lutyens Bel Geddes, and Florence returned to studying art and design.

Florence spent 1945 working for the Teatro Municipal Ballet Company in Rio de Janeiro, designing costumes for *The red poppy* and *Papoula Vermelha*, and the set and costumes for *Luta eternal*. She continued to work in Rio de Janeiro until 1947, focusing on theatrical design, including *Judgement of Jupiter*, *Malediction*, *Nocturne* and *Burleska*. She then became a designer for the Foxhole Ballet and Grant Mouradoff's ballet company, *Circus*.

The sisters moved to London in 1952, where Florence gave up theatre design to concentrate on painting, and returned to Australia in 1972.

Unknown photographer
Kathleen and Florence Martin
in *The Philadelphia Inquirer* 1945
National Gallery of Australia Research Library, Canberra, papers of Kathleen and Florence Martin

André Masson

André Masson (b Balagny, Oise, France, 4 January 1896 – d Paris, 28 October 1987) studied painting at the Académie des Beaux-Arts, Brussels before moving to Paris, in 1912, to study at the Ecole des Beaux-Arts. During the First World War he was seriously wounded, an experience which left an indelible mark on his psyche and art. Hence, by 1922 he had begun an association with the Surrealist group.

Masson's first ballet commission was for the Ballets Russes de Monte Carlo's production of *Les Présages* (1933), followed by set designs for Armand Salacrou's play *La Terre est ronde* (*The earth is round*) (1938). After the Second World War, Masson returned to theatre work, producing set and costume designs for Hamlet and Jean-Paul Sartre's play *Morts sans sépulture* (*The victors*) (1946).

In 1958 he appeared as a cameo role in the film *André Masson et les quatres éléments* (*André Masson and the four elements*), while also completing designs for Jean-Louis Barrault's production of *Tête d'or* (*Head of gold*). In 1965 he again returned to the theatre, this time producing designs for the ceiling of the Théâtre de l'Odéon in Paris. During the 1970s Masson continued to produce theatre designs and his work also appeared in several films, one of which, *A la source, la femme aimée* (*At the source, the beloved*) (1966–67) about his erotic drawings, was censored.

Robert Doisneau
André Masson in Aix-en-Provence, during preparations of Iphigenia in Tauris 1953
Atelier Robert Doisneau, Paris

Henri Matisse

Henri-Emile-Benoît Matisse (b La Cateau-Cambrésis, France 31 December 1869 – d Cimiez, France, 3 November 1954) attended morning drawing classes at the Ecole Quentin Latour in 1889. He started at the Académie Julian in Paris a year later and in 1892 began drawing classes with Gustave Moreau at the Ecole des Beaux-Arts.

After previously exhibiting at the inaugural Salon d'Automne (1903) with friends such as André Derain, Matisse was part of in the famous Fauve exhibition in 1905. Gertrude Stein introduced Matisse to Pablo Picasso with whom he exchanged paintings. Matisse also began to be collected by the Russian art patron S I Shchukin, who commissioned his works *Dance* and *Music* in 1909, installing them in his Moscow home in 1910.

In 1920 he was invited by Diaghilev to design the Ballets Russes' 1920 production of *Le Chant du rossignol* and travelled frequently between Nice and Monte Carlo to consult the impresario about the project. In 1937 Matisse was again invited, this time by the Ballets Russes de Monte Carlo, to design scenery and costumes for its ballet *Rouge et noir* (*Red and black*).

In 1931 Matisse accepted an important commission from Albert C Barnes to paint a mural, *The dance II*, for the walls of the Barnes Foundation in Merion, Pennsylvania. Matisse was diagnosed with cancer in 1941 and was forced to use a wheelchair after an operation to remove a tumour. From this time onward Matisse worked extensively with cut-out coloured paper, a design technique that he had first used when developing his costume and scenery designs for *Le Chant du rossignol*.

Oliver Messel

Oliver Hilary Sambourne Messel (b London, 13 January 1904 – d Barbados, 13 July 1978) studied painting at Slade School of Fine Art in London from 1922–24. There he began making masks and in 1925 some of these where shown in the Claridge Gallery exhibition *Character masks*. Both Diaghilev and the English impresario Sir Charles Blake Cochran saw this exhibition and Diaghilev commissioned Messel to create masks and symbols for the Ballets Russes' London production of *Zéphire et Flore* (1925).

Messel continued to work for Cochran, producing masks for his annual revues at the London Pavilion in the late 1920s. He produced set and costume designs for Cochran's production of the opera-bouffe *Helen* (1926) and *The miracle* (1932). In 1937 he was commissioned by the Ballets Russes de Monte Carlo to produce designs for its ballet, *Francesca da Rimini*, at Covent Garden, London.

From 1932, while continuing to design for the theatre and ballet, he branched out into film, designing sets and costumes for the MGM film version of Shakespeare's *Romeo and Juliet* (1936). In 1944 he began work on *Caesar and Cleopatra* (1945), on which he was costume designer, art director and uncredited as the jewellery designer. In 1960 he was nominated for Best Art Direction-Set Decoration Oscar for his work on *Suddenly, last summer* (1959). He also designed for many Broadway productions in New York, collecting numerous Tony Award nominations and winning the Best Scenic Design award in 1955 for *House of flowers*.

Enriett
Henri Matisse and the Nightingale c 1920 (detail)
page 15 in *Souvenir programme for the Ballets Russes at l'Opéra, May–June 1920*
National Gallery of Australia, Canberra

George Hoyningen-Huene
Costume designer Oliver Messel with theatrical masks c 1929
Condé Nast collection, © Condé Nast Archive/CORBIS

Pablo Picasso

Pablo Ruiz Picasso (b Málaga, Spain, 25 October 1881 – d Mougins, France, 8 April 1973) initially was taught by his father at the School of Fine Arts in Málaga. Later he studied at the School of Fine Arts in La Coruña, in Barcelona, and the Royal Academy of San Fernando. During his long career Picasso's style often changed dramatically—Blue period (1901–04); Rose period (1904–06); Primitive period (1907–09); Analytic Cubism (1909–12); Synthetic Cubism (1912–19); Neoclassical period (1920s); Surrealist period (1930s).

Picasso was introduced to Diaghilev by Jean Cocteau in 1916, leading to his first ballet commission, for *Parade* (1917). Picasso further immersed himself in the world of the Ballets Russes by marrying one of the principal dancers, Olga Khokhlova. Over the years he had several long relationships, and married a second time in 1961. Picasso was also commissioned to work on designs for *Le Tricorne* (1919), *Pulcinella* (1920)—for which he made three different designs—and *Cuadro Flamenco* (1921). His sketches of many Ballets Russes members, including choreographers, dancers and Diaghilev, were published in a number of souvenir programs.

In 1924 he worked on a production of the ballet *Mercure* at the Théâtre de la Cigale for Comte Etienne de Beaumont's *Soirées de Paris*. Picasso's last official design role for the Ballets Russes was the curtain for *Le Train bleu* (1924), the gouache for which he painted two years earlier. In 1946, Picasso returned to theatre work with another curtain design, this time for *Le Rendez-vous* for the Ballets des Champs-Elysées.

Nicholas Roerich

Nicholas Roerich (b St Petersburg, 9 October 1874 – d Nagara, India, 13 December 1947) initially studied painting at the Academy of Fine Arts; at the Imperial Academy of Arts 1893–98; and finally at Fernand Cormon's Paris studio in 1900–01. He began exhibiting in 1895 and became a founding member of *Mir Iskusstva*, exhibiting with the group from 1902–17 and becoming the journal's chairman from 1910–13. A member of the Union of Russian Artists from 1903–10, Roerich exhibited in Paris at the Exposition Universelle in 1900, and at the 1906 and 1907 Salons d'Automne.

His theatrical debut was at the Old Theatre, St Petersburg with designs for *The three magi* (1907). The following year he was commissioned by the Opéra Comique, Paris to produce designs for Rimsky-Korsakov's *Snegurochka* (*The snow maiden*). Diaghilev commissioned him to design several ballets for the Ballets Russes—*Ivan the Terrible* (*The maid of Pskov*) and *Danses polovtsiennes du Prince Igor* (1909) and *Le Sacre du printemps* (*The rite of spring*) (1913). Roerich continued to design for Russian productions and in 1912 began working for the Moscow Art Theatre.

In 1920 Roerich moved to the United States, where he organised several expeditions to Bhutan, Central Asia, China and Mongolia. In 1928 he founded the Urusvati Research Institute for Himalayan Studies in the Kulu Valley and a year later drafted the Pact for the Preservation of Cultural Treasures during Armed Conflicts (also known as the Roerich Pact) which was the basis for the final act of the Hague Convention of 1954.

Brassaï
Picasso in his studio, Rue des Grandes 1939
gelatin silver photograph
36.6 x 27.5 cm
National Gallery of Australia, Canberra, purchased 1980, 1980.2615

Unknown photographer
Nicholas Roerich c 1919
page 27 in *Official program for the Ballets Russes at the Opéra, December 1919–January* 1920
National Gallery of Australia, Canberra

José-María Sert

José-María Sert y Badia (b Barcelona, 21/24 December 1874/76 – d Barcelona November or December 1945) began his career in the studio of his father, producing tapestry cartoons and other fabric designs. He travelled to Italy to study Renaissance fresco painting, before settling in Paris in 1899. Initially a society painter, but after receiving several mural commissions Sert dispensed with easel painting and focused on large-scale works for churches, private houses and public buildings. He received commissions from across Europe and the United States—including the Waldorf Astoria and the Rockefeller Centre in New York and the Council Chamber at the United Nations in Geneva.

He exhibited several times at the Paris Exposition Universelle, was also a contributor to the 1907 Salon d'Automne, and regularly exhibited his work in both London and New York. He was first commissioned to produce theatre designs in 1910 for *La Vida es sueño* (*Life is a dream*), Théâtre d'Art, Paris. In 1914 he was the first non-Russian designer Diaghilev chose to work for the Ballets Russes. He began working with the company on the scenery for its production of *La Légende de Joseph* (costume designs produced by Léon Bakst). He went on to produce designs for two other Diaghilev productions, *Las meniñas* (1916) and *Ballet de l'Astuce féminine / Cimarosiana* (1920). Following Diaghilev's death in 1929, Sert continued to work on ballet productions for de Basil's new Ballets Russes, designing *Pavane* in 1940.

Pavel Tchelitchew

Pavel Fedorovich Tchelitchew (b Kaluya, Russia, 21 September 1898 – d Grottatterrata, Italy, 31 July 1957) began his art training under the guidance of the stage designer Alexandra Exter and at the Kiev Academy as well as private classes with several Russian artists and stage designers. He continued studying in Berlin, Germany from 1921 until 1923, when he moved to Paris, also travelling to Austria, Italy, Bulgaria and Turkey.

By 1921 he had produced designs for six ballets performed in Istanbul and more in Berlin shortly after. These early theatre designs reflect his preoccupation with geometric forms and Cubism. He followed these early experiments with designs for *Le Coq d'or*, performed at the Opera House in Berlin in 1923. Financial support came from Gertrude Stein, who purchased the contents of his studio in 1925 after seeing his entry in the Salon d'Automne. His participation in a 1926 group exhibition at the Galerie Druet, Paris gave rise to the term Neo-Romantic for his work. This style was related to Surrealism and concentrated on fantasy created with the use of everyday objects, increasing the viewer's feeling of unease.

In 1928 Tchelitchew was commissioned by Diaghilev to produce designs for the Ballets Russes production of Ode. Following his move to New York he continued to work in the theatre, designing for George Balanchine's new American Ballet Company and for Arthur Everett Austin Jr at the Wadsworth Atheneum in Hartford, Connecticut, until 1942 when he gave up stage design to concentrate on his painting.

Unknown photographer
José-María Sert on mural site 1933 (detail)
Bettmann collection, © Bettmann/CORBIS

Pavel Tchelitchew
Self-portrait 1925
oil on canvas
61 x 46 cm
private collection
image courtesy of Kournikova Gallery, Moscow

Georgy Yakulov

Georgy Bogdanovich Yakulov (b Tiflis (now Tbilisi), Russia, 2 January 1882 – d Erevan, Russia, 28 December 1928) studied painting for two years at the Moscow School of Painting, Sculpture and Architecture. During his military service, spent partly in northeast China, he developed an appreciation of Eastern light effects and decoration.

In 1907 he began exhibiting with the Moscow Association of Artists, the Union of Russian Artists and *Mir Iskusstva*, and in Paris and Berlin. He travelled to Italy (1910) and to Paris (1912–13), where he met Sonia and Robert Delaunay, discovering that his artistic ideas of light corresponded with their theory of Simultanism.

Yakulov became a member of the Leftist Federation of Painters, organised the decorative, yet abstract interior design of the Café Pittoresque in Moscow, and participated in decorative preparations for various private balls, spectacles and amateur theatrical events in 1910 and 1911. His career in the theatre began officially in 1918, when he designed the sets for Aleksandr Tairov's *Obmen* (*The exchange*) at the Kamerny Theatre. Yakulov's subsequent designs for Tairov, *Princess Brambilla* (1920) and *Giroflé-Girofla* (1922), combined traditional theatrical techniques with modernist abstraction.

In 1925 Yakulov returned to Paris to exhibit in the Exposition Internationale des Arts Décoratifs, and was commissioned by Diaghilev to design for the Ballets Russes production of Le Pas d'acier, eventually performed in 1927 at the Théâtre Sarah Bernhardt. He died a year later in Russia, leaving behind unrealised designs for Vsevolod Meyerhold's play *Misteriya-Buff*.

Unknown photographer
Georgy Yakulov 1923
unknown collection

(opposite) **Natalia Goncharova**
Mantle from costume for King Dodon c 1937 (detail) from *Le Coq d'or*
© Natalia Goncharova/ADAGP. Licensed by Viscopy, 2010

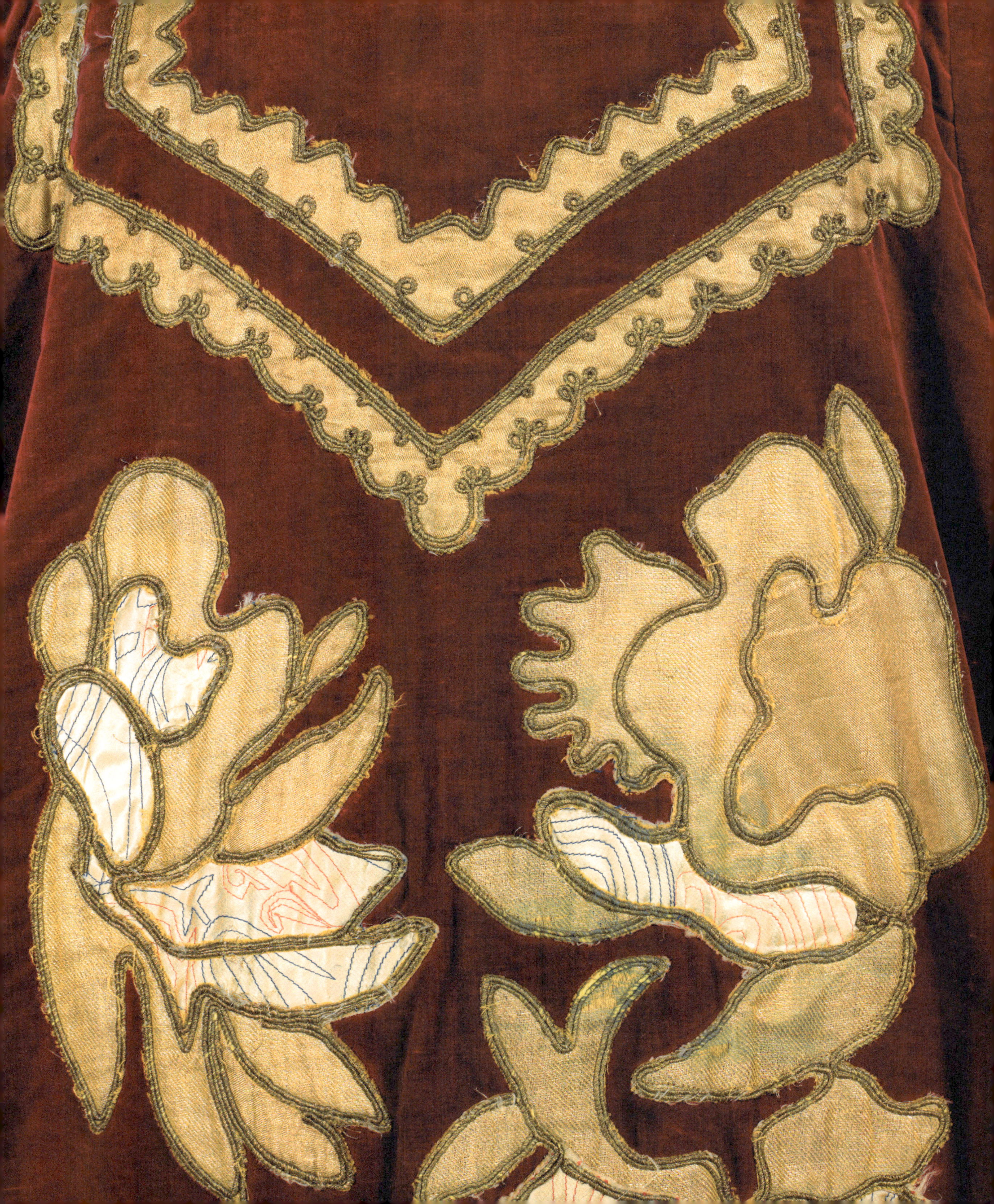

BALLETS RUSSES TIMELINE

Ballets Russes events in bold

1872
31 March	**Sergei Pavlovich Diaghilev born in Selishchenko, Novgorod Province, Russia**

1873
15 May	Composer Nikolai Tcherepnin born in St Petersburg
9 January	Napoleon III, President of the French Second Republic, dies in Kent, England

1874
9 August	Composer Reynaldo Hahn born in Caracas, Venezuela
10 October	Designer and artist Nicholas Roerich born in St Petersburg
15 April	First Impressionist exhibition at the photographer Nadar's studio in Paris

1875
7 March	**Composer Maurice Ravel born in Ciboure, France**
2 August	**Artist and designer Mstislav Dobuzhinsky born in Novgorod Province, Russia (dies 20 November 1957, New York)**
15 January	Charles Garnier's new Palais Garnier on Place de l'Opéra opens in Paris
	Liberty & Co department store opens in London

1876
15 September	**Dancer Nicholas Sergeyev born in St Petersburg**
23 November	**Composer Manuel de Falla born in Cádiz, Spain**
21 December	**Artist and designer José-María Sert born in Barcelona**

10 March	Alexander Graham Bell demonstrates his telephone

1877
	Russo-Turkish War (1877–78)
26 May	Dancer Isadora Duncan born in San Francisco

1878
13 March	**René Blum, founder of the Ballet de l'Opéra, born in Paris**
17 September	**Composer Vincenzo Tommasini born in Rome**
1 May–10 November	The World Fair (Exposition Universelle) held in Paris

1879
9 July	**Composer Ottorino Respighi born in Bologna, Italy**
30 September	**Composer Henri Casadesus born in Paris**
2 October	**Designer Boris Anisfeld born in Beltsy, Moldavia (dies 1973, Waterford, United States of America)**
22 October	Thomas Edison invents the electric light bulb

1880
23 April	**Choreographer and dancer Mikhail Fokine born in St Petersburg**
21 December	**Choreographer and dancer Mikhail Mordkin born in Moscow**
10 June	**Artist and designer André Derain born in Chatou, France (dies 8 September 1954, Garches, France)**

France's first Socialist Party, the French Workers' Party (*Parti Ouvrier Français*) is founded by Jules Guesde and Paul Lafargue (Karl Marx's son-in-law)

Wassily de Basil (Vassily Grigorievich Voskerensky) born in Russia

1881
12 February	**Dancer Anna Pavlova born in St Petersburg**
28 March	**Composer Modest Mussorgsky dies in St Petersburg**
3 June	**Artist, designer and choreographer Mikhail Larionov born in Tiraspol, Russia (dies 10 May 1964, Fontenay-aux-Roses, France)**
4 June	**Artist and designer Natalia Goncharova born in Nagaevo, Russia (dies 17 October 1962, Paris)**
25 October	**Artist and designer Pablo Picasso born in Málaga, Spain (dies 8 April 1973, Mougins, France)**
9 February	Author Fyodor Dostoyevsky dies in St Petersburg
13 March	Russian Tsar Alexander II assassinated; succeeded by Tsar Alexander III
October	First use of electric stage lighting, at the Savoy Theatre in London
18 November	Paris' first cabaret, Le Chat Noir (The Black Cat) opens at 84 Boulevard Rouchechouart Montmartre

1882
13 May	**Artist and designer Georges Braque born in Argenteuil-sur-Seine, France (dies 31 August 1963, Paris)**
17 June	**Composer Igor Stravinsky born in Oranienbaum (later, Lomonosov), Russia (dies 6 April 1971, New York)**
	Sergei Diaghilev's family move to Perm, Russia

1883
8 March	**Designer and ballet patron Count Etienne de Beaumont born in Paris**
5 October	**Serge Grigoriev, theatrical director of the Ballets Russes, born in Tichvin, Russia**
26 December	**Artist and designer Maurice Utrillo born in Paris (dies 5 November 1955, Paris)**
13 February	Composer Wilhelm Richard Wagner dies in Venice, Italy
14 March	Political theorist Karl Marx dies in London
30 April	Artist Edouard Manet dies in Paris
4 October	The *Orient Express* makes its first run from Paris to Constantinople (now Istanbul)

1884
2 January	**Artist and designer Georgy Yakulov born in Tiflis, Georgia**
1 December	First Salon des Indépendants (Group of Independent Artists) is held in Paris

1885
9 March	**Dancer Tamara Karsavina born in St Petersburg**
12 April	**Artist and designer Robert Delaunay born in Paris**
5 October	**Dancer Ida Rubinstein born in St Petersburg**
14 November	**Designer Sonia Delaunay born in Gradizhske (now Poltava Oblast) in the Ukraine (died 5 December 1979, Paris)**
	Savva Mamontov's Private Russian Opera is established in Moscow

1886
27 February	Artist Vincent van Gogh arrives in Paris
15 May	The eighth and last Impressionist exhibition is held in Paris
18 September	Jean Moréas's Symbolist Manifesto appears in *Le Figaro*, Paris
28 October	The Statue of Liberty, a gift from France, is dedicated to New York City
	Artist Paul Gauguin works in Pont-Aven, France

1887
27 February	**Composer Alexander Borodin dies St Petersburg**
23 March	**Artist and designer Juan Gris born in Madrid**
	Vincent van Gogh organises an exhibition of Japanese prints in Paris

1888
12 March	**Dancer and choreographer Vaslav Nijinsky born in Kiev, Ukraine**
10 July	**Artist Giorgio de Chirico born in Volos, Greece (dies 20 November 1978, Rome)**
	Construction on the Eiffel Tower begins in Paris
	The Post-Impressionist avant-garde group, the Nabis, form in Paris

1889
	Alexandre Benois and other students of the May School start the Society for Self Improvement (Nevsky Pickwickians)
8 August	**Dancer Vera Karalli born in Moscow**
5 July	**Writer and designer Jean Cocteau born in Maison-Lafitte, France**
	Production starts on George Eastman's Kodak camera, which uses photographic roll film
6 May–31 October	Exposition Universelle (The World Fair) is held in Paris, at which the first French Symbolist exhibition, organised by painter Paul Gauguin, is shown.

1890
	Sergei Diaghilev begins studying law at St Petersburg University and joins the Society for Self Improvement (Nevsky Pickwickians)
3 January	**Premiere of the ballet *Sleeping beauty* at the Mariinsky Theatre, St Petersburg**

12 March	**Dancer Vaslav Nijinsky born in Kiev, Ukraine**
	Artist Vincent van Gogh commits suicide at Auvers, France

1891
8 January	**Dancer and choreographer Bronislava Nijinska born in Minsk, Belarus (died 22 February 1972, Los Angeles)**
22 March	**Dancer and choreographer Boris Romanov born in St Petersburg (dies 30 January 1957, New York)**
23 April	**Composer Serge Prokofiev born in Sontsovka, Russia (dies 5 March 1953, Moscow)**
	Russian harvests fail, causing widespread famine
	Construction begins on the Trans-Siberian railway
	Artist Paul Gauguin travels to Tahiti
29 March	Georges Seurat dies in Paris

1892
1 July	**Artist and designer Jean Lurçat born in Bruyères, France (dies 6 January 1966, Saint-Paul de Vence, France)**
21 October	**Dancer and choreographer Lydia Lopokova born in St Petersburg (dies 8 June 1981, East Sussex, England)**
	Russia begins period of industrialisation
	The Munich Secession formed in Germany

1893
23 April	**Artist and designer Joan Miró born in Barcelona**
6 November	**Composer Pyotr Ilyich Tchaikovsky dies in St Petersburg**
	Artist Claude Monet begins to create a water garden at Giverny, France
	Talashkino artists' colony established at Smolensk, Russia

1894
1 November	Russian Tsar Alexander III dies; succeeded by Tsar Nicholas II
	First Congress of Russian Artists held in Moscow
	French jeweller René Lalique begins to design Art Nouveau jewellery for actress Sarah Bernhardt

1895
	Sergei Diaghilev graduates from St Petersburg University and embarks on his first tour of Europe
	Cinematography invented by the Lumière brothers (Louis and Auguste)
	Siegfried Bing opens his Maison de l'Art Nouveau shop in Paris
	St Petersburg jeweller, Carl Fabergé, is commissioned by Tsar Nicholas II to create two ornamental Easter eggs, greatly increasing his popularity

1896
4 January	**Artist and designer André Masson born in Balagny-sur-Thérain, France (dies 28 October 1987 in Paris)**
8 August	**Dancer and choreographer Léonide Fedorovich Massine born in Moscow (dies 15 March 1979, Cologne, Germany)**
	Tiffany and Co stained glass is first promoted outside the United States of America
8 January	Symbolist poet Paul Verlaine dies in Paris
3 October	Textile designer William Morris dies in Hammersmith, England

1897
	Secession Group of artists and architects forms in Vienna, Austria

1898
	Sergei Diaghilev founds the magazine *Mir Iskusstva* (*World of Art*). The first issue features the artists Aubrey Beardsley, James Abbott McNeill Whistler, Edgar Degas and Gustave Moreau
28 January	**Composer Vittorio Rieti born in Alexandria, Egypt (dies 19 February 1994, United States of America)**
21 September	**Artist and designer Pavel Tchelitchew born in Moscow (dies 31 July 1957, Rome)**
	The Alexander III Russian Museum opens in St Petersburg
	Paris's Métro subway system opens
16 March	Illustrator Aubrey Beardsley dies in Menton, France
18 April	Symbolist artist Gustave Moreau dies in Paris
17 June	Pre-Raphaelite artist Edward Coley Burne-Jones dies in London

1899
	Sergei Diaghilev starts working at the Imperial Theatres, St Petersburg
February	**First *World of Art* exhibition opens at Stieglitz Museum in St Petersburg**
3 June	**Composer Johan Strauss dies in Vienna, Austria**
	Boer War begins
	Sigmund Freud's *The interpretation of dreams* is published in Vienna

230 BALLETS RUSSES: the art of costume

1900	**First *World of Art* exhibition to feature only Russian art is held in St Petersburg**	**1904**	***Mir Iskusstva* (*World of Art*) magazine closes**
			Dancer Isadora Duncan first performs in St Petersburg
	150th Jubilee of the Russian Theatre founded by Fyodor Volkov in Yaroslav, Russia	3 January	Boris Kochno, librettist, ballet writer, secretary to Diaghilev and artistic advisor to Ballets Russes de Monte Carlo, born in Moscow (dies 8 December 1990, Paris)
	Russian revolutionary Vladimir Ilyich Lenin goes into exile		
20 January	Art critic John Ruskin dies in Brantwood, Cumbria, England	13 January	Artist and designer Oliver Messel born in London (dies 13 July 1978, Barbados)
15 April–12 November	Exposition Universelle (World Fair) is held in Paris. The Finnish pavilion by architects Eliel Saarinen, Herman Gesellius and Armas Lindgren draws attention to Finnish culture and design	22 January	Choreographer George Balanchine born in St Petersburg (dies 30 April 1983, New York)
		27 July	Dancer and choreographer Anton Dolin born in Slinfold, England
	Art Nouveau pioneer, Emile Gallé (1846–1904) wins major awards for his glass at the Paris World Fair	20 November	Dancer Alexandra Dionysievna Danilova born in Peterhof, Russia
19 July	First line of the Paris Métro opens		Sigmund Freud's *Psychopathology of everyday life* is published
25 August	Philosopher Friedrich Nietzsche dies in Weimar, Germany	8 February	Outbreak of Russo-Japanese War
30 November	Author Oscar Wilde dies in Paris	21 July	Trans-Siberian railway completed
		July	Social Democratic Party formed in Russia and immediately splits into the Bolsheviks and the Mensheviks
1901	**Sergei Diaghilev is dismissed from the Imperial Theatres**	15 July	Playwright Anton Chekhov dies in Badenweiler, Germany
	Artist Wassily Kandinsky forms the Phalanx group in Munich, Germany	27 October	New York subway opens
1 January	Australia becomes a Commonwealth	**1905**	
22 January	Queen Victoria dies on the Isle of Wight, England; succeeded by King Edward VII	**6 March**	**Sergei Diaghilev stages historical Russian portrait exhibition at the Tauride Palace, St Petersburg**
31 January	Anton Chekhov's play *Three sisters* is staged at the Moscow Art Theatre	**2 April**	**Dancer and choreographer Serge Lifar born in Kiev, Ukraine (dies 15 December 1986, Lausanne, Switzerland)**
6 September	United States President William McKinley assassinated in Buffalo, New York (dies on 14 September); succeeded by Theodore Roosevelt		
9 September	Sergei Rachmaninov performs his *Second piano concerto*	22 January	Russian Revolution
			Albert Einstein publishes the special theory of relativity
10 December	First Nobel Prizes awarded		French author Jules Verne dies
12 December	Marconi transmits the first trans-Atlantic radio signal		
		1906	**Sergei Diaghilev stages *L'Exposition de l'art russe* at the Salon d'Automne in Paris**
1902	Boer War ends	**25 February**	**Composer Anton Arensky dies in Pertijarvi, Finland**
	French couturier Paul Poiret opens his fashion house in Paris		
		18 April	San Francisco earthquake strikes
1903		7–8 April	Mount Vesuvius erupts near Naples, Italy
4 September	**Designer Kathleen Martin born in Ballarat, Australia**	22 October	Artist Paul Cézanne dies in Aix-en-Provence, France
	First Salon d'Automne (Autumn Salon) held at the Grand Palais in Paris	**1907**	
15 February	The 'teddy bear' is made by Morris and Rose Michtom in the United States of America	**16 May**	**Sergei Diaghilev stages the opera *Boris Godunov* at the Paris Opéra**
17 July	American-born British painter James Abbott McNeill Whistler dies in London		Cubism is created by Pablo Picasso and Georges Braque
1 December	First silent film *The great train robbery* released		Scottish architect Charles Rennie Mackintosh designs the Glasgow School of Art
17 December	The Wright brothers make the first sustained flight in a powered aircraft at Kitty Hawk, North Carolina, United States of America		Spanish designer Mariano Fortuny y Madrazo (1871–1949) presents his *Delphos* pleated dress collection in Venice
	Austrian designers Josef Hoffmann and Koloman Moser co-found the Wiener Werkstätte in Vienna to integrate fine and applied arts		

Timeline 231

1908

28 August	Designer Florence Martin born in Ballarat, Australia (dies 1984, Sydney)
2 March	Premiere of the ballet *Une Nuit d'Egypte* (*A night in Egypt*, later to become *Cleopatra*) at the Mariinsky Theatre in St Petersburg
21 June	Composer Nikolai Rimsky-Korsakov dies in Lyubensk, Russia
30 June	The Tungska Event, a huge unexplained explosion, occurs in Siberia
	Turks revolt in the Ottoman Empire
1 October	Henry Ford produces his first Model T automobile in Detroit

1909

19 May	Sergei Diaghilev presents his first Russian ballet season at the Théâtre du Châtelet, Paris. Premiere of the ballets *Le Pavillon d'Armide* (*Armida's pavilion*), *Le Festin* (*The feast*) and *Danses polovtsiennes du Prince Igor* (*The Polovtsian dances from Prince Igor*)
2 June	Premiere of *Cléopâtre* (*Cleopatra*) at the Théâtre du Châtelet, Paris
4 June	Premiere of *Les Sylphides* at the Théâtre du Châtelet, Paris
20 February	Italian poet FT Marinetti publishes his Futurist Manifesto in *Le Figaro*, in Paris
	Plastic is invented by Leo Hendrik Baekeland
	French couturier Gabrielle 'Coco' Chanel opens her first shop in Paris
	Aviator Louis Blériot makes the first aeroplane flight across the English Channel

1910

20 February	First performance of *Carnaval* (*Carnival*) at the Pavlova Hall, St Petersburg
20 May	Premiere of the ballet *Carnaval* at the Theater des Westens, Berlin
29 May	Mily Balakirev (composer) dies in St Petersburg
4 June	Premiere of the ballets *Carnaval* and *Schéhérazade* at the Théâtre nationale de l'Opéra, Paris
17 June	Premiere of the ballet *Giselle* at the Théâtre nationale de l'Opéra, Paris
25 June	Premiere of the ballets *L'Oiseau de feu* (*The firebird*) and *Les Orientales* at the Théâtre nationale de l'Opéra, Paris
17 July	Choreographer and dancer Marius Petipa dies in Gurzuf, the Crimea (now Ukraine)
25 October	Dancer and choreographer David Lichine born in Rostov na Donu, Russia (dies 1972, Los Angeles)
December 1	Dancer Dame Alicia Markova (Lillian Alicia Marks) born in London
	The tango, which originated in Argentina, gains popularity in Europe and later in the United States of America
20 April	Halley's Comet is visible from Earth
6 May	King Edward VII dies, succeeded by George V
27 August	Thomas Edison demonstrates his Kinetophone, combining sound and motion picture images
11 December	George Claude demonstrates the first neon light

1911

	Diaghilev forms a permanent company. Vaslav Nijinsky is the 'star attraction' First performance of *Papillons* (*Butterflies*) at the Mariinsky Theatre, St Petersburg
19 April	Premiere of the ballet *Le Spectre de la rose* (*Spirit of the rose*) at the Théâtre de Monte Carlo, Monaco
26 April	Premiere of the ballet *Narcisse* (*Narcissus*) at the Théâtre de Monte Carlo, Monaco
16 June	Premiere of the opera *Sadko* at the Théâtre du Châtelet, Paris
13 June	Premiere of the ballet *Petrouchka* (*Petrushka*) at the Théâtre nationale de l'Opéra, Paris Dancer Anna Pavlova's final performance for Diaghilev's Ballets Russes
30 November	Premiere of the ballet *Le Lac des cygnes* (*Swan lake*) at the Royal Opera House, London
24 July	The Inca city of Machu Picchu is 'discovered' in Peru by American historian, Hiram Bingham
21 August	Leonardo da Vinci's *Mona Lisa* is stolen from the Musée du Louvre, Paris
10 October	Chinese Revolution starts (ends 1 January 1912)

1912

13 May	Premiere of the ballet *Le Dieu bleu* (*The blue god*) at the Théâtre nationale de l'Opéra, Paris
20 May	Premiere of the ballet *Thamar* at the Théâtre nationale de l'Opéra, Paris
29 May	Premiere of the ballet *L'Apres-midi d'un faune* (*The afternoon of a faun*) at Théâtre nationale de l'Opéra, Paris
8 June	Premiere of the ballet *Daphnis et Chloé* (*Daphnis and Chloë*) at the Théâtre Nationale de l'Opéra, Paris
15 April	The passenger liner RMS *Titanic* sinks
	Carl Jung's *Theory of psychoanalysis* is published
	Thomas Mann's *Death in Venice* is published

1913

15 May	Premiere of the ballet *Jeux* (*Plays*) at the Théâtre de Champs-Elysées, Paris
29 May	Premiere of *Le Sacre du printemps* (*The rite of spring*) at the Théâtre des Champs-Elysées, Paris
	Diaghilev's Ballets Russes tours South America
12 June	Premiere of the ballet *La Tragédie de Salomé* at the Théâtre des Champs-Elysées, Paris
12 March	Foundation of Canberra as Australia's capital
	The Omega Workshops open in London
	Marcel Proust's *The remembrance of things past (Swann's way)* is published

1914	Dancer Léonide Massine joins Diaghilev's Ballets Russes	**23 May**	**Dancer Tatiana Riabouchinska born in Moscow (dies 24 August 2000, Los Angeles)**
16 April	Premier of the ballet *Papillons* (*Butterflies*) at the Théâtre de Monte Carlo, Monaco	8–12 March	February Revolution in Russia, Abdication of Tsar Nicholas II on 15 March
14 May	Premiere of the ballet *La Légende de Joseph* (*The story of Joseph*) at the Théâtre nationale de l'Opéra, Paris	4 June	First Pulitzer Prize is awarded
24 May	Premiere of the ballet *Le Coq d'or* (*The golden cockerel*) at the Théâtre nationale de l'Opéra, Paris	17 July	Tsar Nicholas II and his family executed at Ekaterinburg
26 May	Premiere of the opera-ballet *Le Rossignol* (*The nightingale*) at the Théâtre nationale de l'Opéra, Paris	27 September	Impressionist painter Edgar Degas dies in Paris
2 June	Premiere of the ballet *Midas* at the Théâtre nationale de l'Opéra, Paris	15 October	Dancer and courtesan Mata Hari is executed for espionage
	Release of *The world, the flesh and the devil*, the first feature length film photographed in colour	26 October	New Soviet Bolshevik government led by Vladimir Lenin takes power
28 June	Assassination of Archduke Franz Ferdinand of Austria, heir to the Austro-Hungarian throne, by a Bosnian-Serb nationalist, Gavrillo Princip, triggering start of the First World War.		*De Stijl* (*The style*) art and design movement founded by Theo van Deosburg, J J P Oud, Gerrit Rietveld and Piet Mondrian in Leiden, The Netherlands.
15 August	The Panama Canal officially opens	**1918**	
		7 February	**Composer Alexander Taneyev dies in Russia**
		25 March	**Composer Claude Debussy dies in Paris**
		5 September	**Revival of *Cléopâtre* at the Coliseum Theatre, London**
1915	Sergei Diaghilev meets FT Marinetti in Rome	11 November	Ceasefire and end of the First World War (peace treaty signed 28 June 1919)
	Sergei Diaghilev establishes a base for his operations at Ouchy, Switzerland		Worldwide influenza epidemic
20 December	Premiere of the ballet *Soleil de nuit* (*Midnight sun*) at the Grand Théâtre, Geneva		
		1919	**Dancer Vaslav Nijinsky gives his last solo performance at St Moritz, Switzerland**
1916		**3 March**	**Dancer Irina Baronova born in Petrograd, Russia**
17 January–6 May	**Diaghilev's Ballets Russes tours the United States of America**	**5 June**	**Premiere of the ballet *La Boutique fantasque* (*The magical toyshop*) at the Alhambra Theatre, London**
21 August	**Premiere of the ballet *Las meninas* at the Teatro Victoria Eugenia, San Sebastián, Spain**	**22 July**	**Premiere in London of *Le Tricorne* (*The three-cornered hat*) at the Alhambra Theatre, London**
25 August	**Premiere of the ballet *Kikimora* at the Teatro Victoria Eugenia, San Sebastián, Spain**		
9 October	**Revival of the ballet *Sadko* at the Manhattan Opera House, New York**	18 May	Dancer Margot Fonteyn is born in Surrey, England
9 Oct–Feb 1917	**Diaghilev's Ballets Russes second tour in the United States**	28 June	Treaty of Versailles ends World War II
23 October	**Premiere of the ballet *Till Eulenspeigel* at the Manhattan Opera House, New York**	September	Adolf Hitler joins the Deutsche Arbeiterpartei (DAP) later commonly referred to as the Nazi Party
1 July–18 November	The Battle of the Somme, France	13 December	Impressionist painter Pierre-Auguste Renoir dies in Cagnes-sur-Mer, France
29 December	Russian mystic Grigori Yefimovich Rasputin murdered in St Petersburg		Architect Walter Gropius founds the Bauhaus School in Weimar, Germany
1917	**Diaghilev's Ballets Russes tours Latin America.**	**1920**	
12 April	**Premiere of the ballets *Le Donne di buon umore* (*Les femmes de bonne humeur* / *The good-humoured ladies*) and *Feu d'artifice* (*Fireworks*) at the Teatro Cosanzi, Rome**	**2 February**	**Premiere of the ballet *Le Chant du rossignol* (*The song of the nightingale*) at the Théâtre nationale de l'Opéra, Paris**
22 April	Artist and designer Sidney Nolan born in Melbourne (dies 28 November 1992, London)	**15 May**	**Premiere of the ballet *Pulcinella* at the Théâtre nationale de l'Opéra, Paris**
11 May	**Premiere of the ballet *Contes russes* (*Russian tales* / *Children's tales*) at the Théâtre du Châtelet, Paris**	**27 May**	**Premiere of the opera-ballet *L'Astuce féminine* (*Women's wiles*) at the Théâtre nationale de l'Opéra, Paris**
18 May	**Premiere of the ballet *Parade* (*Sideshow*) at the Théâtre du Châtelet, Paris**		Prohibition begins in United States of America

	Women gain the vote in the United States of America	21 January	Vladimir Lenin dies in Gorki Leninskiye, Russia
		12 February	Composer George Gershwin's *Rhapsody in blue* is first performed at the Aeolian Hall, New York
1921	**Dancer Léonide Massine leaves Diaghilev's Ballets Russes**		
		1925	
17 May	**Premiere of the ballets *Chout* (*The buffoon*) and *Cuadro flamenco* at the Théâtre de la Gaîté-Lyrique, Paris**	**15 February**	**Premiere of the ballet *Les Contes de fées* (*Fairy tales*) at the Nouvelle Salle de Musique, Monte Carlo Casino, Monaco**
2 November	**Premiere of the ballet *The sleeping princess* at Alhambra Theatre, London**	**18 February**	**Premiere of the ballet *Le Festin* at the Nouvelle Salle de Musique, Monte Carlo Casino, Monaco**
	Costumier Barbara Karinska opens her couture business in Moscow	**7 March**	**Premiere of the ballet *L'Assemblée* (*The gathering*) at the Nouvelle Salle de Musique, Monte Carlo Casino, Monaco**
1922		**11 March**	**Premiere of the ballet *Le Bal du lac des cygnes* (*The ball from Swan lake*) at the Nouvelle Salle de Musique, Monte Carlo Casino, Monaco**
18 May	**Premiere of the ballet *Le Mariage d'Aurore* (*Aurora's wedding*) and *Le Renard* (*The fox*) at the Théâtre nationale de l'Opéra, Paris**		
27 June	Louis II becomes the eleventh sovereign Prince of Monaco	**28 April**	**Premiere of the ballet *Zéphire et Flore* (*Zephyr and Flora*) at the Théâtre de Monte Carlo, Monaco**
24 November	Howard Carter discovers the nearly intact tomb of the twelfth pharaoh of the eighteenth dynasty of Egypt, Tutankhamen, receiving worldwide press coverage and sparking a renewed public interest in ancient Egypt.	**11 December**	**Premiere of the ballet *Barabau* at the Coliseum Theatre, London**
			Léonide Massine re-joins Diaghilev's Ballets Russes
		April-October	Exposition Internationale des Arts Décoratifs et Industriels Modernes (International Exposition of Modern Industrial and Decorative Arts) held in Paris
1923			
19 March	**Premiere of the ballet *Danses russes* (*Russian dances*) at the Palais des Beaux-Arts, Monte Carlo**	2 October	John Logie Baird makes the first television broadcast
19 June	**Premiere of the ballet *Les Noces* (*The wedding*) at the Théâtre de la Gaîté-Lyrique, Paris**		Adolf Hitler's *Mein kampf* is published
		2 October	American dancer Josephine Baker makes her debut performance at the Théâtre des Champs-Élysées in Paris
	Dancer Michel Fokine establishes his ballet school in New York		Sergei M Eisenstein and Grigori Aleksandrov's film *Battleship Potemkin* is released
	Dancer Ninette de Valois joins Diaghilev's Ballets Russes		
		1926	
26 March	Actress Sarah Bernhardt dies in Paris	**March–4 August**	**Dancer Anna Pavlova's first Australian tour**
		4 May	**Premiere of the ballet *Romeo and Juliet* at the Théâtre de Monte Carlo, Monaco**
1924			
3 January	**Premiere of the ballet *Les Tentations de la bergère* (*ou L'amour vainqueur*) (*Temptations of the shepherdess / Victorious love*) at the Théâtre de Monte Carlo, Monaco**	**29 May**	**Premiere of the ballet *La Pastorale* at the Théâtre Sarah Bernhardt, Paris**
		8 June	**Premiere of the ballet *Jack in the box* at the Théâtre Sarah Bernhardt, Paris**
6 January	**Premiere of the ballet *Les Biches* (*The house party*) at the Théâtre de Monte Carlo, Monaco**	**25 November**	**Revival of the ballet *L'Oiseau de feu* (*The firebird*) at the Lyceum Theatre, London**
8 January	**Premiere of *Ballet de l'Astuce féminine* at the Théâtre de Monte Carlo, Monaco**	**3 December**	**Premiere of the ballet *The triumph of Neptune* (*Le Triomphe de Neptune*) at the Lyceum Theatre, London**
19 January	**Premiere of the ballet *Les Fâcheux* (*The bores*) at the Théâtre de Monte Carlo, Monaco**		**Dancer Ninette de Valois leaves Diaghilev's Ballets Russes. She later becomes the founder of the Royal Ballet**
24 January	**Premiere of the ballet *Cimarosiana* in Barcelona**		
13 April	**Premiere of the ballet *La Nuit sur Mont Chauve* (*The night on Mt Chauve*) at the Théâtre de Monte Carlo, Monaco**	5 December	Claude Monet dies in Giverny, France
			AA Milne's *Winnie the Pooh* is published
20 June	**Premiere of the ballet *Le Train bleu* (*The blue train*) at the Théâtre Chamos-Elysées, Paris**		Marcel Duchamp's *The large glass / The bride stripped bare by her bachelors, even* (*La mariée mise à nu par ses célibataires, même*) first exhibited in New York
28 December	**Designer Léon Bakst dies in Paris**		
	André Breton releases the first Surrealist Manifesto		

1927

	Diaghilev's Ballets Russes presents a two-month season at the Princess Theatre, London
3 April	Premiere of the ballet *La Chatte* (*The cat*) at the Théâtre de Monte Carlo, Monaco
11 May	Artist and designer Juan Gris dies in Paris, France
2 June	Premiere of the ballet *Mercure* (*Mercury*) at the Théâtre Sarah Bernhardt, Paris
7 June	Premiere of the ballet *Le Pas d'acier* (*The steel step*) at the Théâtre Sarah Bernhardt, Paris
14 September	Dancer Isadora Duncan dies in Nice, France
6 October	The first 'talkie' film, *The jazz singer*, is released
	German director Fritz Lang's film *Metropolis* is released

1928

6 June	Premiere of the ballet *Ode* at the Théâtre Sarah Bernhardt, Paris
12 June	Premiere of the ballet *Apollon musagète* (*Apollo*) at the Théâtre Sarah Bernhardt, Paris
16 July	Premiere of the ballet *The gods go a-begging* (*Les Dieux mendiants*) at His Majesty's Theatre, London
13 November	Dancer and ballet master Enrico Cecchetti dies in Milan, Italy
28 December	Designer Georgy Yakulov dies in Erevan, Armenia
11 October	The German airship *Graf Zeppelin* completes its first commercial transatlantic flight

1929

7 May	Premier of the ballet *Le Bal* (*The ball*) at the Théâtre de Monte Carlo, Monaco
21 May	Premiere of the ballet *Le Fils prodigue* (*The prodigal son*) at the Théâtre Sarah Bernhardt, Paris
26 July	Diaghilev's Ballets Russes gives its final performance at Covent Garden Theatre, London
19 August	Sergei Diaghilev dies in Venice, Italy
	André Breton releases the second Surrealist Manifesto
October	Wall Street stock market crash in New York

1930

17 April	Artist and designer Aleksandr Golovin dies in Detskoye Selo, Russia
	René Blum forms the Ballet de l'Opéra at Monte Carlo, Colonel Wassily de Basil and Prince Zeretelli present the Opera Russe in Paris (these companies later merge)
30 June–25 August	First International Dada Fair held in Berlin

1931

23 January	Dancer Anna Pavlova dies in The Hague, The Netherlands
23 February	Australian soprano Dame Nellie Melba dies in Sydney

1932

	Léonide Massine joins the Ballets Russes de Monte Carlo
5 January	The Ballets Russes de Monte Carlo participates in the opera season at the Théâtre de Monte Carlo, Monaco
20 April	The Ballet Russe de Monte Carlo (La Societé des Ballets Russes et Ballets de Monte-Carlo) is formally registered in Monaco. The founders are René Blum and Colonel Wassily de Basil
30 April	Revival of the ballet *Pulcinella* at the Théâtre de Monte Carlo, Monaco
9 June	The Ballets Russes de Monte Carlo presents its first Paris season and later tours Belgium, Holland, Germany, and Switzerland
	Sydney Harbour Bridge opens

1933

7 March	Premiere of the ballet *Le Beau Danube* (*The beautiful Danube*) at Théâtre de Monte Carlo, Monaco
13 April	Premiere of the ballet *Les Présages* (*Destiny*) at the Théâtre de Monte Carlo, Monaco
4 July	The Ballets Russes de Monte Carlo presents its premier London season
22 December	The Ballets Russes de Monte Carlo presents its premier American season
	Léonide Massine becomes ballet master for the Ballets Russes de Monte Carlo
	George Balanchine moves to the United States of America
April	Berlin Bauhaus school closes due to pressure from the German Nazi Party

1934

5 April–9 May	The Ballets Russes de Monte Carlo divides into two groups
11 June	Premiere of the ballet *Les Imaginaires* (*The imaginary ones*) at the Théâtre de Champs-Elysée, Paris
25 September	The Ballets Russes de Monte Carlo presents its premier season in Mexico
25 October	The Ballets Russes de Monte Carlo begins a tour of Canada
	Henri Matisse paints *The dance*
	Composer Sergei Prokofiev returns to Russia
	George Balanchine and Lincoln Kerstein establish the School of American Ballet

1935

	The Ballets Russes de Monte Carlo tours to the United States, Spain, London, Cuba, Canada
8 March	Premiere of the ballet *Jardin public* (*The public gardens*) at Auditorium, Chicago
	USSR concludes treaties with the USA, France, Czechoslovakia and Turkey
	Actress Greta Garbo stars in the film of Tolstoy's *Anna Karenina*

28 March	German propaganda film *Triumph of the will* by Leni Riefenstahl is released	17 March	Dancer Rudolf Nureyev born in Irkutsk, Serbia
		9–10 November	Kristallnacht (Night of broken glass) occurs in Germany and Austria

1936 **The Ballets Russes de Monte Carlo presents productions in New York, Barcelona, London, Berlin, and Canada**

The Ballets Russes de Monte Carlo is renamed Colonel de Basil's Ballets Russes

René Blum founds (and directs) The Ballets de Monte Carlo with Michel Fokine serving as ballet master and choreographer

21 March	Composer Alexander Glazunov dies in Paris
18 April	Composer Ottorino Respighi dies in Rome

13 October **Commencement of Monte Carlo Russian Ballet tour in Australia (ends 14 July 1937). Productions given: *L'Amour sorcier*, *L'Après-midi d'une faune*, *Le Beau Danube*, *La Boutique fantasque*, *Carnaval*, *Les cent basiers* (*The hundred kisses*), *Contes russes* (*Children's tales*), *Cotillon* (*The dance*), *Le Lac des cygnes*, *Le Mariage d'Aurore*, *L'Oiseau de feu*, *Petrouchka*, *Port Said*, *Les Présages*, *Prince Igor*, *Schéhérazade*, *Scuola di ballo* (*The school of dance*), *Soleil de nuit*, *Le Spectre de la rose*, *Les Sylphides*, *Thamar***

20 January	Death of King George V, succeeded by Edward VIII
11 June–4 July	International Surrealist Exhibition held at the New Burlington Galleries in London
July	Beginning of Spanish Civil War

1937
15 July **Premiere of the ballet *Francesca da Rimini* at the Royal Opera House, Covent Garden, London**
23 September **Revival of *Le Coq d'or* at Covent Garden Theatre, London**
28 December **Composer Maurice Ravel dies in Paris**
Pablo Picasso paints *Guernica*

1938
February **A personality conflict between Léonide Massine and de Basil splits the Ballets Russes de Monte Carlo company. Blum founds (and directs) the company while Colonel de Basil's company is renamed Covent Garden Russian Ballet.**

28 September **Commencement of the Covent Garden Russian ballet tour to Australia and New Zealand (ends 27 April 1939). Productions given: *Bolero*, *Cendrillon* (*Cinderella*), *Choreartium* (*Choeographic symphony*), *La Concurrence* (*The competition*), *Le Coq d'or*, *Cotillon*, *Danses slaves et tziganes* (*Gypsy dances*), *Les Dieux mendiants*, *Les Femmes de bonne humeur*, *Le Fils prodigue*, *Jeux d'Enfants* (*Children's games*), *Papillons*, *Protée*, *Soleil de nuit*, *Symphonie fantastique*, *Union Pacific***

1939 **Educational Ballets Ltd. purchases de Basil's company and it is renamed Original Ballet Russe (de Basil remains as Director)**

30 December **Commencement of the Original Ballet Russe tour to Australia (ends 21 August 1940). Productions given: *L'Après-midi d'une faune*, *Carnaval*, *Cendrillon*, *Les cent Basiers*, *Choreartium*, *Cimarosiana*, *Coppélia*, *Le Coq d'or*, *Le Danube bleu*, *Les Dieux mendiants*, *Les Femmes de bonne humeur*, *Francesca da Rimini*, *Graduation ball*, *Icare* (*Icarus*), *Le Lac des cygnes*, *La Lutte éternelle* (*The eternal struggle*), *Le Mariage d'Aurore*, *L'Oiseau de feu*, *Paganini*, *Papillons*, *Pavane* (*Pavane of the infantas*), *Pavillon*, *Petrouchka*, *Les Présages*, *Prince Igor*, *Protée*, *Schéhérazade*, *Scuola di ballo*, *Le Spectre de la rose*, *Les Sylphides*, *Symphonie fantastique*, *Thamar***

30 April	New York World's Fair opens
1 September	Beginning of the Second World War

1940
16 February **Premiere of the ballet *Icare* at the Theatre Royal, Sydney, with design by Sidney Nolan**
29 July **Premiere of the ballet *La Lutte éternelle* at the Theatre Royal, Sydney**

May	The Nazi Auschwitz concentration camp becomes operational in Poland
	Walt Disney's animated film *Fantasia* released

1941
25 October **Artist and designer Robert Delaunay dies in Montpellier, France**
The Kirsova Ballet founded by Hélène Kirsova

28 March	Writer Virginia Woolf dies in East Sussex, England
27 December	Dmitri Shostakovich writes *Symphony no 7* during siege of Leningrad

1942
31 April **René Blum dies at Auschwitz concentration camp**
22 August **Dancer Mikhail Fokine dies in New York**

1944 **The Borovansky Australian Ballet Company founded by Edouard Borovansky in Melbourne**

15 July	Choreographer and dancer Mikhail Mordkin dies in New Jersey

16 October	Sergei Prokofiev's opera *War and peace* staged in Moscow	**1949**	9 May Prince Louis II of Monaco dies at Le Marchais, France
13 December	Russian painter Wassily Kandinsky dies		

1945

26 June	**Composer Nikolai Tcherepnin dies in Paris**
27 November	**Artist and designer José-María Sert dies in Barcelona, Spain**
January	Auschwitz concentration camp ceases operation
6 August	United States drops atomic bomb on Hiroshima
2 September	End of the Second World War
	George Orwell writes *Animal farm*
	Evelyn Waugh writes *Brideshead revisited*

1946

14 November	**Composer Manuel de Falla dies in Buenos Aires, Argentina**
	George Balanchine presents the ballet *Nightshadow* in New York
	United States Navy tests atomic bomb at Bikini Atoll
	Jean Cocteau's film *Belle et la bête* is released
	United Nations General Assembly holds its first session in London
	Léon Blum forms socialist government in France

1947

Colonel de Basil's Original Ballets Russes presents its last London season and then disbands (but is briefly revived in 1951–52)

28 January	**Composer Reynaldo Hahn dies in Paris, France**
31 May	**Composer Henri Casadesus dies in Paris, France**
13 December	**Designer Nicholas Roerich dies in the Punjab, India**

Partition of the British-ruled Indian subcontinent along religious lines into Hindu India and Islamic Pakistan

Albert Camus writes *The plague*

The Dead Sea Scrolls are discovered at Wadi Qumran

Pierre Bonnard dies

Swiss architect Le Corbusier builds *Unité d'habitation* housing in Marseilles

French couturier Christian Dior launches his *New look* fashion line

1948

The Jewish state of Israel comes into existence

American artist Jackson Pollock paints *Composition no 1*

Michael Powell directs the film *The red shoes*

Alfred C Kinsey writes *Sexual behaviour in the human male*

1950

8 April	**Vaslav Nijinsky dies in London**
23 December	**Composer Vincenzo Tommasini dies in Rome**

1951

23 June	**Dancer Nicholas Sergeyev dies in Nice, France**
27 July	**Colonel Wassily de Basil dies in Paris**
	Colonel de Basil's Original Ballets Russes is revived briefly by G Kirsta and the Grigorievs

1952

Colonel de Basil's Original Ballets Russes permanently disbands while on tour in Europe

Dancer Kira Bousloff establishes the West Australian Ballet in Perth

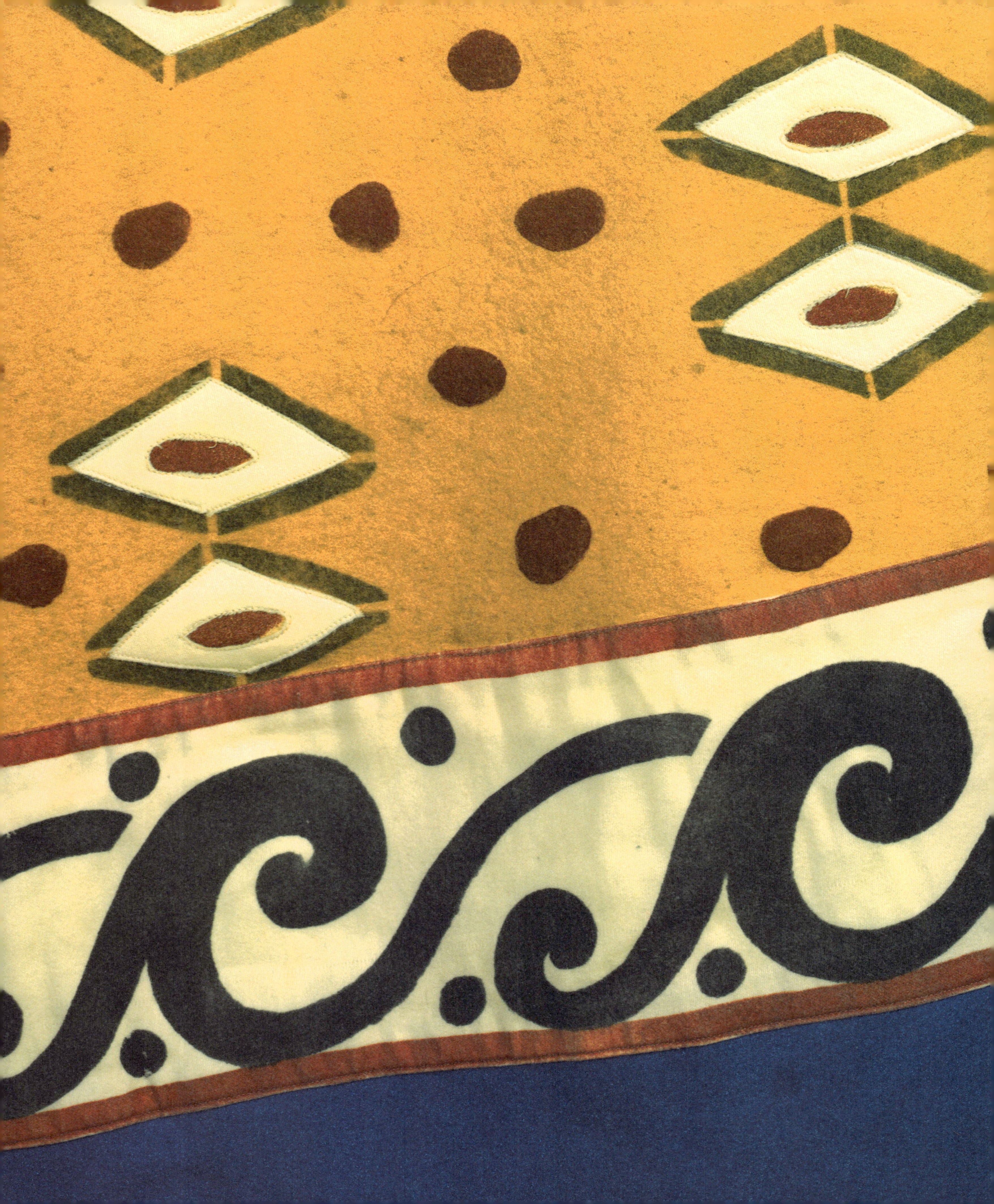

LIST OF WORKS in the exhibition

All works are from the collection of the National Gallery of Australia, unless noted otherwise.

Costumes, and designs for costume and stage decor, are listed chronologically under the ballet productions for which they were made. Dates are provided where they are known and date ranges are given for costumes that were also used in, or modified for, later productions. The ballets are referred to by their premiere titles, followed by English translations. The titles of particular characters are given as they were listed in the premieres or season programs. Costumiers' names are given when known. Associated photographs, posters, books, theatre programs and journals included in the exhibition are listed separately on page 249. Where works are illustrated, page numbers are listed at the end of the relevant entries.

All measurements are in centimetres. Costume measurements are given as the centre-back length for the major element of ensembles, and as the overall length of items such as hats, belts, scarves and boots. Measurements for other works are height before width.

Inscriptions indicate the names, initials or identifiers (in Russian and other languages) of some of the dancers who performed in the costume during the period from its first production to 1951. Inscriptions are generally marked in ink or pencil on the inner surfaces and linings of some costumes. Costumiers' labels, other identifiers of manufacture, and customs stamps on some costumes are also noted.

Costumes from productions from 1909 to 1929 were produced by Les Ballets Russes de Serge Diaghilev (Sergei Diaghilev's Russian Ballet).

Costumes from productions after 1932 were produced (or reproduced or modified from originals made and used by the Ballets Russes de Serge Diaghilev for its original repertoire) by the following companies associated with Colonel Wassily de Basil that operated and performed in various cities from 1932 to 1951:

Les Ballets Russes de Monte Carlo (Monte Carlo 1932)

Ballets Russes de Monte Carlo (Paris and London 1932 and 1933)

Ballets Russes du Col W de Basil (London 1934, 1935, 1936 and 1937)

Monte Carlo Ballet Russe (New York 1934 and 1935)

Col W de Basil's Ballets Russes (New York 1936)

Ballets Russes de Monte Carlo, and Col W de Basil's Monte Carlo Russian Ballet (Australia 1936)

Col W de Basil's Ballet Russe (New York 1937)

Ballets Russes de Léon Woizikovsky (Europe 1937)

Russian Ballet presented by Educational Ballets Ltd (London 1938)

Covent Garden Russian Ballet presented by Educational Ballets Ltd (Australia 1938, London 1939)

Original Ballet Russe Ltd's Col W de Basil's Ballet Company (Australia 1939)

Original Ballet Russe (internationally from 1940)

Léon Bakst
Cloak from costume for a brigand c 1912 (detail) from *Daphnis et Chloé*

Le Pavillon d'Armide
Armida's pavilion

19 May 1909

Alexandre BENOIS, designer
Ivan CAFFI (Imperial Theatres, St Petersburg), costumier

Costume for a spirit of the hours (genie des heures)
c 1909
jacket: brushed cotton, metallic gauze and braid, paint, gelatin, wood, linen; tunic: cotton, silk, lamé, metallic thread, paint, metallic fringe, metallic and gelatin sequins; trunks: cotton, elastic
jacket: 76.4 cm; tunic: 87 cm; trunks: 45.8 cm
inscribed on jacket: 'Pavillon d'Armide', 'Genie des heures', 'archv …', 'Gairel', German customs stamp, 'Cher...', and 'Chernobaieva'; on tunic: 'Pavillon d'Armide, Genie des Heures', 'Lizie', 'Maruarn', and 'Direktion des Russischen Ballets, Sergisi von Diaghilews'; on trunks: 'Pavillon d'Armide', 'Genie des heures', and 'T.R.'
purchased 1973
1973.270.19.A-C

Costume for a spirit of the hours (genie des heures)
c 1909
jacket: brushed cotton, metallic thread, paint, gelatin; tunic: cotton, silk, metallic thread and fabric, paint, gelatin, linen; trunks: cotton, elastic
jacket: 77 cm; tunic 89 cm; trunks: 48 cm
inscribed on jacket: 'Pavillon d'Armide, Genie des Heures', 'Lijic (?)', and customs stamp; on tunic: 'Gairal', 'Pavillon d'Armide', 'Genie des heures', and German customs stamp; on trunks: 'Pavillon d'Armide, Genie des Heures', and 'TK (?)'
purchased 1973
1973.270.20.A-C

Costume for a courtier
c 1909
tunic: silk satin, rayon, cotton lace, lamé, metallic fringe, braid and ribbon, bone; jacket: rayon, cotton, metallic ribbon, wool; garter: metallic thread; belt: metallic fabric
jacket: 88 cm; tunic: 94 cm; garter: 27 (circ), 21 (tassel l), 9 (w) cm; belt: 63 (circ), 25 (tassel l), 6 (w) cm
inscribed on jacket: 'Klaun', 'Ergievsky', 'Klausen', and '…est'; on tunic: 'Chorand', 'Barnett', and 'Wygrin'; on garter: 'Griwwis', 'Feran', and 'Vicka'; on belt: 'Nygren'
purchased 1973
1973.279.27.A-D

Jacket from costume for a musician
c 1909
brushed cotton, wool, paint, linen, imitation jewels (wood, silk velvet, metallic braid, sequins and fringe)
105 cm
inscribed: 'Pavillon d'Armide', 'Musician figuration', 'No 3', and German customs stamp
purchased 1973
1973.270.24

Cloak from costume for a harpist
c 1909
cotton, paint, wood, metallic thread
182 cm
inscribed: 'Pavillon d'Armide', 'Arphiste', 'Be … (?)', 'Belloni', 'Grinwis', 'Fernan', and German customs stamp
purchased 1973
1973.270.25

Danses polovtsiennes du Prince Igor
The Polovtsian dances from Prince Igor

19 May 1909

Nicholas ROERICH, designer

Costume for a Polovtsian warrior
c 1909
jacket: silk ikat, rayon, brass fastener, cotton, paint; trousers: cotton ikat, nickel-plated brass fastener; skullcap: cotton ikat; belt: silk ikat, cotton ikat, metal fasteners
jacket: 85.4 cm; trousers: 85 cm (inner leg), 80 cm (waist circ); skullcap: 57 cm (circ); belt: 81.5 cm (l)
inscribed on jacket: 'Burke'; on trousers: 'Nygren'; on skullcap: 'Seibert'; on belt: 'Lad'
purchased 1973
1973.270.1.C,1.D,3

Costume for a Polovtsian girl
c 1909–37
jacket: wool braid, linen, fur, paint, metal fasteners; blouse: cotton, metallic thread; trousers: cotton, linen, shell, plastic; bonnet: cotton, metal wire, paint, ceramic buttons, linen, elastic
jacket: 99 cm; blouse: 54 cm (shoulder to hem); trousers: 47 cm, 60.6 cm (inner leg); bonnet: 56.4 cm (circ)
inscribed on jacket: 'Roussova'; on blouse: 'Lloyd', 'Evan'; on trousers: 'Sandra'; on bonnet: 'Lloyd'
purchased 1973
1973.270.5.A-D

Costume for a Polovtsian girl
c 1933
jacket: wool braid, linen, fur, paint; blouse: cotton, metallic braid, elastic; trousers: cotton; bonnet: cotton, linen; belt: lamé, cotton
jacket: 100 cm (shoulder to hem); blouse: 45 cm; trousers: 63 cm (inner leg), 82 cm (waist circ); bonnet: 26 cm (circ); belt: 65 x 5 cm
inscribed on jacket: 'Starr', and 'Kosmouska/Louber/Alik'; on trousers: 'Starr', and 'Gou …'; on belt: 'Popov', and 'Newstead'; on bonnet: 'Star'
purchased 1973
1973.270.4.A-D

Cap
c 1909
wool twill
66 cm (circ)
purchased 1976
1976.1054.738

Cléopâtre
Cleopatra

2 June 1909
Revival: 5 September 1918, designs by Sonia Delaunay

Léon BAKST, designer

Costume for a Syrian woman
skirt: 1909; bodice: replaced 1930s
cotton, silk, metal studs, paint
110 cm (l), 43 cm (underarm chest), 33 cm (waist)
inscribed: 'Raya Kousmetiova '37-39", and French customs stamp
purchased 1976
1976.1054.739

Costume for a Greek
c 1909
tunic: silk, silk appliqué, rayon, lamé, metallic braid, metal stays; tights: silk jersey, paint
tunic: 91.6 cm; tights: 83 cm (inner leg)
inscribed: 'Me. de Paoli', and 'Tenor'
purchased 1973
1973.270.11.A-B

Costume for a Greek
1909
silk, lamé, metallic braid
96 cm, 68 cm (underarm chest)
inscribed: 'Mr Carmassi'
purchased 1976
1976.1054.1020

Costume for a Jew
c 1909–20s
jacket: cotton, paint, metallic fringe and braid; waistcoat: silk, paint; metallic fringe, cotton lining
jacket: 81 cm; 9 cm (fringe l), 60 cm (underarm chest); waistcoat: 77 cm, 10 cm (fringe l), 57 cm (underarm chest)
inscribed on both jacket and waistcoat: 'Cleopatre Juif', 'Kobeleff', and German and French customs stamps
purchased 1973
1973.270.6.A-B

Costume for a slave or dancing girl
c 1937
dress: silk faille and chiffon, metallic braid, stencilled paint, metal fasteners; collar: silk faille, metallic and cotton braid, paint, metal fasteners
dress: 115 cm, 43 cm (underarm chest); collar: 6.4 cm (w), 44 cm (circ)
inscribed on dress: 'Radova'
purchased 1976
76.1054.744.A-B

Costume for a slave or dancing girl
1918–c 36
dress: silk faille and chiffon, rayon, metallic braid, stencilled paint, metal fasteners; collar: metallic and cotton, braid, paint, metal fasteners
dress: 115 cm, 40 cm (underarm chest); collar: 37 cm (inner circ)
inscribed on dress: 'Osato', and 'Pat'
purchased 1976
1976.1054.751.A-B

Costume design for Amoun
c 1909
watercolour, gouache, paint, pencil on card
30.4 x 21 cm
purchased 1987
1987.2235

Sonia DELAUNAY, designer

Costume for Amoun
1918–30s
chest strap: cotton velveteen, acetate, linen, metallic braid; skirt: cotton, acetate, leather, silk velvet, silk, metallic braid
chest strap: 31 cm; skirt: 87.6 cm (circ)
purchased 1973
1973.270.13.A-B

Costume for a slave or dancing girl
1918–36
dress: wool, rayon, cotton, lamé, metallic thread, ribbon and braid, paint, elastic; collar: rayon, cotton, metallic thread, metal fasteners; bloomers: synthetic fabric
dress: 94.6 cm; collar 64 cm; bloomers: 36 cm (waist w), 26 cm (outer leg)
inscribed on bloomers and dress: 'Chamie'
purchased 1976
1976.1054.749.A-C

Costume for a slave or dancing girl
1918–36
wool, rayon, lamé, metallic braid, paint, metal, cotton
91 cm
inscribed: 'Volokova'
gift of Elaine Lustig Cohen in memory of Michael Lloyd 1997
1997.633

Carnaval
Carnival
20 February 1910

Léon BAKST, designer
MORRIS ANGEL & SON, costumier

Costume for a lady
c 1920
dress: acetate, rayon, cotton, metal boning, paint; shawl: synthetic fabric
dress: 107 cm (c. front), 34 cm (underarm chest), 30 cm (inner sleeve), 38 cm (outer sleeve); shawl: 38 cm
purchased 1973
1973.270.92.A-B

Costume for Chiarina
c 1910
bodice: acetate, silk crepe and lace, rayon lace, imitation flowers; skirt: silk taffeta, cotton tassels
bodice: 23 cm; skirt: 97 cm (waist)
inscribed on bodice: 'Carmaval', 'L. Tchernicheva'; on skirt: 'Razoumova'
purchased 1973
1973.270.89.A-B

Costume for Pierrot
c 1910
jacket and trousers: wool twill, acetate buttons, plastic buttons, metal buckles, cotton lining; frill: cotton organdie
jacket: 72 cm; trousers: 74 cm; frill: 15 x 39 cm
inscribed: 'Morris Angel & Son Lt', '119', 'Shaftesbury Avenue', 'London. WC'
purchased 1973 (jacket and trousers); purchased 1976 (frill)
1973.270.91.A-B and 76.1054.753

Dress from costume for Columbine
c 1942
acetate, cotton lining, metal boning and fasteners, paint
34 cm (underarm chest), 100 cm (c front)
inscribed: 'Strognova'
purchased 1973
1973.270.93

Schéhérazade
14 June 1910

Léon BAKST, designer
Marie MUELLE, costumier

Costume for the Chief Eunuch
1910
trousers: silk, silk appliqué, cotton; jacket: silk, metallic braid, rayon, cotton; cummerbund: rayon, silk, cotton, metallic paint; overskirt: silk appliqué, acetate, metallic braid, paint, cotton; hat: rayon, silk, metallic braid and ornament, feathers, imitation jewels, cotton wadding, cork, cane, newspaper; keys: wood, metallic and other paint
trousers: 74 cm (inner leg), 39 cm (waist to crotch); jacket: 46 cm; cummerbund: 124 x 32 cm; overskirt: 62 cm; hat: 35 cm (h), 20 cm (circ); keys: 56 x 20 cm
inscribed on trousers: German customs stamp; on overskirt: customs stamp (?)
purchased 1973
1973.270.29, .32, .34, .38, .37, .36

Costume for a servant
1910–35
jacket: cotton, metallic thread, metallic and other paint; trousers: cotton, metallic paint, elastic; belt: cotton, metallic thread; tunic: cotton, metallic paint and braid
trousers: 77 cm (inner leg); jacket: 38 cm; belt: 198 x 19 cm; tunic: 125 cm (l), 55 cm (across shoulders); 49 cm (inner sleeve)
inscribed and jacket and belt: French customs stamp
purchased 1973
1973.270.46.A-D

Costume for a dancing girl (almée) or odalisque
c 1910
one-piece trouser ensemble: rayon, silk, metallic and other paint, metallic and rayon braid, gelatin paillettes, glass beads, metal fasteners; headdress: silk, metallic braid, wire
one-piece trouser ensemble: 71 cm, 65 cm (inner leg); headdress: 65 cm (circ), 100 cm (l)
inscribed on one-piece trouser ensemble: 'Shea'
purchased 1973
1973.270.49.A-B

Costume for a dancing girl (almée) or odalisque
c 1915–30s
cotton, metallic braid, rayon, lamé, metal fasteners
46 cm, 67 cm (inner leg)
inscribed: 'Galvin', 'Abeis', and 'Kolow'
purchased 1973
1973.270.48

Costume for a dancing girl (almée) or odalisque
c 1910
rayon, acetate, metallic thread, cotton
150 cm (c front)
inscribed: 'Arfoy (?)'
purchased 1973
1973.270.42

Costume for Shah Shahriar
1910–30s
coat: silk velvet and appliqué, lamé, metallic braid, painted wooden beads, rayon satin; trousers: rayon satin; hat: silk velvet, rayon, glass and metal imitation jewels
coat: 107 cm; trousers: 56 cm, 72 cm (inner leg); hat: 64 cm (circ)
purchased 1973
1973.270.50.A-C

Costume for Shah's soldier or guard
c 1910
skirt: cotton, acetate, paint; jacket: acetate, metallic paint and braid, cotton
jacket: 58 cm (c front); skirt: 70 cm (c front)
inscribed on jacket: '54', and 'Adre (?)'
purchased 1973
1973.270.45.A-B

Costume for Shah Zeman
1910–30s
coat: silk brocade, satin and embroidery, lamé, metallic braid, cotton lining; trousers: silk satin, metallic braid
coat: 118 cm; trousers: 72 cm (inner back)
purchased 1973
1973.270.52.A-B

Costume for a dancing girl (almée) or odalisque
1930s
rayon, metallic thread and braid, cotton velveteen, wool braid, paint
70 cm, 70.4 cm (inner leg)
inscribed: 'Benks', 'Banks', 'Larom (?)', and 'Markova'
purchased 1973
1973.270.44

Costume for a dancing girl (almée) or odalisque
1930s
one-piece trouser ensemble: rayon, silk, metallic and other paint, metallic and rayon braid, gelatin paillettes, glass beads; headdress: rayon, cotton, silk, paint, wire, elastic
one-piece trouser ensemble: 140 cm (c front); headdress: 102 cm (l), 69 cm (circ)
inscribed on one-piece trouser ensemble: '…onique'; on headdress: 'Chahaska'
purchased 1973
1973.270.41.A-B

Costume design for Shah Zeman
1910
gouache, pencil, watercolour, paint on varnish paper
37 x 22.2 cm
purchased 1980
1980.1942

Costume design for an odalisque
1910
gouache, pencil, paint, paper on cardboard
29 x 19.4 cm
purchased 1980
1980.2691

Giselle
17 June 1910

Alexandre BENOIS, designer

Trunks from costume for Albrecht
c 1910
silk taffeta, velvet
44 cm (waist), 18 cm (inner leg), 48 cm (outer leg)
inscribed: 'Giselle', 'Mr Nijinsky', and '2nd Costume'
purchased 1973
1973.270.54

Costume for The hunt (La chasse) (in Act 1)
c 1910
doublet: cotton velveteen, wool, silk ribbons, cotton lining; trunks: wool, cotton lining
trunks: 42 cm (waist), 45 cm (outer leg), 15 cm (inner leg); doublet: 36 cm (underarm chest), 65 cm (outer sleeve), 44 cm (inner sleeve)
inscribed on trunks: 'Giselle', 'La Chasse', 'Ier Acte', 'Ssep', and 'Gerdssimov'; doublet: 'Giselle', 'La Chasse', 'Ier Acte', 'Gerdssimov', and 'Sep'
purchased 1973
1973.270.57.A-B

Mourning costume for Albrecht
c 1910
tights: silk; trunks: silk pile velvet, plastic buttons; doublet: silk pile velvet, cotton lace and lining, metal fasteners; cape: silk satin, wool lining, cotton ground, silk pile ribbon
tights: 30 cm (waist d), 115 cm (outer leg), 85 cm (inner leg); trunks: 36.5 cm (waist to crotch); doublet: 45 cm (underarm chest); 33 cm (waist), 54 cm (inner sleeve), 68 cm (outer sleeve); cape: 85 x 165 cm
inscribed on doublet: 'Giselle', and 'Bolm'; on tights: 'L.T.C.'
purchased 1973
1973.270.66.A-D

L'Oiseau de feu
The firebird
25 June 1910
Revived: 25 November 1926 with designs by Natalia Goncharova

Léon BAKST, designer
Aleksandr GOLOVIN, designer

Costume for an attendant of the Immortal Köstchei
1910
robe: stencilled cotton, metallic brocade ribbon and fringe, lamé, rayon, paint, metal fasteners, skirt hoop; belt: stencilled cotton, rayon, paint, metal fasteners
robe: 130 cm; belt: 89 cm (waist)
inscribed on dress: 'Young'; on belt: 'Balotine'
purchased 1973
1973.270.74.A-B

Costume for one of Köstchei's women (femmes de Köstchei)
c 1910
silk, paint, cotton, imitation jewels, lamé, metallic braid, gelatin sequins
105 cm, 45 cm (inner sleeve), 55 cm (outer sleeve), 34 cm (underarm chest)
inscribed: 'Moravieva', and 'Joulitska'
purchased 1973
1973.270.77

Costume for a female dancer
c 1910
cotton, silk, wool, metallic and other paint
136 cm
inscribed: 'Chand', and German customs stamp
purchased 1973
1973.270.82

Léon BAKST, designer
Aleksandr GOLOVIN, designer

Dress for a member of Köstchei's entourage
bodice: c 1910, skirt: c 1926
rayon, synthetic fabric, metallic lace, cotton, gelatin sequins, glass beads, plastic jewels, paint
99 cm, 34 cm (underarm chest), 47 cm (inner sleeve), 58 cm (outer sleeve)
inscribed: 'Razoumovitch', 'Bondir', and 'Kamarova'
purchased 1973
1973.270.80

Costume for a female dancer
c 1910, modified c 1934
stencilled cotton, cotton corduroy appliqué, metallic and cotton braid, lamé, metallic and other paint, wool, silk
129 cm
inscribed: German customs stamp
purchased 1973
1973.270.83

Costume for a princess
c 1910, modified c 1934
wool twill, silk, rayon, metallic braid, metallic and other paint, cotton and wool linings
104 cm, 51 cm (underarm chest), 53 cm (inner sleeve), 71 cm (outer sleeve)
purchased 1973
1973.270.87

Natalia GONCHAROVA, designer
Vera SUDEIKINA, costumier

Costume for one of Köstchei's warriors
c 1926
lamé, metallic braid and cord, cotton, silk, plastic
130 cm, 46 cm (underarm chest), 60 cm (inner sleeve), 86 cm (outer sleeve)
inscribed: 'Milt', 'Run', and 'Farrell'
purchased 1973
1973.270.71

Costume for the finale
c 1926
tunic: wool twill, cotton appliqué and lining, metallic braid and paint, painted wood beads; trousers: cotton, elastic, metal fasteners
tunic: 120 cm, 122 cm (front l), 58 cm (inner sleeve), 72 cm (outer sleeve); trousers: 28 cm (waist), 68 cm (inner leg), 96 cm (outer leg)
inscribed on tunic: '88', and '5'
purchased 1973
1973.270.72.A-B

Robe for costume for a guard
c 1926
wool, cotton, metallic paint and braid, cotton and silk muslin, metal fasteners, plastic, glass beads, rayon, cotton twill, brushed cotton
123 cm, 60 cm (underarm chest), 62 cm (inner sleeve), 75 cm (outer sleeve)
inscribed: '5'
purchased 1973
1973.270.70

Narcisse
Narcissus
26 April 1911

Costume for a Boeotian youth
c 1911
wool, wood, metallic braid
74 cm
inscribed: 'Yazvinskna', 'Narcisse Echo', 'G. Varzhinski', 'Mr Varzinsky', and German customs stamp
purchased 1973
1973.270.15

Costume for a Boeotian girl
c 1911
dress: wool, cotton, metal buttons, elastic; headdress: silk, metallic braid, cotton, metal wire
dress: 140 cm, 90 cm (w); headdress: 65 cm (circ)
inscribed on dress: 'Doreen', and 'Kamerova'; on headdress: 'Tarueberais', 'Jackevska', 'Narcisse', and 'Beothiennes'
purchased 1973
1973.270.16.A-B

Cloak for costume for Echo
c 1911
wool, bronze powder paint
213 x 317 cm
purchased 1973
1973.270.18

Petrouchka
Petrushka
13 June 1911

Alexandre BENOIS, designer
Ivan CAFFI and VOROBIER, costumiers

Costume for Petrouchka
c 1911
tunic: silk satin, cotton and cotton lace, metal fasteners; trousers: silk satin, rayon patches, plastic buttons; boots: silk, metal eyelets, cotton, leather
tunic: 77 cm; trousers: 37.6 cm, 59.4 cm (inner leg); boots: 19 (h) x 26 cm (l), 0.4 cm (heel height)
inscribed on trousers: 'Per', and 'Nijinski'; on boots: 'Petrouchka', 'Y-Y-Petrouch (1) (7)', and 'C. Bottinos'
80.3592.1-3.A-B

Costume design for a merchant
c 1920
watercolour, pen and ink, pencil on paper
32 x 21.2 cm
purchased 1987
1987.517

Costume design for a peasant woman
c 1920
watercolour, pen and ink, pencil on paper
31.6 x 23 cm
purchased 1987
1987.518

Costume design for a reveller in a pig mask
c 1920
watercolour, pen and ink, pencil on paper
31 x 23.6 cm
purchased 1987
1987.519

Set design for the Moor's room (*in Scene 3*)
c 1920s
pen and ink, gouache, watercolour on paper
14.2 x 21.8 cm
purchased 1981
1981.1045

Set design for proscenium arch (*in Scene 1*)
after 1911
watercolour, pencil, pen and ink, gouache on paper
30.8 x 47.6 cm
purchased 1981
1981.2853

Costume design for a devil
c 1920
brush and ink, pen and ink, watercolour, pencil on paper
31.8 x 21.4 cm
purchased 1987
1987.520

Backdrop and wings scenery
1911
cotton, distemper, dyes, charcoal, metal
940 x 1175 cm
purchased 1973
1973.270.287.A-E

Le Dieu bleu
The blue god
13 May 1912

Léon BAKST, designer
M LANDOFF and Marie MUELLE, costumiers

Costume for The Blue God
c 1912
tunic: silk, silk moiré faille, satin, velvet ribbon, braid and embroidery thread, rayon, metallic embroidery thread and ribbon, metal studs and fasteners, gelatin imitation mother-of-pearl discs; crown: metallic gauze, braid and paillettes, silk embroidery thread, gelatin sequins, metal studs, metallic and other paint
tunic: 76.6 cm; crown: 50 cm (h)
inscribed: 'Nijinsky' and German customs stamp
purchased 1987
1987.2239.A-B

Costume design for the Sacrificial Bearer
1911
gouache, pencil, paint on paper
28.4 x 23 cm
purchased 1988
1988.1956

Thamar
20 May 1912

Léon BAKST, designer
Marie MUELLE, costumier

Costume for Queen Thamar
c 1912
dress: acetate, silk, rayon, cotton, metallic braid, lamé, metal medallions, elastic; overskirt: silk, rayon, cotton, lamé, metallic braid, metal buckle, imitation turquoise; cropped vest: silk, lamé, metallic braid, metal medallions; crown: acetate, cotton, lamé, metallic braid, metal medallions, imitation jewels, wire; veil: silk, paint; scarf: silk
dress: 102 cm; overskirt: 60 cm; cropped vest: 15.4 cm; crown: 23 cm (c front); veil: 216 x 98 cm; scarf: 210 x 106 cm
purchased 1973
1973.270.114.A-F

Costume for a friend of Queen Thamar
c 1912
dress: silk, silk and cotton lining, cellulose diacetate, paint, viscose, silk ribbon, metallic braid, metal pressed shapes; hat: cotton, silk/cotton satin, metallic braid
dress: 105 cm; hat: 9 cm
purchased 1976
1976.1054.755.A-B

Costume for a Lezghin
c 1912
coat: silk, acetate, rayon, metallic braid, cotton; trousers: silk, metallic braid, cotton, paint; belt: silk, metallic braid, cotton, leather, glass, metal; hat: silk, wool, metallic braid, cotton, elastic
coat: 97 cm; trousers: 55 cm; belt: 97 cm (l); hat: 57 cm (circ)
inscribed on trousers: 'Fisher', 'Thamar', 'X1a', 'musikant', 'shtany', and German customs stamp
purchased 1973
1973.270.103.A, .104.B, .102, .107

L'Après midi d'un faune
The afternoon of a faun
29 May 1912

Léon BAKST, designer

Costume for a nymph
c 1912
silk chiffon, paint, lamé, metallic ribbon, cotton
94 cm
inscribed: 'Goloven', and 'Deni'
purchased 1973
1973.270.116

Costume for a nymph
c 1912
silk chiffon, lamé, metallic ribbon, cotton
94 cm
inscribed: 'Osato', 'Olrich', and 'Couprina'
purchased 1973
1973.270.117

Costume for a nymph
c 1912
silk chiffon, lamé, metallic ribbon, cotton
90 cm
inscribed: 'Milton', 'Stepanova', and 'Lvova'
purchased 1973
1973.270.118

Daphnis et Chloé
Daphnis and Chloë
8 June 1912

Léon BAKST, designer
Marie MUELLE, costumier

Costume for a brigand
c 1912
tunic: wool, paint; belt: cotton, paint, metal buckle
tunic: 91 cm; belt: 65 cm (l)
inscribed on tunic: 'Zvirev'; on belt: 'Kevgler', and German customs stamp
purchased 1973
1973.270.119.A-B

Costume for a brigand
c 1912
tunic and belt: wool, cotton, paint, metal buckle
tunic: 92.8 cm; belt: 102.4 cm (l)
inscribed on tunic: 'Loboika'; on belt: 'Kovalski';
German customs stamp (on both pieces)
purchased 1973
1973.270.120.A-B

Costume for a brigand
c 1912
tunic, breeches and belt: wool, cotton, metal fasteners
tunic: 96.5 cm; breeches: 42.2 cm (waist to crotch), 33.4 cm (inner leg); belt: 93 cm (l)
inscribed on breeches: 'Zyrev'; on breeches and belt: 'Kremnev', and German customs stamp
purchased 1973
1973.270.121.A-C

Costume for a brigand
c 1912
tunic: wool, cotton, metal and plastic fastener, paint; breeches: wool, cotton, plastic and metal fasteners; belt: wool, cotton, metal fasteners; cloak: wool, paint
tunic: 93 cm; breeches: 38 cm (waist to crotch), 32.6 cm (inner leg); belt: 91 (l); cloak: 269 cm (l)
inscribed on breeches: 'Kostetski'; on breeches and belt: German customs stamp
purchased 1973
1973.270.122.A-D

Cloak from costume for a brigand
c 1912
cotton, wool, paint
294 x 100 cm
inscribed: German customs stamp
purchased 1973
1973.270.125

Cloak from costume for a brigand
c 1912
cotton, wool, paint
88.4 cm (max l)
inscribed: German customs stamp
purchased 1973
1973.270.126

Cloak from costume for a brigand
c 1912
cotton, wool, paint
88.4 cm (max l)
inscribed: German customs stamp
purchased 1973
1973.270.127

Papillons
Butterflies
16 April 1914

Léon BAKST, designer

Cape from costume for a lady
c 1914
silk, metal fasteners, cotton trim
97 cm
purchased 1973
1973.270.128

Le Coq d'or
The golden cockerel
23 September 1937

Natalia GONCHAROVA, designer
Barbara KARINSKA, costumier

Costume for King Dodon
c 1937
robe: cotton velveteen, silk grosgrain, wool, lamé, metallic braid; mantle: cotton velveteen, silk, lamé, rayon, acetate, metallic braid, brushed cotton lining, ermine tails
robe: 143 cm; mantle: 145 cm
purchased 1973
1973.1279.1.A-B

Costume for a female subject of King Dodon
c 1937
blouse: linen; pinafore and overbodice: cotton, wool, cotton lace, wool braid
blouse: 48 cm; pinafore: 114 cm; overbodice: 37 x 48 cm
inscribed on blouse and pinafore: 'Reynold's House, Karinska, 5 Great Newport St, WC'; on blouse: '18-RO'; on pinafore: 'Evans', 'Roy', 'Larkina', and 'Nelidov'; on overbodice: 'Ex'
purchased 1973
1973.1279.3.A-C

Costume for a nursemaid to King Dodon
c 1937
blouse: cotton; skirt: cotton, wool, metal, linen
blouse: 53 cm; skirt: 80 cm
inscribed on blouse: 'Reynolds House', 'Karinska', and 'S. Great Newport St WC'; on skirt: 'Barlow'
purchased 1973
1973.1279.4.A-B

Costume for a peasant woman
c 1937
dress and blouse: cotton, wool, metal fasteners, linen, paint
dress: 124 cm; blouse: 48 cm
inscribed on dress and blouse: 'Reynolds House', 'Karinska', and 'S. Great Newport St WC'; on dress: 'Gal-wan', and 'Francis'
purchased 1973
1973.1279.5.A-B

Costume for an Oriental dancer to the Queen of Shemakhan
c 1937
acetate taffeta, cotton, felt, paint, braid, metal fasteners
160 cm
inscribed: 'V.L.'
Julian Robinson Collection, purchased 1976
1976.1054.802

Costume design for a peasant woman
1914
gouache and pencil on cardboard
37.8 x 26.8 cm
purchased 1986
1986.1819

Costume design for a peasant woman, back view
c 1914
gouache and pencil on paper
25.2 x 8.2 cm
purchased 1980
1981.1331

Costume design for a peasant woman, front view
c 1914
gouache and pencil on paper
25.4 x 8.2 cm
purchased 1980
1981.1330

Sadko
9 October 1916

Natalia GONCHAROVA, designer

Costume for a seahorse
c 1916
headdress, blouse and cape: silk-cotton satin, lamé, paint, wire, wadding; trousers: silk-cotton satin, paint
headdress: 83 x 60 x 25 cm; blouse: 59.8 cm; cape: 166 cm (l); trousers: 78 cm (inner leg)
inscribed on headdress: 'Mr Novak', and 'D8-1230-3', on blouse: 'Kavezk', and 'D8-1230'; on trousers: 'Kawecki', and 'D8-1230-1'
purchased 1995
1995.914.1-4

Headdress from a costume for a fish
c 1916
silk, cotton, lamé, wire, paint, gelatin sequins
60 cm (h)
purchased 1996
1996.1254

Costume for a squid
c 1916
silk, lamé, wire, paint
117 cm (h)
purchased 1996
1996.215

La Boutique fantasque
The magical toyshop
5 June 1919

André DERAIN, designer

Costume for the White Poodle
c 1919
bodysuit, snout and gloves: woollen fur, wire supports, cotton jersey, elastic, paint, flax, mohair, linoleum (snout)
bodysuit: cm; snout: 17 cm (l); gloves: 21 cm (l)
inscribed on snout: 'A. & L. Corne, Hat makers, 68 Belvedere Rd., Lambeth, London, SE1'; on gloves: '2RRoRo'
purchased 1973
1973.270.133.A-C

Costume for the Brown Poodle
c 1919
bodysuit and gloves: cotton jersey, wool, wire supports, brass zipper, elastic, paint, rabbit hair
bodysuit: 54 cm (outer sleeve), 43 cm (inner sleeve), 98 cm (outer leg), 70 cm (inner leg), 65 cm (neck to crutch), 21 cm (c front); gloves: 23 cm
purchased 1973
1973.270.134.A-B (IRN 107557)

Costume design for the Can-Can Dancer
c 1919
watercolour, pen and ink, pencil on paper
31.6 x 24.8 cm
purchased 1980
1980.4319

Le Chant du rossignol
The song of the nightingale
2 February 1920

Henri MATISSE, designer
Marie MUELLE, costumier

Costume for a Mandarin
c 1920
silk, cotton, lamé, ink, Bakelite
114 cm
purchased 1973
1973.270.143

Costume for a court lady
c 1920
silk satin and velvet, cotton wadding and lining, lamé, metal fasteners
88 cm
inscribed: 'Clenentovich Msikechka Idvyiska'
purchased 1973
1973.270.146

Costume for a court lady
c 1920
silk, cotton, lamé, graphite
150 x 90 cm
inscribed: 'Isomane Estomania Lubov 96'
purchased 1973
1973.270.145

Costume for a mourner
c 1920
robe and headdress: cotton-wool felt, cotton-silk velvet, sized cotton, steel wire, cotton lining
robe: 166.5 cm
inscribed: 'I. Ya'
purchased 1973
1973.270.147.A-B

Costume for a chamberlain
c 1920
robe: silk satin and ribbon, lamé appliqué, cotton, paint; hat: silk, wool, metallic braid, paint, wire
robe: 138 cm; hat: 65 cm
inscribed on robe: 'Slia', 'Dodr', and 'Dodf'
purchased 1973
1973.270.144.A-B

Hat from costume for a courtier
c 1920
wool felt, paint, wire
28 cm
purchased 2008
2008.233

Ballet de l'Astuce féminine / Cimarosiana
Women's wiles / Cimarosiana
8 January 1924 / 24 April 1924, expanded ballet productions

José-María SERT, designer
Marie MUELLE, costumier

Costume for Dr Romualdo
1920–24
jacket: silk, cotton, metallic braid, metal fasteners, paint; breeches: cotton, paint
jacket: 112 cm; breeches: 49 cm, 50 cm (inner leg)
purchased 1973
1973.270.136.A-B

Lorgnette
1920–24
wood, paint, metal, silk, shellac
22 x 17 cm
purchased 1973
1973.270.142

Hat
1920–24
silk and cotton velvet, rayon, metallic thread, cotton, animal hair felt, paper, baste fibre
65 cm (circ)
purchased 1973
1973.270.139

Hat
1920–24
silk, cotton, metal, wood, wax (?), paint, feathers, starch
52 cm (circ)
purchased 1973
1973.270.141

Top hat from a costume for Giampaolo
1920–24
silk, cotton, wire
28 cm (h), 60 cm (circ)
purchased 1973
1973.270.140

Hat for costume for the military corps
1920–24
wool, cotton, elastic, card, feather, wire
59 cm (circ)
purchased 1973
1973.270.177.B

Dress
1920–24
cotton, wool, silk, acetate
120 cm, 84 cm (underarm chest)
purchased 1973
1973.270.172

Costume for Pierrot
1920–24
jacket and trousers: cotton, silk, wool, metal fasteners
jacket: 53 cm; trousers: 55 cm (inner leg)
inscribed: 'Property of Educational Ballets Ltd'
purchased 1973
1973.270.175.A-B

Chout
The buffoon
17 May 1921

Mikhail LARIONOV, designer
Germaine BONGARD (MAISON JOVE), costumier

Pannier and collar from costume for a buffoon's daughter
c 1921
pannier: cotton, buckram, cane, paint; collar: buckram, cane, paint
pannier: 80 cm; collar: 73 x 84 cm (approx)
purchased 1973
1973.270.164.A-B

Costume for a buffoon's wife
c 1921
bodice: cotton, metal fasteners; trousers: silk, buckram, cotton, cane, paint; wings: cotton, cane, paint; collar: silk, cotton, resin coated fabric, elastic, buckram
bodice: 37.6 cm; trousers: 39 cm, 47.4 cm (inner leg); wings: 130 x 120 cm; collar: 55 (w)
purchased 1973
1973.270.156.A, 156.C, .157.C, 156.D

Costume for a soldier
c 1921
jacket: cotton buckram, brushed cotton, paint, leatherette; breeches: brushed cotton, leatherette, cotton; headpiece: buckram, cotton sateen, paint
jacket: 60 cm; breeches: 36 cm, 65 cm (inner leg); headpiece: 38 cm (h)
inscribed on jacket and headpiece: 'Pavlov'; on breeches: '80', and 'Banter'
purchased 1973
1973.270.159.A-C

Blouse and cape from a costume for a bridesmaid
c 1921
blouse: cotton sateen, paint, cotton sateen buttons; cape: cotton, cane, paint
blouse: 48 cm; cape: 120 cm
inscribed on blouse: 'Lyda'
purchased 1973
1973.270.161.A-B

List of works **245**

The sleeping princess
2 November 1921

Léon BAKST, designer
MUELLE ROSSIGNOL, Pierre PITOEFF, Lovat FRASER, Miss NORMAN, costumiers

Costume for a lady-in-waiting
c 1921
bodice and skirt: silk satin, chiffon and velvet, metallic braid and fringe, swansdown feathers, fur, wood, paint, metal, glass, gelatin discs and lacquer imitation jewels
bodice: 14 cm; skirt: 125 x 100 cm
inscribed on bodice: 'Rosenski', and 'Ros'
purchased 1973
1973.270.150.A-B

Costume for a court lady
c 1921
dress: cotton velveteen, cotton-silk satin, cotton lining, metallic braid and discs, paint, metal fasteners, wood, lacquer; underskirt: silk, cotton, metal, paint
dress: 234 cm; underskirt: 107 cm
inscribed on dress: 'Mon. Muelle Rossignol Sr, Costumier de l'Opera, 12 Rue de la Victoire, Paris', 'Nemtchinova', 'Lyda [?] 5 Act', and 'L. Piat'; on underskirt: 'Savitika'
purchased 1973
1973.270.151.A-B

Costume for the page to the Hummingbird Fairy
c 1921
silk, cotton, metal fasteners
72 cm
purchased 1973
1973.270.152

Dress for a court lady
c 1921
silk, cotton, metal fasteners
96 cm
inscribed: 'Mon. Muelle Rossignol Sr', 'Costumier de l'Opéra, 12 Rue de la Victoire, Paris', and 'Anoni'
purchased 1973
1973.270.153

Costume for the Bluebird
c 1921
doublet: silk, cotton, metallic braid, imitation jewels, gelatin pearls, elastic; cap: silk, metallic braid, gelatin pearls, imitation jewels, cotton, wire
doublet: 74 cm; cap: 60 (circ)
purchased 1980
1980.2167.1-2

Costume design for the Queen and her page (in Act I)
1921
watercolour, pencil, metallic paint on paper adhered to card
29.2 x 44.6 cm
purchased 1984
1984.839

Le Mariage d'Aurore
Aurora's wedding
18 May 1922

Alexandre BENOIS, designer
Léon BAKST, designer
Ivan CAFFI, costumier

Costume for the Bluebird
c 1922
doublet: silk, acetate, wool, metallic thread, cotton, imitation jewels, gelatin pearls; cap: cotton velvet, gelatin pearls, glass rubies, metallic thread
doublet: 60 cm; cap: 46 cm (circ)
purchased 1973
1973.270.166.A-B

Overdress from costume for Aurora
c 1922
silk, rayon, cotton, lamé
69 cm
purchased 1973
1973.270.167

Costume for a prince
c 1922
tunic: acetate, rayon, cotton, cotton lace, silk, metallic thread, plastic buttons and decorations, gelatin sequins; trunks: acetate, metallic braid, cotton lining, metal fasteners
tunic: 74 cm; trunks: 40.5 cm (l), 63 cm (waist circ)
inscribed on : 'Oleg'
purchased 1973
1973.270.169, .168

Natalia GONCHAROVA, designer

Costume for the Wolf
c 1922
jacket: rayon, acetate, silk, cotton, elastic, metallic thread, metal fasteners; trousers: acetate, cotton; hood: acetate, rayon, cotton, metal fasteners, elastic
jacket: 78 cm; breeches: 55 cm (inner leg); hood: 95 cm
inscribed on jacket: 'Balin', and 'Hoyer'
purchased 1976
1976.1054.760.A-C

Costume for a cavalier
c 1920s
doublet: rayon, acetate, metal fasteners, elastic, metallic paint; trunks: silk, cotton; tights: wool, elastic
doublet: 41 cm; trunks: 42 cm; tights: 83 cm (inner leg)
inscribed on doublet: 'Wass', and 'Celada'; on trunks: 'Balin', 'Lorain', and 'Arap'; on tights: '18Ro'
purchased 1976
1976.1054.763.A-C

Costume for an Ivan
c 1920s
tunic: silk, cotton, metallic thread; trousers: acetate, cotton, elastic, boots: leather
tunic: 79 cm; trousers: 37 cm, 58 cm (inner leg); boots: 42 x 28 cm
inscribed on tunic: 'Rose Schogeli, Paris, 31 West 56th St, New York', 'Harvey', 'Klimof, Rueda, TL', and '64.2, Joukovsky'; on trousers: 'Klimof', 'Orskov', 'Rueda', 'T/L 64/2'; on boots: 'Anello & Davide, London', W C Crompton', 'Jouko', and 'Castano'
purchased 1976
1976.1054.761.A, 762.B, 761.C

Les Tentations de la bergère, ou l'Amour vainqueur
The temptations of the shepherdess, or Victorious love
3 January 1924

Juan GRIS, designer
Marie MUELLE, attrib. costumier

Costume for the Countess
c 1924
bodice, skirt and cape: silk, cotton, metallic braid, lamé
bodice: 60.4 cm; skirt: 162 cm; cape: 75 cm
purchased 1973
1973.270.171.A-C

Costume design for a maiden
c 1923
coloured chalk, gouache, pencil on paper
24 x 16 cm
purchased 1973
1973.581

Costume design for Barons
1923
watercolour over pencil on paper
31.2 x 25.4 cm
purchased 1983
1983.286

Costume design for the Marquis
1923
watercolour over pencil on paper
31.2 x 25.6 cm
purchased 1983
1983.285

Zéphire et Flore
Zephyr and Flora
28 April 1925

Georges BRAQUE, designer

Costume for Boreas
c 1925
trunks: lamé, cotton, elastic, metal; helmet: papier-mâché, cane, feathers, cotton, paint
trunks: 38 cm; helmet: 69 (circ)
inscribed on trunks: 'Zephyr et Flores', and 'S. Lifar'
purchased 1973
1973.270.178.A-B

Cap from a costume for Zéphire
c 1925
lamé, cotton, wire
59 cm (circ)
purchased 1973
1973.270.179

Overskirt from a costume for Zéphire
c 1925
lamé, cotton, paper, paint, metal
27.6 cm; 54cm (waist)
purchased 1973
1973.270.180

Headdress from costume for a muse
c 1925
lamé, metallic braid and paint, silk, cotton, glass, elastic
28 x 18 cm
purchased 1973
1973.270.182

Oliver MESSEL, designer

Mask from costume for a muse
c 1925
cardboard, paper, plaster, paint, elastic
26 x 23 cm
inscribed: 'Zepher et Flores'
purchased 1973
1973.270.183

Le Pas d'acier
The Steel step
7 June 1927

Georgy YAKULOV, designer
A YOUKINE, costumier

Costume for a female worker
c 1927
dress: silk, cotton, metal fasteners; apron: vinyl (?), cotton, elastic, metal fasteners
dress: 114 cm (l), 38 cm (chest) cm; apron: 85 cm (l), 43.5 cm (w) cm
purchased 1973
1973.270.185, .186

Costume for a female worker
c 1927
dress: silk, cotton, metal fasteners; cap: vinyl (?), cotton, elastic, buckram
dress: 98 cm (l), 37 cm (chest); cap: 52 cm (circ)
inscribed on dress: 'Klemetska', and 'Choulgina'
purchased 1973
1973.270.224, .201

Costume for a male worker
c 1927
trousers: wool, cotton, plastic buttons; bib and apron: vinyl (?), cotton, elastic, metal fasteners
trousers: 105 cm (l); bib: 84.5 cm (circ); apron: 105 cm (circ)
purchased 1973
73.270.196, .206, .207

Hat from costume for the Sailor
c 1925
wool, cotton ribbon
14.5 cm (h.), 52 cm (circ)
purchased 1973
1973.270.200.3.B

Cap from costume for a male worker
c 1927
faux fur (cotton with animal fibre), unknown stiffening, cotton lining and padding
52 cm (circ)
purchased 1973
1973.270.184

Cap from costume for a male worker
c 1927
wool, cotton
46 cm (circ), 7 cm (h)
purchased 1973
1973.270.218

Cap from costume for a female worker
c 1927
cotton
54 cm (circ)
purchased 1973
1973.270.215

Ode
6 June 1928

Pavel TCHELITCHEW, designer
A YOUKINE, costumier

Costume for a constellation
c 1928
leotard and tights: cotton, zinc and barium paint, metal fasteners; mask: wire mesh, elastic
leotard: 70 cm; tights: 40 cm; mask: 25 cm
inscribed on leotard: 'Hor. Ya'; on tights: 'Petr'
purchased 1973
1973.270.228.A-B, .239

Costume for a star
c 1928
dress: cotton, mirrored Bakelite, metal fasteners, flax; mask: wire mesh, elastic
dress: 190 x 31 x 41 cm; mask: 25 cm (h)
inscribed on dress: 'Pab'
purchased 1973
1973.270.234, .240

Costume for a star
c 1928
dress: cotton, mirrored Bakelite, metal fasteners, flax; mask: wire mesh, elastic
dress: 190 x 31 x 41 cm; mask: 25 cm (h)
purchased 1973
1973.270.236, .238

Le Bal
The ball
7 May 1929

Giorgio de CHIRICO, designer
A YOUKINE, costumier

Costume for a male guest
1929
dickey, jacket and trousers: wool, cotton grosgrain, rayon ribbon, linen, Bakelite, paint
dickey: 45.5 cm; jacket: 80.2 cm; trousers: 110 cm
inscribed on jacket: 'Lad', and 'Borov'; on trousers: 'S. Ingrao, Monte Carlo', 'Borovski', and 'Ladre'
purchased 1984
1984.3029.A-C

Jacket from costume for the Young Man
c 1929
wool, cotton, metallic trim, hessian (stiffening), metal fasteners
63 cm
inscribed: 'Anton Dolin'
purchased 1985
1985.258

Pulcinella
30 April 1932

Giorgio de CHIRICO, designer

Tunic
1932
wool, cotton, paint
51 x 47 cm
purchased 2007
2007.40

Costume
1932
cotton, paint, raffia
141 cm
inscribed: 'Milenko', and 'G. Diaz'
purchased 1973
1973.270.247

Dress
1932
wool, cotton, paint
71 cm (l)
purchased 2007
2007.38

Coat
1932
wool, cotton, paint
116 cm
purchased 2007
2007.45

Les Présages
Destiny
13 April 1933

André MASSON, designer
Barbara KARINSKA, costumier

Costume for a male (in Scene 1)
1933
jacket: wool, cotton, metal fasteners; tights: cotton, elastic; helmet: wool, metal supports, wire
jacket: 53 cm; tights: 128 cm; helmet: 61 cm (circ)
inscribed on jacket: 'P Sota', and '92-73'; on tights: 'Was'
purchased 1973
1973.270.258.A-C

Costume for a male (in Scene 1)
1933
jacket: wool, cotton, metal fasteners; tights: cotton, elastic; helmet: wool, metal supports, wire
jacket: 57 cm; tights: 133 cm; helmet: 61 cm
inscribed on jacket: 'Eglev', and '92-71'; on tights: 'Jasin', and 'Ele'
purchased 1973
1973.270.257.A-C

Costume for a male (in Scene 1)
1933
jacket: wool, cotton, metal fasteners; tights: cotton, elastic; helmet: wool, metal supports, wire
jacket: 55.4 cm; tights: 124 cm; helmet: 61.4 cm (circ)
inscribed on jacket: 'Chabelevsky', and '92-67'; on tights: 'Nik', and 'McK'; on helmet: 'Selada', 'Gordon', 'And', and 'Nik'
purchased 1973
1973.270.259.A-C

Costume for a female (in Scene 1)
1933; headband 1940s remake
dress: rayon, cotton, metal fasteners; headband: rayon, elastic, unknown stiffening
dress: 102 cm; headband: 54 cm (circ)
inscribed on dress: 'Voronova', 'Charaska', and 'Bentley'
purchased 1973
1973.270.261.A-B

Costume for a female (in Scene 2)
1933; headband 1940s remake
dress: silk, rayon, metal fasteners, elastic; headband: silk, elastic
dress: 97 cm; headband: 48.8 cm (circ)
inscribed on dress: 'June King', 'Wassipeva', and 'Oukow'
purchased 1973
1973.270.268.A-B

Costume for a female (in Scene 2)
1933
dress: silk, rayon, metal fasteners, elastic; headband: silk, elastic, unknown stiffening
dress: 94 cm; headband: 54 cm (circ)
inscribed on dress: 'Evans', and 'Constantine'
purchased 1973
1973.270.267.A-B

Dress from costume for Action
c 1933
rayon, cotton lining
116 cm (l)
inscribed: 'Herida', and 'May'
purchased 1973
1973.270.264

Le Beau Danube
The beautiful Danube
7 March 1933 [15 April 1933]

Etienne de BEAUMONT, designer

Costume for the Huzzar
c 1935
jacket and trousers: wool, brass fasteners, cotton, elastic, wood, paint, plastic buttons
jacket: 41 cm; trousers: 71 cm (inner leg)
inscribed on jacket and trousers: 'Morris Angel & Son Ltd, 119 Shaftesbury Avenue, London WC, Date – 16/7/35, Massine'
purchased 1973
1973.270.252.A-B

Le Tricorne
The three-cornered hat
22 July 1919
Revived 20 February 1934

Pablo PICASSO, designer for 1919 production

Jacket
1919–c 33
wool, cotton
55 cm (l), 49.5 cm (width of chest)
inscribed: '1618'
purchased 2007
2007.37.1

Waistcoat
1919–c 33
wool, cotton
53 cm (l), 49 cm (width of chest)
inscribed: '1595'
purchased 2007
2007.37.4

Waistcoat
1919–c 33
wool, cotton
51.5 cm (l), 86 cm (chest)
inscribed: '1583'
purchased 2007
2007.37.2

Cropped vest
1919–c 33
wool, cotton
53 cm (l), 49 cm (width of chest)
inscribed: '947'
purchased 2007
2007.37.5

Breeches
1919–c 33
cotton velveteen
84.5 cm (l); 38.5 cm (waist)
inscribed: '1586'
purchased 2007
2007.37.6

Shorts
1919–c 33
wool
60 cm (l); 42 cm (waist)
inscribed: '1585'
purchased 2007
2007.37.8

Shorts
1919–c 33
wool, cotton
52.5 cm (l); 33 cm (waist)
inscribed: '1588'
purchased 2007
2007.37.11

Shorts
1919–c 33
wool, cotton
55 cm (l); 37 cm (waist)
inscribed: '1592'
purchased 2007
2007.37.12

Pair of spats
1919–c 33
wool, cotton
36 cm (l)
inscribed: '1582'
purchased 2007
2007.37.14.A-B

Pair of spats
1919–c33
cotton
38.5 cm (l)
inscribed: '1594'
purchased 2007
2007.37.15.A-B

Pair of spats
1919–c33
wool, cotton
41.7 cm (l)
inscribed: '1591'
purchased 2007
2007.37.16.A-B

Jardin public
The public garden
8 March 1935

Jean LURÇAT, designer
Helen PONS, costumier

Costume for a street cleaner
c1935
shirt and hood: cotton, cotton jersey; tights: cotton knit; overalls: cotton twill; tabard: vinyl (?), cotton
shirt and hood: 91 cm (full l); tights: 38 cm (waist), 122.5 cm (outer leg); overalls: 86 cm (waist), 139.5 cm (l); tabard: 52 cm (l)
inscribed on overalls: 'Helene Pons Studio. New York', 'Bousloff', and 'Street Cleaner'
purchased 1973
1973.270.271.A-D

Costume for a military musician
c1935
jacket: cotton rayon, cotton flannelette, cotton lining, metal fasteners, paint, unknown stiffening (collar and epaulets); trousers: cotton flannelette, cotton twill, cotton lining, metal fasteners
jacket: 67.5 cm; trousers: 36 cm (waist); 101.5 cm (outer leg)
inscribed on jacket and trousers: 'Helene Pons', 'New York', and 'Katcharoff'
purchased 1973
1973.270.272.A-B

Costume for the Old Man
c1935
coat: cotton, cotton flannelette, plastic, synthetic; trousers: cotton, plastic, metal fastenings, elastic, synthetic; tie: plastic, metal fastenings, synthetic, stiffening; waistcoat: cotton, cotton flannelette, metal; shirt: cotton, plastic (?)
coat: 104 cm; trousers: 34 cm (waist), 107 cm (outer leg); tie: 50.5 cm (l); waistcoat: 60.5 cm (overall l); shirt: 75 cm (l), 56.5 cm (outer sleeve)
inscribed on trousers: 'Jasinsky'; on shirt: 'Plymouth'; on waistcoat: 'Bousloff'; on trousers, coat and waistcoat: 'Helene Pons Studio, New York'
purchased 1973
1973.270.275.A-E

Francesca da Rimini
15 July 1937

Oliver MESSEL, designer
Barbara KARINSKA, costumier

Costume for a courtier
1937
jacket: wool, silk crepe de chine, metal decoration, paint, leather, wooden beads, acetate lining; tights: mercerised cotton
jacket: 73 cm, 88 cm (chest); tights: 139 cm (outer leg)
inscribed on jacket: 'Katcharoff, and 'Adama'; on tights: 'Burk'
purchased 1973
1973.270.279.A-B

Dress from costume for a court lady
c1937
acetate moiré, metallic braid, lamé, cotton velveteen, metal buttons, paint, leather, wool felt, cotton and rayon net, stiffening, metal wrapped cord (woollen centre), acetate lining
68 cm (waist), 92.5 cm (c front)
inscribed: 'Karinska', and 'Lara'
purchased 1973
1973.270.282

La Lutte éternelle
The eternal struggle
29 July 1940

Florence MARTIN, designer
Kathleen MARTIN, designer

Costume design for Obsessions
c1939
gouache and pencil on card
37.9 x 27.8 cm
purchased 1978
1978.1169

PAINTINGS AND WORKS ON PAPER

Léon BAKST
Russia/Lithuania border (now Belarus) 1866 – France 1924

Dioné: dessin de Bakst réalisé par Paquin (Dioné: drawing by Bakst carried out by Paquin)
1913
plate 73 from *Journal des Dames et des Modes, no 34, 1913*
pochoir on paper
17 x 9 cm
Julian Robinson Collection, purchased 1976
1976.1055.48.13.2

Souvenir program for The Sleeping Princess at the Alhambra Theatre
1921
illustrated book
31 x 24.5 cm

Souvenir program for Serge de Diaghileff's Ballet Russe
1916–17
illustrated book
31.2 x 23.2 cm

Official program of the Ballets Russes at the Théâtre du Châtelet June 1911 (Programme officiel des Ballets Russes Théâtre du Châtelet Juin 1911)
1911
illustrated book
34.4 x 23.2 cm

Official program of the Ballets Russes at the Théâtre du Châtelet May–June 1912 (Programme officiel des Ballets Russes Théâtre du Châtelet Mai–Juin 1912)
1912
illustrated book
31.8 x 24.4 cm

Official program for the ninth season of the Ballets Russes May–June 1914 (Les Ballets Russes programme officiel 9 saison Mai–Juin 1914)
1914
illustrated book
31.6 x 24.6 cm

Souvenir program XXIIe Saison des Ballets Russes de Serge Diaghilev
1928
illustrated book
31.4 x 24.5 cm

Official program for the Ballets Russes at the Opéra, December 1919–January 1920 (Programme officiel pour le Ballet Russe à l'Opéra, Décembre 1919–Janvier 1920)
1919–20
illustrated book
32 x 24.6 cm

Souvenir program for the Ballets Russes at L'Opéra, May–June 1920 (*Ballets Russes à L'Opéra, Mai–Juin 1920*)
1920
illustrated book
31.2 x 24.4 cm

Official program for The Ballets Russes, Théâtre national de l'Opéra (*Programme officiel de Les Ballets Russes, Théâtre national de l'Opéra*)
1910
illustrated book
32.1 x 24.9 cm

Ballets Russes supplement from 15 June 1910 edition of Comoedia Illustré (*Les Ballets Russes supplément au Comoedia Illustré du 15 Juin 1910*)
1910
illustrated book
31.8 x 24.5 cm

Grande saison d'art Ballets Russes de Serge de Diaghilew de la VIIIe olympiade Champs Elysées Mai–Juin 1924
1924
illustrated book
27.2 x 21.4 cm
TEMP.5334

Souvenir program XXI Saison des Ballets Russes de Serge Diaghilev
1928
illustrated book, pin-pricked by hand
31.7 x 24.5 cm

Vene BECK
1896 Australia – ?

Riabouchinska as the Golden Cockerel in Le Coq d'or
1938
gelatin silver photograph
19 x 11.4 cm
gift of Mrs Haydn Beck and daughter Mrs Norman Johnstone, 1982

Riabouchinska waiting in the wings during a performance of Le Coq d'or
1938
gelatin silver photograph
19 x 11.4 cm
gift of Mrs Haydn Beck and daughter Mrs Norman Johnstone, 1982

Auguste BERT, photographer
1856 France – ?
THE FINE ARTS SOCIETY, LONDON, publisher

Scheherazade – M. Nijinsky
plate 15 from *Studies from the Russian Ballet*
1910
rotogravure
20.4 x 14 cm
purchased 1983
1983.3743.15

Auguste BERT, photographer
1856 France – ?
THE FINE ARTS SOCIETY, LONDON, publisher

Le Spectre de la rose – M. Nijinsky
plate 8 from *Studies from the Russian Ballet*
1913
rotogravure
20.4 x 13.6 cm
purchased 1983
1983.3743.8

Jean COCTEAU
France 1889–1963

Vaslav Nijinsky
1911
planograph
197.2 x 123 cm
purchased 1982
1982.2054

Adrian FEINT
Australia 1894–1971

not titled (*The Queen of Shemakhan in the ballet Le Coq d'or*)
ink, pen and wash, gouache and pencil on card
26.6 x 11.1 cm
purchased 1979
1979.1620A

not titled (*Albrecht in the ballet Giselle*)
ink, pen and wash and pencil on card
26.7 x 12.7 cm
purchased 1979
1979.1615

not titled (*Action in the ballet Les Présages*)
ink, pen and wash and pencil on card
28.6 x 13.7 cm
purchased 1979
1979.1611

not titled (*Vanessa Imperialis in the ballet Papillons*)
ink, pen and wash and pencil on card
purchased 1979
1979.1619

not titled (*Estrella in the ballet Carnaval*)
ink, pen and brush and pencil on card
26.8 x 12.9 cm
purchased 1979
1979.1610

not titled (*The Firebird in the ballet L'Oiseau de feu*)
ink, pen and wash, pencil on card
24.1 x 10 cm
purchased 1979
1979.1618

not titled (*Ballerina in large red hat and long train*)
ink, pen and wash, pencil on card
26 x 12.8 cm
purchased 1979
1979.1616

Natalia GONCHAROVA

The bull
1911
watercolour, pencil, pastel on wove paper
68.8 x 56.8 cm
gift of Orde Poynton Esq. CMG 1997
1997.1757

Valentine GROSS
France 1890–1968

Tamar Karsavina dans Le Coq d'or (*Tamar Karsavina in The golden cockerel*)
1914
from *La Gazette du Bon Ton*, issue no 7, Paris, 1914
pochoir, coloured on paper
16.5 x 13 cm
Julian Robinson Collection, purchased 1976
1976.1056.56.19.4

E O HOPPÉ, photographer
Germany 1878 – England 1972
THE FINE ARTS SOCIETY, LONDON, publisher

Cleopatra – Madame Fedorova
1913
plate 14 from *Studies from the Russian Ballet*
rotogravure
20.4 x 14.4 cm
purchased 1983
1983.3743.14

Le Carnaval – Monsieur Adolph Bolm
1913
plate 14 from *Studies from the Russian Ballet*
rotogravure
20.4 x 14.6 cm
purchased 1983
1983.3743.11

Le Pavillon d'Armide – Madame Thamar Karsavina
1909
plate 10 from *Studies from the Russian Ballet*
rotogravure
20.4 x 15.2 cm
purchased 1983
1983.3743.10

Le Pavillon d'Armide – Madame Thamar Karsavina and Adolph Bolm
1909
plate 9 from *Studies from the Russian Ballet*
rotogravure
20.4 x 15 cm
purchased 1983
1983.3743.9

Le Spectre de la rose – Madame Thamar Karsavina
1913
plate 7 from *Studies from the Russian Ballet*
rotogravure
20.4 x 14.6 cm
purchased 1983
1983.3743.7

L'Oiseau de feu – Madame Thamar Karsavina and M Adolph Bolm
1913
plate 3 from *Studies from the Russian Ballet*
rotogravure
20.4 x 15.4 cm
purchased 1983
1983.3743.3

L'Oiseau de feu – Madame Thamar Karsavina
1913
plate 2 from *Studies from the Russian Ballet*
rotogravure
20.6 x 11.4 cm
purchased 1983
1983.3743.2

L'Oiseau de feu – Madame Thamar Karsavina
1913
plate 1 from *Studies from the Russian Ballet*
rotogravure
18.4 x 15.4 cm
purchased 1983
1983.3743.1

L'Oiseau de feu – Monsieur Adolph Bolm
1913
plate 4 from *Studies from the Russian Ballet*
rotogravure
20.4 x 15.4 cm
purchased 1983
1983.3743.4

Prince Igor – Madame Fedorova
1913
plate 12 from *Studies from the Russian Ballet*
rotogravure
20.4 x 15.4 cm
purchased 1983
1983.3743.12

Prince Igor – Monsieur Adolph Bolm
1913
plate 13 from *Studies from the Russian Ballet*
rotogravure
20.4 x 15.2 cm
purchased 1983
1983.3743.13

Thamar – Madame Thamar Karsavina and M Adolph Bolm
1913
plate 6 from *Studies from the Russian Ballet*
rotogravure
20.4 x 15.4 cm
purchased 1983
1983.3743.6

Thamar – Monsieur Adolph Bolm
1913
plate 5 from *Studies from the Russian Ballet*
rotogravure
20.4 x 15.4 cm
purchased 1983
1983.3743.5

Georges LEPAPE
France 1887–1971

L'Habit persan (Persian costume)
1912
plate 11 in *Modes et Manières d'Aujourd'hui*, vol 1, 1912
pochoir over a lithographic base, gouache on paper
20.5 x 13.5 cm
Julian Robinson Collection, purchased 1976
1976.1056.38.12

Les coussins (Cushions)
1912
plate 5 in *Modes et Manières d'Aujourd'hui*, vol 1, 1912
pochoir over a lithographic base, gouache on paper
20.5 x 13.5 cm
Julian Robinson Collection, purchased 1976
1976.1056.38.6

Daryl LINDSAY
Australia 1889–1976

Baronova in rehearsal for Le Coq d'or at Covent Garden
1937
pencil on paper
28.6 x 18.2 cm
gift of Sir Daryl Lindsay 1972
1972.36

Baronova in Le Coq d'or, seven studies
1937
pencil on paper
28.6 x 18.2 cm
gift of Sir Daryl Lindsay 1972
1972.31

Prince Igor
1937
pencil on paper
51.2 x 37.9 cm
gift of Sir Daryl Lindsay 1972
1972.28

Robert MONTGOMERY
Australia 1912–1964

Algeranoff as the Astrologer
c 1938–40
watercolour on paper
19 x 28 cm
purchased 1978
1978.364

Riabouchinska as Le Coq d'or
c 1938–40
watercolour on paper
21.2 x 23.8 cm
purchased 1978
1978.361

Pablo PICASSO
Spain 1881 – France 1973
MOURLOT POSTERS

Ballets Russes de Diaghilev 1909–29
1939
lithograph on paper
59.8 x 39.9 cm
purchased 1976
1976.89.502

Sidney NOLAN
Australia 1917 – England 1992

Set design for the ballet Icare
1940
gouache, brush and ink, pencil and collage on card
37.8 x 41.2 cm
purchased 1984
1984.879

Teddy PIAZ
Poster of Serge Lifar
c 1930
lithograph
152.8 x 112.7 cm
gift of Lady Nolan 1998
1998.76

Hermann LEISER, publisher, est Berlin

Postcard of Nijinsky and Karsavina wearing Cleopatra costumes
c 1910
collotype
13.7 x 8.7 cm
gift of Andrew Paterson 1983
1983.1157.1

ELLIOTT & FRY
London 1863–1963

Nijinsky in the role of Petrouchka
c 1913
gelatin silver photograph
14.8 x 11.2 cm
gift of Mrs Diana Woollard 1980
1981.968

Portrait of Vaslav Nijinsky
c 1913
gelatin silver photograph
14.4 x 10.7 cm
purchased 1981
1981.1553

List of works 251

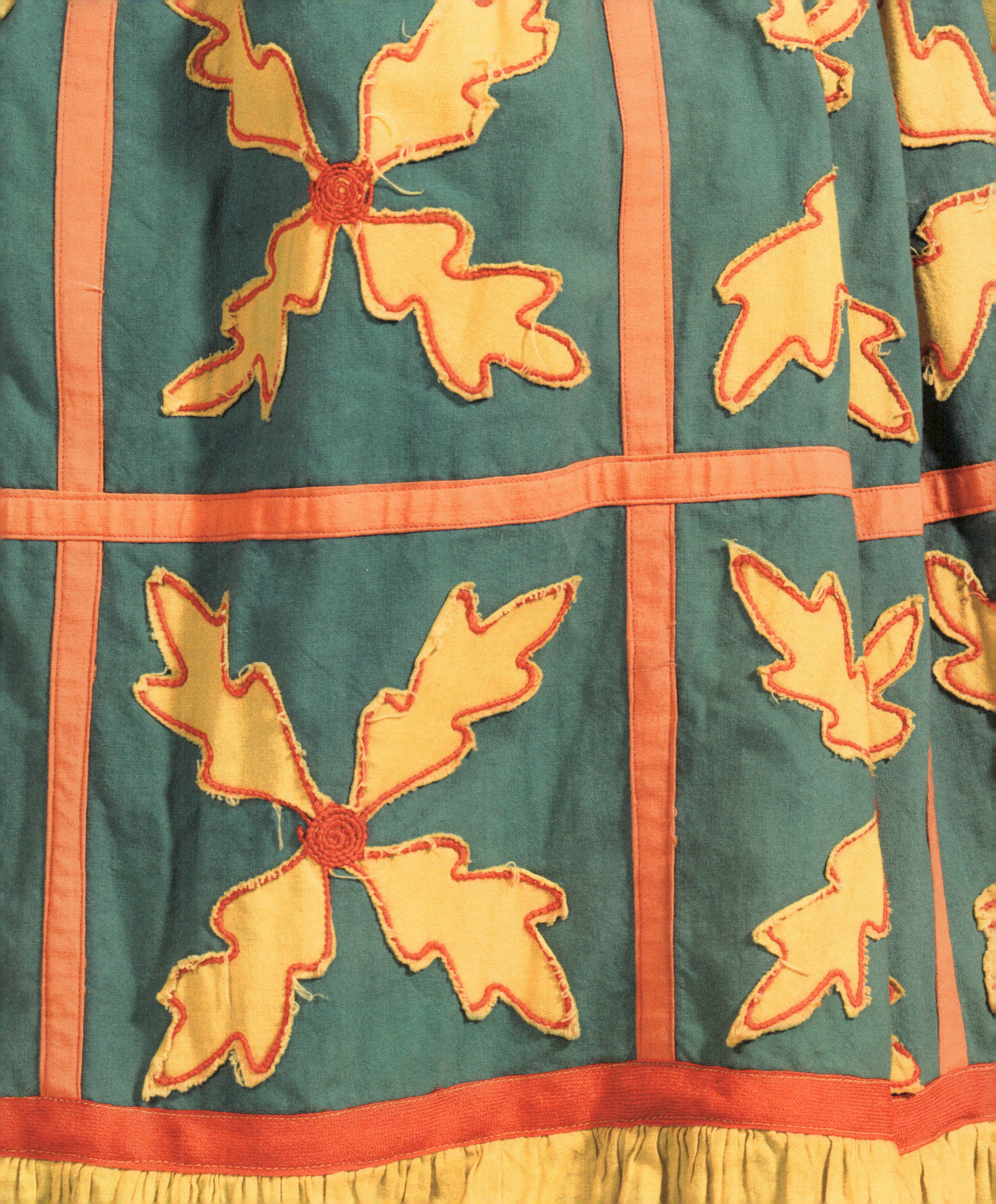

SELECTED BIBLIOGRAPHY

Acocella, Joan, *The reception of Diaghilev's Ballets Russes by artists and intellectuals in Paris and London 1909–1914*, unpub PhD thesis, Rutgers University, NJ, 1984.

Acocella, Joan, *The diary of Vaslav Nijinsky*, Allen Lane, London, 1999.

Acocella, Joan & Lynn Garofola, *André Levinson on dance: writings from Paris in the twenties*, Wesleyan University Press and University Press of New England, Hanover, NH, 1991.

Alexandre, Arsène & Jean Cocteau, *The decorative art of Léon Bakst*, Harry Melvill, Dover, New York, 1972.

Anderson, Jack, *The one and only: the Ballet Russes de Monte Carlo*, Dance Horizons, New York, 1981.

Axsom, Richard H, *Parade: Cubism as theater*, Garland, New York, 1979.

Baer, Nancy van Norman (ed), *Bronislava Nijinska: a dancer's legacy*, exhibition book, San Francisco Fine Arts Museum, San Francisco, 1986.

Baer, Nancy van Norman (ed), *The art of enchantment: Diaghilev's Ballets Russes 1909–1929*, exhibition book, San Francisco Fine Arts Museum, San Francisco, 1988.

Baer, Nancy van Norman, *Theatre in revolution: Russian avant-garde stage design 1913–1935*, Thames and Hudson/The Fine Arts Museums of San Francisco, New York, 1991.

Bann, Stephen, *Romanticism and the rise of history*, Twayne Publishers, New York, 1995.

Baronova, Irina, *Irina: ballet, life and love*, Penguin, Melbourne, 2005.

Barron, Stephanie and Maurice Tuchman (eds), *The avant-garde in Russia 1910–1930: new perspectives*, exhibition book, Los Angeles County Museum of Art, Los Angeles, 1980.

Beaumont, Cyril, *Complete book of ballets: a guide to the principal ballets of the nineteenth and twentieth centuries*, Putnam, London, 1937.

Beaumont, Cyril, *The Diaghilev ballet in London: a personal record*, Putnam, London, 1940.

Beaumont, Cyril, *Bookseller at the Ballet: Memoirs 1891–1929*, CW Beaumont, London, 1975.

Beaumont, Cyril, *Michel Fokine and his ballets*, Dance Horizons, New York, 1981.

Bell, Robert, 'Diaghilev's Ballets Russes costumes make a triumphant return to Europe', *Artonview*, 42, 2005, pp 34–5.

(opposite) **Natalia Goncharova**
Costume for a nursemaid to King Dodon c 1937 (detail) from *Le Coq d'or*
© Natalia Goncharova/ADAGP. Licensed by Viscopy, 2010

Bellow, Juliet, *Clothing the corps; how the avant-garde and the Ballets Russes fashioned the modern body*, unpub PdD thesis, University of Pennsylvania, 2005.

Benois, Alexandre, *Reminiscences of the Russian Ballet*, trans Mary Britineva, Putnam, London, 1941.

Benois, Alexandre, *Memoirs*, trans Moura Budberg, Chatto & Windus, London, 1960.

Benois, Alexandre, *Memoirs*, vol. II, trans Moura Budberg, Chatto & Windus, London, 1964.

Benois, Alexandre, 'The origins of the Ballets Russes', in Boris Kochno, *Diaghilev and the Ballets Russes*, trans Adrienne Foulke, Harper & Row, New York/Evanston, 1970, pp 4–18.

Benois, Alexandre, *Vozniknoveniye Mira iskusstva*, reprint, Iskusstvo, Moscow, [1928] 1998.

Bentley, Toni, *Costumes by Karinska*, Harry N Abrams Inc, New York, 1995.

Bernays, Edward L, *Biography of an idea: memoirs of public relations counsel*, Simon & Schuster, New York, 1965.

Boissel, Jessica, *Nathalie Gontcharova, Michel Larionov*, Editions du Centre Pompidou, Paris, 1995.

Bowlt, John E, *The silver age: Russian art of the early twentieth century and the 'World of Art' group*, Oriental Research Partners, Newtonville, MASS, 1982.

Bowlt, John E (ed), *Russian stage design: scenic innovation, 1904–1930; from the collection of Mr and Mrs Nikita D Lobanov-Rostovsky*, exhibition book, Mississippi Museum of Art, Jackson, 1982.

Bowlt, John E, *The Russian avant-garde: theory and criticism 1902–1934*, Abrams, London, 1988.

Bowlt, John E, *Painters of Russian theater 1880–1930: collection of Nikita and Nina Lobanov-Rostovsky*, Iskusstvo, Moscow, 1994.

Bowlt, John E, *Theater of reason, theater of desire: the art of Alexandre Benois and Léon Bakst*, Skira Editore, Milan, 1998.

Bowlt, John E, *Moscow, St Petersburg: the Russian Silver Age*, Vendome, New York, 2008.

Bowlt, John E, *A feast of wonders: Sergei Diaghilev and the Ballets Russes*, Skira Editore, Milan, 2009.

Brezgin, Oleg, *Diaghileva v khudozhestvennoi kulture Rossi, Zapadnoi Evropy i Ameriki* (*Diaghilev's personality in the artistic culture of Russia, Western Europe and America*), Perm Art Gallery, Perm, 2007.

Brissenden, Alan & Keith Glennon, *Australia Dances: Creating Australian dance 1945–1965*, Wakefield Press, Adelaide, 2010.

Buckle, Richard, *In search of Diaghilev*, Sidgwick & Jackson, London, 1955.

Buckle, Richard, *The Diaghilev Ballet in England*, Norwich and London, 1979.

Buckle, Richard, *Diaghilev*, Tony Mayer, J-C Lattès, Paris, 1980.

Buckle, Richard, *Alexandre Benois, 1870–1960: drawings for the ballet*, Hazlitt, Gooden & Fox, London, 1980.

Buckle, Richard, *In the wake of Diaghilev*, Collins, London, 1982.

Buckle, Richard, *Diaghilev*, Atheneum, New York, 1984.

Buckle, Richard, *Nijinsky*, Phoenix, London, 1988.

Buckle, Richard, *George Balanchine: ballet master*, Random House, New York, 1988.

Carmeli, Haviva et al, *Leon Bakst: the sleeping beauty*, exhibition book, Museum of Art, Tel Aviv, 1992.

Castle, Charles, *Oliver Messel: a biography*, Thames & Hudson, London, 1986.

Chamot, Mary (ed), *Retrospective exhibition of paintings and designs for the theatre: Larionov and Gontcharova*, exhibition book, Arts Council of Great Britain, London, 1961.

Chamot, Mary, *Gontcharova: stage designs and paintings*, Oresko Books, London, 1979.

Christofis, Lee (ed), *The Ballets Russes in Australia 1936–1940*, exhibition book, National Library of Australia, Canberra, 2009.

Clark, Maribeth, 'The role of *Gustave, ou Le bal masqué* in restraining the body of the July Monarchy', *Music and Culture* 88, 2006, pp 204–31.

Clarke, Mary & Clement Crisp, *Design for ballet*, Hawthorn Books, New York, 1978.

Cogniat, Raymond, *Décors de théâtre*, Editions Chroniques du Jour, Paris, 1930.

Cooper, Douglas, *Picasso theatre*, Harry N Abrams, New York, 1987.

Crisp, Clement et al, *Artists design for dance 1909–1984*, exhibition book, Arnolfini Gallery, Bristol, 1984.

Damase, Jacques, *Sonia Delaunay: fashion and fabrics*, Thames & Hudson, London, 1991.

Decter, Jacqueline, *Nicholas Roerich: the life and art of a Russian master*, Park Street Press, Rochester, VT, 1989.

de la Haye, Amy, Lou Taylor & Eleanor Thompson, *A family of fashion: the Messels: six generations of dress*, Philip Wilson Publishers, London, 2005.

dell'Arco, Maurizio Fagiolo, *De Chirico: gli anni trenta*, Edizione Gabriele Mazzotta, Verona, 1998.

Dixon, Christine, *Museum pieces? The Russian Ballet collection*, in Pauline Green (ed), *Building the collection*, National Gallery of Australia, Canberra, 2003, pp 176–89.

Dobrovolskaia, Galina, *Mikhail Fokin: russkii period* (*Mikhail Fokine: the Russian period*), Hyperion, St Petersburg, 2004.

Dolin, Anton, *Last words: a final autobiography*, Century Publishing, London, 1985.

Drummond, John, *Speaking of Diaghilev*, Faber & Faber, London and Boston, 1997.

Dudakov, Valerian, *Il simbolismo russo: Sergej Djagilev e l'età d'argento nell'arte*, Olivetti & Electa, Milan, 1992.

Dyer, Philip, *Report on the collection of Diaghilev and de Basil theatre costumes held by the Australian National Gallery Canberra*, Australian National Gallery, Canberra, 1974?

Elshevskaia, Galina, *Mir Iskusstva* (*The World of Art*), Belyi Gorod, Moscow, 2008.

Emery, Elizabeth & Laura Morowitz, *Consuming the past: The medieval revival in fin-de-siècle France*, Ashgate, Aldershot, UK and Burlington, VT, 2003.

Erlande-Brandenburg, Alain, Pierre-Yves Le Pogam & Dany Sandron, *Musée national du Moyen Age Thermes de Cluny*, Réunion des Musées Nationaux, Paris, 1993.

Féderovsky, Vladimir, *L'histoire secrète des Ballets Russes*, Rocher, Monaco, 2002.

Féderovsky, Vladimir, *Sergei Diaghilev ili zakulisnaia istoriia russkogo baleta* (*Sergei Diaghilev or a backstage history of Russian ballet*), Exmo, Moscow, 2003.

Féderovsky, Vladimir, *Diaghilev et Monaco*, Rocher, Monaco, 2004.

Fokine, Michel, *Fokine: memories of a ballet master*, trans Vitale Fokine, Constable, London, 1961.

Franko, Mark, *Dance as text: ideologies of the Baroque body*, Cambridge University Press, Cambridge, 1993.

Fulcher, Jane, *French grand opera as politics and as politicized art*, Cambridge University Press, Cambridge, 1987.

Gaeta, Caserma Cosenz, *The Russian ballet: the heyday of the Ballets Russes*, Palace Editions Europe, Bad Breisig, 2008.

Garafola, Lynn, *Art and enterprise in Diaghilev's Ballets Russes*, Da Capo Press, New York, 1988.

Garafola, Lynn, *Diaghilev's Ballets Russes*, Oxford University Press, London, 1989.

Garafola, Lynn & Nancy van Norman Baer, *The Ballets Russes and its world*, Yale University Press, New Haven and London, 1999.

Garafola, Lynn & Vicente García-Márquez, *España y los Ballets Russes*, Ministerio de Cultura, Madrid, 1989.

García-Márquez, Vicente, *The Ballets Russes: Colonel de Basil's Ballets Russes de Monte Carlo 1932–1952*, Alfred A Knopf Inc, New York, 1990.

García-Márquez, Vicente, *Massine*, Nick Hern Books, London, 1996.

George, Waldemar, *Larionov*, Bibliothèque des Arts, Paris, 1966.

Gosling, Nigel, *Paris 1900–1914: the miraculous years*, Weidenfeld & Nicholson, London, 1978.

Gottlieb, Robert, *Balanchine: the ballet master*, Atlas Books, Harper Press, London, 2006.

Green, Christopher (ed), *Juan Gris*, exhibition book, Whitechapel Art Gallery, London, 1992.

Grigoriev, Serge, *The Diaghilev ballet 1909–1929*, trans Vera Bowen, Constable, London, 1953.

Grigoriev, Sergei, *Balet Diaghileva 1909–1929*, ART, Moscow, 1993.

Hammond, Helena, 'Cecchetti, Carabosse and beauty', *Dancing Times*, May 2007, pp 32–5.

Haskell, Arnold, *Dancing round the world: memoirs of an attempted escape from ballet*, Victor Gollancz, London, 1937.

Haskell, Arnold, *Waltzing Matilda: a background to Australia*, Adam & Charles Black, London, 1944.

Haskell, Arnold, *Ballet*, Penguin, London, 1955.

Haskell, Arnold, *Diaghileff*, Victor Gollancz, London, 1955.

Healy, Robyn & Michael Lloyd (ed), *From studio to stage: costumes and designs from the Russian Ballet in the Australian National Gallery*, exhibition book, Australian National Gallery, Canberra, 1990.

Houston Museum of Fine Arts (ed), *The Diaghilev heritage: selections from the collection of Robert L B Tobin*, exhibition book, Houston Museum of Fine Arts, Houston, 1981.

Howard, Deborah, 'A sumptuous revival: Bakst's designs for Diaghilev's *Sleeping princess*', *Apollo*, 91, April 1970, pp 301–8.

Howard, Marjorie, 'Muelle—known to every singer; and every other stage favorite, too, who wants a distinctive Paris costume in which to create a new role', *New York Times*, 25 April 1915.

Huesca, Roland, *Triomphes et scandales: la belle époque des Ballets Russes*, Hermann, Paris, 2001.

Ingles, Elizabeth, *Bakst*, Grange Books, Rochester, Kent, 2007.

Järvinen, Hanna, '"The Russian Barnum": Russian opinions on Diaghilev's Ballets Russes, 1909–14', *Dance Research*, vol 26.1, Summer 2008, pp 18–41.

Jeschke, Claudia, *Spiegelungen: die Ballets Russes und die Künste*, Vorwerk 8 Publishing House, Berlin, 1997.

Joseph, Charles M, *Stravinsky and Balanchine*, Yale University Press, New Haven, CT, 2002.

Kahane, Martine, *Les Ballets Russes à l'Opéra 1909–1929*, Bibliothèque Nationale, Hazan, Paris, 1992.

Karsavina, Tamara, *Theatre street*, Constable, London, 1930.

Kennedy, Janet, *The 'Mir iskusstva' group and Russian art, 1989–1912*, Garland, New York, 1977.

Kirker, Anne, *Natalia Gontcharova*, National Art Gallery, Wellington, 1987.

Kochno, Boris, *Diaghilev and the Ballets Russes*, trans Adrienne Foulke, Harper & Row, New York/Evanston, 1970.

Kodicek, Ann (ed), *Diaghilev: creator of the Ballets Russes*, exhibition book, Barbican Art Gallery and Lund Humphries, London, 1996.

Kohnweiler, Daniel-Henry, *Juan Gris: his life and work*, trans Douglas Cooper, Thames & Hudson, London, 1969.

Koutsomallis, Kyriakos & Margarita Katanga (eds), *André Masson and ancient Greece*, Umberto Allemandi, Turin, 2007.

Kovtun, Yevgeny, *Mikhail Larionov 1881–1964*, Parkstone Press, London, 1998.

Laskin, Aleksandr, *V poiskakh Diaghileva* (*In search of Diaghilev*), St Petersburg Academy of Culture, St Petersburg, 1997.

Léal, Brigitte et al, *Picasso: Le Tricorne*, exhibition book, Musée des Beaux-Art, Lyon, 1992.

Leong, Roger et al, *From Russia with love: costumes for the Ballets Russes 1909–1933*, exhibition book, National Gallery of Australia, Canberra, 1998.

Lepape, Claude & Thierry Defert, *From the Ballets Russes to Vogue: the art of Georges Lepape*, trans Jane Brenton, Vendome, New York, 1984.

Levinson, André, *The story of Leon Bakst's life*, Alexander Kogan Publishing Company 'Russian Art', Berlin, 1922.

Levinson, André, *The designs of Léon Bakst for 'The sleeping princess', a ballet in five acts after Perrault, music by Tchaikovsky*, preface by André Levinson, Benn Brothers Ltd, London, 1923.

Lieven, Prince Peter, *The birth of the Ballets-Russes*, trans L Zarine, George Allen & Unwin Ltd, London, 1936.

Lifar, Serge, *Serge Diaghilev: his life, his work, his legend*, Putnam, London, 1940.

Lifar, Serge, *Serge de Diaghilev*, Editions d'Aujourd'Hui, Monaco, 1982.

London (Alhambra Theatre, Leicester Square), *Souvenir Programme: The Sleeping Princess*, 1921.

Macdonald, Nesta, *Diaghilev observed by critics in England and the United States 1911–1929*, New York Dance Books Ltd, London and New York, 1975.

Mackrell, Judith, *Bloomsbury ballerina: Lydia Lopokova*, Weidenfeld & Nicholson, London, 2008.

Massine, Léonide, *My life in ballet*, Macmillan, London, 1968.

Mayer, Charles, *The theatrical designs of Léon Bakst*, Columbia University, 1977.

McQuillan, Melissa, *Painters and the ballet, 1917–1926: an aspect of the relationship between art and theatre*, University Microfilms International, Ann Arbor, MICH, 1988.

Migel, Parmenia, *Pablo Picasso: designs for The three-cornered hat* (*Le Tricorne*), Dover and Stravinsky-Diaghilev Foundation, New York, 1978.

Mississippi Museum of Art, *Russian stage design: scenic innovation 1900–1930*, exhibition book, Mississippi Museum of Art, Jackson, 1982.

Museo Nacional Centro de Arte Reina Sofía, *Painters in the theatre of the European avant-garde*, Museo Nacional Centro de Arte Reina Sofía, Madrid, 2000.

Näslund, Erik, *Överdådets konst II: The art of extravagance II: kostymer från Diaghilews Ryska Baletten i Paris*, Dansmuseet, Stockholm, 2004.

Näslund, Erik, *Ballets Russes: the Stockholm collection*, Dansmuseet, in collaboration with Bokförlaget Langenskiöld, Stockholm, 2009.

Näslund, Erik et al, *Leon Bakst: sensualismens triumf*, trans Märta Sahlberg, exhibition book, Dansmuseet, Stockholm, 1993.

Nestiev, Izrail, *Diaghilev i musykalnyi teatr 20-go veka* (*Diaghilev and musical theatre of the twentieth century*), Muzyka, Moscow, 1994.

Nijinska, Bronislava, *Bronislava Nijinska: early memoirs*, trans Irina and Jean Rawlinson Nijinska, Faber, London, 1982.

Nijinsky, Vaslav, *The diary of Vaslav Nijinsky*, edited by Romola Nijinsky, Quartet Encounters, London, 1991.

Nommick, Yvan & Antonio Álvarez Cañibano, *Los Ballets Russes de Diaghilev y España*, Archivo Manuel de Falla, Granada and Madrid, 2000.

Ocaña, María Teresa, *Picasso y el teatro: Parade, Pulcinella, Cuadro flamenco, Mercure*, Museo Picasso, Barcelona, 1996.

O'Donoghue, Catherine & Margot Anderson (eds), *Creative Australia and the Ballets Russes*, exhibition book, Victorian Arts Centre Trust, Melbourne, 2009.

Orloff, Alexander & Margaret E Willis, *Russian ballet on tour*, Barrie and Jenkins, London, 1989.

Parton, Anthony, *Michail Larionov and the Russian avant-garde*, Princeton University Press, London, 1993.

Parton, Anthony, *Natalia Gontcharova and the Russian Ballet*, J Barran, London, 1997.

Pask, Edward H, *Enter the colonies dancing: a history of dance in Australia 1835–1940*, Oxford University Press, Melbourne, 1979.

Pask, Edward H, *Ballet in Australia: the second act 1940–1980*, Oxford University Press, Melbourne, 1982.

Pastori, Jean-Pierre, *La danse: des Ballets Russes a l'avant-garde*, Gallimard, Paris, 1997.

Petrov, Vsevold, *Russian Art Nouveau: the World of Art and Diaghilev's painters*, Parkstone Press, Bournemouth, 1997.

Petrov, Vsevolod & Aleksandr Kamensky, *The World of Art movement in early 20th-century Russia*, Aurora, Leningrad, 1991.

Pinkham, Roger (ed), *Oliver Messel*, exhibition book, Victoria and Albert Museum, London, 1983.

Plouffe, David Allen, *Textiles in the work of Henri Matisse 1894 to 1940*, MA thesis, California State University, Fullerton, CA, 2008.

Polunin, Vladimir, *The Continental method of scene painting*, Dance Books, London, 1980.

Pospelov, Gleb & Evgenia Iliukhina, *Mikhail Larionov*, Galart/RA, Moscow, 2005.

Potter, Michelle, *The Russian ballet in Australia 1936–40*, Australian National University, Canberra, 1987.

Pozharskaia, Militsa & Tatiana Volodina, *The art of the Ballets Russes: the Russian season in Paris 1908–1929*, Aurum, London, 1990.

Press, Stephen D, *Prokofiev's ballets for Diaghilev*, Ashgate, Aldershot, UK and Burlington, VT, 2006.

Pritchard, Jane & Geoffrey Marsh, *Diaghilev and the golden age of the Ballets Russes: 1909–1929*, V&A Publishing, London, 2010.

Propert, Walter, *The Russian ballet in western Europe*, Bodley Head, London, 1921.

Propert, Walter, *The Russian ballet 1921–1929*, Bodley Head, London, 1931.

Proust, Marcel, 'The captive and the fugitive', *In search of lost time*, vol V, trans C K Scott Moncrieff & Terence Kilmartin, revised D J Enright, Vintage Books, London, 2000.

Pruzhan, Irina, *Léon Bakst: set and costume designs, book illustrations, paintings and graphic works*, trans Arthur Shkarovski-Raffé, Penguin, Harmondsworth, Middlesex, 1988.

Purvis, Alston, Peter Rand & Anna Winestein (eds), *The Ballets Russes and the art of design*, The Monacelli Press, New York, 2009.

Ries, Frank W D, *The dance theatre of Jean Cocteau*, UMI Research Press, Ann Arbor, MICH, 1986.

Robb, Graham, *Parisians: an adventure history of Paris*, Picador, London, 2010.

Rothschild, Deborah Menaker, *Picasso's 'Parade': from street to stage*, Sotheby's Publications, London, 1991.

San Francisco Fine Arts Museum (ed), *The art of enchantment: Diaghilev's Ballets Russes, 1909–1929*, exhibition book, San Francisco Fine Arts Museum, San Francisco, 1988.

Shead, Richard, *Ballets Russes*, Apple Press, London, 1989.

Scheijen, Sjeng, *Working for Diaghilev*, BAI, Groningen, 2004.

Scheijen, Sjeng, *Diaghilev: a life*, trans Jane Hedley-Prôle & S J Leinbach, Profile Books Ltd, London, 2009.

Schouvaloff, Alexander (ed), *Set and costume designs for ballet and theatre and the Thyssen-Bornemisza Collection*, exhibition book, Sotheby & Co, London, 1987.

Schouvaloff, Alexander, *Léon Bakst*, Scala, Paris, 1991.

Schouvaloff, Alexander, *The art of Ballets Russes: the Serge Lifar Collection of theater designs, costumes and paintings at the Wadsworth Atheneum, Hartford, Connecticut*, Yale University Press, New Haven, CT, 1997.

Schouvaloff, Alexander & Victor Borovsky, *Stravinsky on stage*, Stainer & Bell, London, 1982.

Schwartz, Selma, *The Waddesdon companion guide*, The National Trust, Waddesdon Manor, Bucks, UK, 2003.

Sitwell, Sacheverell, 'The sleeping beauty at the London Alhambra, 1921', *Ballet—to Poland*, ed Arnold Haskell, London, 1940, pp 17–9.

Souhami, Diana, *Bakst: The Rothschild panels of 'The sleeping beauty'*, Philip Wilson, London, 1992.

Senelick, Laurence, *Wandering stars: Russian emigré theatre 1905–1940*, University of Iowa Press, Iowa City, 1992.

Sezon Museum of Art, *Diaghilev's Ballets Russes*, Sezon Museum of Art, Tokyo, 1998.

Shead, Richard, *Ballets Russes*, Apple, London, 1989.

Singleton, John, *The world textile industry*, Routledge, London and New York, 1997.

Smalley, Lionel & Alan McCulloch, *Ballet bogies*, Lionel Smalley, Melbourne, 1938.

Sokolova, Lydia, *Dancing for Diaghilev: the memoirs of Lydia Sokolova*, ed Richard Buckle, John Murray, London, 1960.

Sokolova, Lydia, *Dancing for Diaghilev: the memoirs of Lydia Sokolova*, ed Richard Buckle, Mercury House, San Francisco, 1989.

Sotheby & Co (ed), *Costumes and curtains from Diaghilev and de Basil Ballets*, sale catalogue, Sotheby & Co, London, 1969.

Spangenberg, Kristin (ed), *The golden age of costume and set design for the Ballet Russe de Monte Carlo 1938 to 1944*, exhibition book, Cincinnati Museum of Art, Cincinnati, OH, 2002.

Spencer, Charles, *Leon Bakst*, Academy Editions, London, 1973.

Spencer, Charles, *The world of Serge Diaghilev*, Paul Elek, London, 1974.

Spencer, Charles, *Léon Bakst and the Ballets Russes*, Academy Books, London, 1995.

Strong, Roy, Ivor Guest, Richard Buckle et al, *Designing for the dancer*, Elron Press, London, 1981.

Taper, Bernard, *Balanchine*, second rev edn, University of California Press, Berkeley and Los Angeles, 1996.

Taruskin, Richard, *Stravinsky and the Russian traditions*, Oxford University Press, Oxford, 1996.

Taruskin, Richard, *Defining Russia musically: historical and hermeneutical essays*, Princeton University Press, Princeton, NJ, 1997.

The State Russian Museum, *The age of Diaghilev*, Palace Editions, St Petersburg, 2001.

Tye, Larry, *The father of spin: Edward L Bernays and the birth of public relations*, Crown Publishers, New York, 1998.

Tyler, Parker, *The divine comedy of Pavel Tchelitchew: a biography*, Weidenfeld & Nicholson, London, 1969.

Vincent Astor Gallery (ed), *Artist of the theatre: Alexandra Exter*, exhibition book, New York Public Library, New York, 1974.

Vlasova, Raisa, *Russkoe teatralno-dekorativnye iskusstvo nachala 20-go veka* (*Russian theatrical and decorative art of the early twentieth century*), Russian Federation of Artists, Leningrad, 1984.

von Maur, Karin, 'Music and theatre in the work of Juan Gris' in Christopher Green (with contributions by Christian Derouet & Karin von Maur), *Juan Gris*, Whitechapel Art Gallery, London, 1992, pp 268–85.

Wachtel, Andrew, *Petrushka: sources and contexts*, Northwestern University Press, Evanston, ILL, 1998.

Walker, Kathrine Sorley, *De Basil's Ballets Russes*, Hutchinson & Co, London, 1982.

Walsh, Stephen, *Igor Stravinsky: a creative spring: Russia and France 1882–1934*, Jonathan Cape, London, 2000.

Wild, Nicole & Jean-Michel Nectoux, *Diaghilev: Les Ballets Russes*, Bibliothèque Nationale, Paris, 1979.

Wiley, John Roland, *Tchaikovsky's ballets: Swan Lake, Sleeping beauty, Nutcracker*, Oxford University Press, Oxford, 1985.

Wiley, John Roland, *A century of Russian ballet: documents and eyewitness accounts 1810–1910*, Oxford University Press, Oxford, 1990.

Zilbershtein, Ilia & Vladimir Samkov, *Sergei Diaghilev i russkoe iskusstvo* (*Sergei Diaghilev and Russian art*), Izobrazitelnoe Iskusstvo, Moscow, 1982.

CONTRIBUTORS

Robert Bell is Senior Curator, Decorative Arts and Design at the National Gallery of Australia, covering all aspects of the decorative arts. He has curated numerous exhibitions on crafts and design including *Material culture: aspects of contemporary Australian craft and design* (2002) and *Transformations: the language of craft* (2005). He has particular interests in twentieth-century design and contemporary craft. He has a PhD from the Australian National University and in 2010 was made a Member of the Order of Australia for service to crafts, design and museums.

Christine Dixon is Senior Curator, International Painting and Sculpture at the National Gallery of Australia. She was the editor for the catalogue of European and American Painting and Sculpture in Gallery's collection. Most recently she co-curated and wrote for the books for the major exhibitions *Turner to Monet: the triumph of landscape painting in the nineteenth century* (2008) and *Masterpieces from Paris: Van Gogh, Gauguin, Cézanne and beyond—Post-Impressionism from the Musée d'Orsay* (2009). Her particular interest is European Modernism 1890–1940; she is currently working on the surrealist artist Max Ernst.

Helena Hammond (D Phil Oxon) is Lecturer in Dance History at the University of Surrey, UK. Her current research centres on the politics of historical representation in dance, in which connection she was Visiting Fellow at the Australian National University in 2007 and awarded the Fulbright Association's 2010 Selma Jeanne Cohen Fund endowed lectureship in international dance. She has contributed to journals and publications, most recently as contributor to *Fifty contemporary choreographers* (Routledge, 2011) and she serves on the editorial board of the journal *Australian Studies*.

Simeran Maxwell is the Exhibition Assistant for *Ballets Russes: the art of costume*. She has previously worked on, and contributed to the exhibition books for *Masterpieces from Paris: Van Gogh, Cézanne, Gauguin and beyond* (2009), *Degas: master of French art* (2009), *Turner to Monet: the triumph of landscape painting* (2008) and *Birth of the modern poster* (2008).

Michelle Potter is an independent dance historian, curator and writer with a doctorate in Art History and Dance History from the Australian National University. She was inaugural Curator of Dance at the National Library of Australia, 2001–06, and Curator, Jerome Robbins Dance Division, New York Public Library for the Performing Arts, 2006–08. Her extensive writing about the Ballets Russes has been published in Australia, the United States and the United Kingdom. She trained as a dancer under former Ballets Russes soloist, Valrene Tweedie.

Debbie Ward is Head of Conservation at the National Gallery of Australia. She has a BA (Sydney University) and a Masters of Applied Science in Materials Conservation (University of Canberra) and has worked in the field of conservation, specialising in textiles, since the early 1980s. She has worked on all past Gallery theatre arts exhibitions and lectured in textile conservation in Australia and overseas. Due to her extensive work on the Gallery's textile collection, her areas of expertise are theatre costumes and Asian textiles.

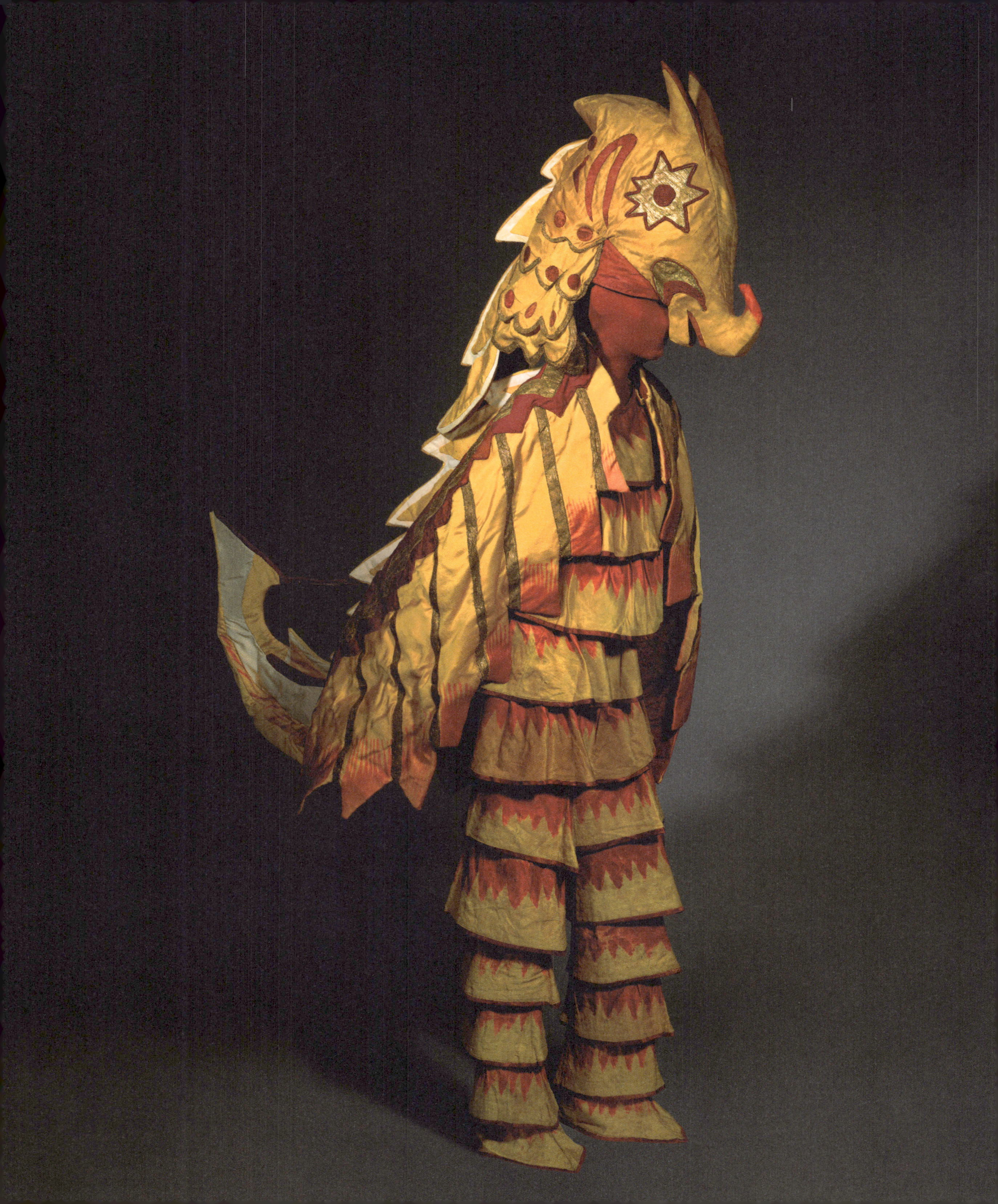

ACKNOWLEDGMENTS

The exhibition *Ballets Russes: the art of costume* and this book are the results of the efforts of many— developing, researching, conserving, photographing, exhibiting, documenting and interpreting the National Gallery of Australia's Ballets Russes costume collection.

I am grateful to have been able draw upon the work of those who have preceded me in developing the collection: former curators Diana Woollard, Robyn Healy, Michael Lloyd and Roger Leong. The support of the Gallery's former directors, a commitment continued by Ron Radford, has ensured the collection's prominence.

Helena Hammond, Christine Dixon, Michelle Potter and Debbie Ward have drawn on their wealth of experience to provide new insights into the complex history of the Ballets Russes. Exhibition Assistant Simeran Maxwell has written for the catalogue and managed the myriad tasks involved in sourcing and preparing images, cataloguing and departmental liaison to keep the project on schedule. Karie Wilson assisted with the re-cataloguing begun by Sarah Edge.

Costume conservation is a continuous and demanding process. Head of Conservation Debbie Ward and Senior Textile Conservator Micheline Ford have for many years coordinated a rigorous program by conservators Jane Wild, Chandra Obie, Hannah Barrett, Stefanie Woodruff, Carmela Mollica and Debra Spoehr, resulting in more than fifty unrestored costumes being made ready for display. Blaide Lallemand and David McRoberts made costume mounts, Jan Mackay coordinated handling and volunteer Gudrun Genée made storage supports. Conservators Andrea Wise, James Ward, Fiona Kemp and David Wise prepared costume design drawings, original programs and backdrops for presentation.

Brenton McGeachie, and other Imaging team members Steve Nebauer, John Tassie and Barry Le Lievre, provided the fine images of the costumes and other works seen here and on the exhibition website developed by Andrew Powrie and Kylie Doherty. Nick Nicholson organised image clearances.

Emma Doy's powerful exhibition design enhances the costumes' visual and physical drama. Designer Kirsty Morrison ensured that the exuberance and colour of the Ballets Russes were reflected in the book's design. Editor Anne Savage contributed to shaping the text and publisher Julie Donaldson steered the book through the process.

Program managers Simon Elliott, Shanthini Naidoo and Adam Worrall, and section managers Dominique Nagy (Exhibitions), Peter Naumann (Education and Public Programs), David Pang (Imaging), Patrice Riboust (Exhibition Design), Kirsten Downie (Marketing) and Joy Volker (Research Library) provided enthusiastic support. I thank Katrina Power for exhibition project management and Tui Tahi for the exhibition lighting.

I thank our Decorative Arts and Design volunteers for being so generous with their time. Meredith Hinchliffe updated catalogue records, while Jane Herring assisted with general research on the Ballets Russes and its dancers, sourcing related music, film and images for the exhibition.

I welcomed the interest in the project and advice from Lee Christofis, Michelle Potter, Vincent Plush and Erik Näslund and thank Eugenie Keefer Bell for her constant support.

Robert Bell

Natalia Goncharova
Costume for a seahorse c 1916
© Natalia Goncharova/ADAGP.
Licensed by Viscopy, 2010

INDEX

Locators in italic indicate illustrations of costumes; locators in bold indicate biographies of designers.

Abramtsevo 28
Abricossova, Kira *see* Bousloff, Kira
Académie Royale de la Danse 62
Alfonso XIII (King of Spain) 40
Anderson, Joseph Ringland 47
Anello & Davide 197–8
Angels (costumier) 197–8
Anisfeld, Boris 131
L'Après-midi d'un faune (*The afternoon of a faun*) 35, *118–21*
Arensky, Anton 89
artists and designers 32, 33, 35, 36, 39, 40, 43, 44, 47, 53, 63, 65, 71–81, **216–26** *see also names of specific artists*
artists' design drawings 20
Arts and Crafts movement 28
Astruc, Gabriel 61
Australian Ballet 47, 65
Australian tours 45–7, 65, 171, 179, 183–93

'baby ballerinas' 45, 46
Los Bailes-Rusos 40
Bakst, Léon *6–7, 10–12, 18,* 20, 27, 29, *34,* 35–7, 39, *41,* 43, 53–5, 59, 61, *61,* 63–5, *66,* 67, 71, 76, 81, *88,* 89, *90–100, 104–5, 107–9, 114–25,* 132, *140–3, 186–7,* **216**
Le Bal (*The ball*) 44, *48–9, 78,* 80, *162–3*
Balakirev, Mily Alexeyevich 116
Balanchine, George 43–4, 45, 80
Balla, Giacomo 39
ballet, history of 25–6, 31; in Australia 46–7

Ballet Australia 47
ballet d'action 25–6
ballet de cour 25, 63, 64
Ballet de l'Astuce féminine/Cimarosiana (*Feminine wiles*) 150–3
Ballet de l'Opéra Russes à Paris 45, 80, 167
Ballet Russe de Diaghileff 35
Ballets de Monte Carlo 45
Ballets Russes de Léon Woizikovsky 189
Ballets Russes de Monte Carlo 44–5, 65, *166–79,* 189 *see also* Monte Carlo Russian Ballet
Ballets Russes de Serge Diaghilev 13, 26, 35, *84–163*
Ballets Russes in Australia: our cultural revolution (research project) 47
Ballets Russes timeline 228–37
Ballets Suédois 209
Baronova, Irina 45, 46, 185
Basil, Wassily de *see* de Basil, Wassily
Bauchant, André 39
Le Beau Danube (*The beautiful Danube*) 170–1
Beaumont, Cyril 65
La Belle au bois dormant see The sleeping beauty
Benois, Alexandre 20, 27, 29, *30,* 32, 33, 35, 36, *42,* 45, 53–6, *57,* 59, 61, 63–4, 65, *66,* 71, 81, *84–5, 102–3, 111–12,* 140, *144,* 148, **217**
Bérain, Jean 65, 85, 141
Bernays, Edward L 183, 193
Bert, Auguste 96
Bibiena, Ferdinando Galli 141
Les Biches (*The house party*) 43
Bilibin, Ivan 56
Blum, René 44, 45
Boker, George Henry 176
Bolm, Adolph 33, 36
Bongard, Germaine 21

Boquet, Louis-René 65, 85, 141
Boris Godunov (opera) 32, 56
Borodin, Alexander 33, 86
Borovansky, Edouard 47
Borovansky Australian Ballet Company Ltd 47, 222
Bousloff, Kira 47
La Boutique fantasque (*The magical toyshop*) 43, 76, *132–3*
Braque, Georges 39, 76, *154,* **217**
Buck family 185–7
Buckle, Richard 20
Burdett, Basil 190

Caffi, Ivan 85, 111, 145
Caffi and Vorobier 21, 111
Canada, tours to 40
Carnaval (*Carnival*) *6–7, 92–5,* 125
Casadesus, Henri 148
Cecchetti, Enrico 36
Chanel, Gabrielle 'Coco' 21, 44
Le Chant du rossignol (*The song of the nightingale*) *15,* 38, 43, 76–7, *134–7*
Charbonnier, Pierre 159
La Chatte (*The cat*) 44
Chopiniana 32 *see also Les Sylphides*
choreography and choreographers 31–2, 35, 36, 39, 40, 43, 44, 45 *see also names of specific choreographers*
Chout (*The buffoon*) *16,* 21, 43, *74,* 75, *138–9*
Cimarosa, Domenico 151
Cimarosiana (*Women's wiles*) 150–3
Cinderella 31
Clarke, Vera *see* Savina, Vera
classicism 53, 54, 55, 56, 62, 67
Cléopâtre (*Cleopatra*) 32, 35, *41,* 59, *61,* 70, 75–6, *88–91*

260 Ballets Russes: the art of costume

Cocteau, Jean 40, 73, 76

Col W de Basil's Ballets Russes 45

Col W de Basil's Monte Carlo Russian Ballet 13

Colonel Wassily de Basil's Covent Garden Ballet 47

composers 33–4, 35, 71 *see also names of specific composers*

concerts 32, 56

Constructivism 44, 78, 81, 157, 159

Le Coq d'or (*The golden cockerel*) *2*, 39, 71, 72–3, *126–9*

costumes

    conservation/restoration 14, 20, 197–207

    construction 200–1

    fabrics 75, 80, 127, 138, 157, 198–200, 204–5

    repairs and replicas 21, 204, 205

costumiers 20–1, 25–6, 33, 45, 197–8 *see also names of specific costumiers*

Covent Garden Russian Ballet 45

Cuadro flamenco 21

Cubism 39, 40, 43, 73, 76, 81, 138

dancers 32, 33, 35–6, 43–7, 71, 185–6, 188–9 *see also names of specific dancers*

Danilova, Alexandra 169, 189

Danses polovtsiennes du Prince Igor (*The Polovtsian dances from Prince Igor*) 32, *86–7*

Le Danube bleu 170

Daphnis et Chloé (*Daphnis and Chloë*) 35, 39, 81, *122–3*

de Basil, Wassily 13, 19, 45, 46, 47, 65, 183, 188, 189–90, 193

de Beaumont, Etienne *170–1*, **216**

de Chirico, Giorgio 39, 44, 45, *48–9*, 71, *78*, 80–1, *162–3*, *166–7*, **218**

de Coubertin, Pierre 58

de Falla, Mañuel 40, 76

de Montéclair, Michel 62, 148

de Polignac, Pierre 43

de Polignac, Princesse (Winnaretta Singer) 43

de Pulzsky, Romola 39

de Rothschild, James 64–5

de Valois, Ninette 65

Deane, Daphne 45

Debussy, Claude 35, 119

Delaunay, Robert 39, 40, 71, 75

Delaunay, Sonia 39, 40, 45, *70*, 71, 75–6, *88*, **218**

Denham, Serge 45

Derain, André 20, 39, 43, 45, 76, *132–3*, **219**

designers *see* artists and designers

Desormière, Roger 45

Diaghilev, Sergei 19, 20, 26–9, 71–81

    early life and travels 26–8, 29

    entrepreneurship 28–9, 31, 33, 40–1, 43, 47, 53, 55–6, 65, 73, 140–1, 145

    exhibitions 28, 29, 32, 53, 55–6

    ill-health and death 44

    personal relationships 31, 35, 39, 43, 44

    productions and tours 31–3, 35–6, 39–40, 43–4, 47, 56, 71

    professional partnerships 31–2, 35, 43, 53–4, 63, 127

    publisher 28–9, 31, 55

Diaghilev and de Basil Ballet Foundation 19

Diamantidi, Anthony 19–20

Didelot, Charles-Louis 154

Le Dieu bleu (*The blue god*) 21, 35, *37*, 39, *114–15*

Doisneau, Robert 221

Dolin, Anton 43, 46

Don Quixote 31

Du Sommerard, Edmond 59

Dukelsky, Vladimir 154, 175

Duncan, Isadora 31, 32, 108

Dupain, Max 47, 191–3

Dyer, Philip 20

Educational Ballets Ltd 19, 45

Ernst, Max 39

Etude 184

exhibitions 19, 20, 28, 29, 32, 44, 53, 55–6

Fauré, Gabriel 40

Fauvism 35, 72, 81, 132

Le Festin (*The feast*) 32

La Fête Merveilleuse 61–3

Filosofov, Dima 27, 28, 29

Le Fils prodigue (*The prodigal son*) 44

Fokin, Mikhail *see* Fokine, Michel

Fokina, Vera 33

Fokine, Michel 9, 31–2, 33, 35, 36, 39, 45, 46, 56, 72, 89, 108, 115, 125, 131, 176

Francesca da Rimini 176–7

Fraser, Grace Lovat 21, 140

Fuller, Loïe 32

Futurism 39, 72, 76, 81, 138, 168

Gabo, Nuam 39, 80

Gautier, Théophile 56, 85

Genée, Adeline 188

Gesamtkunstwerk 33, 54–67, 73

Gevergeyeva, Tamara 44

Gide, André 175

Giselle 31, 32, 35, *102–3*

Glazunov, Alexander 86, 89, 93

Glinka, Mikhail 89

Goetz, E Ray 19

Golovin, Aleksandr *34*, 71, *104–5*, *107*, 131, **219**

Goncharova, Natalia *2–3*, 20, *24*, *34*, 39, 40, 43, 45, 65, 71–3, 75, *104*, *106*, *126–31*, *146–7*, **220**

Grigoriev, Serge 36, 44, 45

Gris, Juan 20, 39, *61*, 62, 76, *148–9*, **220**

Guerard, Roland *146*

Hahn, Reynaldo 35, 115

Hall, Hugh P 47

Haskell, Arnold 189–90, 193

Healey-Kay, Sydney l *see* Dolin, Anton

Henry Buck's (store) 185–7

historicism 54, 56, 58–9, 61, 63–5, 67

Hoppé, E O 39, 89, 107, 216

Icare (*Icarus*) *46*, 47, 184

Imperial Ballet School 31

Imperial Russian Ballet 31, 33

Imperial Theatres 29, 32, 35, 55, 56

Ivan the terrible (*The maid of Pskov*) (opera) 32

J C Williamson Theatres Ltd 46, 187–9, 193

Jardin public (*The public gardens*) 174–5

Les Jeux 61

Jmoudsky, Varvara Andreievna *see* Karinska, Barbara

journals 28

Jove (firm) 21

Judith (opera) 32

Karinska, Barbara 21, 45, 80

Karsavina, Tamara 33, 35, 103

Khokhlova, Olga 40

Kirsova, Hélène 47, 184

Kochno, Boris 43, 44, 45

Lami, Eugène 26

Landoff, M 21, 115

Lang, Fritz 157

Lapauze, Henry 61

Index **261**

Larionov, Mikhail *16*, 31, 39, 40, 43, 45, 71, *74*, 75, *138–9*, 145, *188*, **221**

Larose, Olga 179

Laurencin, Marie 39

Laurens, Henri 39

Lavrova, Irina *see* Tweedie, Valrene

La Légende de Joseph (*The story of Joseph*) 76, 218, 225

Levinson, André 54–6

Levitsky, Dmitry 55

Liadov, Anatol 93

Lichine, David 176

Lieven, Peter 53, 55, 59, 61, 65

Lifar, Serge 44, *155*, *157*, *160*

Louis XIV (King of France) 25, 54, 61–2

lubok 71, 126

Lurçat, Jean *174–5*, **221**

La Lutte eternelle (*The eternal struggle*) 47, *178–9*

McCulloch, Alan 185–7

McCulloch, Wilfred 186–8

Malevich, Kazimir 73

Mamontov, Savva 28, 29

Man Ray 216, 217, 220, 221

Marcovitch 217

Le Mariage d'Aurore (*Aurora's wedding*) *3*, 62, 65, *66*, *144–7*

Mariinsky Theatre 31, 32, 56, 140, 176

Marinetti, Filippo 40, 72

Martin, Florence and Kathleen 47, *178–9*, **222**

Martin, Jean-Baptiste 65

Massine, Léonide 19, 39, 40, 43, 45, 71, 78, 80, 168, 171, 172

Masson, André *81*, *168–9*, 184, **222**

Matisse, Henri *15*, *38*, 39, 43, 71, 72, 76–7, *134–7*, **223**

Las meniñas 40

Messel, Oliver 45, 154, *176–7*, **223**

Metropolis (film) 157

Mir Iskusstva (journal) 28–9, 31, 55

miriskusniki 29, 31, 32, 39, 54, 55, 96, 108, 148

Miró, Joan 39, 45

Modernism 39–43, 61, 71, 73, 127, 168

Monte Carlo, Monaco 35, 43

Monte Carlo Opera 44

Monte Carlo Russian Ballet 45–6, 171, 188–90 *see also* Ballets Russes de Monte Carlo

Mordkin, Mikhail 33

Morris Angel & Son 197–8

Muelle, Marie 21, 115, 198

Muelle & Rossignol 21

Murray-Will, Ewan 47

Musée des Thermes et de l'Hôtel de Cluny 58–9, 65

'museumification' 65

Mussorgsky, Modest 32, 33

Myasin, Leonid *see* Massine, Léonide

Nabokov, Nikolai 80, 159

Narcisse (*Narcissus*) 36, *108–9*

National Library of Australia 47

Nevsky Pickwickians 27–8, 54

New Zealand tours 45–6

Nicholas II (Tsar) 29, 35, 55

Nijinska, Bronislava 36, 43, 44, 45, 64, *121*, 189

Nijinsky, Vaslav 21, 32, 33, 35–6, 39, 43, 56, 71, 96, 103, 111, *113*, 115, 119, *121*, 201

Les Noces (*The wedding*) 43, 61

Nolan, Sidney *46*, 47, 184

North America, tours to 40–1, 179

Nouvel, Walter 27, 29, 44

The nutcracker 31

Ode 44, *158–61*

L'Oiseau de feu (*The firebird*) *24*, *34*, 35, *104–7*

opera 32

Opéra Russe à Paris *see* Ballet de l'Opéra Russes à Paris

Les Orientales 35

Orientalism 32, 39, 71, 76

Original Ballet Russe 45, 47, 184

Papillons (*Butterflies*) *124–5*

Paquin, Jeanne 21

Parade (*Side show*) 21, 40, 43, 67, 73

Paris Opéra 25, 26, 32, 62

Le Pas d'acier (*Step of steel*) 44, 78, 80, *156–7*

Le Pavillon d'Armide (*Armida's pavilion*) *30*, 31, 32, *42*, *52*, 56, *57*, 58, 59, 65, *84–5*, 145

Pavlova, Anna 31, 32, 33, 64, 103, 140, 188, 190

Pergolesi, Giovanni Battista 167

Petipa, Marius 31, 43, 103, 140

Petrouchka (*Petrushka*) 36, 43, 67, *110–13*

Pevsner, Anton 39, 80

Philipoff, Olga 189, 190

Picasso, Pablo 39, 40, 43, 71, 72, 73, 76, 167, *172–3*, 219, **224**

Pignolet de Montéclair, Michel *see* de Montéclair, Michel

Piranesi, Giovanni Battista 65

Pitoeff, Pierre 21, 140

Poiret, Paul 35

Polunin, Vladimir 77

Pons, Helen 21, 175

Les Présages (*Destiny*) *81*, *168–9*, 184

productions 71–81, gather programs and ephemera 20

Prokofiev, Serge 43, 44, 71, 78

promotion 188–93

Proust, Marcel 58, 59

Pulcinella 43, 80, *80*, *166–7*

Ravel, Maurice 35, 122

Rayonnism 72, 73

Le Renard (*The fox*) 43, 145

research resources 20

Respighi, Ottorino 132

Revalles, Flora 183

Riabouchinska, Tatiana 45, 46

Richter, Johann Paul 125

Rieti, Vittorio 80, 162

Rimsky-Korsakov, Nikolai 28, 33, 35, 39, 73, 96, 131

Robinowitz, Theodora *see* Deane, Daphne

Roerich, Nicholas 27, 33, 39, 71, 86, *87*, **224**

Romanov, Boris 167

Romantic movement 26, 71, 116

Rosai, Georgi 33

Rosenberg, Lev Samoilovich *see* Bakst, Léon

Le Rossignol (*The nightingale*) (opera) 76, 135

Rossini, Gioacchino 132

Rouault, Georges 39, 44, 45

Royal Ballet 65

Rubinstein, Ida 33, 89

Ruslan and Ludmila (opera) 32

Russian Ballet 45

Russian Ballet Development Company 19

Le Sacre du printemps (*The rite of spring*) 39, 43, 61, 71

Sadko 36, *130–1*

Sainthill, Loudon 184

Salon d'Automne 32, 56

Satie, Eric 40, 71, 73

Savina, Vera 43

Schéhérazade 35, *96–101*, 187, *206–7*

Schollar, Ludmila 33

Schumann, Robert 71, 93, 179

Schwezoff, Igor 47, 179

Sergei Diaghilev's Russian Ballet see Ballets Russes de Serge Diaghilev; Diaghilev, Sergei

Sert, José-María 39, 40, *150–3*, **225**

Sert, Misia 40, 44

sexuality 31, 33

Singer, Winnaretta 43

Sitwell, Sacheverell 64, 67

Slavinsky, Thadée 43, 75, 138

The sleeping beauty 53–4, 56, 62, 63, 65, 67, 140

The sleeping princess 18, 43, 63–5, 67, *140–3*, 145

Smith, Sydney Ure see Ure Smith, Sydney

La Société des Ballets Russes et Ballets de Monte-Carlo see Ballets Russes de Monte Carlo

Society for Self Education see Nevsky Pickwickians

Sokolova, Lydia 20

Somov, Konstantin 27

South America, tours to 40, 43, 179

Spain, sojourn in 40, 172

Le Spectre de la rose (*The spirit of the rose*) 36, 43

Spessivtseva, Olga 188

Stoll, Oswald 65, 141

Strauss, Johan 171

Stravinsky, Igor 35, 36, 39, 40, 43, 63–4, 71, 76, 107, 111, 135, 145, 148, 167

Sudeikina, Vera 21, 104

Surrealism 168, 175

Svetlov, Valerian 55

Swan lake 31

La Sylphide 26, 103

Les Sylphides 32, 61, 189

Sylvia 29

Taglioni, Marie 26, 103

Talashkino 28

Taneyev, Alexander 89

Tatlin, Vladimir 73

Tchaikovsky, Pyotr Il'yich 33, 54, 63–4, 71, 80, 140, 145, 168, 176

Tchelitchew, Pavel 39, 45, 75, 80, *158–61*, **225**

Tcherepnin, Nicholas 33, 93

Tchernicheva, Lubov 46, 205

Tenisheva, Maria Klavdievna 28, 29

Les Tentations de la bergère (*The temptations of the shepherdess*) 61, 62, *148–9*

Thamar 10–12, 39, *116–17*, 186

Théâtre du Châtelet 32, 33

timeline of Ballets Russes 228–37

'total work of art' concept 54–67, 73 see also Gesamtkunstwerk

Toumanova, Tamara 45, 46, 189

tours 40, 43
        Australia and NZ 45–7, 65, 171, 179, 183–93
        North America 40–1, 179
        South America 40, 43, 179

Le Train bleu (*The blue train*) 21, 43

Le Tricorne (*The three-cornered hat*) 43, 76, *172–3*

Tweedie, Valrene (Irina Lavrova) 47

Une Nuit d'Egypte (*Egyptian nights*) 32 see also *Cléopâtre* (*Cleopatra*)

University of Adelaide 47

Ure Smith, Sydney 189–90, 193

Utrillo, Maurice 39

van Praagh, Peggy 47, 65

Velázquez, Diego 40

Verchinina, Nina 184

Versailles 59, 61, 62–3, 65

Villa Bellerive, Ouchy Switzerland 40

Volkonsky, Sergei 29, 55

Voskerensky, Vassily Grigorievich see de Basil, Wassily

Vsevolozhsky, Ivan 31, 54

Wagner, Richard 28, 63–4, 67

West Australian Ballet 47

Williamson (J C) Theatres Ltd 46, 187–9, 193

Woizikowsky, Léon 45, 46, 189

Yakulov, Georgy 71, 78, 80, *156–7*, **226**

Youkine, A 21

Zéphire et Flore (*Zephyr and Flora*) 76, *154–5*

Zeretelli, Alexis 45

© National Gallery of Australia, Canberra 2010

All rights reserved. No part of this publication may be reproduced or transmitted in any form or by any means, electronic or mechanical (including photocopying, recording or any information storage and retrieval system), without permission from the publisher.

National Gallery of Australia is an Australian Government agency

nga.gov.au

Produced by NGA Publishing
National Gallery of Australia, Canberra

Editing: Anne Savage
Design and production coordination: Kirsty Morrison*
Photography: Brenton McGeachie* and NGA Imaging Services
Rights & permissions: Nick Nicholson*
Index: Sherrey Quinn
Publishing manager: Julie Donaldson*
Printer: Blue Star Print, Melbourne
*National Gallery of Australia

National Library of Australia cataloguing-in-Publication entry
Author: Bell, Robert, 1946-
Title: Ballets Russes: the art of costume / Robert Bell.
ISBN: 9780642541574 (hbk)
Notes: Includes bibliographical references and index.
Subjects: Ballets Russes. Ballets Russes du Col W de Basil. Ballet–Costume.
Other authors/contributors: Christine, Dixon, Helena Hammond, Michelle Potter, Debbie Ward, Simeran Maxwell
Dewey Number: 792.8026

Published in conjunction with the exhibition
Ballets Russes: the art of costume
10 December 2010–20 March 2011
National Gallery of Australia, Canberra

Distributed in Australia by
Thames & Hudson
11 Central Boulevard Business Park
Port Melbourne, Victoria, 3207

Distributed in UK and Europe by
Thames & Hudson
181A High Holborn
London, WC1V7QX

Distributed in the USA by
University of Washington press
4333 Brooklyn Avenue, NE
Seattle, Washington 98195-5096

(jacket)
Giorgio de Chirico
Costume for a male guest
c 1929 (detail)
© Giorgio de Chirico/SIAE. Licensed by Viscopy, 2010